The Works of James Arminius
Volume 2 - Private Disputations
By Jacobus Arminius
Edited by Anthony Uyl

Devoted Publishing

Woodstock, Ontario, 2017

The Works of James Arminius
Volume 2 - Private Disputations
By Jacobus Arminius (1560-1609)
Edited by Anthony Uyl

Originally Published in 1853

What kind of philosophies do you have?
Let us know!

Contact us at: devotedpub@hotmail.com
Visit our shop on Facebook: @DevotedPublishing

Published in Woodstock, Ontario, Canada 2017

For bulk educational rates, please contact us at the above email address.

ISBN: 978-1-77356-027-4

Table of Contents

Disputations

DISPUTATION I - ON THEOLOGY

As we are about again to commence our course of theological disputations under the auspices of our gracious God, we will previously treat a little on theology itself. II. By the word "theology" we do not understand a conception or a discourse of God himself, of which meaning it would properly admit; but we understand by it, "a conception" or "a discourse about God and things divine," according to its common use. III. It may be defined, the doctrine or science of the truth which is according to godliness, and which God has revealed to man that he may know God and divine things, may believe on him and may through faith perform to him the acts of love, fear, honour, worship and obedience, and obtain blessedness from him through union with him, to the divine glory. IV. The proximate and immediate object of this doctrine or science is, not God himself, but the duty and act of man which he is bound to perform to God. In theology, therefore, God himself must be considered as the object of this duty. V. On this account, theology is not a theoretical science or doctrine, but a practical one, requiring the action of the whole man, according to all and each of its parts -- an action of the most transcendent description, answerable to the excellence of the object as far as the human capacity will permit. VI. From these premises, it follows that this doctrine is not expressed after the example of natural science, by which God knows himself, but after the example of that notion which God has willingly conceived within himself from all eternity, about the prescribing of that duty and of all things required for it.

DISPUTATION II - ON THE MANNER IN WHICH THEOLOGY MUST BE TAUGHT

It has long been a maxim with those philosophers who are the masters of method and order, that the theoretical sciences ought to be delivered in a synthetical order, but the practical in an analytical order, on which account, and because theology is a practical science, it follows that it must be treated according to the analytical method. II. Our discussion of this doctrine must therefore commence with its end, about which we must previously treat, with much brevity, both on its nature or what it is, and its qualities; we must then teach, throughout the entire discourse, the means for attaining the end, to which the obtaining of the end must be subjoined, and, at this, the whole discussion must terminate. III. For, according to this order, not only the whole doctrine itself, but likewise all its parts, will be treated from its principal end, and each article will obtain that place which belongs to it according to the principal relation which it has to its total and to the end of the whole. IV. But though we are easily satisfied with all treatises in which the body of divinity is explained, provided they agree according to the truth, at least in the chief and fundamental things, with the Scripture itself; and though we willingly give to all of them praise and commendation; yet, if on account only of inquiry into the order, and for the sake of treating the subject with greater accuracy, we may be allowed to explain what are our views and wishes. V. In the first place, the order in which the theology ascribed to God, and to the actions of God, is treated, seems to be inconvenient. Neither are we pleased with the division of theology into the pathological, and the therapeutic after a preface of the doctrine about the principles, the end and the efficient; nor with that, how accommodating soever it may be, in appearance, in which, after premising as its principles the word of God, and God himself, as the causes of our salvation, and therefore the works and effects of God, and man who is its subject is placed as a part of it. So neither do we receive satisfaction from the partition of theological science into the knowledge of God and of man; nor from that by which theology is said to exercise itself about God and the church; nor that by which it is previously determined that we must treat about God, the motion of a rational creature to him, and about Christ; nor does that which prescribes us to a discourse about God, the creatures, and principally about man and his fall, about his reparation through Christ, and about the sacraments and a future life.

DISPUTATION III - ON BLESSEDNESS, THE END OF THEOLOGY

The end of theology is the blessedness of man; and that, not animal or natural, but spiritual and supernatural. II. It consists in fruition, the object of which is a perfect, chief, and sufficient good, which is God. III. The foundation of this fruition is life, endowed with understanding and with intellectual feeling. IV. The connective or coherent cause of fruition is union with God, by which that life is so greatly perfected, that they who obtain this union are said to be "partakers of the divine nature and of life eternal." V. The medium of fruition is understanding and emotion or feeling -- understanding, not by species or image, but by clear vision, which is called that of face to face; and feeling, corresponding with this vision. VI. The cause of blessedness is God himself, uniting himself with man; that is, giving himself to be seen, loved, possessed, and thus to be enjoyed by man. VII. The antecedent or only moving cause is the goodness and the remunerative justice of God, which have the wisdom of God as their precursor. VIII. The executive cause is the power of God, by which the soul is enlarged after the capacity of God, and the animal body is transformed and transfigured into a spiritual body. IX. The end, event, or consequence is two-fold, (1.) a demonstration of the glorious wisdom, goodness, justice, power, and likewise the universal perfection of God; and (2.) his glorification by the beatified. X. Its adjunct properties are, that it is eternal, and is known to be so by him who possesses it; and that it at once both satisfies every desire, and is an object of continued desire.

DISPUTATION IV - ON RELIGION

Omitting all dispute about the question, "whether it be possible for God to render man happy by a union with himself without the intervening act of man," we affirm that it has pleased God not to bless man except by some duty performed according to the will of God, which God has determined to reward with eternal blessedness. II. And this most equitable will of God rests on the foundation of the justice and equity according to which it seems lawful and proper, that the Creator should require from his creature, endowed with reason, an act tending to God, by which, in return, a rational creature is bound to tend towards God, its author and beneficent lord and master. III. This act must be one of the entire man, according to each of his parts -- according to his soul, and that entirely, and each of his faculties, and according to his body, so far as it is the mute instrument of the soul, yet itself possessing a capacity for happiness by means of the soul. This act must likewise be the most excellent of all those things which can proceed from man, and like a continuous act; so that whatever other acts those may he which are performed by man through some intervention of the will, they ought to be performed according to this act and its rule. IV. Though this duty, according to its entire essence and all its parts, can scarcely be designated by one name, yet we do not improperly denominate it when we give it the name of Religion This word, in its most enlarged acceptation, embraces three things -- the act itself, the obligation of the act, and the obligation with regard to God, on account of whom that act must be performed. Thus, we are bound to honour our parents on account of God. V. Religion, then, is that act which our theology places in order; and it is for this reason justly called "the object of theological doctrine." VI. Its method is defined by the command of God, and not by human choice; for the word of God is its rule and measure. And as in these days we have this word in the Scriptures of the Old and New Testament alone, we say that these Scriptures are the canon according to which religion is to be conformed. We shall soon treat more fully about the Scriptures how far it is required that we should consider them as the canon of religion. VII. The opposites to religion are, impiety, that is, the neglect and contempt of God, and eqeloqrhskeia will-worship, or superstition, that is, a mode of religion invented by man. Hypocrisy is not opposed to the whole of religion, but to its integrity or purity; because that in which the entire man ought to be engaged, is performed only by his body.

DISPUTATION V - ON THE RULE OF RELIGION, THE WORD OF GOD, AND THE SCRIPTURES IN PARTICULAR

As religion is the duty of man towards God, it is necessary that it should be so prescribed by God in his sure word as to render it evident to man that he is bound by this prescript as it proceeds from God; or, at least, it may and ought to be evident to man. II. This word is either endiaqeton, [an inward or mental reasoning,] or wroforikon, [a spoken or delivered discourse] the former of them being engrafted in the mind of man by an internal inscription, whether it be an increation or a superinfusion; the latter being openly pronounced. III. By the engrafted word, God has prescribed religion to man, first by inwardly persuading him that God ought, and that it was his will, to be worshipped by man; then, by universally disclosing to the mind of man the worship that is pleasing to himself, and that consists of the love of God and of one's neighbour; and, lastly, by writing or sealing a remuneration on his heart. This inward manifestation is the foundation of all external revelation. IV. God has employed the outward word, First, that he might repeat what had been engrafted -- might recall it to remembrance, and might urge its exercise. Secondly, that he might prescribe to him other things besides, which seem to be placed in a four-fold difference. (1.) For they are either such things as are homogeneous to the law of nature, which might easily be raised up on the things engrafted, or which man could not with equal ease deduce from them. (2.) Or they may appear to be such things as these, yet such as it has pleased God to circumscribe, lest, from the things engrafted, conclusions should be drawn that were universally, or at least for that time, repugnant to the will of God. (3.) Or they are merely positive, having no communion with these engrafted things, although they rest on the general duty of religion. (4.) Or, lastly, according to some state of man, they are suitable to him, particularly for that into which man was brought by the fall from his primeval condition. V. God communicates this external word to man, either orally, or by writing. For, neither with respect to the whole of religion, nor with respect to its parts, is God confined to either of these modes of communication; but he sometimes uses one and sometimes another, and at other times both of them, according to his own choice and pleasure. He first employed oral enunciation in its delivery, and afterwards, writing, as a more certain means against corruption and oblivion. He has also completed it in writing; so that we now have the infallible word of God in no other place than in the Scriptures, which are therefore appropriately denominated "the instrument of religion." VI. These Scriptures are contained in those books of the Old and the New Testament which are called "canonical:" They consist of the five books of Moses; the books of Joshua, Judges, and of Ruth; the First and Second of Samuel; the First and Second of Kings; the First and Second of Chronicles; the books of Ezra and of Nehemiah, and the first ten chapters of that of Esther; fifteen books of the prophets, that is, the three Major and the twelve Minor Prophets; the books of Job, the Psalms, Proverbs, Ecclesiastes, the Canticles, Daniel, and of the Lamentations of Jeremiah: All these books are contained in the Old Testament. Those of the New Testament are the following: The four Evangelists; one book of the Acts of the Apostles; thirteen of St. Paul's Epistles; the Epistle to the Hebrews; that of St. James; the two of St. Peter; the three of St. John; that of St. Jude; and the Apocalypse by St. John. Some of these are without hesitation accounted authentic; but about others of them doubts have been occasionally entertained. Yet the number is quite sufficient of those about which no doubts were ever indulged. VII. The primary cause of these books is God, in his Son, through the Holy Spirit. The instrumental causes are holy men of God, who, not at their own will and pleasure, but as they were actuated and inspired by the Holy Spirit, wrote these books, whether the words were inspired into them, dictated to them, or administered by them under the divine direction. VIII. The matter or object of the Scriptures is religion, as has already been mentioned. The essential and internal form is the true intimation or signification of the will of God respecting religion. The external is the form or character of the word, which is attempered to the dignity of the speaker, and accommodated to the nature of things and to the capacity of men. IX. The end is the instruction of man, to his own salvation and the glory of God. The parts of the whole instruction are doctrine, reproof, institution or instruction, correction, consolation, and threatening.

DISPUTATION VI - ON THE AUTHORITY AND CERTAINTY OF THE HOLY SCRIPTURES

The authority of the word of God, which is comprised in the Scriptures of the Old and New Testament, lies both in the veracity of the whole narration, and of all the declarations, whether they be those about things past, about things present, or about those which are to come, and in the power of the commands and prohibitions, which are contained in the divine word. II. Both of these kinds of authority can depend on no other than on God, who is the principal author of this word, both because he is truth without suspicion of falsehood, and because he is of power invincible. III. On this account, the knowledge alone that this word is divine, is obligatory on our belief and obedience; and so strongly is it binding, that this obligation can be augmented by no external authority. IV. In what manner or respect soever the church may be contemplated, she can do nothing to confirm this authority; for she, also, is indebted to this word for all her own authority; and she is not a church unless she have previously exercised faith in this word as being divine, and have engaged to obey it. Wherefore, in any way to suspend the authority of the Scriptures on the church, is to deny that God is of sufficient veracity and supreme power, and that the church herself is a church. V. But it is proved by various methods, that this word has a divine origin, either by signs employed for the enunciation or declaration of the word, such as miracles, predictions and divine appearances -- by arguments engrafted on the word itself, such as the matters which it contains, the style and character of the discourse, the agreements between all the parts and each of them, and the efficacy of the word itself; and by the inward testification or witness of God himself by his Holy Spirit. To all these, we add a secondary proof -- the testimony of those persons who have received this word as divine. VI. The force and efficacy of this last testimony is entirely human, and is of importance equal to the quantum of wisdom, probity and constancy possessed by the witnesses. And on this account the authority of the church can make no other kind of faith than that which is human, but which may be preparatory to the production of faith divine. The testimony of the church, therefore, is not the only thing by which the certainty of the Scriptures is confirmed to us; indeed it is not the principle thing; nay, it is the weakest of all those which are adduced in confirmation. VII. No arguments can be invented for establishing the divinity of any word, which do not belong by most equitable reason to this word; and, on the other hand, it is impossible any arguments can be devised which may conduce even by a probable reason to destroy the divinity of this word. VIII. Though it be not absolutely necessary to salvation to believe that this or that book is the work of the author whose title it bears; yet this fact may be established by surer arguments than are those which claim the authorship of any other work for the writer. IX. The Scriptures are canonical in the same way as they are divine; because they contain the rule of faith, charity, hope, and of all our inward and outward actions. They do not, therefore, require human authority in order to their being received into the canon, or considered as canonical. Nay, the relation between God and his creatures, requires that his word should be the rule of life to his creatures. X. We assert that, for the establishment of the divinity of the Scriptures of the Old and New Testament, this disjunctive proposition is of irrefutable validity: Either the Scriptures are divine, or (far be blasphemy from the expression!) they are the most foolish of all writings, whether they be said to have proceeded from man, or from the evil spirit. COROLLARIES I. To affirm "that the authority of the Scriptures depends upon the church, because the church is more ancient than the Scriptures," is a falsehood, a foolish speech, an implication of manifold contradictions and blasphemy. II. The authority of the Roman pontiff to bear witness to the divinity of the Scriptures, is less than that of any bishop who is wiser and better than he, and possessed of greater constancy.

DISPUTATION VII - ON THE PERFECTION OF THE SCRIPTURES

We denominate that which comprehends all things necessary for the church to know, to believe, to do and to hope, in order to salvation, "THE PERFECTION OF THE SACRED SCRIPTURES." II. As we are about to engage in the defense of this perfection, against inspirations, visions, dreams and other novel enthusiastic things, we assert, that, since the time when Christ and his apostles sojourned on earth, no inspiration of any thing necessary for the salvation of any individual man, or of the church, has been given to any single person or to any congregation of men whatsoever, which thing is not in a full and most perfect manner comprised in the sacred Scriptures. III. We likewise affirm, that in the latter ages no doctrine necessary to salvation has been deduced from these Scriptures which was not explicitly known and believed from the very commencement of the Christian church. For, from the time of Christ's ascent into heaven, the church of God was in an adult state, being capable indeed of increasing in the knowledge and belief of things necessary to salvation, but not capable of receiving accessions of new articles; that is, she was capable of increase in that faith by which the articles of religion are believed, but not in that faith which is the subject of belief. IV. Whatever additions have since been made, they obtain only the rank of interpretations and proofs, which ought themselves not to be at variance with the Scriptures, but to be deduced from them; otherwise, no authority is due to them, but they should rather be considered as allied to error; for the perfection, not only of the propositions, but likewise of the explanations and proofs which are comprised in the Scriptures, is very great. V. But the most compendious way of forming a judgment about any enunciation or proposition, is, to discern whether its subject and predicate be either expressly or with equal force contained in them, that proposition may be rejected at least as not necessary to salvation, without any detriment to one's salvation. But the predicate may be of such a kind, that, when ascribed to this subject, it cannot be received without detriment to the salvation. For instance, "The Roman pontiff is the head of the church." "The virgin Mary is the mediatrix of grace."

DISPUTATION VIII - ON THE PERSPICUITY OF THE SCRIPTURES I

The perspicuity of the Scriptures is a quality agreeing with them as with a sign, according. to which quality they are adapted clearly to reveal the conceptions, whose signs are the words comprised in the Scriptures, to those persons to whom the Scriptures are administered according to the benevolent providence of God. II. That perspicuity is a quality which agrees with the Scriptures, is proved from its cause and its end. (1.) In cause, we consider the wisdom and goodness of the author, who, according to his wisdom knew, and according to his goodness willed, clearly and well to enunciate or declare the meanings of his own mind. (2.) In the end is the duty of those to whom the Scriptures are directed, and who, through the decree of God, cannot attain to salvation without this knowledge. III. This perspicuity comes distinctly to be considered both with regard to its object and its subject. For all things [in the Scriptures] are not equally perspicuous, nor is every thing alike perspicuous to all persons; but in the epistle of St. Paul, some things occur which "are hard to be understood;" and "the gospel is hid, or concealed, to them who are lost, in whom the god of this world hath blinded the minds of them who believe not" IV. But those senses or meanings, the knowledge and belief of which are simply necessary to salvation, are revealed in the Scriptures with such plainness, that they can be perceived even by the most simple of mankind, provided they be able duly to exercise their reason. V. But they are perspicuous to those alone who, being illuminated by the light of the Holy Spirit, have eyes to see, and a mind to understand and discern. For any colour whatever, though sufficiently illuminated by the light, is not seen except by the eye which is endued with the power of seeing, as with an inward light. VI. But even in those things which are necessary to be known and believed in order to salvation, the law must be distinguished from the gospel, especially in that part which relates to Jesus Christ crucified and raised up again. For even the gentiles, who are aliens from Christ, have "the work of the law written in their hearts," though this is not saving, except by the addition of the internal illumination and inspiration of God; but "the doctrine of the cross, which is foolishness and a stumbling block to the natural man," is not perceived without the revelation of the Spirit. VII. In the Scriptures, some things may be found so difficult to be understood, that men of the quickest and most perspicacious genius may, in attaining to an understanding of those things, have a subject on which to bestow their labours during the whole course of their lives. But God has so finely attempered the Scripture, that they can neither be read without profit, nor, after having been perused and reperused innumerable times, can they be put aside through aversion or disgust.

DISPUTATION IX - ON THE MEANINGS AND INTERPRETATION OF THE HOLY SCRIPTURES

The legitimate and genuine sense of the holy Scriptures is, that which the Holy Ghost, the author of them, intended, and which is collected from the words themselves, whether they be received in their proper or in their figurative signification; that is, it is the grammatical sense, as it is called. II. From this sense, alone, efficacious arguments may be sought for the proof of doctrines. III. But, on account of the analogical similitude of corporeal, carnal, natural, and earthly things, and those belonging to the present life, to things spiritual, heavenly, future and eternal, it happens that a double meaning, each of them certain and intended by the author, lies under the very same words in the Scriptures, of which the one is called "the typical," the other "the meaning prefigured in the type" or "the allegorical." To this allegorical meaning, we also refer the analogical, as opposed in a similar manner to that which is typical. IV. From these meanings, that which is called "the ethiological" and "the tropological" do not differ, since the former of them renders the cause of the grammatical sense, and the latter contains an accommodation of it to the circumstances of persons, place, time, &c. V. The interpretation of Scripture has respect both to its words and to its sense or meaning. VI. The interpretation of its words is either that of single words, or of many words combined; and both of these methods constitute either a translation of the words into another language, or an explanation [or paraphrase] through other words of the same language. VII. Let translation be so restricted, that, if the original word has any ambiguity, the word into which it is translated may retain it: or, if that cannot be done, let it have something equivalent by being noted in the margin. VIII. In the explanation [or paraphrase] which shall be made by other words, endeavours must be used that explanatory words be sought from the Scriptures themselves. For this purpose, attention to the synonymy and phraseology will be exceedingly useful. IX. In the interpretation of the meanings of the words, it must be sedulously attempted both to make the sense agree with the rule or "form of sound words," and to accommodate it to the scope or intention of the author in that passage. To this end, in addition to a clear conception of the words, a comparison of other passages of Scripture, whether they be similar, is conducive, as is likewise a diligent search or institution into its context. In this labour, the occasion [of the words] and their end, the connection of those things which precede and which follow, and the circumstances, also, of persons, times and places, will be principally observed. X. As "the Scriptures are not of private or peculiar explanation," an interpreter of them will strive to "have his senses exercised" in them; that the interpretation of the Scriptures, which, in those sacred writings, comes under the denomination of "prophecy," may proceed from the same Spirit as that which primarily inspired the prophecy of the Scriptures. XI. But the authority of no one is so great, whether it be that of an individual or of a church, as to be able to obtrude his own interpretation on the people as the authentic one. From this affirmation however, by way of eminence, we except the prophets and the apostles. For such interpretation is always subjected to the judgment of him to whom it is proposed, to this extent -- that he is bound to receive it, only so far as it is confirmed by strength of arguments. XII. For this reason, neither the agreement of the fathers, which can, with difficulty, be demonstrated, nor the authority of the Roman pontiff, ought to be received as the rule of interpretation. XIII. We do not wish to introduce unbounded license, by which it may be allowable to any person, whether a public interpreter of Scripture or a private individual, to reject, without cause, any interpretations whatsoever, whether made by one prophet, or by more; but we desire the liberty of prophesying [or public expounding] to be preserved entire and unimpaired in the church. This liberty, itself, however, we subject to the judgment of God, as possessing the power of life and death, and to that of the church, or of her prelates who are endowed with the power of binding and loosing.

DISPUTATION X - ON THE EFFICACY OF THE SCRIPTURES

When we treat on the force and efficacy of the word of God, whether spoken or written, we always append to it the principal and concurrent efficacy of the Holy Spirit. II. The object of this efficacy is man, but he must be considered either as the subject in whom the efficacy operates, or as the object about whom this efficacy exercises itself. III. The subject of this efficacy in whom it operates, is man according to his understanding and his passions, and as being endowed with a capacity, either active or passive. (1.) According to his understanding, by which he is able to understand the meanings of the word, and to apprehend them as true and good for himself: (2.) According to his passions, by which he is capable of being carried by his appetites to something true and good which is pointed out, to embrace it, and to repose in it. IV. This efficacy is not only preparatory, by which the understanding and the passions are prepared to apprehend something else that is yet more true and good, and that is not comprised in the external word; but it is likewise perfective, by which the human understanding and affections are so perfected, that man cannot attain to an ulterior perfection in the present life. Therefore, we reject [the doctrine of] those who affirm that the Scriptures are a dead letter, and serve only to prepare a man, and to render him capable of receiving another inward word. V. This efficacy is beautifully circumscribed in the Scriptures by three acts, each of which is two-fold. (1.) That of teaching what is true, and of confuting what is false. (2.) That of exhorting to what is good, dissuading from what is evil, and of reproving if any thing has been done beyond or contrary to one's duty. (3.) That of administering consolation to a contrite spirit, and of denouncing threats against a lofty spirit. VI. The object of this efficacy, about which it exercises itself, is the same man, placed before the tribunal of divine justice, that, according to this word, he [reporter] may bear away from it a sentence either of justification or of condemnation.

DISPUTATION XI - ON RELIGION IN A STRICTER SENSE

We have treated on religion generally, and on its principles as they are comprehended in the scriptures of the Old and New Testament. We must now treat upon it in a stricter signification. I. As religion contains the duty of man towards God, it must necessarily be founded in the mutual relation which subsists between God and man. If it happen that this relation is varied, the mode of religion must also be varied, the acts pertaining to the substance of every religion always remaining, which are knowledge, faith, love, fear, trust, dread and obedience. II. The first relation between God and man is that which flows from the creation of man in the divine image, according to which religion was prescribed to him by the comprehensive law that has been impressed on the minds of men, and that was afterwards repeated by Moses in the ten commandments. For the sake of proving man's obedience, God added to this a symbolical law, about not eating the fruit of the tree of the knowledge of good and evil. III. Through the sin of man, another relation was introduced between him and God, according to which, man, being liable to the condemnation of God, needs the grace of restoration. If God bestow this grace on man, the religion which is to be prescribed to man must now be also founded on that act, in addition to creation. Since this act [on the part of God] requires from man an acknowledgment of sin and thanksgiving for deliverance, it is apparent that, in this new relation, the mode of religion ought likewise to be varied, as, through the appointment of God, it has in reality been varied. IV. It was the pleasure of God so to administer this variation, that it should not immediately exhibit this grace in a complete manner, but that it should retain man for a season under the sealed dominion of guilt, yet with the addition of a promise of grace to be exhibited in his own time. Hence, arises the difference of the religion which was prescribed by Moses to the children of Israel, and that which was delivered by Christ to his followers -- of which the former is called "the religion of the Old Testament and of the promise," and the latter," that of the New Testament and of the gospel;" the former is also called the Jewish religion; the latter, the Christian. V. The use of the ceremonial law under Moses, and its abrogation under Christ, teach most clearly that this religion or mode of religion differs in many acts. But as the Christian religion prevails at this time, and as [its obligations are] to be performed by us, we will treat further about it, yet so as to intersperse, in their proper places, some mention, both of the primitive religion and of that of the Jews, so Jar as they are capable, and ought to serve to explain the Christian religion. VI. But it is not our wish for this difference to be extended so far as to have the attainment of salvation, without the intervention of Christ, ascribed to those who served God under the pedagogy of the Old Testament and by faith in the promise; for the subjoined affirmation has always obtained from the time when the first promise was promulgated: "There is none other name under heaven, given among men, than that of our Lord Jesus Christ, by which men must be saved." VII. It appears, from this, that the following assertion, which was used by one of the ancients, is false and untheological: "Men were saved at first by the law of nature, afterwards, by that of Moses, and at length, by that of grace." This, also, is further apparent, that such a confusion of the Jewish and Christian religions as was introduced by it, is completely opposed to the dispensation or economy of God.

DISPUTATION XII - ON THE CHRISTIAN RELIGION, ITS NAME AND RELATION

Beginning now to treat further on the Christian religion, we will first declare what is the meaning of this term, and we will afterwards consider the matter of this religion, each in its order. II. The Christian religion, which the Jews called "the heresy of the Nazarenes," obtained its name from Jesus of Nazareth, whom God hath appointed as our only master, and hath made him both Christ and Lord. III. But this name agrees with him in two ways -- from the cause and from the object. (1.) From the cause; because Jesus Christ, as "the Teacher sent from God," prescribed this religion, both by his own voice, when he dwelt on earth, and by his apostles, whom he sent forth into all the world. (2.) From the object; because the same Jesus Christ, the object of this religion, according to godliness, is now exhibited, and fully or perfectly manifested; whereas, he was formerly promised and foretold by Moses and the prophets, only as being about to come. IV. He was, indeed, a teacher far transcending all other teachers -- Moses, the prophets, and even the angels themselves -- both in the mode of his perception, and in the excellence of his doctrine. In the mode of his perception; because, existing in the bosom of the Father, admitted intimately to behold all the secrets of the Father, and endued with the plenitude of the Spirit, he saw and heard those things which he speaks and testifies. But other teachers, being endued, according to a certain measure with the Spirit, have perceived either by a vision, by dreams, by conversing "face to face," or by the intervention of an angel, those things which it was their duty to declare to others; and this Spirit itself is called "the Spirit of Christ." V. In the excellence of his doctrine, also, Christ was superior to all other teachers, because he revealed to mankind, together and at once, the fullness of the very Godhead, and the complete and latest will of his Father respecting the salvation of men; so that, either as it regards the matter or the dearness of the exposition, no addition can be made to it, nor is it necessary that it should. VI. From their belief in this religion, and their profession of it, the professors were called Christians. (Acts xi. 26; 1 Pet. iv. 16.) That the excellence of this name may really belong to a person, it is not sufficient for him to acknowledge Christ as a teacher and prophet divinely called. But he must likewise religiously own and worship him as the object of this doctrine, though the former knowledge and faith precede this, and though from it, alone, certain persons are sometimes said to have believed in Christ.

DISPUTATION XIII - ON THE CHRISTIAN RELIGION, WITH REGARD TO THE MATTER GENERALLY

Since God is the object of all religion, in its various modifications, he must likewise be the object of this religion. But Christ, in reference to God, is also an object of it, as having been appointed by God the Father, King and Lord of the universe, and the Head of his church. II. For this reason, in a treatise on the Christian religion, the following subjects come, in due order, under our consideration: (1.) The object itself, towards which faith and religious worship ought to tend. (2.) The cause, on account of which, faith and worship may and ought to be performed to the object. (3.) The very act of faith and worship, and the method of each, according to the command of God and Christ. (4.) Salvation itself, which, as being promised and desired, has the power of an impelling cause, which, when obtained, is the reward of the observance of religion, and from which arises the everlasting glory of God in Christ. III. But man, by whom [the duties of] this religion must be executed, is a sinner, yet one for whom remission of sins and reconciliation have now been obtained. By this mark, it is intended to be distinguished from the religion of the Jews, which God also prescribed to sinners; but it was at a time when remission of sins had not been obtained, on which account, the mode of religion was likewise different, particularly with regard to ceremonies. IV. This religion, with regard to all those things which we have mentioned as coming under consideration in it, is, of all religions, the most excellent; or, rather, it is the most excellent mode of religion. Because, in it, the object is proposed in a manner the most excellent; so that there is nothing about this object which the human mind is capable of perceiving, that is not exhibited in the doctrine of the Christian religion. For God has with it disclosed all his own goodness, and has given it to be viewed in Christ. V. The cause, on account of which, religion may and ought to be performed to this object, is, in every way, the most efficacious; so that nothing can be imagined, why religion may and ought to be performed to any other deity. that is not comprehended in the efficacy of this cause, in a pre-eminent manner. VI. The very act of faith and worship is required, and must be performed, in a manner the most signal and particular; and the salvation which arises from this act, is the greatest and most glorious, both because God will afford a fuller and more perfect sight of himself, than if salvation had been obtained through another form of religion, and because those who will become partakers of this salvation, will have Christ eternally as their head, who is the brother of men, and they will always behold him. On this account, in the attainment and possession of salvation, we shall hereafter become, in some measure, superior to the angels themselves.

DISPUTATION XIV - ON THE OBJECT OF THE CHRISTIAN RELIGION: AND, FIRST, ABOUT GOD, ITS PRIMARY OBJECT, AND WHAT GOD IS I.

The object of the Christian religion is that towards which the faith and worship of a religious man ought to tend. This object is God and his Christ -- God principally, Christ subordinately under God -- God per se, Christ as God has constituted him the object of this religion. II. In God, who is the primary object of the Christian religion, three things come in order under our consideration: (1.) The nature of God, of which the excellence and goodness is such that religion can honourably and usefully be performed to it. (2.) The acts of God, on account of which religion ought to be performed to him. (3.) The will of God, by which he wills religion to be performed to himself, and that he who performs it be rewarded; and, on the contrary, that the neglecter of it be punished. III. To every treatise on the nature of God, must be prefixed this primary and chief axiom of all religion: "There is a God." Without this, vain is every inquiry into the nature of God; for, if the divine nature had no existence, religion would be a mere phantasm of man's conception. IV. Though the existence of God has been intimated to every rational creature that perceives his voice, and though this truth is known to every one who reflects on such an intimation; yet, "that there is a God," may be demonstrated by various arguments. First, by certain theoretical axioms; and because when the terms in which these are expressed have been once understood, they are known to be true, they deserve to receive the name of "implanted ideas." V. The first axiom is, "Nothing is or can be from itself? For thus it would at one and the same time, be and not be, it would be both prior and posterior to itself, and would be both the cause and effect of itself. Therefore, some one being must necessarily be pre-existent, from whom, as from the primary and supreme cause, all other things derive their origin. But this being is God. VI. The second axiom is, "Every efficient primary cause is better or more excellent than its effect." From this, it follows that, as all created minds are in the order of effects, some one mind is supreme and most wise, from which the rest have their origin. But this mind is God. VII. The third axiom is, "No finite force can make something out of nothing; and the first nature has been made out of nothing." For, if it were otherwise, it neither could nor ought to be changed by an efficient or a former; and thus, nothing could be made from it. From this, it follows, either that all things which exist have been from eternity and are primary being, or that there is one primary being. But this being is God. VIII. The same truth is proved by the practical axiom, or the conscience, which has its seat in all rational creatures. It excuses and exhilarates a man in good actions; and, in these which are evil, it accuses and torments -- even in those things [of both kinds] which have not come, and which never will come, to the knowledge of any creature. This stands as a manifest indication that there is some supreme judge, who will institute a strict inquiry, and will pass judgment. But this judge is God. IX. The magnitude, the perfection, the multitude, the variety, and the agreement, of all things that exist, supply us with the fifth argument, which loudly proclaims that all these things proceed from one and the same being and not from many beings. But this being is God. X. The sixth argument is from the order perceptible in things, and from the orderly disposition and direction of all of them to an end, even of those things which, devoid of reason, themselves, cannot act on account of an end, or at least, cannot intend an end. But all order is from one being, and direction to an end is from a wise and good being. But this being is God. XI. The preservation of political, ecclesiastical and economical society among mankind, furnishes our seventh argument. Amidst such great perversity and madness of Satan and of evil men, human society could never attain to any stability or firmness, except it were preserved safe and unimpaired by One who is supremely powerful. But this is God. XII. We take our eighth argument from the miracles which we believe to have been done, and which we perceive to be done, the magnitude of which is so great as to cause them far to exceed the entire force and power of the created universe. Therefore, a cause must exist which transcends the universe and its power or capability. But this cause is God. XIII. The predictions of future and contingent things, and their accurate and strict completion, supply the ninth argument as being things which could proceed from no one except from God. XIV. In the last place, is added, the perpetual and universal agreement of all nations, which general consent must be accounted as equivalent to a law, nay to a divine oracle. COROLLARY On account of the dissensions of very learned men, we allow this question to be discussed, "from the motion which is apparent in the world, and from the fact, that whatever is moved is moved by another, can it be concluded that there is a God?

DISPUTATION XV - ON THE NATURE OF GOD

Concerning God, the primary object of theology, two things must be known, (1.) His nature, or what God is, or rather what qualities does he possess? (2.) Who God is, or to whom this nature must be attributed. These must be known, lest any thing foolish or unbecoming be ascribed to God, or lest another, or a strange one, be considered as the true God. On the first of these we will now treat in a few disputations. II. As we are not able to know the nature of God, in itself, we can, in a measure, attain to some knowledge from the analogy of the nature which is in created things, and principally that which is in ourselves, who are created after the image of God; while we always add a mode of eminence to this analogy, according to which mode God is understood to exceed, infinitely, the perfections of things created. III. As in the whole nature of things, and in man, who is the compendium or abridgment of it, only two things can be considered as essential, whether they be disparted in their subjects, or, in a certain order, connected with each other and subordinate in the same subject, which two things are Essence and Life; we will also contemplate the nature of God according to these two impulses of his nature. For the four degrees, which are proposed by several divines -- to be, to live, to. feel, and to understand -- are restricted to these two causes of motion; because the word "to live," embraces within itself both feeling and understanding. IV. We say the essence of God is the first impulse of the divine nature, by which God is purely and simply understood to be. V. As the whole nature of things is distributed according to their essence, into body and spirit, we affirm that the divine essence is spiritual, and from this, that God is a Spirit, because it could not possibly come to pass that the first and chief being should be corporeal. From this, one cannot do otherwise than justly admire the transcendent force and plenitude of God, by which he is capable of creating even things corporeal that have nothing analogous to himself. VI. To the essence of God no attribute can be added, whether distinguished from it in reality, by relation, or by a mere conception of the mind; but only a mode of pre-eminence can be attributed to it, according to which it is understood to comprise within itself and to exceed all the perfections of all things. This mode may be declared in this one expression: "The divine essence is uncaused and without commencement." VII. Hence, it follows that this essence is simple and infinite; from this, that it is eternal and immeasurable; and, lastly, that it is unchangeable, impassable and incorruptible, in the manner in which it has been proved by us in our public theses on this subject. VIII. And since unity and goodness reciprocate with being, and as the affections or passions of every being are general, we also affirm that the essence of God is one, and that God is one according to it, and is, therefore, good -- nay, the chief good, from the participation of which all things have both their being, and their well being. IX. As this essence is itself pure from all composition, so it cannot enter into the composition of any thing. We permit it to become a subject of discussion, whether this be designated in the Scriptures by the name of "holiness," which denotes separation or a being separated. X. These modes of pre-eminence are not communicable to any thing, from the very circumstance of their being such. And when these modes are contemplated in the life of God, and in the faculties of his life, they are of infinite usefulness in theology, and are not among the smallest foundations of true religion.

DISPUTATION XVI - ON THE LIFE OF GOD I

Life is that which comes under our consideration, in the second impulse of the divine nature; and that it belongs to God, is not only evident from its own nature, but is likewise known, per se, to all those who have any conception of God. For it is much more incredible that God is something senseless and dead, than that there is no God. And the life of God is easily proved. For, as whatever is beside God is from him, we must also attribute life to him, because among his creatures are many things which have life; and we affirm that God is a living substance, and that life belongs to him, not only eminently but also formally, since life is simply perfection. II. But, as life is taken, either in the second act, and is called "operation," or in the first, principal and radical act, and thus is the very nature and form of a living thing, we attribute this, of itself, primarily and adequately to God; so that he Is the life of himself, not having it from His union with another thing; (for that is the part of imperfection,) but existing the same as it does -- he being life itself, and living by the first act, but bestowing life by the second act. III. The life of God, therefore, is most simple, so that it is not, in reality, distinguished from his essence; and according to the confined capacity of our conception, by which it is distinguished from his essence, it may, in some degree, be described as being "an act that flows from the essence of God," by which is intimated that it is active in itself; first, by a reflex act on God himself, and then on other objects, on account of the most abundant copiousness, and the most perfect activity of life in God. IV. The life of God is the foundation and the proximate and adequate principle not only of ad intra et ad extra, an inward and an outward act, but likewise of all fruition by which God is said to be blessed in himself. This seems to be the cause why God wished himself, principally in reference to life, to be distinguished from false gods and dead idols, and why he wished men to swear by his name, in a form composed thus: "The Lord liveth." V. As the essence of God is infinite and most simple, eternal, impassable, unchangeable and incorruptible, we ought likewise to consider His life with these modes of being and life; on which account we attribute to him per se immortality, and a most prompt, powerful, indefatigable and insatiable desire, strength and delight to act and to enjoy, and in action and enjoyment, if it be lawful, thus to express ourselves. VI. By two faculties, the understanding and the will, this life is active towards God himself; but towards other things it is active by three faculties, power, or capability, being added to the two preceding. But the faculties of the understanding and the will are accommodated to fruition, and this chiefly as they tend towards God himself; secondarily, and because it thus pleases him of his abundant goodness, as they tend towards the creatures.

DISPUTATION XVII - ON THE UNDERSTANDING OF GOD I

The understanding of God is that faculty of his life which is first in nature and order, and by which the living God distinctly understands all things and every one, which, in what manner soever, either have, will have, have had, can have, or might hypothetically have, a being of any kind, by which he also distinctly understands the order, connection, and relation of all and each of them between each other, and the entities of reason, those beings which exist, or which can exist, in the mind, imagination, and enunciation. II. God knows all things, neither by intelligible representations, nor by similitude, but by his own and sole essence; with the exception of evil things, which he knows indirectly by the good things opposed to them, as privation is known by means of our having been accustomed to any thing. III. The mode by which God understands, is, not by composition and division, not by gradual argumentation, but by simple and infinite intuition, according to the succession of order and not of time. IV. The succession of order, in the objects of the divine knowledge, is in this manner: First. God knows himself entirely and adequately, and this understanding is his own essence or being. Secondly. He knows all possible things, in the perfection of his own essence, and, therefore, all things impossible. In the understanding of possible things, this is the order: (1.) He knows what things can exist by his own primary and sole act. (2.) He knows what things, from the creatures, whether they will come into existence or will not, can exist by his conservation, motion, assistance, concurrence, and permission. (3.) He knows what things he can do about the acts of the creatures consistently with himself or with these acts. Thirdly. He knows all entities, even according to the same order as that which we have just shown in his knowledge of things possible. V. The understanding of God is certain and infallible; so that he sees certainly and infallibly, even, things future and contingent, whether he sees them in their causes, or in themselves. But this infallibility depends on the infinity of the essence of God, and not on his unchangeable will. VI. The act of understanding of God is occasioned by no external cause, not even by its object; though if there be not afterwards an object, neither will there be any act of God's understanding about it. VII. How certain soever the acts of God's understanding may themselves be, this does not impose any necessity on things, but rather establishes contingency in them. For, as he knows the thing itself and its mode, if the mode of the thing be contingent, he must know it as such, and, therefore, it remains contingent with respect to the divine knowledge. VIII. The knowledge of God may be distinguished according to its objects. And, First, into the theoretical, by which he understands things under the relation of entity and truth; and into the practical, by which he considers things under the relation of good, and as objects of his will and power. IX. Secondly. One [quality of the] knowledge of God is that of simple intelligence, by which he understands, himself, all possible things, and the nature and essence of all entities; another is that of vision, by which he beholds his own existence and that of all other entities or beings. X. The knowledge by which God knows his own essence and existence, all things possible, and the nature and essence of all entities, is simply necessary, as pertaining to the perfection of his own knowledge. But that by which he knows the existence of other entities, is hypothetically necessary, that is, if they now have, have already had, or shall afterwards have, any existence. For when any object, whatsoever, is laid down, it must, of necessity, fall within the knowledge of God. The former of these precedes every free act of the divine will; the latter follows every free act. The schoolmen; therefore, denominate the first "natural," and the second "free knowledge." XI. The knowledge by which God knows any thing if it be or exist, is intermediate between the two [kinds] described in theses 9 & 10; In fact it precedes the free act of the will with regard to intelligence. But it knows something future according to vision, only through its hypothesis. XII. Free knowledge, or that of vision, which is also called "prescience," is not the cause of things; but the knowledge which is practical and of simple intelligence, and which is denominated "natural," or "necessary," is the cause of all things by the mode of prescribing and directing to which is added the action of the will and of the capability. The middle or intermediate [kind of] knowledge ought to intervene in things which depend on the liberty of created choice or pleasure. XIII. From the variety and multitude of objects, and from the means and mode of intelligence and vision, it is apparent that infinite knowledge and omniscience are justly attributed to God; and that they are so proper or peculiar to God according to their objects, means and mode, as not to be capable of appertaining to any created thing.

DISPUTATION XVIII - ON THE WILL OF GOD

The will of God is spoken of in three ways: First, the faculty itself of willing. Secondly, the act of willing. Thirdly, the object willed. The first signification is the principal and proper one, the two others are secondary and figurative. II. It may be thus described: It is the second faculty of the life of God, flowing through the understanding from the life that has an ulterior tendency; by which faculty God is borne towards a known good -- towards a good, because this is an adequate object of every will -- towards a known good, not only with regard to it as a being, but likewise as a good, whether in reality or only in the act of the divine understanding. Both, however, are shown by the understanding. But the evil which is called that of culpability, God does not simply and absolutely will. III. The good is two-fold. The chief good, and that which is from the chief. The first of these is the primary, immediate, principal, direct, peculiar and adequate object of the divine will; the latter is secondary and indirect, towards which the divine will does not tend, except by means of the chief good. IV. The will of God is borne towards its objects in the following order: (1.) He wills himself. (2.) He wills all those things which, out of infinite things possible to himself he has, by the last judgment of his wisdom, determined to be made. And first, he wills to make them to be; then he is affected towards them by his will, according as they possess some likeness with his nature, or some vestige of it. (3.) The third object of the will of God is those things which he judges fit and equitable to be done by creatures who are endowed with understanding and with free will, in which is included a prohibition of that which he wills not to be done. (4.) The fourth object of the divine will is his permission, that chiefly by which he permits a rational creature to do what he has prohibited, and to omit what he has commanded. (5.) He wills those things which, according to his own wisdom, he judges to be done concerning the acts of his rational creatures. V. There is out of God no inwardly moving cause of his will; nor out of him is there any end. But the creature, and its action or passion, may be the outwardly moving cause, without which God would supersede or omit that volition or act of willing. VI. But the cause of all other things is God, by His understanding and will, by means of His power or capability; yet so, that when he acts either through his creatures, with them or in them, he does not take away the peculiar mode of acting, or of suffering, which he has divinely placed within them; and that he suffers them, according to their peculiar mode, to produce their own effects, and to receive in themselves the acts of God, either necessarily, contingently, or freely. As this contingency and liberty do not make the prescience of God to be uncertain, so they are destroyed by the volition of God, and by the certain futurition of events with regard to the understanding of God.

DISPUTATION XIX - ON THE VARIOUS DISTINCTIONS OF THE WILL OF GOD

Though the will of God be one and simple, yet it may be variously distinguished, from its objects, in reference to the mode and order according to which it is borne towards its objects. Of these distinctions the use is important in the whole of the Scriptures, and in explaining many passages in them. II. The will of God is borne towards its object either according to the mode of nature, or that of liberty. In reference to the former, God tends towards his own primary, proper and adequate object, that is, towards himself. But, according to the mode of liberty, he tends towards other things -- and towards all other things by the liberty of exercise, and towards many by the liberty of specification; because he cannot hate things, so far as they have some likeness of God, that is, so far as they are good; though he is not necessarily bound to love them, since he might reduce them to nothing whenever it seemed good to himself. III. The will of God is distinguished into that by which he absolutely wills to do any thing or to prevent it; and into that by which he wills something to be done or omitted by his rational creatures. The former of these is called "the will of his good pleasure," or rather "of his pleasure;" and the latter, "that of his open intimation." The latter is revealed, for this is required by the use to which it is applied. The former is partly revealed, partly secret, or hidden. The former employs a power that is either irresistible, or that is so accommodated to the object and subject as to obtain or insure its success, though it was possible for it to happen otherwise. To these two kinds of the divine will, is opposed the remission of the will, that is, a two-fold permission, the one opposed to the will of open intimation, the other to that of good pleasure. The former is that by which God permits something to the power of a rational creature by not circumscribing some act by a law; the latter is that by which God permits something to the will and capability of the creature, by not placing an impediment in its way, by which the act may in reality be hindered. IV. Whatever things God wills to do, he wills them (1.) either from himself, not on account of any other cause placed beyond him, (whether that be without the consideration of any act perpetrated by the creature, or solely from the occasion of the act of the creature,) (2.) or on account of a preceding cause afforded by the creature. In reference to this distinction, some work is said to be "proper to God," some other "extraneous, strange and foreign." But there is a two-fold difference in those things which he wills to be done; for they are pleasing and acceptable to God, either in themselves, as in the case of moral works; or they please accidentally and on account of some other thing, as in the case of things ceremonial. V. The will of God is either peremptory, or with a condition. (1.) His peremptory will is that which strictly and rigidly obtains, such as the words of the gospel which contain the last revelation of God: "The wrath of God abides on him who does not believe;" "He that believes shall be saved;" also the words of Samuel to Saul: "The Lord hath rejected thee from being king over Israel." (2.) His will, with a condition, is that which has a condition annexed, whether it be a tacit one, such as, "Yet forty days, and Nineveh shall be overthrown." "Cursed is every one that continueth not in all things which are written in the book of the law to do them," that is, unless he be delivered from this curse as it is expressed in Gal. iii. 13. See also Jer. xviii. 7-10. VI. One will of God is absolute, another respective. His absolute will is that by which he wills any thing simply, without regard to the volition or act of the creature, such as is that about the salvation of believers. His respective will is that by which he wills something with respect to the volition or the act of the creature. It is also either antecedent or consequent. (1.) The antecedent is that by which he wills something with respect to the subsequent will or act of the creature, as, "God wills all men to be saved if they believe." (2.) The consequent is that by which he wills something with respect to the antecedent volition or act of the creature, as, "Woe to that man by whom the Son of man is betrayed! Better would it have been for that man if he had never been born! Both depend on the absolute will, and according to it each of them is regulated. VII. God wills some things, so far as they are good, when absolutely considered according to their nature. Thus he wills alms-giving, and to do good to man so far as he is his creature. He also wills some other things, so far as, all circumstances considered, they are understood to be good. According to this will, he says to the wicked man, "What hast thou to do, that thou shouldst take my covenant in thy mouth?" And he speaks thus to Eli: "Be it far from me that thy house, and the house of thy father, should walk before me for ever; for them that honour me I will honour, and they that despise me shall be lightly esteemed." This distinction does not differ greatly from the antecedent will of God, which has been already mentioned. VIII. God wills some things per se or per accidens. Of themselves, he wills those things which are simply relatively good. Thus He wills salvation to that man who is obedient. Accidentally, those things which, in some respect are evil, but have a good joined with them, which God wills more than the respective good things that are opposed to those evil. Thus he wills the evils of punishment, because he chooses that the order of justice be preserved in punishment, rather than that a sinning creature should escape punishment, though this impunity might be for the good of the creature. IX. God wills some things in their antecedent causes, that is, he wills their causes relatively, and places them in such order that effects may follow from them; and if they do follow, he wills that they, of themselves, be pleasing to him. God wills other things in themselves. This distinction does not substantially differ from that by which the divine will is distinguished into absolute and selective. COROLLARIES I. Is it possible for two affirmatively contrary volitions of God to tend towards one object which is the same and uniform? We answer in the negative. II. Can one volition of God, that is, one formally, tend towards contrary objects? We reply, It can tend towards objects physically contrary, but not towards objects morally contrary. III. Does God will, as an end, something which is beyond himself, and which does not proceed from his free will? We reply in the negative.

DISPUTATION XX - ON THE ATTRIBUTES OF GOD WHICH COME TO BE CONSIDERED UNDER HIS WILL AND, FIRST, ON THOSE WHICH HAVE AN ANALOGY TO THE AFFECTIONS OR PASSIONS IN RATIONAL CREATURES

Those attributes of God ought to be considered, which are either properly or figuratively attributed to him in the Scriptures, according to a certain analogy of the affections and virtues in rational creatures. II. Those divine attributes which have the analogy of affections, may be referred to two principal kinds, so that the first class may contain those affections which are simply conversant about good or evil, and which may be denominated primitive affections; and the second may comprehend those which are exercised about good and evil in reference to their absence or presence, and which may be called affections derived from the primitive. III. The primitive affections are love, (the opposite to which is hatred,) and goodness; and with these are connected grace, benignity and mercy. Love is prior to goodness towards the object, which is God himself; goodness is prior to love towards that object which is some other than God. IV. Love is an affection of union in God, whose objects are not only God himself and the good of justice, but also the creature, imitating or related to God either according to likeness, or only according to impress, and the felicity of the creature. But this affection is borne onwards either to enjoy and to have, or to do good; the former is called "the love of complacency;" the latter, "the love of friendship," which falls into goodness, God loves himself with complacency in the perfection of His own nature, wherefore he likewise enjoys himself. He also loves himself with the love of complacency in his effects produced externally; both in acts and works, which are specimens and evident, infallible indications of that perfection. Wherefore he may be said, in some degree, likewise to enjoy these acts and works. Even the justice or righteousness performed by the creature, is pleasing to him; wherefore his affection is extended to secure it. V. Hatred is an affection of separation in God, whose many object is injustice or unrighteousness; and the secondary, the misery of the creature. The former is from "the love of complacency;" the latter, from "the love of friendship." But since God properly loves himself and the good of justice, and by the same impulse holds iniquity in detestation; and since he secondarily loves the creature and his blessedness, and in that impulse hates the misery of the creature, that is, he wills it to be taken away from the creature; hence, it comes to pass, that he hates the creature who perseveres in unrighteousness, and he loves his misery. VI. Hatred, however, is not collateral to love, but necessarily flowing from it; since love neither does nor can tend towards all those things which become objects to the understanding of God. It belongs to him, therefore, in the first act, and must be placed in him prior to any existence of a thing worthy of hatred, which existence being laid down, the act of hatred arises from it by a natural necessity, not by liberty of the will. VII. But since love does not perfectly fill the whole will of God, it has goodness united with it; which also is an affection in God of communicating his good. Its first object externally is nothing; and this is so necessarily first, that, when it is removed, no communication can be made externally. Its act is creation. Its second object is the creature as a creature; and its act is called conservation, or sustentation, as if it was a continuance of creation. Its third object is the creature performing his duty according to the command of God; and its act is the elevation to a more worthy and felicitous condition, that is, the communication of a greater good than that which the creature obtained by creation. Both these advances of goodness may also be appropriately denominated "benignity," or "kindness." Its fourth object is the creature not performing his duty, or sinful, and on this account liable to misery according to the just judgment of God; and its act is a deliverance from sin through the remission and the mortification of sin. And this progress of goodness is denominated mercy, which is an affection for giving succour to a man in misery, sin presenting no obstacle. VIII. Grace is a certain adjunct of goodness and love, by which is signified that God is affected to communicate his own good and to love the creatures, not through merit or of debt, not by any cause impelling from without, nor that something may be added to God himself, but that it may be well with him on whom the good is bestowed and who is beloved, which may also receive the name of "liberality." According to this, God is said to be "rich in goodness, mercy," &c. IX. The affections which spring from these, and which are exercised about good or evil as each is present or absent, are considered as having an analogy either in those things which are in the concupiscible part of our souls, or in that which is irascible. X. In the concupiscible part are, first, desire and that which is opposed to it; secondly, joy and grief. (1.) Desire is an affection of obtaining the works of righteousness from rational creatures, and of bestowing a remunerative reward, as well as of inflicting punishment if they be contumacious. To this is opposed the affection according to which God execrates the works of unrighteousness, and the omission of a remuneration. (2.). Joy is an affection from the presence of a thing that is suitable or agreeable -- such as the fruition of himself, the obedience of the creature, the communication of his own goodness, and the destruction of His rebels and enemies. Grief, which is opposed to it, arises from the disobedience and the misery of the creature, and in the occasion thus given by his people for blaspheming the name of God among the gentiles. To this, repentance has some affinity; which is nothing more than a change of the thing willed or done, on account of the act of a rational creature, or, rather, a desire for such change. XI. In the irascible part are hope and its opposite, despair, confidence and anger, also fear, which is affirmatively opposed to hope. (1.) Hope is an earnest expectation of a good, due from the creature, and performable by the grace of God. It cannot easily be reconciled with the certain foreknowledge of God. (2.) Despair arises from the pertinacious wickedness of the creature, opposing himself to the grace of God, and resisting the Holy Spirit. (3.) Confidence is that by which God with great animation prosecutes a desired good, and repels an evil that is hated. (4.) Anger is an affection of depulsion in God, through the punishment of the creature that has transgressed his law, by which he inflicts on the creature the evil of misery for his unrighteousness, and takes the vengeance which is due to him, as an indication of his love towards justice, and of his hatred to sin. When this affection is vehement, it is called "fury." (5.) Fear is from an impending evil to which God is averse. XII. Of the second class of these derivative affections, (See Thesis 11) some belong to God per se, as they simply contain in themselves perfection; others, which seem to have something of imperfection, are attributed to him after the manner of the feelings of men, on account of some effects which he produces analogous to the effects of the creatures, yet without any passion, as he is simple and immutable and without any disorder and repugnance to right reason. But we subject the use and exercise of the first class of those affections (See Thesis 10) to the infinite wisdom of God, whose property it is to prefix to each of them its object, means, end and circumstances, and to decree to which, in preference to the rest, is to be conceded the province of acting.

DISPUTATION XXI - ON THOSE ATTRIBUTES OF GOD WHICH HAVE SOME ANALOGY TO THE MORAL VIRTUES, AND WHICH ACT LIKE MODERATORS OF THE AFFECTIONS, CONSIDERED IN THE PRECEDING DISPUTATION

But these attributes preside generally over all the affections, or specially relate to some of them. The general is justice, or righteousness, which is called "universal" or "legal," and concerning which it was said by the ancients, that it contains, in itself, all the virtues. The special are, particular justice, patience, and those which are the moderators of anger, and of chastisements and punishments. II. The justice of God, considered universally, is a virtue of God, according to which he administers all things correctly and in a suitable manner, according to that which his wisdom dictates as befitting himself. In conjunction with wisdom, it presides over all his acts, decrees and deeds; and according to it, God is said to be "just and right," his way "equal," and himself to be "just in all his ways." III. The particular justice of God is that by which he consistently renders to every one his own -- to God himself that which is his, and to the creature that which belongs to itself. We consider it both in the words of God and in his deeds. In this, the method of the decrees is not different; because, whatever God does or says, he does or says it according to his own eternal decree. This justice likewise contains a moderator partly of his love for the good of obedience, and partly of his love for the creature, and of his goodness. IV. Justice In deeds may be considered in the following order: That the first may be in the communication of good, either according to the first creation, or according to regeneration. The second is in the prescribing of duty, or in legislation, which consists in the requisition of a deed, and in the promise of a reward, and the threat of a punishment. The third is in the judging about deeds, which is retributive, being both communicative of a reward and vindicative. In all these, the magnanimity of God is to be considered. In communication, in promise, and in remuneration, his liberality and magnificence are also to come under consideration; and they may be appropriately referred partly to distributive, and partly to commutative justice. V. Justice in words is also three-fold. (1.) Truth, by which he always enunciates or declares exactly as the thing is, to which is opposed falsehood. (2.) Sincerity and simplicity, by which he always declares as he inwardly conceives, according to the meaning and purpose of his mind, to which are opposed hypocrisy and duplicity of heart. And (3.) Fidelity, by which he is constant in keeping promises and in communicating privileges, to which are opposed inconstancy and perfidy. VI. Patience is that by which he patiently endures the absence of that Good, that is, of the prescribed obedience which he loves, desires, and for which he hopes, and the presence of that evil which he forbids, sparing sinners, not only that he may execute the judicial acts of His mercy and severity through them, but that he may also lead them to repentance, or that he may punish the contumacious with greater equity and severity. And this attribute seems to attemper the love [which God entertains] for the good of justice. VII. Long suffering, gentleness or lenity, clemency and readiness to pardon, are the moderators of anger, chastisements and punishments. VIII. Long suffering is a virtue by which God suspends his anger, lest it should instantly hasten to the depulsion of the evil, as soon as the creature has by his sins deserved it. IX. Gentleness or lenity is a virtue, by which God preserves moderation concerning anger in taking vengeance, lest it should be too vehement -- lest the seventy of the anger should certainly correspond with the magnitude of the wickedness perpetrated. X. Clemency is a virtue by which God so attempers the chastisements and punishments of the creature, even at the very time when he inflicts them, that, by their weight and continuance, they may not equal the magnitude of the sins committed; indeed, that they may not exceed the strength of the creature. XI. Readiness to forgive is a virtue by which God shows himself to be exorable to his creature, and which fixes a measure to the limits of anger, lest it should endure for ever, agreeably to the demerit of the sins committed. COROLLARIES Does the justice of God permit him to destine to death eternal, a rational creature who has never sinned? We reply in the negative. Does the justice of God allow that a creature should be saved who perseveres in his sins? We reply in the negative. Cannot justice and mercy, in some accommodated sense, be considered, as, in a certain respect, opposed? We reply in the affirmative.

DISPUTATION XXII - ON THE POWER OR CAPABILITY OF GOD I

When entering on the consideration of the power or capability of God, as we deny the passive power which cannot belong to God who is a pure act, so we likewise omit that which is occupied with internal acts through necessity of nature; and at present we exhibit for examination that power alone which consists in the capacity of external actions, and by which God not only is capable of operating beyond himself, but actually does operate whenever it is his own good pleasure. II. And it is a faculty of the divine life, by which, (subsequently to the understanding of God that shows and directs, and to his will that commands,) he is capable of operating externally what things soever he can freely will, and by which he does operate whatever he freely wills. III. The measure of the divine capability is the free will of God, and that is truly an adequate measure; so that the object of the capability may be, and, indeed, ought to be, circumscribed and limited most appropriately from the object of the free will of God. For, whatever cannot fall under his will, cannot fall under his capability; and whatever is subject to the former, is likewise subject to the latter. IV. But the will of God can only will that which is not opposed to the divine essence, (which is the foundation both of His understanding and of his will,) that is, it can will nothing but that which exists, is true and good. Hence, neither can his capability do any other. Again, since, under the phrase "what is not opposed to the divine essence," is comprehended whatsoever is simply and absolutely possible, and since God can will the whole of this, it follows that God is capable of every thing which is possible. V. Those things are impossible to God which involve a contradiction, as, to make another God, to be mutable, to sin, to lie, to cause some thing at once to be and not to be, to have been and not to have been, &c., that this thing should be and not be, that it and its contrary should be, that an accident should be without its subject, that a substance should be changed into a pre-existing substance, bread into the body of Christ, that a body should possess ubiquity, &c. These things partly belong to a want of power to be capable of doing them, and partly to a want of will to do them. VI. But the capability of God is infinite -- and this not only because it can do all things possible, which, indeed, are innumerable, so that as many cannot be enumerated as it is capable of doing, [or after all that can be numbered, it is capable of doing still more]; nor can such great things be calculated without its being able to produce far greater, but likewise because nothing can resist it. For all created things depend upon him, as upon the efficient principle, both in their being and in their preservation. Hence, omnipotence is justly ascribed to him. VII. This can be communicated to no creature.

DISPUTATION XXIII - ON THE PERFECTION, BLESSEDNESS AND GLORY OF GOD

Next in order, follows the perfection of God, resulting from the simple and infinite circuit of all those things which we have already attributed to God, and considered with the mode of pre-eminence -- not that perfection by which he has every individual thing most perfectly, (for this is the office of simplicity and infinity,) but that by which he has all things simply denoting some perfection in the most perfect manner. And it may be appropriately described thus: It is the interminable, and, at the same time, the entire and perfect possession of essence and life. II. And this perfection of God infinitely transcends every created perfection, in three several ways: (1.) Because it has all things. (2.) It has them in a manner the most perfect. And (3.) It does not derive them from any other source. But as the creatures have, through participation, a perfection from God, faintly shadowed forth after its archetype, so, of consequence, they neither have every perfection, nor in a manner the most perfect; yet some creatures have a greater perfection than others; and the more of it they possess, the nearer are they to God, and the more like him. III. From this perfection of God, by means of some internal act, his blessedness has its existence; and by means of some relation of it ad extra, his glory exists. IV. Blessedness is an act of God, by which he enjoys his own perfection, that is fully known by his understanding, and supremely loved by his will, with a delightful satisfaction in it. It is, therefore, through the act of the understanding, and of the will; of the understanding, indeed, reaching to the essence of the object, but the act of which would not be an act of felicity, unless it had this, its being an act of felicity[sic.], from the will which perpetually desires to behold the beatified object, and is delightfully satisfied in it. V. But this blessedness is so peculiar to God that it cannot be communicated to any creature. Yet he is, himself, with respect to the object, the beatified good of creatures endowed with understanding, and the effector of the act which tends to the effect, and which is delightfully satisfied in it. Of these, consists the blessedness of the creature. VI. Glory is the divine excellence above all things, which he makes manifest by external acts, in various ways. VII. But the modes of manifestation, which are declared to us in the Scriptures, are principally two -- the one, by an effulgence of unusual light and splendour, or by the opposite to it, a dense darkness and obscurity; the other, by the production of works which agree with his perfection and excellence. VIII. This description of the divine nature is the first foundation of all religion. For it is concluded, from this perfection and blessedness of God, that the act of religion can be worthily and usefully exhibited to God, to the knowledge of which matter, we are brought, through the manifestation of the divine glory. The candid reader will be able, in this place, to supply from the preceding public disputations, the theses on the Father and the Son, and those on the Holy Spirit, the Holy and undivided Trinity.

DISPUTATION XXIV - ON CREATION

We have treated on God, who is the first object of the Christian religion. And we would now treat on Christ, who, next to God, is another object of the same religion; but we must premise some things, without which, Christ would neither be an object of religion, nor would the necessity of the Christian religion be understood. Indeed, the cause must be First explained, on account of which God has a right to require any religion from man; THEN the religion, also, that is prescribed in virtue of this cause and right, and, LASTLY, the event ensuing, from which has arisen the necessity of constituting Christ our saviour, and the Christian religion, employed by God, through his own will, who hath not, by the sin of man, lost His right which he obtains over him by creation, nor has he entirely laid aside his affection for man, though a sinner, and miserable. II. And since God is the object of the Christian religion, not only as the Creator, but likewise as the Creator anew, (in which latter respect, Christ, also, as constituted by God to be the saviour, is the object of the Christian religion,) it is necessary for us first to treat about the primitive creation, and those things which are joined to it according to nature, and, after that, about those which resulted from the conduct of man, before we begin to treat on the new creation, in which the primary consideration is that of Christ as Mediator. III. Creation is an external act of God, by which he produced all things out of nothing, for himself, by his Word and Spirit. IV. The primary efficient cause is God the Father, by his Word and Spirit. The impelling cause, which we have indicated in the definition by the particle "for," is the goodness of God, according to which he is inclined to communicate his good. The ordainer is the divine wisdom; and the executrix, or performer, is the divine power, which the will of God employs through an inclination of goodness, according to the most equitable prescript of his wisdom. V. The matter from which God created all things, must be considered in three forms: (1.) The first of all is that from which all things in general were produced, into which, also, they may all, on this account, relapse and be reduced; it is nothing itself, that our mind, by the removal of all entity, considers as the first matter; for, that, alone, is capable of the first communication of God ad extra; because, God would neither have the right to introduce his own form into matter coeval [with himself], nor would he be capable of acting, as it would then be eternal matter, and, therefore, obnoxious to no change. (2.) The second matter is that from which all things corporeal are now distinguished, according to their own separate forms; and this is the rude chaos and undigested mass created at the beginning. (3.) The third consists both of these simple and secret elements, and of certain compound bodies, from which all the rest have been produced, as from the waters have proceeded creeping and flying things, and fishes -- from the earth, all other living things, trees, herbs and shrubs -- from the rib of. Adam, the woman, and from seeds, the perpetuation of the species. VI. The form is the production itself of all things out of nothing, which form pre existed ready framed, according to the archetype in the mind of God, without any proper entity, lest any one should feign an ideal world. VII. From an inspection of the matter and form, it is evident, First, that creation is the immediate act of God, alone, both because a creature, who is of a finite power is incapable of operating on nothing, and because such a creature cannot shape matter in substantial forms. Secondly. The creation was freely produced, not necessarily, because God was neither bound to nothing, nor destitute of forms. VIII. The end -- not that which moved God to create, for God is not moved by any thing external, but that which incessantly and immediately results from the very act of creation, and which is, in fact, contained in the essence of this act -- this end is the demonstration of the divine wisdom, goodness and power. For those divine properties which concur to act, shine forth and show themselves in their own nature action -- goodness, in the very communication -- wisdom, in the mode, order and variety -- and power, in this circumstance, that so many and such great things are produced out of nothing. IX. The end, which is called "to what purpose," is the good of the Creatures themselves, and especially of man, to whom are referred most other creatures, as being useful to him, according to the institution of the divine creation. X. The effect of creation is this universal world, which, in the Scriptures, obtains the names of the heaven and the earth, sometimes, also, of the sea, as being the extremities within which all things are embraced. This world is an entire something, which is perfect and complete, having no defect of any form, that can bear relation to the whole or to its parts; nor is redundant in any form which has no relation to the whole and its parts. It is, also, a single, or a united something, not by an indivisible unity, but according to connection and co-ordination, and the affection of mutual relation, consisting of parts distinguished, not only according to place and situation, but likewise according to nature, essence and peculiar existence. This was necessary, not only to adumbrate, in some measure, the perfection of God in variety and multitude, but also to demonstrate that the Lord omnipotent did not create the world by a natural necessity, but by the freedom of his will. XI. But this entire universe is, according to the Scriptures, distributed in the best manner possible into three classes of objects, (1.) Into creatures purely spiritual and invisible; of this class are the angels. (2.) Into creatures merely corporeal. And (3.) Into natures that are, in one part of them, corporeal and visible, and in another part, spiritual and invisible; men are of this last class. XII. We think this was the order observed in creation: Spiritual creatures, that is, the angels, were first created. Corporeal creatures were next created, according to the series of six days, not together and in a single moment. Lastly, man was created, consisting both of body and spirit; his body was, indeed, first formed; and afterwards his soul was inspired by creating, and created by inspiring; that as God commenced the creation in a spirit, so he might finish it on a spirit, being himself the immeasurable and eternal Spirit. XIII. This creation is the foundation of that right by which God can require religion from man, which is a matter that will be more certainly and fully understood, when we come more specially to treat on the primeval creation of man; for he who is not the creator of all things, and who, therefore, has not all things under his command, cannot be believed, neither can any sure hope and confidence be placed in him, nor can he alone be feared. Yet all these are acts which belong to religion. COROLLARIES I. The world was neither created from all eternity, nor could it be so created; though God was, from eternity, furnished with that capability by which he could create the world, and afterwards did create it; and though no moment of time can be conceived by us, in which the world could not have been created. II. He who forms an accurate conception, in his mind, of creation, must, in addition to the plenitude of divine wisdom, goodness and power, or capability, conceive that there was a two-fold privation or vacuity -- the First, according to essence or form, which will bear some resemblance to an infinite nothing that is capable of infinite forms; the SECOND, according to place, which will be like an infinite vacuum that is capable of being the receptacle of numerous worlds. III. Hence, this, also, follows, that time and place are not Separate Creatures, but are created with things themselves, or, rather, that they exist together at the creation of things, not by an absolute but a relative entity, without which no created thing can be thought upon or conceived. IV. This creation is the first of all the divine external acts, both in the intention of the Creator, and actually or in reality; and it is an act perfect in itself, not serving another more primary one, as its medium; though God has made some creatures, which, in addition to the fact of their having been made by the act of creation, are fitted to be advanced still further, and to be elevated to a condition yet more excellent. V. If any thing be represented as the object of creation, it seems that nothing can be laid down more suitably than those things which, out of all things possible, have, by the act of creation, been produced from non-existence into existence.

DISPUTATION XXV - ON ANGELS IN GENERAL AND IN PARTICULAR

Angels are substances merely spiritual, created after the image of God, not only that they might acknowledge, love and worship their Creator, and might live in a state of happiness with him, but that they might likewise perform certain duties concerning the rest of the creatures according to the command of God. II. We call them "substances," against the Sadducees and others, who contend that angels are nothing more than the good or the evil motions of spirits, or else exercises of power to aid or to injure. But this is completely at variance with the whole Scripture, as the actions, (which are those of supposititious beings,) the appearances, and the names which they ascribe to them, more than sufficiently demonstrate. III. We add that they are "merely spiritual," that we may separate them from men, the species opposite to them, and may intimate their nature. And though composition out of matter and form does not belong to angels, yet, we affirm that they are absolutely compound substances, and that they are composed, (1.) Of being and essence. (2.) Of act and power, or capability. (3.) Lastly, of subject and inhering accident. IV. But because they are creatures, they are finite, and we measure them by place, time, and number. (1.) By PLACE, not that they are in it corporeally, that is, not that they occupy and fill up a certain local space, commensurate with their substance; but they are in it intellectually, that is, they exist in a place without the occupying and repletion of any local space, which the schoolmen denominate by way of definition, "to be in a place." But, as they cannot be in several places at once, but are sometimes in one place, and sometimes in another, so they are not moved without time, though it is scarcely perceptible. (2.) We measure them by TIME, or by duration or age, because they have a commencement of being, and the whole age in which they continue they have in succession, by parts of past, present and future; but the whole of it is not present to them at the same moment and without any distance. (3.) Lastly. We measure them by NUMBER, though this number is not defined in the pages of the sacred volume, and, therefore, is unknown to us, but known to God; yet it is very great, for it is neither diminished nor increased, because the angels are neither begotten nor die. V. We say that they were "created after the image of God;" for they are denominated "the sons of God." This image, we say, consists partly in those things which belong to their natures, and partly in those things which are of supernatural endowment. (1.) To their nature, belong both their spiritual essence, and the faculty of understanding, of willing, and of powerfully acting. (2.) To supernatural endowment, belong the light of knowledge in the understanding, and, following it, the rectitude or holiness of the will. Immortality itself, is of supernatural endowment; but it is that which God has determined to preserve to them, in what manner soever they may conduct themselves towards him. VI. The end subjoined is two-fold -- that, standing around the throne of God as his apparitors or messengers, for the glory of the divine Majesty, the angels may perpetually laud and celebrate [the praises of] God, and that they may, with the utmost swiftness, execute, at the beck of God, the offices of ministration which he enjoins upon them. VII. We are informed in the Scriptures themselves, that there is a certain order among angels; for they mention angels and archangels,-and attribute even to the devil his angels. But we are willingly ignorant of that distinction into orders and various degrees, and what it is which constitutes such distinction. We also think that if [the existence of] certain orders of angels be granted, it is more probable that God employs angels of different orders for the same duties, than that he appoints distinct orders to each separate ministry; though we allow that those who hold other sentiments, think so with some reason. VIII. For the performance of the ministries enjoined on them, angels have frequently appeared clothed in bodies, which bodies they have not formed and assumed to themselves out of nothing, but out of pre-existing matter, by a union neither essential nor personal, but local, (because they were not then beyond those bodies,) and, according to an instrumental purpose, that they might use them for the due performance of the acts enjoined. IX. These bodies, therefore, have neither been alive, nor have the angels, through them, seen, heard, tasted, smelled, touched, conceived phantasms or imaginations, &c. through the organs of these bodies, they produced only such acts as could be performed by an angel inhabiting them, or, rather, existing in them, as the mover according to place. On this account, perhaps, it is not improperly affirmed, that bodies, truly human, which are inhabited by a living and directing spirit, can be discerned, by human judgment, from these assumed bodies. X. God likewise prescribed a certain law to angels, by which they might order their life according to God, and not according to themselves, and by the observance of which they might be blessed, or, by transgressing it, might be eternally miserable, without any hope of pardon. For it was the good pleasure of God to act towards angels according to strict justice, and not to display all his goodness in bringing them to salvation. XI. But we do not decide whether a single act of obedience was sufficient to obtain eternal blessedness, as one act of disobedience was deserving of eternal destruction. XII. Some of the angels transgressed the law under which they were placed; and this they did by their own fault, because by that grace with which they were furnished, and by which God assisted them, and was prepared to assist them, they were enabled to obey the law, and to remain in their integrity. XIII. Hence, is the division made of angels into the good and the evil. The former are so denominated, because they continued steadfast in the truth, and preserved "their own habitation." But the latter are called "evil angels," because they did not continue in the truth, and "deserted their own habitation." XIV. But the former are called "good angels," not only according to an infused habit, but likewise according to the act which they performed, and according to their confirmation in habitual goodness, the cause of which we place in the increase of grace, and in their holy purpose, which they conceived partly through beholding the punishment which was inflicted on the apostate angels, and partly through the perception of increased grace. [If it be asked,] Did they not also do this, through perfect blessedness, to which nothing could be added?, we do not deny it, on account of the agreement of learned men, though it seems possible to produce reasons to the contrary. XV. The latter (Thesis 13) are called "evil angels," First, by actual wickedness, and then by habitual wickedness and pertinacious obstinacy in it; hence, they take a delight in doing whatever they suppose can tend to the reproach of God and the destruction of their neighbour. But this fixed obstinacy in evil seems to derive its origin partly from an intuition of the wrath of God and from an evil conscience which springs out of that, and partly from their own wickedness. XVI. But, concerning the species of sin which the angels perpetrated, we dare not assert what it was. Yet we say, it may with some probability be affirmed, that it was the crime of pride, from that argument which solicited man to sin through the desire of excellence. XVII. When it is the will of God to employ the assistance of good angels, he may be said to employ not only those powers and faculties which he has conferred on them, but likewise those which are augmented by himself. But we think it is contradictory to truth, if God be said to furnish the devils, whose service he uses, with greater knowledge and power than they have through creation and their own experience. COROLLARIES I. We allow this to become a subject of discussion: Can good angels be said sometimes to contend among themselves, with a reservation of that charity which they owe to God, to each other, and to men? II. Do angels need a mediator? and is Christ the mediator of angels? We reply in the negative. III. Are all angels of one species? We think this to be more probable than its contrary.

DISPUTATION XXVI - ON THE CREATION OF MAN AFTER THE IMAGE OF GOD

Man is a creature of God; consisting of a body and a soul, rational, good, and created after the divine image -- according to his body, created from pre-existing matter, that is, earth mixed and besprinkled with aqueous and ethereal moisture, -- according to his soul, created out of nothing, by the breathing of breath into his nostrils. II. But that body would have been incorruptible, and, by the grace of God, would not have been liable to death, if men had not sinned, and had not, by that deed, procured for himself the necessity of dying. And because it was to be the future receptacle of the soul, it was furnished by the wise Creator with various and excellent organs. III. But the soul is entirely of an admirable nature, if you consider its origin, substance, faculties, and habits. (1.) Its origin; for it is from nothing, created by infusion, and infused by creation, a body being duly prepared for its reception, that it might fashion matter as with form, and, being united to the body by a native bond, might, with it, compose one ufisamenon, production. Created, I say, by God in time, as he still daily creates a new soul in each body. IV. Its substance, which is simple, immaterial, and immortal. Simple, I say, not with respect to God; for it consists of act and power or capability, of being and essence, of subject and accidents; but it is simple with respect to material and compound things. It is immaterial, because it can subsist by itself, and, when separated from the body, can operate alone. It is immortal, not indeed from itself, but by the sustaining grace of God. V. Its faculties, which are two, the understanding and the will, as in fact the object of the soul is two-fold. For the understanding apprehends eternity and truth both universal and particular, by a natural and necessary, and therefore by a uniform act. But the will has an inclination to good. Yet this is either, according to the mode of its nature, to universal good and to that which is the chief good; or, according to the mode of liberty, to all other [kinds of] good. VI. Lastly. In its habits, which are, First, wisdom, by which the intellect clearly and sufficiently understood the supernatural truth and goodness both of felicity and of righteousness. Secondly. Righteousness and the holiness of truth, by which the will was fitted and ready to follow what this wisdom commanded to be done, and what it showed to be desired. This righteousness and wisdom are called "original," both because man had them from his very origin, and because, if man had continued in his integrity, they would also have been communicated to his posterity. VII. In all these things, the image of God most wonderfully shone forth. We say that this is the likeness by which man resembled his Creator, and expressed it according to the mode of his capacity -- in his soul, according to its substance, faculties and habits -- in this body, though this cannot be properly said to have been created after the image of God who is pure spirit, yet it is something divine, both from the circumstance that, if man had not sinned, his body would never have died, and because it is capable of special incorruptibility and glory, of which the apostle treats in 1 Corinthians 15, because it displays some excellence and majesty beyond the bodies of other living creatures, and, lastly, because it is an instrument well fitted for admirable actions and operations -- in his whole person, according to the excellence, integrity, and the dominion over the rest of the creatures, which were conferred upon him. VIII. The parts of this image may be thus distinguished: Some of them may be called natural to man, and others supernatural; some, essential to him, and others accidental. It is natural and essential to the soul to be a spirit, and to be endowed with the power of understanding and of willing, both according to nature and the mode of liberty. But the knowledge of God, and of things pertaining to eternal salvation, is supernatural and accidental, as are likewise the rectitude and holiness of the will, according to that knowledge. Immortality is so far essential to the soul, that it cannot die unless it cease to be; but it is on this account supernatural and accidental, because it is through grace and the aid of preservation, which God is not bound to bestow on the soul. IX. But the immortality of the body is entirely supernatural and accidental; for it can be taken away from the body, and the body can return to the dust, from which it was taken. Its excellence above other living creatures, and its peculiar fitness to produce various effects, are natural to it, and essential. Its dominion over the creatures which belongs to the whole man as consisting of body and soul, may he partly considered as belonging to it according to the excellence of nature, and partly as conferred upon it by gracious gift, of which dominion this seems to be an evidence, that it is never taken wholly away from the soul, although it be varied, and be augmented and diminished according to degrees and parts. X. Thus was man created, that he might know, love and worship his Creator, and might live with him for ever in a state of blessedness. By this act of creation, God most manifestly displayed the glory of his wisdom, goodness and power. XI. From this description of man, it appears, that he is both fitted to perform the act of religion to God, since such an act is required from him -- that he is capable of the reward which may be properly adjudged to those who perform [acts of] religion to God, and of the punishment which may be justly inflicted on those who neglect religion; and therefore that religion may, by a deserved right, be required from man according to this relation; and this is the principal relation, according to which we must, in sacred theology, treat about the creation of man after the image of God. XII. In addition to this image of God, and this reference to supernatural and spiritual things, comes under our consideration the state of the natural life, in which the first man was created and constituted, according to the apostle Paul, "that which is natural was first, and afterwards, that which is spiritual." (1 Cor. xv. 46.) This state is founded in the natural union of body and soul, and in the life which the soul naturally lives in the body; from which union and life it is that the soul procures for its body, things which are good for it; and, on the other hand, the body is ready for offices which are congruous to its nature and desires. According to this state or condition, there is a mutual relation between man and the good things of this world, the effect of which is, that man can desire them, and, in procuring them for himself, can bestow that labour which he deems to be necessary and convenient.

DISPUTATION XXVII - ON THE LORDSHIP OR DOMINION OF GOD

Through creation, dominion over all things which have been created by himself, belongs to the Creator. It is, therefore, primary, being dependent on no other dominion or on that of no other person; and it is, on this account, chief because there is none greater; and it is absolute, because it is over the entire creature, according to the whole, and according to all and each of its parts, and to all the relations which subsist between the Creator and the creature. It is, consequently, perpetual, that is, so long as the creature itself exists. II. But the dominion of God is the right of the Creator, and his power over the creatures; according to which he has them as his own property, and can command and use them, and do about them, whatever the relation of creation and the equity which rests upon it, permit. III. For the right cannot extend further than is allowed by that cause from which the whole of it arises, and on which it is dependent. For this reason, it is not agreeable to this right of God, either that he delivers up his creature to another who may domineer over such creature, at his arbitrary pleasure, so that he be not compelled to render to God an account of the exercise of his sovereignty, and be able, without any demerit on the part of the creature, to inflict every evil on a creature capable of injury, or, at least, not for any good of this creature; or that he [God] command an act to be done by the creature, for the performance of which he neither has, nor can have, sufficient and necessary powers; or that he employ the creature to introduce sin into the world, that he may, by punishing or by forgiving it, promote his own glory; or, lastly, to do concerning the creature whatever he is able, according to his absolute power, to do concerning him, that is eternally to punish or to afflict him, without [his having committed] sin. IV. As this is a power over rational creatures, (in reference to whom chiefly we treat on the dominion and power of God,) it may be considered in two views, either as despotic, or as kingly, or patriarchal. The former is that which he employs without any intention of good which may be useful or saving to the creature; that latter is that which he employs when he also intends the good of the creature itself. And this last is used by God through the abundance of his own goodness and sufficiency, until he considers the creature to be unworthy, on account of his perverseness, to have God presiding over him in his kingly and paternal authority. V. Hence, it is, that, when God is about to command some thing to his rational creature, he does not exact every thing which he justly might do, and he employs persuasions through arguments which have regard to the utility and necessity of those persuasions. VI. In addition to this, God enters into a contract or covenant with his creature; and he does this for the purpose that the creature may serve him, not so much "of debt," as from a spontaneous, free and liberal obedience, according to the nature of confederations which consist of stipulations and promises. On this account, God frequently distinguishes his law by the title of a COVENANT. VII. Yet this condition is always annexed to the confederation, that if man be unmindful of the covenant and a contemner of its pleasant rule, he may always be impelled or governed by that domination which is really lordly, strict and rigid, and into which, he who refuses to obey the other [species of rule], justly falls. VIII. Hence, arises a two-fold right of God over his rational creature. The First, which belongs to him through creation; the Second, through contract. The former rests on the good which the creature has received from his Creator; the latter rests on the still greater benefit which the creature will receive from God, his preserver, promoter and glorifier. IX. If the creature happen to sin against this two-fold right, by that very act, he gives to God, his Lord, King and Father, the right of treating him as a sinning creature, and of inflicting on him due punishment; and this is a THIRD right, which rests on the wicked act of the creature against God.

DISPUTATION XXVIII - ON THE PROVIDENCE OF GOD

Not only does the very nature of God, and of things themselves, but likewise the Scriptures and experience do, evidently, show that providence belongs to God. II. But providence denotes some property of God, not a quality, or a capability, or a habit; but it is an act, which is not ad intra nor internal, but which is ad extra and external, and which is about an object different from God, and that is not united to him from all eternity, in his understanding, but as separate and really existing. III. And it is an act of the practical understanding, or of the will employing the understanding, not completed in a single moment, but continued through the moments of the duration of things. IV. And it may be defined the solicitous, everywhere powerful, and continued inspection and oversight of God, according to which he exercises a general care over the whole world, and over each of the creatures and their actions and passions, in a manner that is befitting himself, and suitable for his creatures, for their benefit, especially for that of pious men, and for a declaration of the divine perfection. V. We have represented the object of it to be both the whole world as it is a single thing consisting of many parts which have a certain relation among themselves, and possessing order between each other, and each our the creatures, with its actions and passions. We preserve the distinction of the goodness which is in them, (1.) According to their nature, through creation; (2.) According to grace, through the communication of supernatural gifts, and elevation to dignities; (3.) According to the right use both of nature and grace; yet we ascribe the last two, also, to the act of providence. VI. The rule of providence, according to which it produces its acts, is the wisdom of God, demonstrating what is worthy of God, according to his goodness, His severity, or his love for justice or for the creature, but always according to equity. VII. The acts of providence which belong to its execution, are -- preservation, which appears to be occupied about essences, qualities and quantities -- and government, which presides over actions and passions, and of which the principal acts are motion, assistance, concurrence and permission. The three former of these acts extend themselves to good, whether natural or moral; and the last of them appertains to evil alone. VIII. The power of God serves universally, and at all times, to execute these acts, with the exception of permission; specially, and sometimes, these acts are executed by the creatures themselves. Hence, an act of providence is called either immediate or mediate. When it employs [the agency of] the creatures, then it permits them to conduct their motions agreeably to their own nature, unless it be his pleasure to do any thing out of the ordinary way. IX. Then, those acts which are performed according to some certain course of nature or of grace, are called ordinary; those which are employed either beyond, above, or also contrary to this order, are styled extraordinary; yet they are always concluded by the terms due fitness and suitableness, of which we have treated in the definition. (Thesis 4.) X. Degrees are laid down in providence, not according to intuition or oversight itself, neither according to presence or continuity, but according to solicitude and care, which yet are free from anxiety, but which are greater concerning a man than concerning bullocks, also greater concerning believers and pious persons, than concerning those who are impious. XI. The end of providence and of all its acts, is the declaration of the divine perfections, of wisdom, goodness, justice, severity and power, and the good of the whole, especially of those men who are chosen or elected. XII. But since God does nothing, or permits it to be done in time, which he has not decreed from all eternity, either to do or to permit that decree, therefore, is placed before providence and its acts as an internal act is before one that is external. XIII. The effect, or, rather, the consequence, which belongs to God himself, is his prescience; and it is partly called natural and necessary, and partly free -- FREE, because it follows the act of the divine free will, without which it would not be the object of it -- Natural and Necessary, so far as, (when this object is laid down by the act of the divine will,) it cannot be unknown by the divine understanding. XIV. Prediction sometimes follows this prescience, when it pleases God to give intimations to his creatures of the issues of things, before they come to pass. But neither prediction nor any prescience induces a necessity of any thing that is afterwards to be, since they are [in the divine mind.] posterior in nature and order to the thing that is future. For a thing does not come to pass because it has been foreknown or foretold; but it is foreknown and foretold because it is yet to come to pass. XV. Neither does the decree itself, by which the Lord administers providence and its acts, induce any necessity on things future; for, since it, the decree, (§ 12) is an internal act of God, it lays down nothing in the thing itself. But things come to pass and happen either necessarily or contingently, according to the mode of power, which it has pleased God. to employ in the administration of affairs.

DISPUTATION XXIX - ON THE COVENANT INTO WHICH GOD ENTERED WITH OUR FIRST PARENTS

Though, according to His right and power over man, whom he had created after his own image, God could prescribe obedience to him in all things for the performance of which he possessed suitable powers, or would, by the grace of God, have them in that state; yet, that he might elicit from man voluntary and free obedience, which, alone, is grateful to him, it was his will to enter into a contract and covenant with him, by which God required obedience, and, on the other hand, promised a reward, to which he added the denunciation of a punishment, that the transaction might not seem to be entirely one between equals, and as if man was not completely bound to God. II. On this account, the law of God is very often called a Covenant, because it consists of those two parts, that is, a work commanded, and a reward promised, to which is subjoined the denunciation of a punishment, to signify the right which God had over man and which he has not altogether surrendered, and to incite man to greater obedience. III. God prescribed this obedience, first, by a law placed in and imprinted on the mind of man, in which is contained his natural duty towards God and his neighbour, and, therefore, towards himself also; and it is that of love, with fear, honour and worship towards a superior. For, as true virtue consists in the government or right ordering of the affections, (of which the first, the chief, and that on which the rest depend, is Love,) the whole law is contained in the right ordering of love. And, as no obedience seems to be yielded in the case of a man who executes the whole of his own will without any, even the least resistance, therefore, to try his obedience, that thing was to be prescribed, to which, by a certain feeling, man had an abhorrence; and that was to be forbidden, towards which he was drawn by a certain inclination. Therefore the love of ourselves was to be regulated or rightly ordered, which is the first and proximate cause that man should live in society with his species, or according to humanity. IV. To this law, it was the pleasure of God to add another, which was a symbolical one. A symbolical law is one that prescribes or forbids some act, which, in itself, is neither agreeable nor disagreeable to God, that is, one that is indifferent; and it serves for this purpose that God may try whether man is willing to yield obedience to him, solely on this account, because it has been the pleasure of God to require such obedience, and though it were impossible to devise any other reason why God imposed that law. V. That symbolical law was, in this instance, prohibitive of some act, to which man was inclined by some natural propensity, (that is, to eat of the tree of the knowledge of good and evil,) though "it was pleasant to the eyes and good for food." By the commanding of an indifferent act, it does not seem to have been possible to try the obedience of man with equal advantage. VI. This seems to be the difference between each [of these kinds of] obedience, that the first (Thesis I) is true obedience and, in itself, pleasing to God; and the man who performs it is said truly to live according to godliness; but that the latter (Theses 4 and 5) is not so much obedience, itself, as the external profession of willingly yielding obedience; and it is therefore an acknowledgment, or the token of an acknowledgment, by which man professes himself to be subject to God, and declares that he is willingly subject. Exactly in the same manner, a vassal yields obedience to his lord, for having fought against his enemies, which obedience he confesses that he cheerfully performs to him, by presenting him annually with a gift of small value. VII. From this comparison, it appears that the obedience which is yielded to a symbolical law is far inferior to that which is yielded to a natural law, but that the disobedience manifested to a symbolical law is not the less serious, or that it is even more grievous; because, by this very act, man professes that he is unwilling to submit himself, and indeed not to yield obedience in other matters, and those of greater importance, and of more difficult labour. VIII. The reward that corresponds with obedience to this chief law, the performance of which is, of itself, pleasing to God, (the analogy and difference which exist between God and man being faithfully observed,) is life eternal, the complete satisfying of the whole of our will and desire. But the reward which answers to the observance of the symbolical law, is the free enjoyment of the fruits of Paradise, and the power to eat of the tree of life, by the eating of which man was always restored to his pristine strength. But this tree of life was a symbol of eternal life, which man would have enjoyed, if, by abstaining from eating the fruit, he had professed obedience, and had truly performed such obedience to the moral law. IX. We are of opinion that, if our first parents had remained in their integrity by obedience performed to both these laws, God would have acted with their posterity by the same compact, that is, by their yielding obedience to the moral law inscribed on their hearts, and to some symbolical or ceremonial law; though we dare not specially make a similar affirmation, respecting the tree of the knowledge of good and evil. X. So, likewise, if they had persisted in their obedience to both laws, we think it very probable that, at certain periods, men would have been translated from this natural life, by the intermediate change of the natural, mortal and corruptible body, into a body spiritual, immortal, and incorruptible, to pass a life of immortality and bliss in heaven. COROLLARY We allow this to be made a subject of discussion: Did Eve receive this symbolical command about the tree of the knowledge of good and evil, immediately from God, or through Adam?

DISPUTATION XXX - THE MANNER IN WHICH MAN CONDUCTED HIMSELF FOR FULFILLING THE FIRST COVENANT, OR ON THE SIN OF OUR FIRST PARENTS

When God had entered into this covenant with men, it was the part of man perpetually to form and direct his life according to the conditions and laws prescribed by this covenant, because he would then have obtained the rewards promised through the performance of both those conditions, and would not have incurred the punishment due and denounced to disobedience. We are ignorant of the length of time in which man fulfilled his part; but the Holy Scriptures testify that he did not persevere in this obedience. II. But we say the violation of this covenant was a transgression of the symbolical law imposed concerning his not eating the fruit of the tree of the knowledge of good and evil. III. The efficient cause of that transgression was man, determining his will to that forbidden object, and applying his power or capability to do it. But the external, moving, per se, and principal cause was the devil, who, having accosted the woman, (whom he considered weaker than the man, and who when persuaded herself, would easily persuade him,) employed false arguments for persuasion. One of his arguments was deduced from the usefulness of the good which would ensue from this act; another was deduced from the setting aside of Him who had prohibited it, that is, by a denial of the punishment which would follow. The instrumental cause was the serpent, whose tongue the devil abused to propose what arguments he chose. The accidental cause was the fruit itself, which seemed good for food, pleasant in its flavor, and desirable to the eyes. The occasional cause was the law of God, that circumscribed by its interdict an act which was indifferent in its nature, and for which man possessed inclination and powers, that it might be impossible for this offense to be perpetrated without sin. IV. The only moving or antecedent cause was a two-fold inclination in man, a superior one for the likeness of God, and an inferior one for the desirable fruit, "pleasant to the sight, and good for food." Both of them were implanted by God through creation; but they were to be used in a certain method, order and time. The immediate and proximate cause was the will of man, which applied itself to the act, the understanding preceding and showing the way; and these are the causes which concurred to effect this sin, and all of which, as, through the image of God, he was able to resist, so was it his duty, through the imposing of that law, to have resisted. Not one of these, therefore, nor others, if such be granted in the genus of causes, imposed any necessity on man [to commit that sin]. It was not an external cause, whether you consider God, or something from God, the devil, or man. 5.(1.) It was not God; for since he is the chief good, he does nothing but what is good; and, therefore, he can be called neither the efficient cause of sin, nor the deficient cause, since he has employed whatever things were sufficient and necessary to avoid this sin. (2.) Neither was it something in God; it was neither His understanding nor his will, which commands those things which are just, performs those which are good, and permits those which are evil; and this permission is only a cessation from such an act as would in reality have hindered the act of man, by effecting nothing beyond itself, but by suspending some efficiency. This, therefore, cannot be the cause. (3.) Nor was the devil the cause; for he only infused counsel; he did not impel, or force by necessity. (4.) Eve was not the cause; for she was only able to precede by her example, and to entice by some argument, but not to compel. VI. It was not an internal cause -- whether you consider the common or general nature of man, which was inclined only to one good, or his particular nature, which exactly corresponded with that which is general; nor was it any thing in his particular nature, for this would have been the understanding; but it could act by persuasion and advice, not by necessity. Man, therefore, sinned by his free will, his own proper motion being allowed by God, and himself persuaded by the devil. VII. The matter of that sin was the eating of the fruit of the tree -- an act indifferent, indeed, in its nature, but forbidden by the imposing of a law, and withdrawn from the power of man. lie could also have easily abstained from it without any loss of pleasure. In this, is apparent the admirable goodness of God, who tries whether man be willing to submit to the divine command in a matter which could so easily be avoided. VIII. The form was the transgression of the law imposed, or the act of eating as having been forbidden; for as it had been forbidden, it had gone beyond the order of lawful and good acts, and had been taken away from the [allowable] power of man, that it might not be exercised without sin. IX. There was no end for this sin; for it always assumed the shape or habit of good. An end, however, was proposed by man, (but it was not obtained, that he might satisfy both his superior propensity towards the image of God, and his inferior one towards the fruit of the tree. But the end of the devil was the aversion of man from his God, and, through this, his further seduction into exile, and the society of the evil one. But the permission of God had respect to the antecedent condition of creation, which had made men possessed of free will, and for [the performance of] acts glorious to God, which might arise from it. X. The serious enormity of that sin is principally manifest from the following particulars: (1.) Because it was a transgression of such a law as had been imposed to try whether man was willing to be subject to the law of God, and it carried with it numbers of other grievous sins. (2.) Because, after God had loaded man with such signal gifts, he had the audacity to perpetrate this sin. (3.) Because, when there was such great facility to abstain from sin, he suffered himself to be so easily induced, and did not satisfy his inclination in such a copious abundance of things. (4.) Became he committed that sin in a sanctified place which was a type of the heavenly Paradise, almost under the eyes of God himself, who convened with him in a familiar manner.

DISPUTATION XXXI - ON THE EFFECTS OF THE SIN OF OUR FIRST PARENTS

The first and immediate effect of the sin which Adam and Eve committed in eating of the forbidden fruit, was the offending of the Deity, and guilt -- Offense, which arose from the prohibition imposed -- Guilt, from the sanction added to it, through the denunciation of punishment, if they neglected the prohibition. II. From the offending of the Deity, arose his wrath on account of the violated commandment. In this violation, occur three causes of just anger: (1.) The disparagement of his power or right. (2.) A denial of that towards which God had an inclination. (3.) A contempt of the divine will intimated by the command. III. Punishment was consequent on guilt and the divine wrath; the equity of this punishment is from guilt, the infliction of it is by wrath. But it is preceded both by the wounding of the conscience, and by the fear of an angry God and the dread of punishment. Of these, man gave a token by his subsequent flight, and by "hiding himself from the presence of the Lord God, when he heard him walking in the garden in the cool of the day and calling unto Adam." IV. The assistant cause of this flight and hiding [of our first parents] was a consciousness of their own nakedness, and shame on account of that of which they had not been previously ashamed. This seems to have served for racking the conscience, and for exciting or augmenting that fear and dread. V. The Spirit of grace, whose abode was within man, could not consist with a consciousness of having offended God; and, therefore, on the perpetration of sin and the condemnation of their own hearts, the Holy Spirit departed. Wherefore, the Spirit of God likewise ceased to lead and direct man, and to bear inward testimony to his heart of the favour of God. This circumstance must be considered in the place of a heavy punishment, when the law, with a depraved conscience, accused, bore its testimony [against them], convicted and condemned them. VI. Beside this punishment, which was instantly inflicted, they rendered themselves liable to two other punishments; that is, to temporal death, which is the separation of the soul from the body; and to death eternal, which is the separation of the entire man from God, his chief good. VII. The indication of both these punishments was the ejectment of our first parents out of Paradise. It was a token of death temporal; because Paradise was a type and figure of the celestial abode, in which consummate and perfect bliss ever flourishes, with the translucent splendour of the divine Majesty. It was also a token of death eternal, because, in that garden was planted the tree of life, the fruit of which, when eaten, was suitable for continuing natural life to man without the intervention of death. This tree was both a symbol of the heavenly life of which man was bereft, and of death eternal, which was to follow. VIII. To these may be added the punishment peculiarly inflicted on the man and the woman -- on the former, that he must eat bread through "the sweat of his face," and that "the ground, cursed for his sake, should bring forth to him thorns and thistles;" on the latter, that she should be liable to various pains in conception and child-bearing. The punishment inflicted on the man had regard to his care to preserve the individuals of the species, and that on the woman, to the perpetuation of the species. IX. But because the condition of the covenant into which God entered with our first parents was this, that, if they continued in the favour and grace of God by an observance of this command and of others, the gifts conferred on them should be transmitted to their posterity, by the same divine grace which they had, themselves, received; but that, if by disobedience they rendered themselves unworthy of those blessings, their posterity, likewise, should not possess them, and should be liable to the contrary evils. This was the reason why all men, who were to be propagated from them in a natural way, became obnoxious to death temporal and death eternal, and devoid of this gift of the Holy Spirit or original righteousness. This punishment usually receives the appellation of "a privation of the image of God," and "original sin." X. But we permit this question to be made a subject of discussion: Must some contrary quality, beside the absence of original righteousness, be constituted as another part of original sin? though we think it much more probable, that this absence of original righteousness, only, is original sin, itself, as being that which alone is sufficient to commit and produce any actual sins whatsoever. XI. The discussion, whether original sin be propagated by the soul or by the body, appears to us to be useless; and therefore the other, whether or not the soul be through traduction, seems also scarcely to be necessary to this matter.

DISPUTATION XXXII - ON THE NECESSITY OF THE CHRISTIAN RELIGION

Without religion, man can have no union with God; and without the command and institution of God, no religion can subsist, which, since it appertains to himself, either by the right of creation, or by the additional right of restoration, he can vary it according to his own pleasure; so that, in whatever manner he may appoint religion,. he always obligates man to observe it, and through this obligation, imposes on him the necessity of observing it. II. But the mode of religion is not changed, except with a change of the relation between God and man, who must be united to him; and when this relation is changed, religion is varied, that is, on the previous supposition that man is yet to be united to God; for, as to its substance, (which consists in the knowledge of God, faith, love, &c.,) religion is always the same, except it seem to be referred to the substance, that Christ enters into the Christian religion as its object. III. The first relation, and that which was the first foundation of the primitive religion, was the relation between God and man -- between God as the Creator, and man as created after the image and in a state of innocency; wherefore the religion built upon that relation was that of rigid and strict righteousness and legal obedience. But that relation was changed, through the sin of man, who after this was no longer innocent and acceptable to God, but a transgressor and doomed to damnation. Therefore, after [the commission of] sin, either man could have had no hope of access to God and to a union with him, since he had violated and abrogated the divine worship; or a new relation of man to his Creator was to be founded by God, through his gracious restoration of man, and a new religion was to be instituted on that relation. This is that which God has done, to the praise of his own glorious grace. IV. But, as God is not the restorer of a sinner, except in a mediator, who expiates sins, appeases God, and sanctifies the sinner, I repeat it, except in that "one Mediator between God and men, the man Christ Jesus," it was not the will of our most glorious and most gracious God, alone and without this Mediator, either that there should be any foundation between him and the sinner restored by him, or that there should be an object to the religion, which, to the honour of the restorer and to the eternal felicity of the restored, he would construct upon that relation. For it pleased the Father, through Christ, to reconcile all things to himself, and by him to restore both those things which are in heaven, and those on earth. It also pleased the Father "that all men should honour the Son, even as they honour the Father;" so that whosoever does not honour the Son, does not honour the Father. V. Wherefore, after the entrance of sin, there has been no salvation of men by God, except through Christ, and no saving worship of God, except in the name of Christ, and with regard to him who is the Anointed One for sinners, but the saviour of them who believe on him; so that whosoever is without God is without Christ; and he that is without Christ, is without the faith, the worship and the religion of Christ; and without the faith and hope of this Christ, either promised and shadowed forth in types, or exhibited and clearly announced, neither were the ancient patriarchs saved, nor can we be saved. VI. On this account, as the transgression of the first covenant contains the necessity of constituting another religion, and as this would not have occurred if that first covenant had not been made, it appears that. those things upon which the Scriptures treat, concerning the first covenant, and its transgression on the part of the first human beings, contain the occasion of the restoration which God was to make through Christ, and that they were, therefore, to be thus treated in the Christian religion. This conclusion is easily drawn from the very form of the narration given by Moses. VII. God is also the object of the Christian religion, both as Creator, and as Restorer in Christ, the Son of his love; and these titles contain the reason why God can demand religion from man, who has been formed by his CREATOR a creature, and by his Restorer a new creature. In this object, also, must be considered what is the will of the Glorifier of man, who leads him out from the demerit of sin, and from misery, to eternal felicity. These three names, Creator, Restorer, and Glorifier, contain the most powerful arguments by which man is persuaded to religion. VIII. But because it was the good pleasure of God to make this restoration through his Son, Jesus Christ, the Mediator, therefore, the Son of God, as constituted by the Father Christ and Lord, is likewise an object of the Christian religion subordinate to God; though he on earth, as the Word of his Father, both may be and ought to be considered as existing in the Father from all eternity.

DISPUTATION XXXIII - ON THE RESTORATION OF MAN

Since God is the object of the Christian religion, not only as the Creator, but also and properly as the Restorer, of the human race, and as we have finished our treatise on the creation, we will now proceed to treat on the restoration of mankind, because it is that which contains, in itself, another cause why God by deserved right can require religion from a man and a sinner. II. This restoration is the restitution, and the new or the second creation, of sinful man, obnoxious through sin to death temporal and eternal, and to the dominion of sin. III. The antecedent or only moving cause is the gracious mercy of God, by which it was his pleasure to pardon sin and to succour the misery of his creature. IV. The matter about which [it is exercised] is man, a sinner, and, on account of sin, obnoxious to the wrath of God and the servitude of sin. This matter contains in itself the outwardly moving cause of his gracious mercy, but accidentally, through this circumstance, that God delights in mercy; for in every other respect sin is per se and properly the external and meritorious cause of wrath and damnation. V. We may indeed conceive the form, under the general notion of restitution, reparation, or redemption; but we do not venture to give an explanation of it, except under two particular acts, the first of which is the remission of sins, or the being received into favour; the other is the renewal or sanctification of sinful man after the image of God, in which is contained his adoption into a son of God. VI. The first end is the praise of the glorious grace of God, which springs from, and exists at the same time with, the very act of restitution or redemption; the other end is, that, after men have been thus repaired, they "should live soberly, righteously and godly, in this present world," and should attain to a blissful felicity in the world to come. VII. But it has pleased God not to exercise this mercy in restoring man, without the declaration of his justice, by which he loves righteousness and hates sin; and he has, therefore, appointed that the mode of transacting this restoration should be through a mediator intervening between him and sinful man, and that this restoration should be so performed as to make it certain and evident that God hates sin and loves righteousness, and that it is his will to remit nothing of his own right, except after his justice had been satisfied. VIII. For the fulfilling of this mediation, God has constituted his only begotten Son the mediator between him and men, and indeed a mediator through his own blood and death; for it was not the will of God that, without the shedding of blood and the intervention of the death of the Testator himself, there should be any remission, or a confirmation of the New Testament, which promises remission and the inscribing of the law of God in the hearts [of believers]. IX. This is the reason why the second object of the Christian religion, in subordination to God, is Jesus Christ, the Mediator of this restoration, after the Father had made him Christ [the Anointed One] and had constituted him the Lord and the Head of the church, so that we must, through him, approach to God for the purpose of performing [acts of] religion to him; and the duty of religion must be rendered to him, with God the Father, from which duty we by no means exclude the Spirit of the Father and the Son.

DISPUTATION XXXIV - ON THE PERSON OF OUR LORD JESUS CHRIST

Because our Lord Jesus Christ is the secondary object of the Christian religion, we must further treat on him, as such, in a few disputations. But we account it necessary, in the first place, to consider the person, of what kind he is, in himself. II. We say that this person is the Son of God and the son of man, consisting of two natures, the divine and the human, inseparably united without mixture or confusion, not only according to habitude or indwelling, but likewise by that union which the ancients have correctly denominated hypostatical. III. He has the same nature with the Father, by internal and external communication. IV. He has his human nature from the virgin Mary through the operation of the Holy Spirit, who came upon her and overshadowed her by fecundating her seed, so that from it the promised Messiah should, in a supernatural manner, be born. V. But, according to his human nature, he consists of a body truly organic, and of a soul truly human which quickened or animated his body. In this, he is similar to other persons or human beings, as well as in all the essential and natural properties both of body and soul. VI. From this personal union arises a communication of forms or properties; such communication, however, was not real, as though some things which are proper to the divine nature were effused into the human nature; but it was verbal, yet it rested on the truth of this union, and intimated the closest conjunction of both the natures. COROLLARY The word autoqeov "very God," so far as it signifies that the Son of God has the divine essence from himself, cannot be ascribed to the Son of God, according to the Scriptures and the sentiments of the Greek and Latin churches.

DISPUTATION XXXV - ON THE PRIESTLY OFFICE OF CHRIST

Though the person of Christ is, on account of its excellence, most worthy to be honoured and worshipped, yet, that he might be, according to God, the object of the Christian religion, two other things, through the will of God, were necessary: (1.) That he should undertake some offices for the sake of men, to obtain eternal salvation for them. (2.) That God should bestow on him dominion or lordship over all things, and full power to save and to damn, with an express command, "that all men should honour the Son even as they honour the Father," and that "every knee should bow to him, to the glory of God the Father." II. Both these things are comprehended together under the title of saviour and Mediator. He is a saviour, so far as that comprises the end of both, and a Mediator, as it denotes the method of performing the end of both. For the act of saving, so far as it is ascribed to Christ, denotes the acquisition and communication of salvation. But Christ is the Mediator of men before God in soliciting and obtaining salvation, and the Mediator of God with men in imparting it. We will now treat on the former of these. III. The Mediator of men before God, and their saviour through the soliciting and the acquisition of salvation, (which is also called, by the orthodox, "through the mode of merit,") has been constituted a priest, by God, not according to the order of Levi, but according to that of Melchisedec, who was "priest of the most high God," and at the same time "king of Salem." IV. Through the nature of a true and not of a typical priest was at once both priest and victim in one person, which [duty], therefore, he could not perform except through true and substantial obedience towards God who imposed the office on him. V. In the priesthood of Christ, must be considered the preparation for the office, and the discharge of it. (1.) The Preparation is that of the priest and of the victim; the Priest was prepared by vocation or the imposition of the office, by the sanctification and consecration of his person through the Holy Spirit, and through his obedience and sufferings, and even in some respect by his resuscitation from the dead. The victim was also prepared by separation, by obedience, (for it was necessary that the victim should likewise be holy,) and by being slain. 6.(2.) The Discharge of this office consists in the offering or presentation of the sacrifice of his body and blood, and in his intercession before God. Benediction or blessing, which, also, belonged to the sacerdotal office in the Old Testament, will, in this case, be more appropriately referred to the very communication of salvation, as we read in the Old Testament that kings, also, dispensed benedictions. VII. The results of the fulfillment of the sacerdotal office are, reconciliation with God, the obtaining of eternal redemption, the remission of sins, the Spirit of grace, and life eternal. VIII. Indeed, in this respect, the priesthood of Christ was propitiatory. But, because we, also, by his beneficence have been constituted priests to offer thanksgivings to God through Christ, therefore, he is also a eucharistical priest, so far as he offers our sacrifices to God the Father, that, when they are offered by his hands, the Father may receive them with acceptance. IX. It is evident, from those things which have been now advanced, that Christ, in his sacerdotal office, has neither any successor, vicar, nor associate, whether we consider the oblation, both of his propitiatory sacrifice which he offered of those things which were his own, and of his eucharistical sacrifice which he offered of those also, which belonged to us, or whether we consider his intercession. COROLLARIES I. We deny that the comparison between the priesthood of Christ and that of Melchisedec, consisted either principally or in any manner in this, that Melchisedec offered bread and wine when he met Abraham returning from the slaughter of the kings. II. That the propitiatory sacrifice of Christ is bloodless, implies a contradiction, according to the Scriptures. III. The living Christ is presented to the Father in no other place than in heaven. Therefore, he is not offered in the mass.

DISPUTATION XXXVI - ON THE PROPHETICAL OFFICE OF CHRIST

The prophetical office of Christ comes under consideration in two views -- either as he executed it in his own person while he was a sojourner on earth, or as he administered it when seated in heaven, at the right hand of the Father. In the present disputation, we shall treat upon it according to the former of these relations. II. The proper object of the prophetical office of Christ was not the law, though [he explained or] fulfilled that, and freed it from depraved corruptions; neither was it epaggelia the promise, though he confirmed that which had been made to the fathers; but it was the gospel and the New Testament itself, or "the kingdom of heaven and its righteousness. III. In this prophetical office of Christ are to be considered both the imposition of the office, and the discharge of it. 1. The imposition has sanctification, instruction or furnishing, inauguration, and the promise of assistance. IV. Sanctification is that by which the Father sanctified him to his office, from the very moment of his conception by the

Holy Spirit, (whence, he says, "To this end was I born, and for this cause came I into the world, that I should bear witness unto the truth,") and, indeed, in a manner far more excellent than that by which Jeremiah and John are said to have been sanctified. V. Instruction, or furnishing, is a conferring of those gifts which are necessary for discharging the duties of the prophetical office; and it consists in a most copious effusion of the Holy Spirit upon him, and in its abiding in him -- "the Spirit of wisdom and understanding, of counsel and might, of knowledge and of the fear of the Lord;" by which Spirit it came to pass that it was his will to teach according to godliness all those things which were to be taught, and that he had the courage to teach them -- his mind and affections, both concupiscible and irascible, having been sufficiently and abundantly instructed or furnished against all impediments. VI. But the instruction in things necessary to be known is said, in the Scriptures, to be imparted by vision and hearing, by a familiar knowledge of the secrets of the Father, which is intimated in the phrase in which he is said to be in the bosom of the Father, and in heaven. VII. His inauguration was made by the baptism which John conferred on him, when a voice came from the Father in heaven, and the Spirit, "in a bodily shape, like a dove, descended upon him." These were like credential letters, by which the power of teaching was asserted and claimed for him as the ambassador of the Father. VIII. To this, must be subjoined the promised perpetual assistance of the Holy Spirit, resting and remaining upon him in this very token of a dove, that he might administer with spirit an office so arduous. IX. In the Discharge of this office, are to be considered the propounding of the doctrine, its confirmation and the result. X. The propounding of the doctrine was made in a manner suitable, both to the things themselves, and to persons -- to his own person, and to the persons of those whom he taught with grace and authority, by accepting the person of no man, of whatsoever state or condition he might be. XI. The confirmation was given both by the holiness which exactly answers to the doctrine, and by miracles, predictions of future things, the revealing of the thoughts of men and of other secrets, and by his most bitter and contumelious death. XII. The result was two-fold: The First was one that agreed with the nature of the doctrine itself -- the conversion of a few men to him, but without such a knowledge of him as the doctrine required; for their thoughts were engaged with the notion of restoring the external kingdom. The Second, which arose from the depraved wickedness of his auditors, was the rejection of the doctrine, and of him who taught it, his crucifixion and murder. Wherefore, he complains concerning himself, in Isa. xlix. 4 "I have laboured in vain, I have spent my strength for nought." XIII. As God foreknew that this would happen, it is certain that he willed this prophetical office to serve, for the consecration of Christ, through sufferings, to undertake and administer the sacerdotal and regal office. And thus the prophetical office of Christ, so far as it was administered by him through his apostles and others of his servants, was the means by which his church was brought to the faith, and was saved. COROLLARY We allow this question to become a subject of discussion: Did the soul of Christ receive any knowledge immediately from the Logos operating on it, without the intervention of the Holy Spirit, which is called the knowledge of union?

DISPUTATION XXXVII - ON THE REGAL OFFICE OF CHRIST

As Christ, when consecrated by his sufferings, was made the author of salvation to all who obey him; and as for this end, not only the solicitation and the obtaining of blessings were required, (to which the sacerdotal office was devoted,) but also the communication of them, it was necessary for him to be invested with the regal dignity, and to be constituted Lord over. all things, with full power to bestow salvation, and whatever things are necessary for that purpose. II. The kingly office of Christ is a mediatorial function, by which, the Father having constituted him Lord over all things which are in heaven and in earth, and peculiarly the King and the head of his church, he governs all things and the church, to her salvation and the glory of God. We will view this office in accommodation to the church, because we are principally concerned in this consideration. III. The functions belonging to this office seem to be the following: Vocation to a participation in the kingdom of Christ, legislation, the conferring of the blessings in this life necessary to salvation, the averting of the evils opposed to them, and the last judgment and the circumstances connected with it. IV. Vocation is the first function of the regal office of Christ, by which he calls sinful men to repent and believe the gospel -- a reward being proposed concerning a participation of the kingdom, and a threatening added of eternal destruction from the presence of the Lord. V. Legislation is the second function of the regal office of Christ, by which he prescribes to believers their duty, that, as his subjects, they are bound to perform to him, as their Head and Prince -- a sanction being added through rewards and punishments, which properly agree with the state of this spiritual kingdom. VI. Among the blessings which the third function of the regal office of Christ serves to communicate, we number not only the remission of sins and the Spirit of grace inwardly witnessing with our hearts that we are the children of God, but likewise all those blessings which are necessary for the discharge of the office; as illumination, the inspiring of good thoughts and desires, strength against temptations, and, in brief, the inscribing of the law of God in our hearts, In addition to these, as many of the blessings of this natural life, as Christ knows will contribute to the salvation of those who believe in him. But the evils over the averting of which this function presides, must be understood as being contrary to these blessings. VII. Judgment is the last act of the regal office of Christ, by which, justly, and without respect of persons, he pronounces sentence concerning all the thoughts, words, deeds and omissions of all men, who have been previously summoned and placed before his tribunal; and by which he irresistibly executes that sentence through a just and gracious rendering of rewards, and through the due retribution of punishments, which consist in the bestowing of life eternal, and in the infliction of death eternal. VIII. The results or consequences which correspond with these functions, are, (1.) The collection or gathering together of the church, or the building of the temple of Jehovah; this gathering together consists of the calling of the gentiles, and the bringing back or the restoration of the Jews, through the faith which answers to the divine vocation. (2.) Obedience performed to the commands of Christ by those who have believed in the Lord, and who have, through faith, been made citizens of the kingdom of heaven. (3.) The obtaining of the remission of sins, and of the Holy Spirit, and of other blessings which conduce to salvation, as well as a deliverance from the evils which molest [believers] in the present life. (4.) Lastly. The resurrection from the dead, and a participation of life eternal. IX. The means by which Christ administers his kingdom, and which principally come under our observation in considering the church, are the word, and the Holy Spirit, which ought never to be separated from each other. For this Spirit ordinarily employs the word, or the meaning of the word, in its external preaching; and the word alone, without the illumination and the inspiration of the Holy Spirit, is insufficient. But Christ never separates these two things, except through the fault of those who reject the word and resist the Holy Spirit. X. The opposite results to these consequences are, the casting away of the yoke [of Christ], the imputation of sin, the denial or the withdrawing of the Holy Spirit, and the delivering over to the power of Satan to a reprobate mind, and to hardness of heart, with other temporal evils, and, lastly, death eternal. XI. From these things, it appears that the prophetical office, by which a church is collected through the word, ought to be a reserve or accessory to the regal office; and, therefore, that the administrators of it are rightly denominated "the apostles and the servants of Christ," as of him who sends them forth into the whole world, over which he has the power, and who puts words into their mouths, whose continued assistance is likewise necessary, that the word may produce such fruit as agrees with its nature. XII. This regal office is so peculiar to Christ, under God the Father, that he admits no man, even subordinately, into a participation of it, as if he would employ such an one for a ministerial head. For this reason, we say, that the Roman pontiff, who calls himself the head and spouse, though under Christ, is Antichrist.

DISPUTATION XXXVIII - ON THE STATES OF CHRIST'S HUMILIATION AND EXALTATION

Respecting the imposition and the execution of the offices which belong to Christ, two states of his usually come under consideration, both of them being required for this purpose - - that he may be able to bear the name of saviour according to the will of God, and, in reality, to perform the thing signified under this name. One of these states is that of his humiliation, and is, according to the flesh, natural; the other is that of glory, according to the Spirit, and is spiritual. II. To the first state, that of his humiliation, belong the following articles of our belief: "He suffered under Pontius Pilate, was crucified, dead and buried; he descended into hell." To the latter state, that of his exaltation, belong these articles: "He arose again from the dead; he ascended into heaven, and sitteth on the right hand of God the Father Almighty; from thence he shall come to judge the quick and the dead." III. The sufferings of Christ contain every kind of reproaches and torments, both of soul and body, which were inflicted on him partly by the fury of his enemies, and partly by the immediate chastisement of his Father. We say that these last are not contrary to the good of the natural life, but to that of the spiritual life. But we deduce the commencement of these sufferings from the time when he was taken into custody; for we consider those things which previously befell him, rather to have been forerunners of his sufferings, by which it might be put to the test, whether, with the prescience of those things which were to be endured, and, indeed, through an experimental knowledge, he would still be ready by voluntary obedience to endure other sufferings. IV. The crucifixion has the mode of murder, by which mode we are taught, that Christ was made a curse for us, that we, through his cross, might be delivered from the curse of the law; for this seems to have been the entire reason why God pronounced him accursed who hung on a tree or cross, that we might understand that Christ, having been crucified rather by divine appointment, than by human means, was reckoned accursed for our sake, by God himself. V. The death of Christ was a true separation of his soul from the body, both according to its effects and according to place. It would indeed have ensued from crucifixion, and especially from the breaking of his legs; on which account, he is justly said to have been killed by the Jews; but death was anticipated, or previously undertaken, by Christ himself, that he might declare himself to have received power from God the Father to lay down his soul and life, and that he died a voluntary death. The former of these seems to relate to the confirmation of the truth which had been announced by him as a prophet, and the latter, to the circumstances of his priestly office. VI. The burial of Christ has relation to his certain death; and his remaining in the grave signifies, that he was under the dominion of death till the hour of his resurrection. This state, we think, was denoted by the existence of Christ among the dead, of which his descent into hell [or hades] was the commencement, as his interment was that of his remaining in the tomb. This interpretation is confirmed, both by the second chapter of the Acts of the Apostles, and by the consent of the ancient church, who, in the symbol of her belief, had only the one or the other of these expressions, either "He descended into hell," or "He was buried." Yet if any man thinks the meaning of this article -- "He descended into hell" -- to be different from that which we have given, we will not contradict his opinion, provided it be agreeable to the Scriptures and to the analogy of faith. VII. This state [of humiliation] was necessary, both that he might yield obedience to his Father, and that, having been tempted in all things without sin, he might be able to sympathize with those who are tempted, and, lastly, that he might, by suffering, be consecrated as priest and king, and might enter into his own glory. VIII. But this state of glory and exhaltation contains three degrees -- his resurrection, ascension into heaven, and sitting at the right hand of the Father. IX. The commencement of his glory was his deliverance from the bonds of the grave, and his rising again from the dead, by which his body, that was dead and had been laid in the sepulcher, after the effects of death had been destroyed in it, was reunited to his soul, and brought back again to life, not to this natural, but to a spiritual life; though, from the overflowing force of natural life, he was able to perform its functions as long as it was necessary for him to remain with his disciples in the present life, after having "arisen again from the dead," to impart credibility to his resurrection. We ascribe this resurrection, not only to the Father through the Holy Spirit, but likewise to Christ himself, who had the power of taking up his life again. X. The assumption of Christ into heaven contains the progress of his exaltation. For, as he had finished, on earth, the office enjoined, and had received a body -- not a natural, earthly, corruptible, fleshly and ignominious body, but one spiritual, heavenly, incorruptible and glorious, and as other duties, necessary for procuring the salvation of men, were to be performed in and concerning heaven, it was right and proper that he should rise and be exalted to heaven, and should remain there until he comes to judgment. From these premises, the dogma of the papists concerning transubstantiation, and that of the Ubiguitarians concerning consubstantiation, or the bodily presence of Christ in, with and, under the bread, are refuted. XI. The exaltation of Christ to the right hand of the Father is the supreme degree of his exaltation; for it contains the consummate glory and power which have been communicated to Christ himself by the Father -- glory, in his being seated with the Father in the throne of majesty, both because the regal office has been conferred on him, with full command, and on earth above all and over all created things, and because the dignity was conferred on him of further discharging [the duties of] the sacerdotal office, in that action which was to be performed in heaven by a more sublime High Priest constituted in heaven itself. XII. In relation to the priesthood, the state of humiliation was necessary; because it was the part of Christ to appear in heaven before the face of his Father, sprinkled with his own blood, and to intercede for believers. It was also necessary, in relation to his regal office; because, (and in this behold the administration of the prophetical office placed in subordination to the regal!) because it was his duty to send the word and the Spirit from heaven, and to administer from the throne of his majesty all things in the name of his Father, and especially his church, by conferring on those who obey him, the blessings promised in his word and sealed by his Spirit, and by inflicting evils on the disobedient after they have abused the patience of God as long as his justice could bear it. Of this administration, the last act will be the universal judgment, for which we are now waiting. "Come, Lord Jesus!"

DISPUTATION XXXIX - ON THE WILL, AND COMMAND OF GOD THE FATHER AND OF CHRIST, BY WHICH THEY WILL AND COMMAND THAT RELIGION BE PERFORMED TO THEM BY SINFUL MAN

In addition to the things that God has done in Christ, and Christ has done through the command of the Father, for the redemption of mankind, who were lost through sin, by which both of them have merited that religious homage should be performed to them by sinful man -- and in addition to the fact that the Father has constituted Christ the saviour and Head, with full power and capability of saving through the administration of his priestly and regal offices, on account of which power, Christ is worthy to be worshipped with religious honours, and able to reward his worshipers, that he may not be worshipped in vain, it was requisite that the will of God the Father and of Christ should be subjoined, by which they willed and commanded that religious worship should be offered to them, lest the performance of religion should be "will-worship," or superstition. II. It was the will of God that this command should be proposed through the mode of a covenant, that is, through the mutual stipulation and promise of the contracting parties -- of a covenant, indeed, which is never to be disannulled or to perish, which is, therefore, denominated "the new covenant," and is ratified by the blood of Jesus Christ as Mediator. III. On this account, and because Christ has been constituted by the Father, a prince and Lord, with the full possession of all the blessings necessary to salvation, it is also called "a Testament" or "Will;" therefore, he, also, as the Testator, is dead, and by his death, has confirmed the testamentary promise which had previously been made, concerning the obtaining of the eternal inheritance by the remission of sins. IV. The stipulation on the part of God and Christ is, that God shall be God and Father in Christ [to a believer] if in the name, and by the command of God, he acknowledges Christ as his Lord and saviour, that is, if he believe in God through Christ, and in Christ, and if he yield to both of them love, worship, honour, fear, and complete obedience as prescribed. V. The promise, on the part of God the Father, and of Christ, is, that God will be the God and Father, and that Christ will be the saviour, (through the administration of his sacerdotal and regal offices,) of those who have faith in God the Father, and in Christ, and who, through faith, yield obedience to them; that is, God the Father, and Christ, will account the performance of religious duty to be grateful, and will crown it with a reward. VI. On the other hand, the promise of sinful man is that he will believe in God and in Christ, and through faith will yield compliance or render obedience. But the stipulation is that God be willing to be mindful of his compact and holy declaration. VII. Christ intervenes between the two parties; on the part of God, he proposes the stipulation, and confirms the promise with his blood; he likewise works a persuasion in the hearts of believers, and affixes to it his attesting seal, that the promise will be ratified. But, on the part of sinful man, he promises [to the Father] that, by the efficacy of his Spirit he will cause man to perform the things which he has promised to his God; and, on the other hand, he requires of the Father, that, mindful of his own promise, he will deign to bestow on those who answer this description, or believers, the forgiveness of all their sins, and life eternal. He likewise intervenes, by presenting to God the service performed by man, and by rendering it grateful and acceptable to God through the odour of his own fragrance. VIII. External seals or tokens are also employed to which the ancient Latin fathers have given the appellation of "Sacraments," and which, on the part of God, seal the promise that has been made by himself; but, on the part of men, they are "the hand-writing," or bond of that obligation by which they had bound themselves that nothing may in any respect be wanting which seems to be at all capable of contributing to the nature and relation of the covenant and compact into which the parties have mutually entered. IX. From all these things, are apparent the most sufficient perfection of the Christian religion and its unparalleled excellence above all other religions, though they also be supposed to be true. Its sufficiency consists in this -- both that it demonstrates the necessity of that duty which is to be performed by sinful man, to be completely absolute, and on no account to be remissible, by which the way is closed against carnal security -- and that it most strongly fortifies against despair, not only sinners, that they may be led to repentance, but also those who perform the duty, that they may, through the certain hope of future blessings, persevere in the course of faith and of good works upon which they have entered. These two [despair and carnal security] are the greatest evils which are to be avoided in the whole of religion. X. This is the excellence of the Christian religion above every other, that all these things are transacted by the intervention of Christ our mediator, priest and king, in which, numerous arguments are proposed to us, both for the establishment of the necessity of its performance, and for the confirmation of hope, and for the removal of despair, that cannot be shown in any other religion. On this account, therefore, it is not wonderful that Christ is said to be the wisdom of God and the power of God, manifested in the gospel for the salvation of believers. COROLLARY No prayers and no duty, performed by a sinner, are grateful to God, except with reference to Christ; and yet, people have acted properly in desiring and in beseeching God, that he would be pleased to bless King Messiah and the progress of his kingdom.

DISPUTATION XL - ON THE PREDESTINATION OF BELIEVERS

As we have hitherto treated on the object of the Christian religion, that is, on Christ and God, and on the formal reasons why religion may be usefully performed to them, and ought to be, among which reasons, the last is the will of God and his command that prescribes religion by the conditions of a covenant; and as it will be necessary now to subjoin to this a discourse on the vocation of men to a participation in that covenant, it will not be improper for us, in this place, to insert one on the Predestination, by which God determined to treat with men according to that prescript, and by which he decreed to administer that vocation, and the means to it. First, concerning the former of these. II. That predestination is the decree of the good pleasure of God, in Christ, by which he determined, within himself, from all eternity, to justify believers, to adopt them, and to endow them with eternal life, "to the praise of the glory of his grace," and even for the declaration of his justice. III. This predestination is evangelical, and, therefore, per- emptory and irrevocable; and, as the gospel is purely gracious, this predestination is also gracious, according to the benevolent inclination of God in Christ. But that grace excludes every cause which can possibly be imagined to be capable of having proceeded from man, and by which God may be moved to make this decree. IV. But we place Christ as the foundation of this predestination, and as the meritorious cause of those blessings which have been destined to believers by that decree. For the love with which God loves men absolutely to salvation, and according to which he absolutely intends to bestow on them eternal life, this love has no existence except in Jesus Christ, the Son of his love, who, both by his efficacious communication, and by his most worthy merits, is the cause of salvation, and not only the dispenser of recovered salvation, but likewise the solicitor, obtainer, and restorer of that salvation which was lost. Therefore, sufficient is not attributed to Christ, when he is called executor of the decree which had been previously made, and without the consideration of him as [the person] on whom that decree is founded. V. We lay down a two-fold matter for this predestination -- divine things, and the persons to whom the communication of them has been predestinated. (1.) Those divine things are the spiritual blessings which usually receive the appellations of grace and glory. (2.) The persons are the faithful, or believers; that is, they believe in God who justifies the ungodly, and in Christ raised from the dead. But faith, that is, the faith which is on Christ, the mediator between God and men, presupposes sin, and likewise the knowledge or acknowledgment of it. VI. We place the form of this predestination in the internal act itself of God, who foreordains to believers this union with Christ their Head, and a participation in his benefits. But we place the end in "the praise of the glory of the grace of God;" and as this grace is the cause of that decree, it is equitable that it should be celebrated by glory, though God, by using it, has rendered it illustrious and glorious. In this place, too, occurs the mention of justice itself, as that by the intervention of which Christ was given as mediator, and faith in him was required; because, without this mediator, God has neither willed to shew mercy, nor to save men without faith in him. VII. But, as this decree of predestination is according to election, which necessarily includes reprobation, we must likewise advert to it. As opposed to election, therefore, we define reprobation to be the decree of God's anger or of his severe will, by which, from all eternity, he determined to condemn to eternal death all unbelievers and impenitent persons, for the declaration of his power and anger; yet so, that unbelievers are visited with this punishment, not only on account of unbelief, but likewise on account of other sins from which they might have been delivered through faith in Christ. VIII. To both these is severally subjoined the execution of each; the acts of which are performed in that order in which they have been ordained by God in the decree itself; and the objects, both of the decree and of its execution, are completely the same and uniform, or they are invested with the same formal reason, though they are considered in the decree, as in the mind of God, through the understanding, but, in the execution of it, as such, actually in existence. IX. This predestination is the foundation of Christianity, of salvation, and of the certainty of salvation; and St. Paul treats upon it in his epistle to the Romans, (viii, 28-30) in the ninth and following chapters of the same epistle, and in the first chapter of that to the Ephesians.

DISPUTATION XLI - ON THE PREDESTINATION OF THE MEANS TO THE END

After we have finished our discussion on the predestination by which God has determined the necessity of faith in himself and in Christ, for the obtaining of salvation, according to which faith is prescribed to be performed as the bounden duty of man to God and Christ; it follows, that we treat on the predestination by which God determines to administer the means to faith. II. For, as that act of faith is not in the power of a natural, carnal, sensual, and sinful man, and as no one can perform this act except through the grace of God, but as all the grace of God is administered according to the will of God -- that will which he has had within himself from all eternity -- for it is an internal act, therefore, some certain predestination must be preconceived in the mind and will of God, according to which he dispenses that grace, or the means to it. III. But we can define this predestination, that it is the eternal decree of God, by which he has wisely and justly resolved, within himself, to administer those means which are necessary and sufficient to produce faith in [the hearts of] sinful men, in such a manner as he knows to be comportable with his mercy and with his severity, to the glory of his name and to the salvation of believers. IV. The object of this predestination is, both the means of producing this faith, and the sinful men to whom he has creed either to give or not to give this faith, as the object of the predestination discussed in the preceding disputation was faith itself, existing in the preconception of the mind of God. V. The antecedent, or only moving cause, impelling to make the decree, is not only the mercy of God, but also his severity. But his wisdom prescribes the mode which his justice administers, that what is justly due to mercy may be attributed to it, and that, in the mean time, regard may be had to severity, according to which God threatens that he will send a famine of the word on the earth. VI. The matter is the conceded or the denied dispensation of the means. The form is the ordained dispensation itself, according to which it is granted to some men and denied to others, or it is granted or denied on this and not on that condition. VII. The end for the sake of which, and the end which, are conjoined to the administration itself at the very same moment, and are the declaration of the mercy of God, and of his severity, wisdom and justice. The end for which it was intended, and which follows from the administration, is the salvation of believers. The results are, the condemnation of unbelievers, and the still more grievous condemnation of some men. VIII. But the proper and peculiar means destined, are the word and Spirit; to which, also, may be joined the good and the evil things of this natural life, which God employs for the same end, and of the nature and efficacy of which we shall treat in the disputation on Vocation, where they are used. IX. To these means, we attribute two epithets, "necessity" and "sufficiency," (§ 3,) which belong to them according to the will and nature of God, and which we also join together. (1.) Necessity is in them; because, without them, a sinner cannot conceive faith. (2.) Sufficiency also is in them; because they are employed in vain, if they be not sufficient; yet we do not account it necessary to place this sufficiency in the first moment in which they begin to be used, but in the entire progress and completion. X. God destines these means to no persons on account of, or according to, their own merits, but through mere grace alone; and he denies them to no one, except justly, on account of previous transgressions.

DISPUTATION XLII - ON THE VOCATION OF SINFUL MEN TO CHRIST, AND TO A PARTICIPATION OF SALVATION IN HIM

The vocation or calling to the communion of Christ and its benefits, is the gracious act of God, by which, through the word and His Spirit, he calls forth sinful men, subject to condemnation and placed under the dominion of sin, from the condition of natural life, and out of the defilements and corruptions of this world, to obtain a supernatural life in Christ through repentance and faith, that they may be united in him, as their head destined and ordained by God, and may enjoy the participation of his benefits, to the glory of God and to their own salvation. II. The efficient cause of this vocation is God and the Father in the Son; the Son, also, himself, as constituted Mediator and King by God the Father, calls men by the Holy Spirit, as he is the Spirit of God given to the mediator, and the Spirit of Christ, the King and the Head of His church, by whom the Father and the Son both "work hitherto." But this vocation is so administered by the Spirit, that he also, is properly denominated the author of it. For he appoints bishops in the church, he sends teachers, he furnishes them with gifts, he grants them divine aid, and imparts force and authority to the word. III. The antecedent or only moving cause is the grace, mercy and philanthropy of God, by which he is inclined to succour the misery of sinful men, and to bestow blessedness upon him. But the disposing cause is, the wisdom and the justice of God, by which he knows the method by which it is proper for this vocation to be administered, and by which he wills to dispense it as it is proper and fight. From this, arises the decree of his will concerning its administration and mode. IV. The instrumental cause of vocation is the word of God administered by the aid of man, either by preaching or by writing; and this is the ordinary instrument; or it is the divine word immediately proposed by God, inwardly to the mind and will, without human aid or endeavour; and this is extraordinary. The word employed, in both these cases, is that both of the law and of the gospel, subordinate to each other in their separate services. V. The matter of vocation is men constituted in their sensual life, as worldly, natural, sensual, and sinful. VI. The boundary from which they are called, is, both the state of sensual or natural life, and that of sin and of misery on account of sin; that is, from condemnation and guilt, and afterwards from the bondage and dominion of sin. VII. The boundary to which they are called, is, the communication of grace, or of supernatural good, and of every spiritual blessing, the plenitude of which resides in Christ -- also their power and force, as well as the inclination to communicate them. VIII. The proximate end of vocation is, that men may love, fear, honour and worship God and Christ -- may in righteousness and true holiness, according to the command of the word of God, render obedience to God who calls them, and may, by this means, make their calling and election sure. IX. The remote end is the salvation of those who are called, and the glory of God and of Christ who calls; both of which are placed in the union of God and man. For as God unites himself to man, and declares himself to be prepared to unite himself to him, he makes his own glory illustrious; and, as man is united to God, he obtains salvation. X. This vocation is both external and internal. The external vocation is by the ministry of men propounding the word. The internal vocation is through the operation of the Holy Spirit illuminating and affecting the heart, that attention may be paid to those things which are spoken, and that credence may be given to the word. From the concurrence of both these, arises the efficacy of vocation. XI. But that distribution is not of a genus into its species, but of a whole into its parts; that is, the distribution of the whole vocation into partial acts concurring together to one result, which is obedience yielded to the vocation. Hence, the company of those who are called and who answer to the call, is denominated "a Church." XII. The accidental issue of vocation is, the rejection of the doctrine of grace, contempt of the divine counsel, and resistance manifested against the Holy Spirit, of which the proper and per se cause is, the wickedness and hardness of the human heart; and to this not unfrequently is added the just judgment of God, avenging the contempt shown to his word, from which arise blindness of mind, hardening of the heart, and a delivering up to a reprobate mind, and to the power of Satan.

DISPUTATION XLIII - ON THE REPENTANCE BY WHICH MEN ANSWER TO THE DIVINE VOCATION

As, in the matter of salvation, it has pleased God to treat with man by the method of a covenant, that is, by a stipulation, or a demand and a promise, and as even vocation has regard to a participation in the covenant; it is instituted on both sides and separately, that man may perform the requisition or command of God, by which he may obtain [the fulfillment of] his promise. But this is the mutual relation between these two -- the promise is tantamount to an argument, which God employs, that he may obtain from man that which he demands; and the compliance with the demand, on the other hand, is the condition, without which man cannot obtain what has been promised by God, and through [the performance of] which he most assuredly obtains the promise. II. Hence, it is apparent that the first of all which accepts this vocation is the faith, by which a man believes that, if he complies with the requisition, he will enjoy the promise, but that if he does not comply with it, he will not be put in possession of the things promised, nay, that the contrary evils will be inflicted on him, according to the nature of the divine covenant, in which there is no promise without a punishment opposed to it. This faith is the foundation on which rests the obedience that is to be yielded to God; and it is, therefore, the foundation of religion. III. But divines generally place three parts in this obedience. The first is repentance, for it is the calling of sinners to righteousness. The second is faith in Christ, and in God through Christ; for vocation is made through the gospel, which is the word of faith. The third is the observance of God's commands, in which consists holiness of life, to which believers are called, and without which no man shall see God. IV. Repentance is grief or sorrow on account of sins known and acknowledged, the debt of death contracted by sin, and on account of the slavery of sin, with a desire to be delivered. Hence, it is evident, that three things concur in penitence - - the first as an antecedent, the second as a consequence, and the third as properly and most fully comprising its nature. V. That which is tantamount to an antecedent is the knowledge or acknowledgment of sin. This consists of a two-fold knowledge: (1.) A general knowledge by which is known what is sin universally and according to the prescript of the law. (2.) A particular knowledge, by which it is acknowledged that sin had been committed, both from a recollection of the bad deeds perpetrated and of the good omitted, and from the examination of them according to the law. This acknowledgment, has, united with it, a consciousness of a two-fold demerit, of damnation or death, and of the slavery of sin; "for the wages of sin is death;" and "he who sins is the slave of sin." This acknowledgment is either internal, and made in the mind, or it is external, and receives the appellation of "confession." VI. That which intimately comprises the nature of repentance is, sorrow on account of sin committed, and of its demerit, which is so much the deeper, as the acknowledgment of sin is clearer, and more copious. It is also produced from this acknowledgment by means of a two-fold fear of punishment: (1.) A fear not only of bodily and temporal punishment, but likewise of that which is spiritual and eternal. (2.) The fear of God, by which men are afraid of the judgment of such a good and just being, whom they have offended by their sins. This fear may be correctly called "initial;" and we believe that it has some hope annexed to it. VII. That which follows as a consequence, is the desire of deliverance from sin, that is, from the condemnation of sin and from its dominion, which desire is so much the more intense, by how much the greater is the acknowledgment of misery and sorrow on account of sin. VIII. The cause of this repentance is, God by his word and Spirit in Christ. For it is a repentance tending not to despair, but to salvation; but such it cannot be, except with respect to Christ, in whom, alone, the sinner can obtain deliverance from the condemnation and dominion of sin. But the word which he uses at the beginning is the word of the law, yet not under the legal condition peculiar to the law, but under that which is annexed to the preaching of the gospel, of which the first word is, that deliverance is declared to penitents. The Spirit of God may, not improperly, be denominated "the Spirit of Christ," as he is Mediator; and it first urges a man by the word of the law, and then shows him the grace of the gospel. The connection of the word of the law and that of the gospel, which is thus skillfully made, removes all self-security, and forbids despair, which are the two pests of religion and of souls. IX. We do not acknowledge satisfaction, which the papists make to be the third part of repentance, though we do not deny that the man who is a real penitent will endeavour to make satisfaction to his neighbour against whom he owns that he has sinned, and to the church that he has injured by the offense. But satisfaction can by no means be rendered to God, on the part of man, by repentance, sorrow, contrition, almsgiving, or by the voluntary susception and infliction of punishments. If such a course were prescribed by God, the consciences of men must necessarily be tormented with the continual anguish of a threatening hell, not less than if no promise of grace had been made to sinners. But God considers this repentance, which we have described, if it be true, to be worthy of a gracious deliverance from sin and misery; and it has faith as a consequence, on which we will treat in the subsequent disputation. COROLLARY Repentance is not a sacrament, either with regard to itself, or with regard to its external tokens.

DISPUTATION XLIV - ON FAITH IN GOD AND CHRIST

In the preceding disputation, we have treated on the first part of that obedience which is yielded to the vocation of God. The second part now follows, which is called "the obedience of faith." II. Faith, generally, is the assent given to truth; and divine faith is that which is given to truth divinely revealed. The foundation on which divine faith rests is two-fold -- the one external and out of or beyond the mind -- the other internal and in the mind. (1.) The external foundation of faith is the very veracity of God who makes the declaration, and who can declare nothing that is false. (2.) The internal foundation of faith is two-fold -- both the general idea by which we know that God is true -- and the knowledge by which we know that it is the word of God. Faith is also two-fold, according to the mode of revelation, being both legal and evangelical, of which the latter comes under our present consideration, and tends to God and Christ. III. Evangelical faith is an assent of the mind, produced by the Holy Spirit, through the gospel, in sinners, who, through the law, know and acknowledge their sins, and are penitent on account of them, by which they are not only fully persuaded within themselves that Jesus Christ has been constituted by God the author of salvation to those who obey him, and that he is their own saviour if they have believed in him, and by which they also believe in him as such, and through him on God as the benevolent Father in him, to the salvation of believers and to the glory of Christ and God. IV. The object of faith is not only the God and Father of our Lord Jesus Christ, but likewise Christ himself who is here constituted by God the author of salvation to those that obey him. V. The form is the assent that is given to an object of this description; which assent is not acquired by a course of reasoning from principles known by nature; but it is an assent infused above the order of nature, which, yet, is confirmed and increased by the daily exercises of prayers and mortification of the flesh, and by the practice of good works. Knowledge is antecedent to faith; for the Son of God is beheld before a sinner believes on him. But trust or confidence is consequent to it; for, through faith, confidence is placed in Christ, and through him in God. VI. The author of faith is the Holy Spirit, whom the Son sends from the Father, as his advocate and substitute, who may manage his cause in the world and against it. The instrument is the gospel, or the word of faith, containing the meaning concerning God and Christ which the Spirit proposes to the understanding, and of which he there works a persuasion. VII. The subject in which it resides, is the mind, not only as it acknowledges this object to be true, but likewise to be good, which the word of the gospel declares. Wherefore, it belongs not only to the theoretical understanding, but likewise to that of the affections, which is practical. VIII. The subject to which [it is directed], or the object about which [it is occupied], is sinful man, acknowledging his sins, and penitent on account of them. For this faith is necessary for salvation to him who believes; but it is unnecessary to one who is not a sinner; and, therefore, no one except a sinner, can know or acknowledge Christ for his saviour, for he is the saviour of sinners. The end, which we intend for our own benefit, is salvation in its nature. But the chief end is the glory of God through Jesus Christ. COROLLARY "Was the faith of the patriarchs under the covenants of promise, the same as ours under the New Testament, with regard to its substance?" We answer in the affirmative.

DISPUTATION XLV - ON THE UNION OF BELIEVERS WITH CHRIST

As Christ is constituted by the Father the saviour of those that believe, who, being exalted. in heaven to the right hand of the Father, communicates to believers all those blessings which he has solicited from the Father, and which he has obtained by his obedience and pleading, but as the participation of blessings cannot be through communication, unless where there has previously been an orderly and suitable union between him who communicates and those to whom such communications are made, it is, therefore, necessary for us to treat, in the first place, upon the union of Christ with us, on account of its being the primary and immediate effect of that faith by which men believe in him as the only saviour. II. The truth of this thing, and the necessity of this union, are intimated by the names with which Christ is signally distinguished in a certain relation to believers. Such are the appellations of head, spouse, foundation, vine, and others of a similar kind; from which, on the other hand, believers are called members in his body, which is the entire church of believers, the spouse of Christ, lively stones built on him, and young shoots or branches. By these epithets, is signified the closest and most intimate union between Christ and believers. III. We may define or describe it to be that spiritual and most strict and therefore mystically essential conjunction, by which believers, being immediately connected, by God the Father and Jesus Christ through the Spirit of Christ and of God, with Christ himself, and through Christ with God, become one with him and with the Father, and are made partakers of all his blessings, to their own salvation and the glory of Christ and of God. IV. The author of this union is not only God the Father, who has constituted his Son the head of the church, endued him with the Spirit without measure, and unites believers to his Son; but also Christ, who communicates to believers that Spirit whom he obtained from the Father, that, cleaving to him by faith, they may be one Spirit. The administrators are prophets, apostles and other dispensers of the mysteries of God, who lay Christ as the foundation, and bring his spouse to him. V. The parties to be united are, (1.) Christ, whom God the Father has constituted the head, the spouse, the foundation, the vine, etc, and to whom he has given all perfection, with a plenary power and command to communicate it; (2.) And sinful man, and therefore destitute of the glory of God, yet a believer, and owning Christ for his saviour. VI. The bond of union must be considered both on the part of believers, and on the part of God and Christ. (1.) On the part of believers, it is faith in Christ and God, by which Christ is given to dwell in our hearts. (2.) On the part of God and Christ, it is the Spirit of both, who flows from Christ as the constituted head, into believers, that he may unite them to him as members. VII. The form of union is a compacting and joining together, which is orderly, harmonious, and in every part agreeing with itself by joints fitly supplied, according to the measure of the gifts of Christ. This conjunction receives various appellations, according to the various similitudes which we have already adduced. With respect to a foundation and a house built upon it, it is a being built up into [a spiritual house]. With respect to a husband and wife, it is a participation of flesh and bones; or, it is flesh of the flesh of Christ, and bone of his bones. With respect to a vine and its branches, or to an olive tree and its boughs, it is an engrafting and implanting. VIII. The proximate and immediate end is the communion of the parts united among themselves; this, also, is an effect consequent upon that union, but actively understood, as it flows from Christ, and positively, as it flows into believers, and is received by them. The cause of this is, that the relation is that of disquiparency, where the foundation is Christ, who possesses all things, and stands in need of nothing; the term, or boundary, is the believer in want of all things. The remote end is the external salvation of believers, and the glory of God and Christ. IX. But not only does Christ communicate his blessings to the believers, who are united to him, but he likewise considers, on account of this most intimate and close union, that the good things bestowed, and the evils inflicted on believers, are also done to himself. Hence, arise commiseration for his children, and certain succour, but anger against those who afflict, which abides upon them unless they repent, and beneficence towards those who have given even a draught of cold water, in the name of Christ, to one of his followers.

DISPUTATION XLVI - ON THE COMMUNION OF BELIEVERS WITH CHRIST, AND PARTICULARLY WITH HIS DEATH

The union of believers with Christ tends to communion with him, which contains, in itself, every end and fruit of union, and flows immediately from the union itself. II. Communion with Christ is that by which believers, when united to him, have, in common with himself all those things which belong to him; yet the distinction is preserved, which exists between the head and the members, between him who communicates, and them who are made partakers, between him who sanctifieth, and those who are sanctified. III. This communion must, according to the Scriptures, be considered in two views, for it is either a communion of his death, or of his life; because Christ must be thus considered in two relations, either according to the state in the body of his flesh, which was crucified, dead, and buried, or, according to his glorious state and the new life to which he was raised up again. IV. The communion of his death is that by which, being planted together in the likeness of his death, we participate of his power, and of all the benefits which flow from his death. V. This planting together is the crucifixion, the death and the burial of "our old man," or of "the body of sin," in and with the body of the flesh of Christ. These are the degrees by which the body of the flesh of Christ is abolished; that may also in its own measure, be called "the body of sin," so far as God has made Christ to be sin for us, and has given him to bear our sins, in his own body, on the tree. VI. The strength and efficacy of the death of Christ consist in the abolishing of sin and death, and of the law, which is "the hand-writing that is against us;" and the strength or force of sin is that by which sin kills us. VII. The efficacious benefits of the death of Christ which believers enjoy through communion with it, are principally the following: The First is the removal of the curse, which we had deserved through sin. This includes, or has connected with it, our reconciliation with God, perpetual redemption, remission of sins, and justification. VIII. The SECOND. is deliverance from the dominion and slavery of sin, that sin may no longer exercise its power in our crucified, dead and buried body of sin, to obtain its desires by the obedience which we have usually yielded to it in our body of sin, according to the old man. IX. The THIRD is deliverance from the law, both as it is "the hand-writing which was against us," consisting of ceremonial institutions, and as it is the rigid exactor of what is due from us, and useless and inefficacious as it is on account of our flesh, and the body of sin, according to which we were carnal, though it was spiritual, and as sin, by its wickedness and perversity, abused the law itself to seduce and kill us.

DISPUTATION XLVII - THE COMMUNION OF BELIEVERS WITH CHRIST IN REGARD TO HIS LIFE

Communion with the life of Christ is that by which, being engrafted into him by a conformity to his life, we become partakers of the whole power of his life, and of all the benefits which flow from it. II. Our conformity to the life of Christ, is either that of the present life, or of that which is future. (1.) That of the present life is the raising of us up into a new life, and our being seated, with regard to the Spirit, "in heavenly places" in Christ our head. (2.) That of the life to come is our resurrection into a new life according to the body, and our being elevated to heavenly places with regard to the entire man. III. Hence, our conformity to Christ is according to the same two-fold relation: in this life, it is our resurrection to newness of spiritual life, and our conversation in heaven according to the Spirit; after the present life, it is the resurrection of our, bodies, their conformity to the glorious body of Christ, and the fruition of celestial blessedness. IV. The blessings which flow from the life of Christ, fall partly within the limits of this life, and partly within the continued duration of the life to come. V. Those which fall within the limits of the present life are, adoption into sons of God, and the communication of the Holy Spirit. This communication composes within itself three particular benefits: First. Our regeneration, through the illumination of the mind and the renewal of the heart. Secondly. The perpetual aid of the

Holy Spirit to excite and co-operate. Thirdly. The testimony of the same Spirit with our hearts, that we are the children of God, on which account he is called "the Spirit of adoption." VI. Those which fall within the boundless duration of the life to come, are our preservation from future wrath, and the bestowing of life eternal;' though this preservation from wrath may seem to be a continued act, begun and carried on in this world, but consummated at the period of the last judgment. VII. Under the preservation from wrath, also, is not unsuitably comprehended continued justification from sins through the intercession of Christ, who, in his own blood, is the propitiation for our sins, and our advocate before God.

DISPUTATION XLVIII - ON JUSTIFICATION

The spiritual benefits which believers enjoy in the present life, from their union with Christ through communion with his death and life, may be properly referred to that of justification and sanctification, as in those two is comprehended the whole promise of the new covenant, in which God promises that he will pardon sins, and will write his laws in the hearts of believers, who have entered into covenant with him. II. Justification is a just and gracious act of God as a judge, by which, from the throne of his grace and mercy, he absolves from his sins, man, a sinner, but who is a believer, on account of Christ, and the obedience and righteousness of Christ, and considers him righteous, to the salvation of the justified person, and to the glory of divine righteousness and grace. III. We say that "it is the act of God as a judge," who though as the supreme legislator he could have issued regulations concerning his law, and actually did issue them, yet has not administered this direction through the absolute plenitude of infinite power, but contained himself within the bounds of justice which he demonstrated by two methods, First, because God would not justify, except as justification was preceded by reconciliation and satisfaction made through Christ in his blood; Secondly, because he would not justify any except those who acknowledged their sins and believed in Christ. IV. We say that "it is a gracious and merciful act; "not with respect to Christ, as if the Father, through grace as distinguished from strict and rigid justice, had accepted the obedience of Christ for righteousness, but with respect to us, both because God, through his gracious mercy towards us, has made Christ to be sin for us, and righteousness to us, that we might be the righteousness of God in him, and because he has placed communion with Christ in the faith of the gospel, and has set forth Christ as a propitiation through faith. V. The meritorious cause of justification is Christ through his obedience and righteousness, who may, therefore, be justly called the principal or outwardly moving cause. In his obedience and righteousness, Christ is also the material cause of our justification, so far as God bestows Christ on us for righteousness, and imputes his righteousness and obedience to us. In regard to this two-fold cause, that is, the meritorious and the material, we are said to be constituted righteous through the obedience of Christ. VI. The object of justification is man, a sinner, acknowledging himself, with sorrow, to be such an one, and a believer, that is, believing in God who justifies the ungodly, and in Christ as having been delivered for our offenses, and raised again for our justification. As a sinner, man needs justification through grace, and, as a believer, he obtains justification through grace. VII. Faith is the instrumental cause, or act, by which we apprehend Christ proposed to us by God for a propitiation and for righteousness, according to the command and promise of the gospel, in which it is said, "He who believes shall be justified and saved, and he who believeth not shall be damned." VIII. The form is the gracious reckoning of God, by which he imputes to us the righteousness of Christ, and imputes faith to us for righteousness; that is, he remits our sins to us who are believers, on account of Christ apprehended by faith, and accounts us righteous in him. This estimation or reckoning, has, joined with it, adoption into sons, and the conferring of a right to the inheritance of life eternal. IX. The end, for the sake of which is the salvation of the justified person; for that act is performed for the good of the man himself who is justified. The end which flows from justification without any advantage to God who justifies, is the glorious demonstration of divine justice and grace. X. The most excellent effects of this justification are peace with God and tranquillity of conscience, rejoicing under afflictions in hope of the glory of God and in God himself, and an assured expectation of life eternal. XI. The external seal of justification is baptism; the internal seal is the Holy Spirit, testifying together with our spirits that we are the children of God, and crying in our hearts, Abba, Father! XII. But we have yet to consider justification, both about the beginning of conversion, when all preceding sins are for, given, and through the whole life, because God has promised remission of sins to believers, those who have entered into covenant with him, as often as they repent and flee by true faith to Christ their propitiator and expiator. But the end and completion of justification will be at the close of life, when God will grant to those who end their days in the faith of Christ, to find his mercy, absolving them from all the sins which had been perpetrated through the whole of their lives. The declaration and manifestation of justification will be in the future general judgment. XIII. The opposite to justification is condemnation, and this by an immediate contrariety, so that between these two no medium can be imagined. COROLLARIES I. That faith and works concur together to justification, is a thing impossible. II. Faith is not correctly denominated the formal cause of justification; and when it receives that appellation from some divines of our profession, it is then improperly so called. III. Christ has not obtained by his merits that we should be justified by the worthiness and merit of faith, and much less that we should be justified by the merit of works: But the merit of Christ is opposed to justification by works; and, in the Scriptures, faith and merit are placed in opposition to each other.

DISPUTATION XLIX - ON THE SANCTIFICATION OF MAN

The word "sanctification" denotes an act, by which any thing is separated from common use, and is consecrated to divine use. II. Common use, about the sanctification of which [to divine purposes] we are now treating, is either according to nature itself, by which man lives a natural life; or it is according to the corruption of sin, by which he lives to sin and obeys it in its lusts or desires. Divine use is when a man lives according to godliness, in a conformity to the holiness and righteousness in which he was created. III. Therefore, this sanctification, with respect to the boundary from which it proceeds, is either from the natural use, or from the use of sin; the boundary to which it tends, is the supernatural and divine use. IV. But when we treat about man, as a sinner, then sanctification is thus defined: It is a gracious act of God, by which he purifies man who is a sinner, and yet a believer, from the darkness of ignorance, from indwelling sin and from its lusts or desires, and imbues him with the Spirit of knowledge, righteousness and holiness, that, being separated from the life of the world and made conformable to God, man may live the life of God, to the praise of the righteousness and of the glorious grace of God, and to his own salvation. V. Therefore, this sanctification consists in these two things: In the death of: the old man" who is corrupt according to the deceitful lusts," and in the quickening or enlivening of "the new man, who, after God, is created in righteousness and the holiness of truth." VI. The author of sanctification is God, the Holy Father himself, in his Son who is the Holy of holies, through the Spirit of holiness. The external instrument is the word of God; the internal one is faith yielded to the word preached. For the word does not sanctify, only as it is preached, unless the faith be added by which the hearts of men are purified. VII. the object of sanctification is man, a sinner, and yet a believer -- a sinner, because, being contaminated through sin and addicted to a life of sin, he is unfit to serve the living God -- a believer, because he is united to Christ through faith in him, on whom our holiness is founded; and he is planted together with Christ and joined to him in a conformity with his death and resurrection. Hence, he dies to sin, and is excited or raised up to a new life. VIII. The subject is, properly, the soul of man. And, first, the mind, which is illuminated, the dark clouds of ignorance being driven away. Next, the inclination or the will, by which it is delivered from the dominion of indwelling sin, and is filled with the spirit of holiness. The body is not changed, either as to its essence or its inward qualifies; but as it is a part of the man, who is consecrated to God, and is an instrument united to the soul, having been removed by the sanctified soul which inhabits it from the purposes of sin, it is admitted to and employed in the service of God, "that our whole spirit and soul and body may be preserved blameless unto the day of our Lord Jesus Christ." IX. The form lies in the purification from sin, and in a conformity with God in the body of Christ through his Spirit. X. The end is, that a believing man, being consecrated to God as a priest and king, should serve him in newness of life, to the glory of his divine name, and to the salvation of man. XI. As, under the Old Testament, the priests, when approaching to render worship to God, were accustomed to be sprinkled with blood, so, likewise, the blood of Jesus Christ, which is the blood of the New Testament, serves for this purpose-to sprinkle us, who are constituted by him as priests, to serve the living God. In this respect, the sprinkling of the blood of Christ, which principally serves for the expiation of sins, and which is the cause of justification, belongs also to sanctification; for in justification, this sprinkling serves to wash away sins that have been committed; but in sanctification, it serves to sanctify men who have obtained remission of their sins, that they may further be enabled to offer worship and sacrifices to God, through Christ. XII. This sanctification is not completed in a single moment; but sin, from whose dominion we have been delivered through the cross and the death of Christ, is weakened more and more by daily losses, and the inner man is day by day renewed more and more, while we carry about with us in our bodies, the death of Christ, and the outward man is perishing. COROLLARY We permit this question to be made the subject of discussion: Does the death of the body bring the perfection and completion of sanctification -- and how is this effect produced?

DISPUTATION L - ON THE CHURCH OF GOD AND OF CHRIST: OR ON THE CHURCH IN GENERAL AFTER THE FALL

As, through faith, which is the first part of our duty towards God and Christ, we have obtained the blessings of justification and sanctification from our union and communion with Christ, by which benefits we are, from children of wrath and the slaves of sin, not only constituted the children of God and the servants of righteousness, (on which account it is fit that we should render obedience and worship to our Parent and our Lord,) and as we have likewise obtained power and confidence for the performance of such obedience and worship, it would follow that we should now treat on obedience and worship as on another part of our duty. II. But as there are multitudes of those who have, through these benefits, been made the sons and the servants of God, and who have been united, among themselves, by the same faith and the Spirit of Christ, as members in one body, which is called the church, and of which the Scriptures make frequent mention, it appears to be the most proper course to treat, First, upon this church, because, as she derives her origin from this faith, she comprehends within her embraces all those to whom the performance of worship to God and Christ is to be prescribed. III. And as it has pleased God to institute certain signs by which may be sealed or testified, both the communion of believers with Christ and among themselves, and a participation of these benefits, and, on the other hand, their service of gratitude towards God and Christ, we shall deem it proper, NEXT, to treat upon these signs or tokens, before we proceed to the worship, itself, which is due to God and Christ. First, then, let us consider the church. IV. This word, in its general acceptation, denotes a company or congregation of men who are called out, and not only the act and the command of him who calls them out, but likewise the obedient compliance of those who answer the call; so that the result or effect of that act is included in the word "church. " V. But it is thus defined: A company of persons called out from a state of natural life and of sin, by God and Christ, through the Spirit of both, to a supernatural life to be spent according to God and Christ in the knowledge and worship of both, that by a participation with both, they may be eternally blessed, to the glory of God through Christ, and of Christ in God. VI. The efficient cause of this evocation, or calling out, is God the Father, in his Son Jesus Christ, and Christ himself, through the Spirit, both of the Father and of the Son as he is Mediator and the Head of the church, sanctifying and regenerating her to a new life. The impulsive cause is the gracious good pleasure of God the Father, in Christ, and the love of Christ towards those whom he has acquired for himself by his own blood. VII. The executive cause of this gracious good pleasure of God in Christ, which may also, in this respect, according to its distribution, be called "the administrative cause," is the Spirit of God and of Christ by the word of both; by which he requires outwardly a life according to God and Christ, with the addition of the promise of a reward and the threatening of a punishment; and he inwardly illuminates the mind to a knowledge of this life, imparts to us the feelings of love and desire for this life, and bestows on the whole man strength and power to live such a life. VIII. The matter about which [it is occupied], or the object of the vocations, are natural and sinful men, who, indeed, according to nature, are capable of receiving instruction from the Spirit through the word, but who are, according to the life of the present world and the state of sin, darkened in their minds and alienated from the life of God. This state requires that the beginning of preaching be made from preaching the law as it reproves sin and convinces of sin, and thus that progress be made to the preaching of the gospel of grace. IX. The form of the church resides in the mutual relation of God and Christ who calls, and of the church who obeys that call, according to which, God in Christ, by the Spirit of both, infuses into her supernatural life, feeling or sensation, and motion; and she, on the other hand, being quickened and under the influence of feeling and motion, begins to live and to walk according to godliness, and in expectation of the blessings promised. X. The end of this evocation, which also contains the chief good of the church, is blessedness perfected and consummated through a union with God in Christ. From this, results the glory of God, who unites the church to himself and beatifies her, which glory is declared in the very act of union and beatification -- also the glory of the same blessed God, when the church in her triumphant songs ascribes to him praise, honour and glory forever and ever. XI. From the act of this evocation and from the form of the church arising out of it, it appears that a distinction must be made among the men or congregation, as they are men, and as they are called out and obey the call; and they must be so distinguished that the company to whom the name of "the church" at any time belonged, may so decline from that obedience as to lose the name of "the church," God "removing their candlestick out of its place," and sending a bill of divorce to his disobedient and adulterous wife. Hence it is evident that the glorying of the papists is vain on this point -- that the church of Rome cannot err and fall away

DISPUTATION LI - ON THE CHURCH OF THE OLD TESTAMENT, OR UNDER THE PROMISE

As Jesus Christ is the same yesterday, to-day, and ever -- as he is the chief or deepest corner-stone, upon which the superstructure of the church is raised, being built up both by prophets and apostles, and as he is the head of all those who will be partaken of salvation, the whole church, therefore, may, in this sense, be called "Christian," though under this appellation, peculiarly, comes the church as she began to be collected together after the actual ascent of Christ into heaven. II. But though the church be one with respect to its foundation, and of those things which concern the substance itself yet, because it has pleased God to govern it according to different methods, in reference to this the church may, in the most suitable manner, be distinguished into the church which existed in the times of the Old Testament before Christ, and into that which flourished in the times of the New Testament and after Christ appeared on earth. III. "The church, prior to the advent of Christ, under the dispensation of the Old Testament," is that which was called out, (by the word of promise concerning the seed of the woman and the seed of Abraham, and concerning the Messiah who was subsequently to come,) from the state of sin and misery, to a participation of the righteousness of faith and salvation, and to the faith placed in that promise -- and by the word of the law, to render worship to God in confidence of obtaining mercy in this blessed Seed and the promised Messiah, in a manner suitable to the infantile age of the church herself. IV. The word of promise was propounded, in the beginning, in a very general manner and with much obscurity, but in succeeding ages, more specially and with greater distinctness, and still more so, as the times of the advent of the Messiah in the flesh drew nearer. V. The law which contributed to this calling, was both the moral and the ceremonial; (for, in this place, the forensic does not come under consideration;) and both of them as delivered orally, and as comprised and proposed in writing by Moses, in which last respect, the law is principally treated upon in the Scriptures of the Old and the New Testament. VI. The moral law serves this office in a two-fold manner: First, by demonstrating the necessity of the gracious promise, which it does by convincing [men] of sins against the law, and of the weakness [of man] to perform the law. To this purpose it has been rigidly and strictly propounded; and it is considered as so proposed, according to these passages: "The man that doeth them shall live in them," and "Cursed is every one that continueth not in all things which are written in the book of the law to do them." Secondly, by ewieikwv moderately, or with clemency, requiring the observance of it from those who were parties to the covenant of promise. VII. Though the observance of the ceremonial law be not, of itself, and on account of itself, pleasing to God, yet the observance of it was prescribed for two purposes: (1.) That it might convince of the guilt of sins and of the curse, and might thus declare the necessity of the gracious promise. (2.) And that it might sustain believers by the hope of the promise, which hope was confirmed by the typical presignification of future things. In the former of these two respects, the ceremonial law was the seal of sins; but in the latter, it was the seal of grace and remission. VIII. The church of those times must, therefore, be considered, both as it is called the heir, and as called the infant, either according to its substance, or according to the dispensation and economy suitable to those times. According to the former of these respects, the church was under the promise or the covenant of promise; and according to the latter respect, she was under the law and under the Old Testament, in regard to which, that people is called servile, or in bondage, and the infant heir "differing in nothing from a servant," as, in regard to the promise, the same people are denominated free, born of a free woman, and according to Isaac "counted for the seed" to whom the promise was made. IX. According to the promise, the church was a willing people -- according to the Old Testament, a carnal people; according to the former relation, the heir of spiritual and heavenly blessings; according to the latter, the heir of spiritual and earthly blessings, especially of the land of Canaan and of its benefits. According to the former relation, the church was endowed with the Spirit of adoption; according to the latter, she had this Spirit intermixed with that of bondage as long as the promise continued. X. The open consideration of these relations, and a suitable comparison and opposition between the covenant of promise, and the law or the Old Testament, contributes much to the [correct] interpretation of several passages of Scripture, which, otherwise, can scarcely be at all explained, or at least with great difficulty COROLLARIES I. Because the Old Testament was forced to be abrogated, therefore it was to be confirmed, not by the blood of a testator or mediator, but of brute animals. II. "The Old Testament" is never used in the Scriptures for the covenant of grace. III. The confounding of the promise and of the Old Testament is productive of much obscurity in Christian theology, and is the cause of more than a single error.

DISPUTATION LII - ON THE CHURCH OF THE NEW TESTAMENT, OR UNDER THE GOSPEL

The Church of the New Testament is that which, from the time when that Testament was confirmed by the blood of Christ the mediator of the New Testament, or from the period of his ascension into heaven, began to be called out from a state of sin which was plainly manifested by the word of the gospel, and by the Spirit that was suited to the heirs who had attained to the age of adults -- to a participation of the righteousness of faith and of salvation, through faith placed in the gospel, and to render worship to God and Christ in the unity of the same Spirit; and this church will continue to be called out in the same manner to the end of the world, to the praise of the glory of the grace of God and of Christ. II. The efficient cause is the God and Father of our Lord Jesus Christ, who has now most plainly manifested himself to be Jehovah and the Father of our Lord Jesus Christ; and it is Christ himself, elevated to the right hand of the Father, invested with full power in heaven and on earth, and endowed with the word of the gospel and with the Spirit beyond measure. The antecedent or only moving cause is the grace and mercy of God the Father and of Christ, and even the justice of God, to which, through the good pleasure of the Father, the fullest satisfaction has now been made in Jesus Christ, and which is clearly manifested in the gospel. III. The Spirit of Christ is the administering cause, according to the economy, as he is the substitute of Christ and receives of that which is Christ's, to glorify Christ by this calling forth in his church, with only a full power to administer all things according to his own pleasure. The Spirit uses the word of the gospel placed in the mouth of his servants, which immediately executes this vocation, and the word of the law, whether written or implanted in the mind; the gospel serves both antecedently that a place may be made for this vocation, and consequently when it has been received by faith. IV. The object of this evocation is, not only Jews, but also gentiles, the middle wall of partition which formerly separated the gentiles from the Jews being taken away by the flesh and blood of Christ; that is, the object is all men generally and promiscuously without any difference, but it is all men actually sinners, whether they be those who acknowledge themselves as such and to whom the preaching of the gospel is constantly exhibited, or those who are yet to be brought to the acknowledgment of their sins. V. Because this church is of adult age, and because she no longer requires a tutor and governor, she is free from the economical bondage of the law, and is governed by the spirit of full liberty, which is, by no means, intermixed with the spirit of bondage; and, therefore, she is free from the use of the ceremonial law, so far as it served for testifying of sins, and as it was "the hand-writing which was against us." VI. This church, also, with unveiled or open face, beholds the glory of the Lord as in a glass, and has the very express image of heavenly things, and Christ, the image of the invisible God, the express image of the Father's person, and the brightness of his glory, and the very body of things to come which is of Christ. She, therefore, does not need the law, which has the shadow of good things to come; on which account, she is free from the same ceremonial law, by which it typically prefigured Christ and good things to come. VII. The church of the New Testament has not experienced, does not now experience, and will not, to the end of the world, experience, in the whole of its course, any change whatever with regard to the word itself or the spirit; For, in these last times, God has spoken to us in his Son, and by those who have heard him. VIII. This same church is called "catholic," in a peculiar and distinct sense in opposition to the church which was under the Old Testament, so far as she has been diffused through the whole world, and has embraced within her boundary all nations, tribes, people and tongues. This universality is not hinder, by the rejection of the greater part of the Jews, as they will also be added to the church, some time hence, in a great multitude, and like an army formed into columns. IX. We may denominate, not unaptly or inappropriately, the state of the church, as she existed from the time of John until the assent of Christ into heaven, "a temporary or intermediate one" between the state of the promise and of the gospel, or that of the Old Testament and of the New. X. On which account, we place the ministry of John between the ministry of the prophets and that of the apostles, and plainly, and in every respect, conformable to neither of them. Hence, also, John is called "a greater prophet," and is said to be "less than the least in the kingdom of heaven. COROLLARY The baptism of John was so far the same with that of Christ, that there was afterwards no need for it to be restored.

DISPUTATION LIII - ON THE HEAD AND THE MARKS OF THE CHURCH

Though the head and the body be of one nature, and though, according to nature, they properly constitute one subsistence, yet he who, according to nature, is the head of the church, cannot have communion of nature with her, for she is his creature. II. But it has been the good pleasure of God, who is both the head of the church according to nature, and her creator, to bestow on his church his Son Jesus Christ, made man, as her head, by whom, likewise, it has been his will to create his church -- that is, a new creature, that the union between the church and her head might be closer, and the communication more free and confiding. III. But a three-fold relation exists between the church and her head: (1.) That the head contains in himself, in a manner the most perfect, all things which are necessary and sufficient for salvation. (2.) That he is fitly united to the church, his body, by "the joints and bands" of the Spirit and of faith. (3.) That the head can infuse the virtue of his own perfection into her, and she can receive it from him according to the order of preordination and subordination fitly corresponding with it according to the difference of both. IV. But these three things belong to Christ alone; nay, not one of the three agrees with any person or thing except with Christ. Wherefore, he, only, is the head of the church, to whom she immediately coheres according to her internal and real essence. V. But no one can, according to this relation, be vicar or substitute to him; neither the apostle Peter, nor any Roman pontiff; nay, Christ can have no one among men as his vicar, according to the external administration of the church; and, what is still more, he cannot have a universal minister, which term is less than that of vicar. VI. Yet we do not deny that those persons who are constituted by this head as his ministers, perform such functions as belong to the head; because it has been his pleasure to gather his church to himself, and to govern it by human means. VII. But, according to her internal essence, this church is known to no one except to her head. She is likewise made known to others by signs and indications which have their origin from her true internal essence itself, if they be real, and not counterfeit and deceptive in their appearance. VIII. These signs are, the profession of the true faith, and the institution or conducting of the life according to the direction and the instigation of the Spirit -- a matter that belongs to external acts, about which, alone, a judgment can be formed by mankind. IX. We say that these are the marks of a church which outwardly conducts herself with propriety. But it may come to pass, that a mere profession of faith may obtain in this church through the public preaching and hearing of the word, through the administration and use of the sacraments, and through prayers and Thanksgivings; and yet in her whole life she may degenerate from the profession; and, lastly, she may in her deeds deny Christ, whom she professes to know in word, in which case, she does not cease to be a church as long as it is the pleasure of God and Christ to bear with her ill manners, and not to send her a bill of divorcement. X. But it has happened that in her profession itself, she begins to intermix falsehoods with truth, and to worship, at the same time, Jehovah and Baal. Then, indeed, her condition is very bad, and "nigh to destruction," and all those who adhere to her are commanded to desert her, so far, at least, as not to become partakers of her abominations, and to contaminate themselves with the pollutions of her idolatry; nay, they are commanded to accuse their mother of being a harlot, and of having violated the marriage compact with her husband. XI. In such a defection as this, those who desert her are not the cause of the dissension, but she who is justly deserted, because she first declined from God and Christ, to whom all believers, and each of them in particular, must adhere by an inseparable connection. XII. The Roman pontiff is not the head of the church; and because he boasts himself of being that head, the name of "Antichrist" on this account most deservedly belongs to him. XIII. The marks of the church of which the papists boast -- antiquity, universality, duration, amplitude, the uninterrupted succession of teachers, and agreement in doctrine-have been invented beyond those which we have laid down, because they are accommodated to the present state of the church of Rome.

DISPUTATION LIV - ON THE CATHOLIC CHURCH, HER PARTS AND RELATIONS

The catholic church is the company of all believers, called out from every language, tribe, people, nation and calling, who have been, are now, and will be, called by the saving vocation of God from a state of corruption to the dignity of the children of God, through the word of the covenant of grace, and engrafted into Christ, as living members to their head through true faith, to the praise of the glory of the grace of God. From this, it appears that the catholic church differs from particular churches in nothing which appertains to the substance of a church, but solely in her amplitude. II. But as she is called "the catholic church" in reference to her matter, which embraces all those who have ever been, are now, and will yet be, made partakers of this vocation, and received into the family of God, so, likewise, is she denominated "the one and holy church," from her form, which consists in the mutual relation of the church, who by faith, embraces Christ as her head and spouse, and of Christ, who so closely unites the church to himself, as his body and spouse, by his Spirit, that the church lives by the life of Christ himself, and is made a partaker of him and of all his benefits. III. The Catholic Church is "ONE," because, under one God and Father, who is above all persons, and through all things, and in all of us, she has been united as one body to one head, Christ the Lord, through one Spirit, and through one faith placed in the same word, through a similar hope of the same inheritance, and through mutual charity, she has been "fitly framed and built for a holy temple, and a habitation of God through the Spirit." Wherefore, the whole of this unity is spiritual, though those who have been thus united together consist partly of body, and partly of spirit. IV. She is "HOLY;" because, by the blessing of the Holy of holies, she has been separated from the unclean world, washed from her sins by His blood, beautified with the presence and gracious indwelling of God, and adorned with true holiness by the sanctification of the Holy Spirit. V. But though this church is one, yet she is distinguished according to the acts of God towards her, so far as she has become the recipient of either of all of those acts, or of some of them. The church that has received only the act of her creation and preservation, is said to be in the way, and is called "the church militant," as being she that must yet contend with sin, the flesh, the world, and Satan. The church that, in addition to this, is made partaker of the consummation, is said to be in her native land, and is called "the church triumphant;" for, after having conquered all her enemies, she rests from her labours, and reigns with Christ in heaven. To that part which is still militant on earth, the title of "catholic" is likewise ascribed, so far as she embraces within her boundaries all particular militant churches. VI. But the catholic church is distributed, according to her parts, into many particular churches, since she consists of many congregations far distant from each other, with respect to place, and quite distinct. But as these particular churches have severally the name of "a church," so they have likewise the thing signified by the name and the entire definition like similar parts which participate in the name and definition of the whole; and the catholic church differs from each particular one solely in her universality, and in no other thing whatever which belongs to the essence of a church. Hence, is easily learned in what manner it may be understood that, as single, particular churches may err, yet the church universal cannot err; that is, in this sense, that there never will be a future time in which some believers will not exist who do not err in the foundation of religion. But from this interpretation, it is apparent that it cannot be concluded from the circumstance of the catholic church, being said to be in this sense, free from error, that any congregation, however numerous soever it may be, is exempt from error, unless there be in it one person, or more, who are so guided into all truth as to be incapable of erring. VII. Hence, since the evocation of the church is made inwardly by the Spirit, and outwardly by the word preached, and since they who are called, answer inwardly by faith, and outwardly by the profession of faith, as they who are called have the inward and the outward man, therefore, the church, in reference to these called persons, is distinguished into the visible and the invisible church, from the subjoined external accident -- invisible, as she "believes with the heart unto righteousness," and visible, as "confession is made with her mouth unto salvation." And this visibility or invisibility belongs neither more nor less to the whole catholic church, than to each church in particular. VIII. Then, since the church is collected out of this world, "which lieth in the wicked one," and often by ministers who, beside the word of God, preach another word, and since this church consists of men liable to be deceived and to fall, nay, of men who have been deceived and are fallen, therefore, the church is distinguished with respect to the doctrine of faith, into an orthodox and heretical church -- with respect to divine worship, into an idolatrous church, and into one that is a right worshiper of God and Christ, and with respect to the morals prescribed in the second table of the law, into a purer church or a more impure one. In all these, are also to be observed the degrees according to which one church is more heretical, idolatrous and impure than another; about all these things a correct judgment must be formed according to the Scriptures. Thus, likewise, the word "catholic" is used concerning those churches that neither labour under any destructive heresy, nor are idolatrous.

DISPUTATION LV - ON THE POWER OF THE CHURCH IN DELIVERING DOCTRINES

The power of the church may be variously considered, according to various objects; for it is occupied either about the delivery of doctrines, the enactment of laws, the convening of assemblies, the appointment of ministers, or, lastly, about jurisdiction. II. In the institution of doctrines, or in the first delivery of them, the power of the church is a mere nullity, whether she be considered generally, or according to her parts; for she is the spouse of Christ, and, therefore, is bound to hear the voice of her husband. She cannot prescribe to herself the rule of willing, believing, doing and hoping. III. But the whole of her power, concerning doctrines, lies in the dispensation and administration of those which have been delivered by God and Christ -- necessarily previous to which is the humble and pious acceptance of the divine doctrines, the consequence of which is, that she justly preserve the name that has once been received. IV. As the acceptance and the preservation of doctrines may be considered either according to the words, or according to the right sense, so, likewise the delivery of the doctrines received and preserved must be distinguished either with respect to the words, or with respect to their correct meaning. V. The delivery or tradition of doctrines according to the words, is when the church declares or publishes the very words which she has received, (after they have been delivered to her by God, either in writing or orally,) without any addition, diminution, change or transposition, whether from the repositories in which she has concealed the divine writings, or from her own memory, in which she had carefully and faithfully preserved those things which had been orally delivered. At the same time, she solemnly testifies that those very things which she has received from above are [when transmitted through her] pure and unadulterated, (and is prepared even by death itself to confirm this her testimony,) as far as the variations of copies in the original languages permit a translator into other languages [thus to testify]; yet they do not concern the foundation so much as to be able to produce doubts concerning it on account of these variations. VI. The delivery or tradition according to the meaning, is the more ample explanation and application of the doctrines propounded and comprehended in the divine words, in which explanation, the church ought to contain herself within the terms of the very word which has been delivered, publishing no particular interpretation of a doctrine or of a passage, which does not rest on the entire foundation, and which cannot be fully proved from other passages. This she will most sedulously avoid if she adhere as much as possible to the expressions of the word delivered, and if she abstain, as far as she is capable, from the use of foreign words or phrases. VII. To this power, is annexed the right of examining and forming a judgment upon doctrines, as to the kind of spirit by which they have been proposed; in this, also she will employ the rule of the word which bears assured evidences that it is divine, and has been received as such; and indeed, they will employ the rule of this word alone, if she be desirous to institute a proper examination, and to form a correct judgment. But if she employ any human writings whatsoever, for a rule or guide, the morning light will not shine on her, and, therefore, she will grope about in darkness. VIII. But the church ought to be guarded against three things: (1.) To hide from no one the words which have been divinely delivered to her, or to interdict any man from reading them or meditating upon them. (2.) When, for certain reasons, she declares divine doctrines with her own words, not to compel any one to receive or to approve them, except on this condition, so far as they are. consentaneous with the meaning comprehended in the divine words. (3.) And not to prohibit any man who is desirous of examining, in a legitimate manner, the doctrines proposed in the words of the church. Whichsoever of these things she does, she cannot, in that case, evade the criminal charge of having arrogated a power to herself, and of abusing it beyond all law, right and equity. COROLLARY It is one of the fabulous stories of the papists that the Holy Spirit assists the church in such a manner, in forming her judgment on the authentic Scriptures, and in the right interpretation of the divine meanings, that she cannot err.

DISPUTATION LVI - ON THE POWER OF THE CHURCH IN ENACTING LAWS

The laws which may be prescribed to the church, or which may be considered as having been prescribed, are of two kinds, distinguished from each other by a remarkable difference and by a notable doctrine -- according to the matter, that is, the acts which are prescribed -- according to the end for the sake of which they are prescribed, and, lastly, according to the force and necessity of obligation. 2. (1.) For some laws concern the very essence of ordering the life according to godliness and Christianity, and the necessary acts of faith, hope and charity; and these may be called the necessary and primary or principal laws, and are as the fundamental laws of the kingdom of God itself. (2.) But others of them have respect to certain secondary and substituted acts, and the circumstances of the principal acts, all of which conduce to the more commodious and easy observance of those first acts. On this account they deserve to be called positive and attendant laws. III. 1. The church neither has a right, nor is she bound by any necessity, to enact necessary laws, and those which essentially concern the acts of faith itself, of hope and of charity. For this belongs most properly to God and Christ; and it has been so fully exercised by Christ, that nothing can essentially belong to the acts of faith, hope and charity, which has not been prescribed by him in a manner the most copious. IV. The entire power, therefore, of the church is placed in enacting laws of the second kind; about the making and observing of which we must now make some observations. V. In prescribing laws of this kind, the church ought to turn her eyes, and to keep them fixed, on the following particulars: First. That the acts which she will command or forbid be of a middle or an indifferent kind, and in their own nature neither good nor evil; and yet that they may be useful, for the commodious observance of the acts [divinely] prescribed, according to the circumstance of persons, times and places. VI. Secondly. That laws of this description be not adverse to the word of God, but that they rather be conformable to it, whether they be deduced from those things which are, in a general manner, prescribed in the word of God, according to the circumstances already enumerated, or whether they be considered as suitable means for executing those things which have been prescribed in the word of God. VII. Thirdly. That these laws be principally referred to the good order and the decorous administration of the external polity of the church. For God is not the author of confusion; but he is both the author and the lover of order; and regard is in every place to be paid to decorum, but chiefly in the church, which is "the house of God," and in which it is exceedingly unbecoming to have any thing, or to do any thing, that is either indecorous or out of order. VIII. Fourthly. That she do not assume to herself the authority of binding, by her laws, the consciences of men to acts prescribed by herself; for she will thus invade the right of Christ, in prescribing things necessary, and will infringe Christian liberty, which ought to be free from snares of this description. IX. Fifthly. That, by any deed of her own, by a simple promise or by an oath, either orally or by the subscription of the hand, she do not take away from herself the power of abrogating, enlarging, diminishing or of changing the laws themselves. It would not be a useless labour if the church were to enter her protest, at the end of the laws, about the perpetual duration of this her power, in a subjoined clause, such as the civil magistrate is accustomed to employ in political positive laws. X. But with regard to the observance of these laws; as they are already enacted, all and every one of those who are in the church are bound by them so far, that it is not lawful to transgress them through contempt, and to the scandal of others; and the church herself will not estimate the observance of them at so low a value as to permit them to be violated through contempt and to the scandal of others; but she will mark, admonish, reprove and blame such transgressors, as behaving themselves in a disorderly and indecorous manner, and she will endeavour to bring them back to a better mind. COROLLARY Is it not useful, for the purpose of bearing testimony to the power and the liberty of the church, occasionally to make some change in the laws ecclesiastical, lest the observance of them becoming perpetual, and without any change, should produce an opinion of the [absolute] necessity of their being observed?

DISPUTATION LVII - ON THE POWER OF THE CHURCH IN ADMINISTERING JUSTICE, OR ON ECCLESIASTICAL DISCIPLINE

As no society, however rightly constituted and furnished with good laws, can long keep together unless they who belong to it be restrained within their duty by a certain method of jurisdiction or discipline, or be compelled to the performance of their duty, so, in the church, which is the house, the city and the kingdom of God, discipline of the same kind must flourish and be exercised. II. But it is proper that this discipline be accommodated to the spiritual life, and not to that which is natural; and that it should be serviceable for edifying, confirming, amplifying and adorning the church as such, and for directing consciences, without [employing] any force hurtful in any part to the body or to the substance, and to the condition of the animal life; unless, perhaps, it be the pleasure of the magistrate, in virtue of the power granted to him by God, to force an offender to repentance by some other method. Such a proceeding, however, we do not prejudge. III. But ecclesiastical discipline is an act of the church, by which, according to the power instituted by God and Christ, and bestowed on her, and to be employed through a consciousness of the office imposed, she reprehends all and every one of those who belong to the church, if they have fallen into open sin, and admonishes them to repent; or, if they pertinaciously persevere in their sins, she excommunicates them, to the benefit of the whole church, the salvation of the sinner himself, to the profit of those who are without, and to the glory of God himself and Christ. IV. The object of this discipline is all and each of those who, having been engrafted into the church by baptism, are capable of this discipline for the correction of themselves. The cause or formal condition why discipline must be exercised on them is, the offenses committed by them, whether they concern the doctrine of faith, and are pernicious and destructive heresies, or whether they have respect to morals and to the rest of the acts of the Christian life. V. But it is requisite, that these sins be external and manifest, that is, known, and correctly known, to those by whom the discipline shall be administered; and that it be evident, that they are sins according to the laws imposed by Christ on the church, and that they have actually been committed. For God, alone, judges concerning inward sins. VI. Let the form of administering the laws be with all kindness and discretion, also with zeal, and occasionally with severity and some degree of rigor, if occasion require it to be employed. But the intention is, the salvation of him who has sinned, and that of the whole body of the church, to the glory of God and of Christ. VII. The execution of this discipline lies both in admonition and in castigation or punishment, or in censure, which is conveyed only in words, through reprehension, exhortation and communication, or which is given by the privation of some of those things which outwardly belong to the communion of saints, and to the saving edification or building up of every believer in the body of Christ. VIII. Admonitions are accommodated, First, to the persons who have sinned, in which must be observed the difference of age, sex and condition, with all prudence and discretion. Secondly. They are accommodated to those sins which have been committed; for some are more grievous than others. Thirdly. To the mode in which sins have been perpetrated, which mode comes now under our special consideration. IX. For some sins are clandestine, others are public, whether they are offenses only against God, or whether they have, in union with such offense, injury to a man's neighbour. According to this latter respect, it is called "a private sin," that is, an offense committed by one private individual against another-such as is intimated by the word of Christ, in Matt. xviii. 7-18, in which passage is likewise prescribed the mode of reproving an offense. X. A clandestine sin is that which is secretly perpetrated, and with the commission of which very few persons are acquainted; to this belongs a secret reprehension, to be inflicted by those who are acquainted with it. One of the principal ministers of the church, however, will be able to impart authority to the reprehension; yet he can, by no means, refer it to his colleagues; but it will be his duty to deliver this reproof in secret. XI. A public sin is that which is committed when several people are acquainted with it. We allow it to be made a subject of discussion, whether a sin ought to receive the appellation of a public one, when it has been secretly committed but has become known to many persons either through the fault of him who perpetrated it, or through the officiousness of those who divulged it without necessity. XII. But there is still some difference in public sins; for they are known either to some part of the church, or to the whole, or nearly to the whole of it; according to this difference, the admonition to be given ought to be varied. If the sin be known to part of the church, it is sufficient that the sinner be admonished and reproved before the consistory, or in the presence of more persons to whom it had been known. If it be known to the whole church, the sinner must be reprehended before all the members; for this practice conduces both to the shame of him who has sinned, and to deter others from sinning after his example. Some consideration, however, may be had to the shame of any offender, and a degree of moderation be shown; that is, if he is not deeply versed in sinful practices, but if a sin has taken him by surprise, or "he is overtaken in a fault." XIII. As this reproof has the tendency to induce the offender to desist from sinning, if this end is not obtained by the first admonition, it is necessary to repeat it occasionally, until the sinner stands corrected, or makes an open declaration of his contumacy. But some difference of opinion exists on this point among divines: "Is it useful to bring an offender to punishment, when, after having afforded hopes of amendment, he does not fulfill those hopes according to the judgment and the wishes of the church?" But it does not seem possible to determine this so much by settled rules, as by leaving the matter to the discretion of the governors of the church. XIV. But if the offender despise all admonitions, and contumaciously perseveres in his sins, after the church has exercised the necessary patience towards him, she must proceed to punishment; which is excommunication, that is, the exclusion of the contumacious person from the holy communion and even from the church herself. This public exclusion will be accompanied by the avoidance of all intercourse and familiarity with the person excommunicated, to [the observance of] which, each member of the church must pay attention as far as is permitted by the necessary relative duties which either all the members owe to him according to their general vocation, or some of them owe according to their particular obligation. [For a subject is not freed from his obligation toward his prince, on account of the excommunication of the prince; neither, in such circumstances, is a wife freed from the duty which she is bound to perform to her husband; nor are children freed from their duty to parents; and thus in other similar instances.] XV. Some persons suppose, that this excommunication is solely from the privilege of celebrating the Lord's supper. Others suppose it to be of two kinds, the less and the greater -- the less being a partial exclusion from attendance on some of the sacred offices of the church -- the greater, an exclusion from all of them together, and totally from the communion of believers. But others, rejecting the minor excommunication, acknowledge no other than the major; because it appears to them, that there is no cause why a contumacious sinner ought to be rejected from this communion more than from that, since he has rendered himself unworthy to obtain any place in the church and the assembly of saints. We do not interpose our opinion; but we leave this matter to be discussed by the judgment of learned and pious men, that by common consent it may be concluded from the Scriptures what is most agreeable to them, and best suited to the edification of the church. COROLLARIES Excommunication must be avoided, where a manifest fear of a schism exists. "Should not this also be done, where a fear exists of persecution being likely to ensue on account of excommunication?" We think, that, in this case, likewise, excommunication should be avoided.

DISPUTATION LVIII - ON COUNCILS

An ecclesiastical council is an assembly of men gathered together in the name of God, consulting and defining or settling, according to the word of God, about those things which pertain to religion and the good of the church, for the glory of God and the salvation of the church. II. The power of appointing an assembly of this kind resides in the church herself. If she is under the sway of a Christian magistrate, who makes an open profession of religion, or who publicly tolerates it, then we transfer this power to such a magistrate, without whose convocation, those persons that protested to the church concerning the nullity of the Council of Trent have maintained that a council is illegitimate. But if the magistrate is neither a believer, nor publicly tolerates religion, but is an enemy and a persecutor, then those who preside in the church will discharge that office. III. An occasion will be afforded for convening an assembly of this kind, either by some evil men who are an annoyance to the church, whether they be in the church or out of it, or even the perpetual constitution of the church so long as she continues on earth. For as she is liable to error, corruption, and defection from the truth of doctrine, from the purity of divine worship, from moral probity and from Christian concord, to heresies, idolatry, corruption of manners, and schisms, it is useful for assemblies of this kind to be instituted. Yet may they be instituted, not only to correct any corruption if it manifestly appears that it has entered, but likewise to inquire whether something of the kind has not entered; because the enemy sows tares while the men sleep, to whom is entrusted the safe custody of the Lord's field. IV. We say that this is an assembly of men; for, "Let a woman. keep silence in the church, unless she has an extraordinary and divine call; and we say, these men ought to be distinguished by the following marks: First. That they be powerful in the Scriptures, and have their senses exercised in them. Secondly. That they be pious, grave, prudent, moderate, and-lovers of divine truth and of the peace of the church. Thirdly. That they be free, and bound down to no person, church, or confession written by men, but only to God and Christ, and to his word. V. They are men, whether of the ecclesiastical or of the political class -- in the first place, the supreme magistrate himself, and those persons who discharge any public office in the church and the republic. Then, also, private individuals, even those persons not being excluded who maintain some other [doctrine] than that which is the current opinion, provided they be furnished with the endowments which I have described. (Thesis 4.) And we are of opinion that such persons may deliver not only a deliberative but likewise a decisive sentence. VI. The object about which the council will be engaged is, the things appertaining to religion and to the good of the church as such. These are comprised under two chief heads-the primary, comprehending the doctrine, itself, of faith, hope, and charity, and the secondary, the order and polity of the church. VII. The rule, according to which deliberation must be instituted, and decision must be formed, is that single and sole one -- the word of God, who holds absolute dominion in the church. But in things which belong to the good order and eutaxian the discipline of the church, it is allowable for the members attentively to consider the present state of the commonwealth and of the church, and to exercise deliberation and form decisions according to the circumstances of places, times and persons, provided one thing be guarded against-to determine nothing contrary to the word of God. VIII. But, because all things in assemblies of this kind ought to be done in order, it is requisite that some one preside over the whole council. If the chief magistrate be present, this office belongs to him; but he can devolve this charge on some other person, whether an ecclesiastic or layman; nay, he may commit this matter to the council itself, provided he take care that all and each of the members be restrained within the bounds of their duty, lest their judgments be concluded in a tumultuous manner. But it is useful that some bishop be appointed, who may perform the offices of prayer and thanksgiving, may propose the business to be transacted, and may inquire and collect the opinions and votes; indeed, so far, he, as an ecclesiastic, is the more suitable for fulfilling these duties. IX. A place must be appointed for assemblies of this kind, that they may be most commodious to all those who shall come to the synod, unless it be the pleasure of the chief magistrate to choose that place which will be the most convenient to himself. It ought to be a place secure from ambuscade or hostile surprise; and a safe conduct is necessary for all persons, that they may arrive and depart again, without personal detriment, as far as is allowable by the law of God itself, against which the authority of no council, however great, is of the least avail. X. The authority of councils is not absolute, but dependent on the authority of God; for this reason, no one is simply bound to assent to those things which have been decreed in a council, unless those persons be present, as members, who cannot err, and who have the undoubted marks and testimonies of the Holy Spirit to this fact. But every one may, nay, he is bound, to examine, by the word of God, those things which have been concluded in the council; and if he finds them to be agreeable to the divine word, then he may approve of them; but if they are not, then he may express his disapprobation. Yet he must be cautious not easily to reject that which has been determined by the unanimous consent of so many pious and learned men; but he ought diligently to consider, whether it has the Scriptures pronouncing in favour of it with sufficient clearness; and when this is the case, he may yield his assent, in the Lord, to their unanimous agreement. XI. The necessity of councils is not absolute, because the church can be instructed respecting necessary things without them. Yet their utility is very great, if, being instituted in the name of the Lord, they examine all things according to his word, and appoint that which, by common consent, according to that rule, the members have thought proper to pronounce as their decision. For, as many eyes see more than one eye, and as the Lord is accustomed to listen to the prayers of a number who agree together among themselves on earth, it is more probable that the truth will be discovered and confirmed from the Scriptures by some council consisting of many learned and pious men, than by the exertions of a single individual transacting the same business privately by himself. From these premises, we also say that the authority of any council is greater than that of any man who is present at such council, even that of the Roman pontiff, to whom we ascribe no other right in any council, than that which we give to any bishop, even at the time when he performed with fidelity the duties of a true bishop. So far, are we disinclined to believe, that no council can be convened and held without his command, presidency and direction. XIII. No council can prescribe to its successors, that they may not again deliberate about that which has been transacted and determined in preceding councils; because the matter of religion does not come under the denomination of a thing that is prejudged; neither can any council bind itself, by an oath, to the observance of any other word than that of God; much less can it make positive laws, to which it may bind either itself, or any man, by an oath. XIV. It is also allowable for a later ecumenical or general council to call in doubt that which had been decreed by a preceding general council, because it is possible even for general councils to err; nor yet does it follow from these premises that the catholic church errs; that is, that all the faithful universally err.

DISPUTATION LIX - ON THE ECCLESIASTICAL MINISTRATIONS OF THE NEW TESTAMENT AND ON THE VOCATION TO THEM

By The word "ministry," we designate a public auxiliary office or duty, subservient to a superior, who, in this instance, is God and Christ as he is the Lord and Head of the church. It receives the appellation of "ecclesiastical" from its object, which is the church; and we distinguish it from a political ministry, which exercises itself in the civil affairs of the commonwealth. II. But it is the public duty which God has committed to certain men, to collect a church, to attend to it when collected, and to bring it to Christ, its Head, and through him to God, that [the members of] it may attain a life of happiness, to the glory of God and Christ. III. But as a church consists of men who live a natural life, and are called to live while in the body, a spiritual life, which is superior and ought to be as the end of the other, there is a two-fold office to be performed in the church according to the exigencies both of the natural and of the spiritual life: The First is that which is properly, per se, and immediately occupied about the spiritual life, its commencement, progress and confirmation; the Second is that by which the natural life is sustained, and, therefore, it belongs, only by accident and mediately, to the church. The First is always necessary per se. The Second is not necessary [in the church] except by hypothesis; because there are those who need a maintenance from others, and they do not obtain this through some order established in the community, in which case, it ought always to endure; but where any such order is established, it is unnecessary. On the former of these we are now treating; about the latter we have no further remarks to make. IV. The office accommodated to the spiritual life, consists of these three acts: The First is the teaching of the truth which is according to godliness; the Second is intercession before God; the Third is regimen or government accommodated to this institution or teaching. V. Institution or teaching consists in the proposing, explanation and confirmation of the truth, which contains the things that are to be believed, hoped for, and performed, in the refutation of falsehood, in exhortation, reprehension, consolation, and threatening, all of which is accomplished by the word both of the law and the gospel. To this function, we add the administration of the sacraments, which serve for the same purpose. VI. Intercession consists in prayers and Thanksgivings offered to God for the church and each of its members, through Christ our only advocate and intercessor. VII. The government of the church is used for this end, that, in the whole church, all things may be done decently, in order, and to edification; and that each of its members may be kept in their duty, the loiterers may be incited, the weak confirmed, those who have wandered out of the way brought back, the contumacious punished, and the penitents received. VIII. These offices are not always imposed in the same mode, nor administered by the same methods. For, at the commencement of the rising Christian church, they were imposed on some men immediately by God and Christ, and they were administered by those on whom they had been imposed, without binding them to certain churches; hence, also, the apostles were called "ministers," as being the ambassadors of Christ to every creature throughout the world. To these were added the evangelists, as fellow-labourers. Afterwards [the same offices were imposed] immediately on those who were called pastors and teachers, bishops and priests, and who were placed over certain churches. The former of these [the apostles and evangelists] continued only for a season, and had no successors. The latter [pastors, &c.] will remain in perpetual succession to the end of the world, though we do not deny that, when a church is first to be collected for any one, a man may traverse the whole earth in teaching. IX. These offices are so ordered, that one person can discharge all of them at the same time; though, if the utility of the church and the diversity of gifts so require, they can be variously distributed among different men. X. The vocation to such ecclesiastical offices is either immediate or mediate. Immediate vocation we will not now discuss. But that which is mediate is a divine act, administered by God and Christ through the church, by which he consecrates to himself a man separated from the occupations of the natural life and from those which are common, and removes him to the duties of the pastoral office, for the salvation of men and his own glory. In this vocation, we ought to consider the vocation itself, its efficient and its object. XI. The act of vocation consists of previous examination, election, and confirmation. (1.) Examination is a diligent inquiry and trial, whether the person about whom it is occupied be well suited for fulfilling the duties of the office. This fitness consists in the knowledge and approval of things true and necessary, in probity of life, and a facility of communicating to others those things which he knows himself, (which facility contains language and freedom in speaking,) in prudence, moderation of mind, patient endurance of labours, infirmities, injuries, &c. XII. Election, or choice, is the ordination of a person who is legitimately examined and found good and proper, by which is imposed on him the office to be discharged. To this, it is not unusual to add some public inauguration, by prayers and the laying on of hands, and also by previous fasting and is like an admission to the administration of the office itself, which is commonly denominated "confirmation." XIII. The primary efficient is God and Christ, and the Spirit of both as conducting the cause of Christ in the church, on which cause the whole authority of the vocation depends. The administrator is the church itself, in which we number the Christian magistrate, teachers, with the rest of the presbyters, and the people themselves. But in those places in which no magistrate resides who is willing to attend to this matter, there, bishops or presbyters, with the people, can and ought to perform this business. XIV. The object is the person to be called, in whom is required, for the sake of the church, that aptitude or suitableness about which we have already spoken, and on account of it, the testimony of a good conscience, by which he modestly approves the judgment of the church, and is conscious to himself that he enters on this office in the sincere fear of God, and with an intense desire only to edify the church. XV. The essential form of the vocation is that all things may be done according to the rule prescribed in the word of God. The accidental is, that they may all be done decently and suitably, according to the particular relations of persons, places, times, and other circumstances. XVI. Wheresoever all these conditions are observed, the call is legitimate, and on every part approved; but if some one be deficient, the act of vocation is then imperfect; yet the call is to be considered as ratified and firm, while the vocation of God is united by some outward testimony of it, which, because it is various, we cannot define COROLLARY The vocations or calls in the papal church have not been null, though contaminated and imperfect; and the first reformers had an ordinary and mediate call.

DISPUTATION LX - ON SACRAMENTS IN GENERAL

We have thus far treated on the church, her power, and the ministry of the word; it follows that we now discuss those signs or marks which God appends to his word, and by which He seals and confirms the faith which has been produced in the minds of his covenant people. For these signs are commonly called "sacraments" -- a term, indeed, which is not employed in the Scriptures, but which, account of the agreement about it in the church, must not be rejected. I. But this word, "sacrament," is transferred from military usage to that of sacred things; for, as soldiers were devoted to their general by an oath, as by a solemn attestation, so, likewise, those in covenant are bound to Christ by their reception of these signs, as by a public oath. But because the same word is either taken in a relative acceptation, (and this either properly for a sign, or by metonymy for the thing signified,) or in an absolute acceptation, (and this by synecdoche for both,) we will treat about its proper signification. II. A sacrament, therefore, is a sacred and visible sign or token and seal instituted by God, by which he ratifies to his covenant people the gracious promise proposed in his word, and binds them, on the other hand, to the performance of their duty. Therefore, no other promises are proposed to us by these signs than those which are manifested in the word. III. We call it "a sign or token, and a seal, both from the usage of Scripture in Gen. xvii. 11, and Rom. iv. 11, and from the nature of the thing itself, because these tokens, beside the external appearance which they present to our senses, cause something else to occur to the thoughts. Neither are they only naked significant tokens, but seals and pledges, which affect not only the mind, but likewise the heart itself. IV. We call it "sacred" in a two-fold respect: (1.) Because it has been given by God; and

(2.) Because it is given to a sacred use. We call it "visible," because it is of the nature of a sign that it be perceptible to the senses; for that which is not such, cannot be called a sign. V. The author of these signs is God, who alone, is the lord and lawgiver of the church, and whose province it is to prescribe laws, to make promises, and to seal them with those tokens which have seemed good to himself; yet they are so accommodated to the grace to be sealed, as, by a certain analogy, to be significant of it. Therefore, they are not natural signs, which, from their own nature, signify all that of which they are significant; but they are voluntary signs, the whole signification of which depends on the will or option of him who institutes them. VI. The matter is the external element itself created by God, and, therefore, subject to his power, and made suitable to seal that which, according to his wisdom, God wills to be sealed by it. VII. As the internal form of the sacrament is ek twn prov ti of things to their relation, it consists in relation, and is that suitable analogy and similitude between the sign and the thing signified which has regard both to the representation, and to the sealing or witnessing, and the exhibition of the thing signified through the authority and the will of him who institutes it. From this most close analogy of the sign with the thing signified, various figurative expressions are employed in the Scriptures and in the sacraments: as, when the name of the thing signified is ascribed to the sign, thus, "And my covenant shall be in your flesh;" (Gen. xvii. 13;) and, on the contrary, in 1 Corinthians v. 7, "Christ, our passover, is sacrificed for us." Or, when the property of the thing is ascribed to the sign, as "Whosoever drinketh of the water that I shall give him, shall never thirst." (John iv. 14.) And, on the contrary, "Take, eat: this is my body." (Matt. xxvi. 26.) VIII. The end of sacraments is two-fold, proximate and remote. The proximate end is the sealing of the promise made in the covenant. The remote end is, (1.) the confirmation of the faith of those who are in the covenant, and by consequence the salvation of the church that consists of those covenanted members; and (2.) the glory of God. IX. Those for whom the sacraments have been instituted by God, and by whom they are to be used, are those with whom God has entered into covenant, all of them, and they only. To them the use of the sacraments is to be conceded, as long as they are reckoned by God in the number of those who are in covenant; though by their sins they have deserved to be cast off and divorced. X. But these sacraments are to be considered according to the varied conditions of men; for they have either been instituted before the fall, and are of the covenant of works; or, after the fall, and are of the covenant of grace. There was only a single sacrament of the covenant of works, and that the tree of life. Those of the covenant of grace are either so far as they have regard to the promised covenant, and belong to the church while yet in her infancy and placed under pedagogy [the law being her schoolmaster] as were those of circumcision and of the passover; or so far as now they have regard to the covenant confirmed, and belong to the Christian church that is of adult age, as are those of baptism and the Lord's supper. The points of agreement and difference between each of these will be the more conveniently perceived in the discussion of each. COROLLARY Though in some things, sacrifices and sacraments agree together, yet they are by no means to be confounded; because in many respects the latter differ from the former.

DISPUTATION LXI - ON THE SACRAMENTS OF THE OLD TESTAMENT, THE TREE OF LIFE, CIRCUMCISION, AND THE PASCHAL LAMB

The tree of life was created and instituted by God for this end -- that man, as long as he remained obedient to the divine law, might eat of its fruit, both for the preservation and continuance of this natural life against every defect which could happen to it through old age, or any other cause, and to designate or point out the promise of a better and more blissful life. It answered the former purpose, as an element created by God; and the latter, as a sacrament instituted by God. It was adapted to accomplish the former purpose by the natural force and capability which was imparted to it; it was fitted for the latter, on account of the similitude and analogy which subsist between natural and spiritual life. II. Circumcision is the sign of the covenant into which God entered with Abraham to seal or witness the promise about the blessed seed that should be born of him, about all nations which were to be blessed in him, and about constituting him the father of many nations, and the heir of the world through the righteousness of faith; and that God was willing to be his God and the God of his seed after him. This sign was to be administered in that member which is the ordained instrument of generation in the male sex, by a suitable analogy between the sign and the thing signified. III. By that sign all the male descendants from Abraham, were, at the express command of God, to be marked, on the eighth day after their nativity; and a threatening was added, that it should come to pass that the soul of him who was not circumcised on that day should be cut off from his people. IV. But though females were not circumcised in their bodies, yet they were in the mean time partakers of the same covenant and obligation, because they were reckoned among the men, and were considered by God as circumcised. It, therefore, was not necessary that God should institute any other remedy for taking away from females the native corruption of sin, as the papists have the audacity to affirm, beyond and contrary to the Scriptures. V. And this is the first relation of circumcision belonging to the promise. The other is, that the persons circumcised were bound to the observance of the whole law, delivered by God, and especially of the ceremonial law. For it was in the power of God to prescribe, to those who were in covenant with him, a law at his pleasure, and to seal the obligation of its observance by such a sign of the covenant as had been previously instituted and employed; and in this respect circumcision belongs to the Old Testament. VI. The paschal lamb was a sacrament, instituted by God to point out the deliverance from Egypt, and to renew the remembrance of it at a stated time in each year. VII. Beside this use, it served typically to adumbrate Christ, the true Lamb, who was to endure and bear away the sins of the world; on which account, also, its use was abrogated by the sufferings and [the sacrifice of Christ on the cross, as it relates to the right; but it was afterwards, in fact and reality, abrogated with the destruction of the city and the temple. VIII. The sacrament of the tree of life was a bloodless one; in the other two, there was shedding of blood -- both suitable to the diversity of the state of those who were in covenant with God. For the former was instituted before the entrance of sin into the world; but the two latter, after sin had entered, which, according to the decree of God, is not expiated except by blood; because the wages of sin is death, and natural life, according to the Scriptures, has its seat in the blood. IX. The passage under the cloud and through the sea, manna, and the water which gushed from the rock, were sacramental signs; but they were extraordinary, and as a sort of prelude to the sacraments of the New Testament, although of a signification and testification the most obscure, since the things signified and witnessed by them were not declared in express words. COROLLARIES I. It is probable that the church, from the primitive promise and reparation after the fall, until the times of Abraham, had her sacraments, though no express mention is made of them in the Scriptures. II. It would be an act of too great boldness to affirm what those sacraments were; yet if any one should say, that the first of them was the offering of the infant recently born before the Lord, on the very day on which the mother was purified from childbearing, and that another was, the eating of sacrifices and the sprinkling of the blood of the victims; his assertion would not be utterly devoid of probability.

DISPUTATION LXII - ON THE SACRAMENTS OF THE NEW TESTAMENT IN GENERAL

The sacraments of the New Testament are those which have been instituted for giving testimony to the covenant, or the New Testament confirmed by the death and blood of its mediator and testator. II. Wherefore, it was necessary that they should be such as were adapted to give significance and testimony to the confirmation already made; that is, that they should declare and testify that the blood had been shed, and that the death of the mediator had intervened. III. There ought, therefore, to be no shedding of blood in the sacraments of the New Testament; neither ought they to consist of any such thing as is or has been partaker of the life which is in the blood; for as sin has now been expiated, and remission fully obtained through the blood and death of the mediator, no further shedding of blood was necessary. IV. But they were to be instituted before the confirmation of the new covenant was made by the blood of the mediator and the death of the testator himself; both because the institution and the sealing o! the testament ought to precede even the death of the testator; and because the mediator himself ought to be a partaker of these sacraments, to consecrate them in his own person, and more strongly to seal the covenant which is between us and him. V. But as the communion of a sacrifice unto death, offered for sins, is signified and testified by nothing more appropriately than by the sprinkling of the blood and the eating of the sacrifice itself and the drinking of the blood, (if indeed it were allowable to drink blood,) hence, likewise, no signs were more appropriate than water, bread and wine, since the sprinkling of his very blood and the eating of his body could not be done, and, besides, the drinking of his blood ought not to be done. VI. The virtue and efficacy of the sacraments of the New Testament do not go beyond the act of signifying and testifying. There can neither actually be, nor be imagined, any exhibition of the thing signified through them, except such as is completed by these intermediate acts themselves. VII. And, therefore, the sacraments of the New Testament do not differ from those used in the Old Testament; because the former exhibit grace, but the latter typify or prefigure it. VIII. The sacraments of the New Testament have not the ratio of sacraments beyond that very use for the sake of which they were instituted, nor do they profit those who use them without faith and repentance; that is, those persons who are of adult age, and of whom faith and repentance are required. Respecting infants, the judgment is different, to whom it is sufficient that they are the offspring of believing parents, that they may be reckoned in the covenant. IX. The sacraments of the New Testament have been instituted, that they may endure to the end of time; and they will endure till the end of all things. COROLLARY The diversity of sects in the Christian religion does not excuse the omission of the use of the sacraments, though the vehemence of the leaders of any sect may afford a legitimate and sufficient cause to the people to abstain justly and without sin from the use of the sacraments of which such men have to become partakers with them.

DISPUTATION LXIII - ON BAPTISM AND PAEDO-BAPTISM

Baptism is the initial sacrament of the New Testament, by which the covenant people of God are sprinkled with water, by a minister of the church, in the name of the Father, of the Son, and of the Holy Ghost -- to signify and to testify the spiritual ablution which is effected by the blood and Spirit of Christ. By this sacrament, those who are baptized to God the Father, and are consecrated to his Son by the Holy Spirit as a peculiar treasure, may have communion with both of them, and serve God all the days of their life. II. The author of the institution is God the Father, in his Son, the mediator of the New Testament, by the eternal Spirit of both. The first administrator of it was John; but Christ was the confirmer, both by receiving it from John, and by afterwards administering it through his disciples. III. But as baptism is two-fold with respect to the sign and the thing signified -- one being of water, the other of blood and of the Spirit -- the first external, the second internal; so the matter and form ought also to be two-fold -- the external and earthy of the external baptism, the internal and heavenly of that which is internal. IV. The matter of external baptism is elementary water, suitable, according to nature, to purify that which is unclean. Hence, it is also suitable for the service of God to typify and witness the blood and the Spirit of Christ; and this blood and the Spirit of Christ is the thing signified in outward baptism, and the matter of that which is inward. But the application both of the blood and the Spirit of Christ, and the effect of both, are the thing signified by the application of this water, and the effect of the application. V. The form of external baptism is that ordained administration, according to the institution of God, which consists of these two things: (1.) That he who is baptized, be sprinkled with this water. (2.) That this sprinkling be made in the name of the Father, of the Son, and of the Holy Ghost. Analogous to this, is the inward sprinkling and communication both of the blood and the Spirit of Christ, which is done by Christ alone, and which may be called "the internal form of inward baptism." VI. The primary end of baptism is, that it may be a confirmation and sealing of the communication of grace in Christ, according to the new covenant, into which God the Father has entered with us in and on account of Christ. The secondary end is, that it may be the symbol of our initiation into the visible church, and an express mark of the obligation by which we have been bound to God the Father, and to Christ our Lord. VII. The object of this baptism is not real, but only personal; that is, all the covenanted people of God, whether they be adults or infants, provided the infants be born of parents who are themselves in the covenant, or if one of their parents be among the covenanted people of God, both because ablution in the blood of Christ has been promised to them; and because by the Spirit of Christ they are engrafted into the body of Christ. VIII. Because this baptism is an initiatory sacrament, it must be frequently repeated; because it is a sacrament of the New Testament, it must not be changed, but will continue to the end of the world; and because it is a sign confirming the promise, and sealing it, it is unwisely asserted that, through it, grace is conferred; that is, by some other act of conferring than that which is done through typifying and sealing: For grace cannot be immediately conferred by water.

DISPUTATION LXIV - ON THE LORD'S SUPPER

As in the preceding disputation, we have treated on baptism, the sacrament of initiation, it follows that we now discuss the Lord's supper, which is the sacrament of confirmation. II. We define it thus: The Lord's supper is a sacrament of the New Testament immediately instituted by Christ for the use of the church to the end of time, in which, by the legitimate external distribution, taking, and enjoyment of bread and wine, the Lord's death is announced, and the inward receiving and enjoyment of the body and blood of Christ are signified; and that most intimate and close union or fellowship, by which we are joined to Christ our Head, is sealed and confirmed on account of the institution of Christ, and the analogical relation of the sign to the thing signified. But by this, believers profess their gratitude and obligation to God, communion among themselves, and a marked difference from all other persons. III. We constitute Christ the author of this sacrament; for he alone is constituted, by the Father, the Lord and Head of the church, possessing the right of instituting sacraments, and of efficaciously performing this very thing which is signified and sealed by the sacraments. IV. The matter is, bread and wine; which, with regard to their essence, are not changed, but remain what they previously were; neither are they, with regard to place, joined together with the body or blood, so that the body is either in, under, or with the bread, &c.; nor in the use of the Lord's Supper can the bread and wine be separated, that, when the bread is held out to the laity, the cup be not denied to them. V. We lay down the form in the relation and the most strict union, which exist between the signs and the thing signified, and the reference of both to those believers who communicate, and by which they are made by analogy and similitude something united. From this conjunction of relation, arises a two-fold use of signs in this sacrament of the Lord's supper -- the first, that these signs are representative -- the second, that, while representing, they seal Christ to us with his benefits. VI. The end is two-fold: The first is, that our faith should be more and more strengthened towards the promise of grace which has been given by God, and concerning the truth and certainty of our being engrafted into Christ. The second is, (1.) that believers may, by the remembrance of the death of Christ, testify their gratitude and obligation to God; (2.) that they may cultivate charity among themselves; and (3.) that by this mark they may be distinguished from unbelievers.

DISPUTATION LXV - ON THE POPISH MASS

Omitting the various significations of the word "Mass" which may be adduced, we consider, on this occasion, that which the papists declare to be the external and properly called "expiatory sacrifice," in which the sacrificers offer Christ to his Father in behalf of the living and the dead, and which they affirm to have been celebrated and instituted by Christ himself when he celebrated and instituted his last supper. II. First. We say, this sacrifice is falsely ascribed to the institution of the Lord's supper; for Christ did not institute a sacrifice, but a sacrament, which is apparent from the institution itself, in which we are not commanded to offer any thing to God, at least nothing external. Yet we grant, that in the Lord's supper, as in all acts, is commanded, or ought to exist, that internal sacrifice by which believers offer to God prayers, praises and thanksgiving. In this view, the Lord's supper is called "the eucharist." III. Secondly. To this sacrifice are opposed the nature, truth and excellence of the sacrifice of Christ. For, as the sacrifice of Christ is single, expiatory, perfect, and of infinite value; and as Christ was once offered, and "hath by that one oblation perfected for ever them who were once sanctified," as the Scriptures testify, undoubtedly no place has been left either for any other sacrifice, or for a repetition of this sacrifice of Christ. IV. Thirdly. Besides, it is wrong to suppose that Christ can be or ought to be offered by men, or by any other person than by himself; for he, alone, is both the victim and the priest, as being the only one who is truly "holy, harmless, undefiled, and separate from sinners." V. From all these particulars it is sufficiently apparent, that it is not necessary, nay, that it is impious, for any expiatory sacrifice now to be offered by men for the living and the dead. Besides, it is a piece of foolish ignorance, to suppose either that the dead require some oblation; or that they can by it obtain remission of sins, who have not obtained pardon before death. VI. In addition to these three enormous errors committed in the mass, with respect to the sacrifice, to the priest, and to those for whom the sacrifice is offered, there is a fourth, which is one of the greatest turpitude of all, and is committed in conjunction with idolatry -- that this very sacrifice is adored by him who offers it, and by those for whom it is offered, and is carried about in solemn pomp. COROLLARY In these words, "the mass is an expiatory, representative and commemorative sacrifice," there is an opposition in the apposition and a manifest contradiction,

DISPUTATION LXVI - ON THE FIVE FALSE SACRAMENTS

As three things are necessarily required to constitute the essence of a sacrament -- that is, divine institution, an outward and visible sign, and a promise of the invisible grace which belongs to eternal salvation -- it follows that the thing which is deficient in one of these requisites, or in which one of them is wanting, cannot come under the denomination of a sacrament. II. Therefore popish confirmation is not a sacrament, though the external signing of the cross in the forehead of the Christian, and the unction of the chrism, are employed; for these signs have not been instituted by Christ; neither have they been sanctified to typify or to seal any thing of saving grace; nor is promised grace annexed to the use or to the reception of these signs. III. Penitence, indeed, is an act prescribed, by the Lord, to all who have fallen into sin, and has the promise of remission of sins. But because there does not exist in it, through the divine command, any external sign, by which grace is intimated and sealed, it cannot, on this account, receive the appellation of "a sacrament." For the act of a priest, absolving a penitent, belongs to the announcement of the gospel; as does likewise the injunction of those works which are inaccurately styled by the papists satisfactory, that is, fasting, prayers, alms, afflicting the soul, &c. IV. That is called extreme unction, by the papists, which is bestowed on none except on those who are in their last moments; but it has then not the least power or virtue; nor was it ever instituted by Christ to signify the premise of spiritual grace. It cannot, therefore, obtain the appellation of "a sacrament." V. Neither can the order or institution, confirmation or inauguration of any person to the official discharge of some ecclesiastical duties, come under the denomination of a sacrament -- both because it belongs to the particular and public vocation of some persons in the church, and not to the general vocation of all; and because, though it may have been instituted by Christ, yet, whatever external signs may be employed in it, they do not belong to the sealing of that grace which makes a man agreeable [to God] or which is saving, but only to that which is freely given, as they say by way of distinction. VI. Though matrimony between a husband and wife agree by a certain similitude with the spiritual espousals subsisting between Christ and the church; yet it was neither instituted by the Lord for signifying this, nor has it any promise of spiritual grace annexed to it.

DISPUTATION LXVII - ON THE WORSHIP OF GOD IN GENERAL

The first part of our duty to God and Christ was, the true meaning concerning God and Christ, or true faith in God and Christ; the second part is, the right worship to be rendered to both of them. II. This part receives various appellations. Among the Hebrews, it is called h r w k [and μ y h w l a t a d y the honour or worship, and the fear of God. Among the Greek, it is called Eusebeia piety; Qesebeia godliness, or a worshipping of God; Qrhskeia religion; Latreia service rendered to God; Douleia religious homage; Qerapeia divine worship; Timh honour; Fobov fear; Agaph tou Qeou the love of God. Among the Romans it is called, pietas, cultus or cultura dei, veneratio, honos, observantia. III. It may be generally defined to be an observance which must be yielded to God and Christ from a true faith, a good conscience, and from charity unfeigned, according to the will of God which has been manifested and made known to us, to the glory of both of them, to the salvation of the worshiper, and the edification of others. IV. We express the genus by the word "observance," because it contains the express intention of our mind and of our will to God and to his will, which intention partly inspires life into this portion of our duty towards God. V. The object is the same as that of the whole of religion, and of the first part of it, which is faith; and this object is God and Christ, in which the same formal reasons come under consideration, as those which we explained when treating generally on religion. VI. In the efficient or the worshiper, whom we declare to be a Christian man, we require true faith in God and Christ, a good conscience, as having been sanctified and purified through faith by the blood and Spirit of Christ, and a sincere charity; for, without these, no worship which is rendered to God can be grateful and acceptable to him. VII. The matter is, those particular acts in which the worship of God consists; but the very will and command of God gives form to it; for it is not the will of God to be worshipped at the option of a creature, but according to the pleasure and prescript of his own will. VIII. The principal end is, the glory of God and Christ. The less principal is the salvation of the worshiper, and the edification of others, both that they may be won over to Christ, and that, having been brought to Christ, they may the more increase and grow in devotedness. IX. The form is the observance itself, which is framed from the suitable agreement of all these things to the dignity, excellence and merits of the object that is to be worshipped -- from such a disposition of the worshiper according to such prescript, and from the intention of this end. If one of these be wanting the observance is vitiated, and is, therefore, displeasing to God. X. Yet the worship which is prescribed by God must not, on this account, be omitted, though the man, to whom it is prescribed, cannot yet perform it, from such a mind, to this end.

DISPUTATION LXVIII - ON THE PRECEPTS OF DIVINE WORSHIP IN GENERAL

To those who are about to treat on the worship of God, the most commodious way and method seems to be this -- to follow the order of the commands of God in which this worship is prescribed, and to consider all and each of them. For they instruct and inform the worshiper, and they prescribe the matter, form and end of the worship. II. In the precepts which prescribe the worship of God, three things come generally under consideration: (1.) Their foundation, on which rest the right and authority of him who commands, and the equity of his command. (2.) The command itself. (3.) The sanction, through promises and threatenings. The first of these may be called "the preface to the command;" the third, "the appendix to it;" and the second is the very essence of the precept. III. The foundation or preface, containing the authority of Him who commands, and, through this, the equity of the precept, is the common foundation of all religion, and, on this account, also, it is the foundation of faith; for instance,

"I am the Lord thy God," &c. "I, the God omnipotent or all sufficient, will be thy very great reward." "I am thy God, and the God of thy seed." From these expressions, not only may this conclusion be drawn -- "Therefore shalt thou love the Lord thy God," "Therefore walk before me, and be thou perfect" -- but likewise the following: "Therefore believe thou in me." But we must not treat on this subject on this occasion, as it has been discussed in the preceding pages. IV. I say that the other two are, the precept, and the sanction or appendix of the precept. For we must suppose that there are two parts of a precept, the first of which requires the performance or the omission of an act, and the second demands punishment. But we must consider that the latter part, which is called "the appendix," serves for this purpose, that, in the former, God enjoys the thing which he desired, dispensing blessings if he obtain his desire, and inflicting punishments if he does not obtain it. V. With regard to the precepts, before we come to each of them, we must first look generally at that which comes under consideration in every precept. VI. In the first place, the object of every precept is two- fold, the one formal, the other material; or the first formally required, the second materially,. Of these, the former is uniform in all circumstances and in every precept, but the latter is different or distinguishable. VII. The formal object, or that which is formally required, is pure obedience itself without respect of the particular thing or act in which, or about which, obedience must be performed. And we may be allowed to call such obedience "blind," with this exception, that it is preceded solely by the knowledge by which a man knows that this very thing had been prescribed by God. VIII. The material object, or that which is materially required, is the special or particular act itself, in the performance or omission of which obedience lies. IX. From the formal object, it is deduced that the act in which it is the will of God that obedience be yielded to him by its performance, is of such a nature that there is something in man which is abhorrent from its performance; and that the act, the omission of which is commanded by God, is of such a nature that there is something in man which is inclined to perform it. If it were otherwise, neither the performance of the former, nor the omission of the latter, could be called "obedience." X. From these premises, it further follows that the performance and the omission of this act proceed from a cause which overcomes and restrains the nature of man, that is inclined towards the forbidden act, and is abhorrent from that which is prescribed.

DISPUTATION LXIX - ON OBEDIENCE, THE FORMAL OBJECT OF ALL THE DIVINE PRECEPTS

The obedience which is the formal object of all the divine precepts, and which is prescribed in all of them, is properly and adequately prescribed to the will conducting itself according to the mode of liberty; that is, as it is free, that it may regulate the will conducting itself according to the mode of nature, that is, that it may regulate the inclination according to the prescribed obedience. II. This liberty is either that of contradiction or exercise, or that of contrariety or specification. According to the liberty of exercise, the will regulates the inclination, that it may perform some act rather than abstain from it, or the contrary. According to the liberty of specification, the will regulates the inclination, that, by such an act, it may tend towards this rather than towards that object. III. From this formal object of all precepts, and its relation thus considered, arises the first distribution and that a formal one, of all the precepts, into those which command, and those which forbid; that is, those in which the commission or the omission [of an act] is prescribed. IV. A precept which forbids is so binding, as not to allow a man to commit what is forbidden. For we must not perpetrate wickedness that good may come; yet this is the only reason why we might occasionally be allowed to perform what has been forbidden. V. A precept which commands is not equally rigidly binding, so as to require in every single moment of time the performance of what is commanded; for this cannot be done, though the period when man will or will not perform it, is not left to his option; but performance of it must be administered according to the occasions and exigencies which offer. Thus it was not lawful for Daniel to abstain for three days from calling upon his God. VI. When a precept which forbids, and one which commands, are directly contrary -- whether it be according to the act, "Thou shalt love God, and not hate him," "Thou shalt hate the world and not love it;" or, whether it be according to the object, "Thou shalt love God, and not love the world;" "Thou shalt hate the world, but shalt not hate God;" then the transgression of the law which forbids, is more grievous than that which commands, because it recedes further from obedience, and because the commission of an evil which has been forbidden includes in it the omission of a good which has been commanded.

DISPUTATION LXX - ON OBEDIENCE TO THE COMMANDS OF GOD IN GENERAL

Because the yielding of obedience is the duty of an inferior, therefore, for the performance of it, humility is requisite. This, generally considered, is a quality by which any one becomes ready to submit himself to another, to undertake his commands and to execute them; and, in this instance, to submit himself to God. II. Obedience has respect partly to an internal act, and partly to one that is external. The performance of both these is required for entire, true, and sincere obedience. For God is a Spirit, and the inspector of hearts, who demands the obedience of the whole man, both of the inward and the outward man -- obedience from the affections of the heart and from the members of the body. The external act without the internal is hypocrisy; the internal, without the external, is incomplete, unless man be hindered from the performance of the external act without his own immediate fault. III. With this, nearly coincides the expression of the scholastic divines "to perform a command either according to the substance of the act only, or also according to the required quality and mode," in which sense, likewise, Luther seems to have uttered that expression -- "Adverbs save and damn." IV. The grace and special concurrence of God are required for the performance of entire, true, and sincere obedience, even for that of the inner man, of the affections of the heart, and of a lawful mode. But we allow it to be made a subject of discussion, whether revelation, and that assistance of God which is called "general," and which is opposed to this special aid, and is distinguished from it, be sufficient only to perform the external act of the body and the substance of the act. V. Though that special grace which moves, excites, impels and urges to obey, physically moves the understanding and the inclination of man, so that he cannot be otherwise than affected with the perception of it, yet it does not effect or elicit the consent except morally, that is, by the mode of suasion, and by the intervention of the free volition of man, which free volition not only excludes coaction, but likewise all antecedent necessity and determination. VI. But that special concurrence or assistance of grace, which is also called "co-operating and accompanying grace" differs neither in kind nor efficacy from that exciting and moving grace which is called preventing and operating, but it is the same grace continued. It is styled "co-operating" or "concomitant," only on account of the concurrence of the human will which operating and preventing grace has elicited from the will of man. This concurrence is not denied to him to whom exciting grace is applied, unless the man offers resistance to the grace exciting. VII. From these premises, we conclude that a regenerated man is capable of performing more good than he actually performs, and can omit more evil than he omits; and, therefore, that neither in the sense in which it is received by St. Augustine, nor in that in which some of our divines understand it, is efficacious grace necessary for the performance of obedience -- a circumstance which is highly agreeable with the doctrine of St. Augustine. COROLLARY Coaction only circumscribes the liberty of an agent, it does not destroy or take it away; and such circumscription is not made, except through the medium or intervention of the natural inclination; the natural inclination, therefore, is more opposed to liberty than coaction is.

DISPUTATION LXXI - ON THE MATERIAL OBJECT OF THE PRECEPTS OF THE LAW IN GENERAL

As mere obedience, considered in the abstract, is the formal object of all the precepts of the divine law, so the acts in which the obedience that must be performed is prescribed, are the material objects of the same precepts. II. For this reason, these acts will at length be said to be conformable to law, and performed according to law, when obedience has given form to them; that when they have been performed from obedience, or through the intention and desire of obeying. This desire to obey is necessarily preceded by a certain knowledge that those acts have been prescribed by God, according to this expression of the apostle: "Whatsoever is not of faith, is sin." III. Hence, it is apparent that a good intention does not suffice to justify an act, unless it be preceded by a command of God and a knowledge of such command; though, without a good intention, no act, even when commanded by God, can of itself be pleasing to him. But it is our wish that, under the term "actions," omission is also understood to be comprehended. IV. A good work, therefore, universally requires these conditions: (1.) That it be prescribed by God. (2.) That man certainly knows it to have been commanded by God. (3.) That it be performed with the intention and desire of obeying God, which cannot be done without faith in God. To these ought to be added a special condition, which belongs to Christ and to his gospel -- that it be done through faith in Christ, because no work is agreeable to God after the commission of sin in a state of grace, except in Christ, and through faith in him. V. But the acts which are prescribed in the law, are either of themselves and in their own nature indifferent; or they have in them. something why they are pleasing or displeasing to God -- why they are prescribed by him or forbidden. The law, which prescribes the former of these, [the indifferent acts,] is called "positive," "symbolical," and "ceremonial." That which prescribes the latter is styled "the moral law" and "the decalogue;" it is also called "the law of nature." On these last, we shall afterwards treat at greater length. VI. The material acts, in which obedience is prescribed to be performed by the moral law, are either general, and belonging to the observance of the whole law and of all and each of its precepts; or they are special, and peculiarly prescribed in each of the precepts of the decalogue. VII. The general acts are the love, honour and fear of God, and trust in him. The special acts will be treated in the particular explanation of each of the precepts.

DISPUTATION LXXII - THE LOVE, FEAR, TRUST, AND honour WHICH ARE DUE FROM MAN TO GOD

These general acts may be considered either in the first act or in the second. In the first, they come under the denomination of affections; in the second, they retain to themselves the appropriate name of acts. But in consequence of the close union and agreement of nature between an affection and a second act, love, fear, trust and honour, receive the same denomination of "an affection," and "an act." II. The love of God is a dutiful act of man, by which he knowingly and willingly prefers, before all other things, the union of himself with God and obedience to the divine law, to which is subjoined a hatred of separation and of disobedience. III. The fear of God is a dutiful act of man, by which he knowingly and willingly dreads before all things and avoids the displeasing of God, (which is placed in the transgression of his commands,) his wrath and reprehension and any [sinister] inauspicious estimation of him lest he be separated from God. IV. Trust in God is a dutiful act of man, by which he knowingly and willingly reposes on God alone, assuredly hoping for and expecting from him all things which are salutary or saving to himself; in which we also comprehend the removal of evils. V. The honour of God is a dutiful act of man, by which he knowingly and willingly repays to God the reward due for his excellent virtues and acts. VI. The primary object of all these acts, as they are prescribed by law and are man's duty, is God himself; because, for whatever other things these acts are to be performed, they must be performed on account of God and through his command, otherwise no one can truly call them "good." VII. The formal reason of the object, that is, why these acts may and ought to be performed to God, is, the wisdom, goodness, justice, and power of God, and the acts performed by him according to and through them. But we permit this to be made the subject of a pious discussion, Which of these, in requiring simple acts, obtain the precedence, and which of them follow? VIII. The immediate cause of these acts is man, according to his understanding and inclination, and the freedom of his will, not as man is, natural, but as he is spiritual, and formed again after the life of God. IX. The principal cause is the Holy Spirit, who infuses into man, by the act of regeneration, the affections of love, fear, trust, and honour; by exciting grace, excites, moves and incites him to second acts, and by co-operating grace, concurs with man himself to produce such second acts. X. The form of these acts is that they be done through faith, and according to the law of God. Their end is, that they be performed to the salvation of the workers themselves, to the glory of God, and to the benefit and confirmation of others.

DISPUTATION LXXIII - ON PARTICULAR ACTS OF OBEDIENCE, OR THOSE WHICH ARE PRESCRIBED IN EACH PRECEPT, OR CONCERNING THE DECALOGUE IN GENERAL

The special acts of obedience are prescribed in the decalogue, and in each of the commandments. The decalogue, therefore, itself, must be considered by us in order. II. A convenient distribution of the decalogue is that into a preface and precepts. The preface is contained in these words: "I am the Lord thy God, who have brought thee up from the land of Egypt, out of the house of bondage." For we are of opinion that this preface belongs to the entire decalogue, rather than to the first commandment; though we do not consider it advisable to contend about a matter so small and unimportant. III. The preface contains a general argument of suasion, why the children of Israel ought to yield obedience to Jehovah -- and this two-fold -- the first drawn from the right of confederation or covenant -- the second, from a particular and signal benefit recently conferred on him. The former of these is contained in the words, "the Lord thy God;" the latter, in the expression, "who have brought thee out of the land of Egypt," of which benefit a high commendation is given in the description which is added -- that Egypt was to the Israelites "the house of bondage" that by amplifying the misery of that servitude, they might be able to call to mind those things which had happened to them. IV. Though this argument, "thy God," may likewise have respect to creation, and may comprise that benefit, yet it is more probable that it has a special reference to the concluding of a covenant with this people. V. From this preface, may conveniently be deduced those general acts about which we have treated in the preceding disputation -- the love, fear, trust, and honour of God; for, as Jehovah is their God, who delivered them out of Egypt, therefore, most justly, as well as profitably, must he be loved, feared and honoured, and trust must be reposed in him. VI. But some things generally must be observed for the correct performance of all the precepts together. Such are, VII. The law of God requires the entire obedience of the mouth, heart and work, that is, inward and outward obedience -- for God is the God of the whole man, of the soul and body, and looks principally upon the heart. VIII. The explanation of the precepts of the decalogue must be sought from Moses and the prophets, from Christ and his apostles; and it may be procured in sufficient abundance, so that nothing necessary can be imagined, which may not be drawn from the writings of the Old and the New Testament. IX. The meaning of each precept must be taken from the end on account of which it was given; and all those things must be considered as included in it, without which the precept cannot be performed. Therefore, one and the same work may be referred to different precepts, so far as it has respect to different ends. X. In affirmation, its opposite negative seems to be comprised; and, in a negative, the affirmation which is opposed to it; because God not only requires a refraining from evil, but likewise a performance of good, though a reason may be given why God declared some things negatively, and others affirmatively. XI. Homogeneous and cognate acts are commanded or are forbidden in the same precept; and a genus comprehends its species; and a species comprises, in the same command, other species allied to it, unless a just law exists why it must be otherwise determined. XII. An effect in its cause, or a cause in its effect, (if the conversion be necessary and according to nature,) is not commanded and prohibited through accident. XIII. When of those things which have a relation to each other, one is prescribed or forbidden, the other is also commanded or forbidden, because they mutually lay themselves down and remove themselves. XIV. If it happen that the observance of two precepts cannot be paid at the same time to both of them, regard must be had to that which is of the greater moment, and for the performance of which more and juster causes exist.

DISPUTATION LXXIV - ON THE FIRST COMMAND IN THE DECALOGUE

The ten precepts of the decalogue are conveniently distributed into those of the first and those of the second table. To the first table are attributed those precepts which immediately prescribe our duty towards God himself; of this kind, there are four. The second table claims those precepts which contain the duties of men towards their fellow-men; and to it are attributed the last six. II. This is the relation which subsists between the commands of each table -- that, from love to God and in reference to him, we manifest love, and the offices of love towards our neighbour; and if it should happen that we must of necessity relinquish either our duty to God or our neighbour, God should be preferred to our neighbour. Let this relation, however, be understood as concerning those precepts only which are not of the ceremonial worship; otherwise, [respecting ceremonies] this declaration holds good: "I will have mercy, and not sacrifice." III. The first commandment is, "Thou shalt have no other god before my face," or "against my face." IV. It is very certain that, in this negative precept, the subjoined affirmative one is included or presupposed as something preceding and prerequisite: "Thou shalt have me, who am Jehovah, for thy God." This is likewise immediately consequent upon the preface, "I am the Lord thy God;" therefore, "Let me be the Lord thy God;" or, which is the same, "Therefore, have thou me, the Lord, for thy God." V. But "to have the Lord for our God, is the part both of the understanding and of the inclination or the will; and, lastly, of an effect proceeding from both or from each of them. VI. "Another god" is whatever the human mind invents, to which it attributes the divinity that is suitable and appropriate to the true God alone -- whether such divinity be essence and life, or properties, works, or glory. VII. Or whether the thing to which man attributes divinity be something existing or created, or whether it be something non-existent and merely imaginary and a figment of the brain, it is equally "another god" for the entire divinity of that other god lies radically, essentially and virtually in human ascription, and by no means in that to which such divinity is ascribed. Hence is the origin of this phrase, in Scripture, "To go a whoring after their own heart." VIII. But this "other God" may be conceived under a three- fold difference, according to the Scriptures. For those who have him, have (1.) either themselves been the first inventors of him, (2.) have received him from their parents, or (3.) from other nations, when neither they nor their fathers knew him; and this last is done either by force, by persuasion, or by the free and spontaneous choice of the will. IX. For this reason, that "other god" is truly called "an idol;" and the act by which he is accounted another god, is idolatry; whether this be committed in the mind, by estimation, acknowledgment, and belief, or by the affections, love, fear, trust and hope, or by some external effect of honour, worship, adoration and invocation. X. The enormity of this sin is apparent from the fact of its being called "a defection from God," "a forsaking of the living fountain," and "a digging of broken cisterns that hold no water," "a perfidious desertion of holy matrimony," and "a violation of the connubial compact." Nay, the gentiles are said to sacrifice to devils whatsoever they suppose that they offer to God, in this ignorance of God and alienation from the life of God. XI. The cause why men are said to do service unto devils, although they have themselves other thoughts, is this: because Satan is the fountain head, and origin of all idolatry; and is the author, persuader, impeller, approver and defender of all the worship which is expended on another god. Hence, likewise, it is the highest degree of idolatry when any one accounts divine or ascribes divinity to Satan as Satan, displaying himself as Satan and vaunting himself for God. XII. But though the gentiles worshipped angels or devils, not as the supreme God, but as minor deities and his ministers, by whose intervention they might have communication with the supreme God; yet the worship which they paid to them was idolatry, because this worship was due to no one except to the true God. But it does not belong to the definition of idolatry, that any one should pay to another, as to God, that worship which is due to the true God alone; for it is sufficient if he account him as God, by ascribing divine worship to him, though, in his mind, he may account him not to be the supreme God. It is no palliation of the crime, but an aggravation, if any one knowingly performs divine worship to him whom he knows not to be God. XIII. And since Christ must be honoured as the Father is, because he has been constituted by his Father KING and LORD, and has received all judgment, since every knee must bow to him, and since he is to be invoked as Mediator and the Head of his church, so that the church can pay this honour to no one except him, without incurring the crime of idolatry; therefore, the papists, who adore Mary, the angels, or holy men, and who invoke them as the donors and administrators of gifts, or as intercessors through their own merits, are guilty of the crime of idolatry. XIV. Besides, when they adore the bread in the Lord's supper, and receive and account the pope for that personage whom he boasts himself to be, they commit the sin of idolatry.

DISPUTATION LXXV - ON THE SECOND COMMAND IN THE DECALOGUE

The second precept consists of a command and its sanction, from a description of God, who is prompt and powerful to punish the transgressor, and who is greatly inclined to bless him that is obedient. In this are consequently included a threat of punishment and a promise of reward. II. This command is negative: A deed which is displeasing to God is forbidden in these words: "Thou shalt not make unto thee any graven image, or any likeness of any thing that is in the earth beneath, or that is in the water under the earth; thou shalt not bow down thyself to them, nor serve them." III. The sum of the precept is, that no one should adore or offer divine worship to any sculptured, molten or painted image, or one made in any other way, whether it has for its archetype a thing really existing or something fictitious, God or a creature, or whether it resemble its archetype according to some real conformity, or only by institution and opinion, or, which is the same thing, that he do not in or to any image adore or worship that which he considers in the place of a deity and worships as such, whether this be truly or falsely. IV. As, from a comparison of this precept, with other passages of Scripture in which God commands certain images to be made, it appears that the mere formation of every kind of image whatsoever is not forbidden, provided that they be not prostituted to worship; so, from a comparison of this same precept with others which are analogous to it or collateral, it is evident that no image ought to be made to represent God, because this very act is nothing else but a changing of the glory of the incorruptible God into the image or likeness of a corruptible thing. For whatever can be fashioned or framed is visible, therefore corruptible. We are not afraid of making this general affirmation under the sanction of the Scriptures, though with them and from them we know, that now, according to the body, Christ is incorruptible. V. A double distinction is here employed by the papists, of an archetype and its image; and also of an image itself as it is formed of such materials, and as it is an image, that is, calculated and fitted to represent the archetype. From these, they further deduce the distinction of the intention in worshipping; by which the worshiper looks upon either the archetype alone, not its image; or, if he even looks on the image, does not behold it as it is made of such materials, neither on it principally, but in reference to its archetype. We do not attempt to deny that the mind of man can frame a distinction of this kind. VI. But when those who fall down before an image attempt, by such a distinction, to excuse themselves from the transgression of this precept, they accuse God himself of a falsehood, and deride his command. (1.) They charge him with falsehood; because, when God declares that he who falls down before an image, says to the wood and to the stone, "Thou art my Father!" they assert, that the prostrated person does not say this to the wood and the stone, but to their archetype, that is, to God. (2.) They mock God and his command; because by this distinction it comes to pass, that no man at any time, though paying adoration to any kind of images, can be brought in guilty of having violated this precept, unless, according to his own opinion, he has judged that wood really to be God, and therefore that he has himself truly and in reality formed a god, which cannot possibly enter into the conception of one who uses his reason. VII. But they partly annihilate their own excuse which rests on this distinction, when they say that the same honour and worship (whether it be that of latria, of dulia, or of hyperdulia,) must be given to an image as to its archetype. Neither does this prolong its existence by such distinction, when they represent God himself by an image, because that is simply forbidden to be done. VIII. We assert, therefore, that, according to the judgment of God, and express passages of Scripture, the papists are correctly charged with giving a portraiture of the essence of God, when they represent him in the form of an old man, graced with an ample gray beard, and seated on a throne -- though in express words they say, that they know God has not a body, and though they protest that they had fashioned this form, not for the purpose of representing his essence, but that they had instituted this similitude to represent the appearance which he occasionally made to his prophets, and to signify his presence. For the protestation is contrary to facts; since facts are, by nature, not what we feign them to be, but what God, the legislator, declares them to be. But he says those facts are, that he has been assimilated, that a [supposed] likeness of himself has been formed, and that he has been [falsely] set up in a gold or silver graven image. IX. We assert that all those images of which we have spoken - - both those of God, placed only for representation, and those of other things (whether true or fictitious,) exposed for adoration -- are correctly called "idols," not only according to the etymology of the word, but likewise according to the usage of the Scriptures, and that the distinction which is employed by the papists between idols and resemblances or images has been produced from the dark cave of horrid idolatry. X. In the same precept in which it is forbidden to fashion or make any images for divine worship, it is likewise commanded to remove others, if they have been previously made and exposed for worship, these two cautions being always observed, (1.) That it be done, when preceded by a suitable and sufficient teaching. (2.) That it be the work of those who are in possession of the supreme authority in the commonwealth and the church. XI. Though the honour exhibited to such images, or to the deity through such images, be reproachful to the true God himself; yet he, also, who pours contumely on the images which he considers to be correctly formed, and lawfully proposed for worship, pours contumely on the deity himself, whom he presumes to worship, and declares himself to be an atheist. XII. The affirmation seems here to be strictly and directly opposed to the whole negative precept, that we may worship God, because he is a Spirit, with a pure cogitation of mind and abstracted from every imagination. XIII. The sanction of the precept, which includes the threatening, is this: "For I, the Lord thy God, am a jealous God, visiting the iniquity of the fathers upon the children, unto the third and fourth generation of them that hate me;" that is, unless you obey this, my precept, you shall feel that I am jealous of mine honour, and that I will not, with impunity, suffer it to be given to another, or my glory to be communicated to graven images. XIV. The other part of the sanction contains a promise in these words: "I am the Lord thy God, showing mercy unto thousands of them that love me and keep my commandments;" [That is, if you obey this my precept, you shall feel that I will display mercy towards you, and towards your children to the thousandth generation, provided that they also love me.] XV. But mention is made of posterity, that men may be thus the more incited to obedience, since their future compliance with the precept will prove beneficial, not only to themselves, but to their posterity, or their future transgression will be injurious to them and their offspring. XVI. From a comparison of the preceding command with this, it appears that there is a two-fold idolatry -- one, by which a false and fictitious deity is worshipped; another, by which a true or false deity is worshipped in an image, by an image, or at an image. Yet this very image is sometimes called "a false and another god," which the Lord God also seems to intimate in this place, when he endeavours to deter men from a violation of this precept by an argument drawn from his jealousy. COROLLARY Without any exaggeration, the idolatry of the papists may be placed on an equality with that of the Jews and gentiles. If it be urged as an exception, that they have neither made their children pass through the fire, nor have offered living men in sacrifice -- we reply, The horrid tyranny which the papists have exercised in the murder of so many thousand martyrs, with the design of confirming the idolatry that flourishes among them, may be equitably compared to making their children pass through the fire, and the oblation of living men in sacrifice, if not according to the appearance of the deed, at least according to the grievous nature of the crime.

DISPUTATION LXXVI - ON THE THIRD PRECEPT OF THE DECALOGUE

This precept, as well as its predecessor, consists of a command, and of its sanction through the threatening of a punishment. The precept is a negative one, and prohibits a deed which is displeasing to God, in these words: "Thou shalt not take the name of the Lord thy God in vain." II. The reason, and end of the precept is this: Because God is entirely holy, and because his name is full of majesty, we must use it in a holy and reverend manner, and must, by no means, account it common or contaminate it. III. "The name of God" is here received in its most general notion, for every word which, according to the purpose God, is used to signify God and divine things. IV. "To assume" or "to take the name of God," properly, to take that word into our mouth and pronounce it with our tongue. If, under this phrase, any one, by a synecdoche, is desirous, likewise, of comprehending the deeds, in which God and divine things are less religiously treated, he has our full permission; and, we think, he does not depart from the sense of the precept. But we still continue in the explanation of the proper acceptation. V. The particle, "in vain," is variously received -- for that which is done rashly and without just cause -- for what is done in vain and with no useful end -- for what is done with mendacity, dissimulation, falsely, inadvertently, &c. Hence, this prohibition likewise diffuses itself extensively in every direction. VI. But, perhaps with some propriety, every "taking of the name of the Lord in vain" may be reduced to two principal heads or kinds: The First genus comprehends the use of the name of God when no mention of it, whatever, should be made; that is, in a word or deed, in which, it has been the will of God that the mention of his name shall not intervene, either because the word or deed is not lawful, or because it is of minor moment. VII. But the Second genus comprises the incorrect use of the name of God; that is, when it is not truly used in any of our duties in which it may be lawfully used, or in which it ought also to be dutifully used according to the divine direction. VIII. The duties of this class are, the adoration and invocation of God, the narration and preaching of his word or of divine things, oaths, &c. in these, the name of God is taken in vain, in three ways: (1.) Hypocritically, when it is not used sincerely from the whole heart. (2.) With a doubting conscience, when it is used with an uncertain belief that it is lawful to be used in that duty. (3.) Against conscience, as when it is employed to bear testimony to a falsehood. IX. The threatening is expressed in these words: "For the Lord will not leave him unpunished that taketh his name in vain." By this he endeavours to persuade men, that no one should dare to use his name; of which persuasion there is so much the greater necessity, as the heinousness of this offense is not sufficiently considered among men.

DISPUTATION LXXVII - ON THE FOURTH COMMAND IN THE DECALOGUE

This precept contains two parts, a command and a reason for it. But the command is first proposed in few words; it is afterwards more amply explained. The proposition is in these words: "Remember the Sabbath day, to keep it holy." The explanation is thus expressed: "Six days shalt thou labour, and do all thy work," &c. But the reason is comprehended in the following words: "For in six days the Lord made heaven and earth, the seas," &c. II. In the proposition of the precept, three things are worthy of observation: (1.) The act prescribed, which is sanctification. (2.) An anxious and solicitous care about not omitting this act, which is expressed in the words, "remember," and "do not forget." (3.) The object, which is called "the Sabbath," or "the seventh day;" that is, the seventh in the order of the days in which the creation was commenced and perfected. It is also called "the Sabbath," from the circumstance of God having rested at that period, and man was required to repose. III. The explanation contains two things: (1.) A concession or grant, that men may spend six days in labours belonging to the natural life and its sustenance; this concession contains the equity of the command. (2.) A command about resting from those works on the seventh day, with an enumeration of the persons whose duty it is to rest: "Not only thou, but also thy son, thy man servant, thy maid servant, thy cattle, and thy stranger shall rest;" that is, thou shalt cause as many persons to rest as are under thy power. IV. The reason contains, in itself, two arguments: The First is the example of God himself, who rested from his works on the seventh day. The Second is the benediction and sanctification of God, by which it was his pleasure that the seventh should be separated from the rest of the days, and devoted to himself and to his worship. V. "To sanctify the seventh day," is to separate it from common use, and from such as belong to the natural life, and to consecrate it to God, and to acts which belong to God, to things divine, and to the spiritual life. This sanctification consists of various acts. VI. We think that it may be made a most useful point of consideration, how far must abstinence from those works which belong to the natural life be extended?

And though we prescribe nothing absolutely, yet we should wish that the liberty of performing such labour should be restricted as much as possible, and confined to exceedingly few necessary things. For we have no doubt that the Sabbath is in various ways violated among Christians, by not abstaining from such things as are lawful to be done on other days. VII. We think that the acts which belong to the sanctification of the Sabbath may be included in two classes: (1.) Some per se and primarily belong to the worship of God, and are in themselves grateful and acceptable to God. (2.) Others are subordinate to those acts which are to be performed, and they answer the purpose, that those acts may, in the best possible manner, be performed to God by men; such are those which belong to the instruction of believers in their duty. VIII. But this kind of sanctification ought not only to be private and domestic, but also public and ecclesiastical. For it is the will of God, not only that he should be acknowledged, worshipped, invoked and praised by each individual in private, but likewise by all united together in the great church; that he may, by this means, be owned to be the God and Lord not only of each individual, but likewise of the whole of his universal family. IX. But because the neglect of God and of things divine easily creeps upon man, who is too closely intent on this natural life, it was, therefore, necessary that men's memories should be refreshed by this word "Remember," &c. X. But now, with regard to the seventh day, which is commanded to be sanctified. In it, this is moral and perpetual -- that the seventh day, that is, one out of the seven, be devoted to divine worship, and that it be unlawful for any man, at any time, after having expended six days in the labours of the natural life, to continue the seventh day in all the same labours, or in the same manner. XI. But with regard to that day among the seven which followed the six days in which God completed the creation, its sanctification is not of perpetual institution and necessity; but it might be changed into another day, and in its own time it was lawful for it to be changed, that is, into the day which is called "the Lord's day;" because the new creation was then perfected in Christ our head, by his resurrection from the dead; and it was equitable and right that the new people should enter on a new method of keeping the Sabbath. XII. That reason which was taken from the example of God who rested on the seventh day, (that is, when the creation was completed,) endured to the time of the new creation; and, therefore, when it ceased, or at least when a second reason was added to it from the new creation, it was no subject of wonder that the apostles changed it into the following day, on which the resurrection of Christ occurred. For when Christ no longer walks in the flesh, and is not known after the flesh, all things become new. XIII. But the benediction and the sanctification of God are understood to be transferred from the Sabbath to the Lord's day; because all the sanctification which pertains to the new earth, is perfected in Jesus Christ, who is truly the Holy of holies, and in whom all things are sanctified for ever. XIV. Because the reason, by which God afterwards persuaded the people to observe the Sabbath, was for a sign between him and His people that God would engage in the act of sanctifying them; it may likewise be accommodated to the times of the New Testament, and may persuade men to the observance of the [new] Sabbath. XV. If any one supposes that the Lord's day is by no means to be distinguished from the rest of the days [of the week]; or if, for the sake of declaring evangelical liberty, this person has changed it into another day, either into Monday or Tuesday; we think he ought at least to be considered a schismatic in the church of God.

DISPUTATION LXXVIII - ON THE FIFTH COMMAND IN THE DECALOGUE

I. This precept is the first of the second table. It contains the precept itself, and the promise attached to it. The end of the precept is, that a certain order should exist among men, according to which some are superiors and others inferiors, and which consists in the mutual performance of the duties of commanding and obeying that are necessary for the defense of society. II. The precept prescribes an act, and adds an object to which that act must be performed. The act is contained in the word "honour;" the object in these words: "thy father and thy mother." From this, it appears, according to the nature of relations, that this law is prescribed to all those who are relatively opposed to father and mother [as are sons and daughters]. III. The word "honour" is not appropriately employed to signify eminence; for honour is the reward of excellence, and its performance is a sign of recognition; and this word comprehends, either in the wide compass of its signification, all the duties which are due from an inferior to a superior; or, as an end, it comprehends all things necessary to the rendering of such honour. IV. Three things principally are contained in this word: (1.) That reverence be shown to the persons of our parents. (2.) That obedience be performed to their commands. (3.) That gratitude be evinced, in conferring on them all things necessary to the preservation of the present life, with respect to the dignity of their persons and of their office. V. Reverence consists both in the performance of those acts which contain, [on our part] a confession of their pre- eminence and of our submission under them, and in the endurance of their faults and manners, in a connivance at them, in a modest concealment of them, and in kind excuses for them. VI. Obedience lies in the prompt and free performance of those things which they prescribe, and in the omission of those which they prohibit. This obedience must be performed not only "for wrath," or the fear of punishment, but also "for conscience' sake," and this, not so much that we may obey them, as God himself, whose vicegerents they are. VII. Gratitude, which contains the conferring of things necessary for them to the uses of life according to their dignity, ought to extend itself not only to the time when they discharge this duty, but likewise through the whole life -- though it may happen that, through old age or some other cause, they are rendered unfit to discharge the parental office. VIII. The duties of superiors are analogous to those of inferiors -- that they conduct themselves with moderation, seriousness, and decorum, in the whole of their life, public as well as private -- that they observe justice and equity in issuing their commands, and that, in requiring gratitude, they do not transgress the bounds of moderation. But these points will be more particularly discussed in the disputation on the magistracy. IX. The object is enunciated in the words "father," and "mother," in which, likewise, are comprehended all those who are placed above us in human society, whether it be political, ecclesiastical, scholastic or domestic society -- whether in the time of peace or in that of war -- whether such persons discharge the duties of an ordinary or an extraordinary office, or whether they be invested with this power either constantly, or only for a season, however short. X. But all these persons in authority are, in this commandment, fitly, and not without just cause, expressed under the name of "parents," which is an endearing and delightful appellation, and most appropriate both to signify the feeling which it is right for superiors to indulge towards inferiors, and most efficaciously to effect a persuasion in inferiors of the equity of performing their duty towards their superiors. It may be added that the first association among men is that of domestic society, and from this follow the rest by the increase of mankind. XI. Superiors lose no degree of this eminence by any sin, or by any corruption of their own; therefore, this duty of honour, reverence, obedience and gratitude must be performed to superiors, even when they are evil, and abusing their power; provided caution be used that the interest of God be always the more powerful with us, and lest, while that which is Caesar's is given to Caesar, that which belongs to God, be taken from him, or be not given. XII. To this, must necessarily be subjoined another threefold caution -- (1.) That no one commit an error in judgment, by which he persuades himself this or that belongs to God, and not to Caesar. (2.) That he discern correctly between that which he is commanded to do or to tolerate; and, if he must do it, whether or not it be an act about a thing or object which is subject to his power. (3.) That under the name of liberty, no one arrogate to himself the right of a superior, of not obeying in this thing or that, or the power of rising against his superior, either for the purpose of taking away his life, or only his rule and dominion. XIII. The promise which is added to this precept is contained in the following words: "that thy days maybe long upon the land which the Lord thy God will give thee" in which are promised, (1,) to the Jewish believers who perform this precept, length of days in the land of Canaan; (2,) and also to the gentile believers who perform this command, the duration of the present life; (3,) typically, to such persons are promised the eternal or heavenly life, of which the land of Canaan was a type.

DISPUTATION LXXIX - ON THE SIXTH PRECEPT

Order in human society being appointed by the fifth commandment, through the mutual duties of superiors and inferiors in commanding and obeying, God now manifests his care for all those things which, in order to pass one's life in this society, are necessary for the life of each person, for the propagation of the species, for the blessings necessary to life, and for reputation, at the end of which God adds the tenth commandment, in which the coveting of certain things is prohibited. II. By these words, "thou shalt not kill," the sixth precept provides for the preservation of the natural life, and designs the safety of men's bodies that it may be preserved inviolate. III. The sum of the precept is neither in reality to injure the life of another person, and to endanger his safety, nay not even our own, whether we use fraud or violence, nor to wish his injury by our will, to which must be added that we do not intimate this kind of wish by any external token. IV. From this, it appears that the accident must not receive the appellation of "homicide," if, as the Scripture phrase is, any one going into a wood with his neighbour to cut down timber, and the head of his ax slips from the handle and strikes his neighbour so that he dies, nor, if, for the defense of his own life, any one be compelled, at the peril of his life, to repel the force employed against him by another. V. But in this precept, we are commanded to endeavour by all legitimate means and methods, to save the life of our neighbour, as well as our own, and to defend them from all injury. VI. But the cause of this precept, which is universal and always, and in every place, valid, is the following: because man was created after the image of God, which, in this place, principally denotes immortality. To this, may be added similitude of nature, and because all of us derive our origin from one blood. But several particular causes may be adduced, which agree with the spiritual state of men, such as because they have been redeemed by Christ with a price -- because their bodies are a habitation for the Holy Spirit -- because they are all members of one mystical body under one head, &c. VII. But, in the mean time, God reserves to himself the right of disposing of the life of every man according to his own pleasure. Hence, commands have been issued to magistrates concerning killing transgressors, and a command was delivered to Abraham about slaying his son.

COROLLARY

The perpetration of homicide cannot consist with a good conscience, unless pardon for it be sought and obtained by particular repentance,

Dissertation Of The Seventh Chapter Of Romans

DEDICATION

TO THE MOST HONOUR ABLE AND NOBLE WILLIAM BARDESIUS, LIEUTENANT OF WARMENHUYSEN, A NOBLEMAN WHO IS OUR PATRON, AND WHO, ON MANY ACCOUNTS, IS TO BE HONOUR ED BY US. MOST HONOUR ABLE AND NOBLE SIR:

THAT expression of the apostle Paul, by which he designates the doctrine of the gospel as "the truth which is according to godliness," (Tit. i. 1) is very remarkable and worthy of perpetual consideration. From this sentiment, with the leave of all good men, we may collect that this "truth" neither consists in naked theory and inane speculation, nor in those things which, belonging to mere abstract knowledge, only play about the brain of man, and which never extend to the reformation of their will and affections. But it consists in those things which imbue the mind with a sincere fear of God, and with a true love of solid piety, and which render men "zealous of good works." Another passage, not less famous and remarkable, in the same epistle and by the same apostle, tends greatly to confirm and illustrate this view of the matter; it is thus expressed: "For the grace of God that bringeth salvation hath appeared to all men, teaching us that, denying ungodliness and worldly lusts, we should live soberly, righteously and godly in this present world." (Tit. ii. 11,19.) Whosoever they be, therefore, that profess themselves the heralds of this divine "truth," they ought to give additional diligence that, casting aside all curious and thorny questions, and those idle subtilities which derive their origin from human vanity, they commend to their hearers this one and only "godliness," and that they seriously instruct them in faith, hope and charity. And, in return, those of their auditors who are enamored with this "truth," are bound strenuously to conform themselves to this course of conduct--to pass by and to slight all other things which may come across their path, and constantly to aim at this "godliness" alone, and keep their eyes intent upon it. For both clergy and laity may receive this as a principle, that they are yet rude and complete strangers in true theology, unless they have learned so to theologize, that theology may bear the torch before them to that piety and holiness which they sedulously and earnestly pursue. If this admonition ever was necessary, it is undoubtedly the more necessary at this time; because we see impiety overflowing in every direction, like a sea raging and agitated by whirlwinds. Yet, amidst all this storm, such are the stupor and insensibility of men, that not a few who remain exactly the same persons as they formerly were, and who, indeed, have not changed the least particle of the manner of their impure life, still imagine themselves to be in the class of prime Christians, and promise themselves the favour of the supreme God, the possessing of heaven and of life eternal, and of the company of Christ and of the blessed angels, with such great and presumptuous confidence, and with such security of mind, that they consider themselves to be atrociously injured by those who, judging them to be deceived in this their self-persuasion, desire them in any wise to entertain doubts about it. In a condition of affairs thus deplorable, no endeavour appears to be more laudable, than to institute a diligent inquiry into the causes of such a pernicious evil, and, by employing a saving remedy, to arouse erring souls from this diabolical lethargy, and induce them to alter their lives, under the felicitous auspices of the gospel and the Spirit of Christ, to devote their energies to a solid amendment of manners, and thus, at length, from the divine word, to promise themselves, when answering this description, grace with God and eternal glory. The causes of this evil are various, and most of them consist in certain erroneous and false conceptions which, being impressed on their minds, some men carry about with them, being either their own inventions, or furnished to them from some other quarter; yet, either in general or in particular, either directly or indirectly, such erroneous conceptions lay a stumbling-block and an impediment before the true and serious study of piety and the pursuit of virtue. We will not, in this place, introduce any mention of the impious conceptions of some men who do not believe either that there is a life eternal, or that, if it really exists, it is of such great and sublime excellence as it is described to be in the Holy Scriptures--who either despair of the mercy of God towards repentant sinners, or who consider it to be impossible to enter on that way of piety and new obedience which has been prescribed by the prince of our salvation. We say nothing about these persons, because they not only relax the asseverations and the promises of God, which are the true foundations of the Christian religion, but they likewise entirely overturn them, and thus, with one effort, they pluck up, by the roots, all piety, and all desire and love of it, from the hearts of men. We now begin to make some observations on those hypotheses, whether secret or avowed, which are injurious to piety, and which obtain among Christians themselves, whether they be publicly defended or otherwise. Among them, the first which comes under enumeration, is the dogma of unconditional predestination, with those which depend on it by a necessary connection; and, in particular, the so highly extolled perseverance of the saints, in a confidence in which such things are uttered by some persons as we dread to recite, for they are utterly unworthy of entering into the ear of Christians. It is no small impediment which these dogmas place in the way of piety. When, after a diligent and often- repeated perusal of the Holy Scriptures, after long meditations and ardent prayers to God, with fasting, our father, of blessed memory, thought that he had made a sure discovery of the baneful tendency of these dogmas, and had reflected upon them within his own breast, and that, however strenuously they might be urged by certain divines, and generally instilled into the minds of students by scholastic exercises, yet neither the ancient church nor the modern, after a previous lawful examination of them, ever received them or allowed them to pass into matters that had obtained mature adjudication. When he perceived these things, he began by degrees, to propose his difficulties about them, and his objections against them, for the purpose of shewing that they were not so firmly founded in the Scriptures as they are generally supposed to be; and, in process of time, being still more strongly confirmed in the knowledge of the truth, especially after the conference which he had with Doctor Francis Junius, and in which he had seen the weakness of his replies, he began to attack those dogmas with greater boldness; yet on no occasion was he forgetful of the modesty which so eminently became him. But, of the arguments with which he attacked those dogmas, this [on the seventh chapter of St. Paul's epistle to the Romans] in which we have now engaged, was not the last--that is, such was the nature of these doctrines that they were calculated to relax the study of piety, and thus to extinguish it. In that labour he also occasionally employed subtilities. and such reasons as are not at once obvious to the multitude; but they were subtle distinctions, necessary for overturning dogmas which, in his judgment, were very baneful. And, undoubtedly, as love is not conquered except by another love, so that subtlety, which is the inventor and establisher of falsehood, can scarcely be conquered and overturned without the subtlety which is the assertor of the truth and the convictor of falsehood. Therefore, the subtilities which he employed on that occasion, [his conference with Junius,] were useful and necessary--not insignificant, trifling, and invented for pleasure, ostentation or display. But with regard to other things, it is known to all those who were on terms of familiarity with him--especially during the last years of his life, when he was much engaged in the schools, in which it is an established custom principally to pursue subtilities--what a rigid enemy he was of all subtilities and of lofty language; and even those whom he had among his students that differed on some other points from him, could testify, if they would conscientiously relate the truth, that he referred all things to use and to the practice of a Christian life; and thus that piety and the fear of the divine Majesty uniformly breathed in his lectures, in his disputations, (both public and private,) in his sermons, discourses and writings. But it is not necessary for us, in this place, to rehearse the method by which he proved the genius of unconditional predestination and its annexed dogmas to be adverse to godliness; because his writings on this subject are partly extant, and the remainder, under the divine auspices, will soon be published. It is better that prudent readers should listen to him uttering his own words, than to us who are but stammerers about him. The water is sweeter which we taste at the fountain, than that which we drink at a distance from the spring. Various are the other hypotheses which operate as hindrances to piety, and the whole of which we are not able now to mention; but we will briefly discuss a Jew of those which occur, that we may not produce weariness in you, most noble sir, by our prolixity. A capital error which first offers itself, and which closely adheres to the inmost core and fibers of nearly all mankind, is that by which they silently imagine in their own minds that illimitable mercy exists in God; and from this they opine that they will not be rejected, though they have indulged themselves a little too much in vicious pursuits, but that, on the contrary, they will continue to be dear to God and beloved. This error is in reality joined with notorious incredulity, and, in a great measure destroys the Christian religion, which is founded on the blood of Christ. For, in this way, is removed all necessity for a pious life, and a manifest contradiction is given to the declaration of the apostle, in which he affirms that "without holiness no man shall see God." (Heb. xii. 14) Alas for the insanity of men, who have the audacity to bless themselves when they are cursed by God! This is succeeded by the false hypothesis of others, who, revolving in their minds the designs, the morals, and the life of mortals, and reflecting on the multitude, among men of all orders, of those who are wandering in error, conclude that the mercy of God will not permit eternally to perish so many and such infinite myriads of rational creatures, formed after the divine image. The consequence is, that, instead of performing their duty according to the tenor of Christianity, by opposing the torrent of impiety, they, on the contrary, suffer themselves to be carried away by the impulse of such views, and associate with the multitudes of those who are devious in error. They seem to forget that the many walk in the broad way, whose end, according to the truth of God, will be "destruction from the presence of the Lord." A multitude will preserve no man from perdition. Unhappy and most miserable solace, to have many companions in enduring everlasting punishment! Let the force of this deception, likewise, be considered, that vices are dignified with the names of virtues, and, on the other hand, virtues receive the defiling appellation of vices. The effect of this is, that men, who are of themselves, prone to vicious indulgences, pursue them with the greater avidity when they are concealed under the mask of virtues, and, on the contrary, are terrified at virtues, in the attainment of which any difficulty is involved, as though they were clothed in the monstrous garb of the most horrid vices. Thus, among mankind, drunkenness obtains the name of hilarity; and filthy talking, that of cheerful freedom; while sobriety in food and drink, and simplicity in dress, are opprobiously styled hypocrisy. This is really to "call good evil, and evil good," and to seek an occasion, by which a man may cease from the practice of virtue, and devote himself to vicious courses, not only without any reluctance of conscience, but likewise at the impulse and instigation of his [seared] conscience. Into this enumeration, must come that shameful and false reasoning by which unwise men infer, from those passages in Scripture in which we are said to be justified by faith without works, that it is not, therefore, necessary to attend to good works, they being of such a nature that without them we may be justified, and, therefore, saved. They never advert to the fact that, in other passages, it is recorded--True faith, that is, the faith by which we are justified, must be efficacious through charity; and that faith, without works, is dead, and resembles a lifeless carcass. This vain idea also, in no trifling degree, consoles the men who try to flatter themselves in those vices to which they have a constitutional propensity--that they are not given up to all vices, they have not run into every excess of wickedness, but, though addicted to certain vices peculiar to themselves, they feel an abhorrence for all others. As men are most ingenious in the invention of excuses for themselves, in support of this incorrect view are generally cited these common phrases: "No man lives without sin;" "Every man is captivated by that which he finds to be pleasing to himself." Such men, therefore, consider themselves to be true Christians, and that, on this account, it will be eternally well with them, when, as they foolishly persuade themselves, they abstain from most evils, and, as for the rest, they cherish only some one vice, a single Herodias alone. A most absurd invention! since no one is, no one can be, addicted to all vices at once; because some among them are diametrically opposed to others, and are mutual expellers. If this conceit be allowed, no mortal man either will or can be impious. The subjoined passage in the epistle of St. James ought to recur to the remembrance of these persons: "Whosoever shall offend in one point, he is guilty of all." (ii, 10.) We are also commanded to "lay aside," not some one, but "all malice, guile, and hypocrisy," (1 Pet. ii. 1,)that we may thus the more fully devote ourselves to God. Others suppose that, if in some degree their affections be partly drawn out towards God and goodness, they have adequately discharged their duty, though in some other part of their affections they are devoted to the service of the prince of this world and of sin. These men assuredly have forgotten, that God must be adored and loved with the whole affections of the heart--that the Lord God of Heaven, and the prince of this world, are opposing masters, and, therefore, that it is impossible to render service to both of them at once, as our saviour has most expressly declared. Not very dissimilar from this is that invention by which some persons divide their time into portions, and when they have marked off one part for God and Christ, and another part for the flesh and the affections, they imagine that they have most excellently performed their duty. But these men, whosoever they be, never reflect that our whole lives, and all the time of which they are composed, must be consecrated to God, and that we must persevere in the ways of piety and obedience to the close of life; and for this brief obedience of a time which is short at the longest, God has, of grace, covenanted to bestow on the obedient, that great reward of life eternal. Undoubtedly, if at any time a man falls, he cannot return into favour with God until he has not only deplored that fall by a sincere repentance, and is again converted in his heart to God, with this determinations--that he will devote the remaining days of his life to God. Those men must not be forgotten who are in this heresy--that all those things which are not joined with blasphemy to God, and with notorious injury and violence to one's neighbour, and which, with regard to other things, bear the semblance of charity and benevolence, are not to be reckoned among the multitude of sins. According to their doctrine, they are at liberty to indulge their natural relish for earthly things, to serve their belly, to take especial care of themselves, to gratify their sensual and drunken propensities, to live the short and merry life which Epicurus recommends, and to do whatsoever a heart which is inclined to pleasure shall command; provided they abstain from anger, hatred, the desire of revenge, bitterness and malice, and the other passions which are armed for force and injury. If we follow these masters, we shall assuredly discover a far more easy and expeditious way to heaven, than that which has been taught us by the divine ambassador of the great God, whose sole business it was to point out the way to heaven. Occasion is also afforded to unjust conceptions respecting the extreme of piety, by the mode in which some theological subjects are treated, and by some ecclesiastical phrases which are either not sufficiently conformable to the Scriptures, or which are not correctly understood. We must briefly, and without much regard to order, animadvert on a few of these, for the sake of example. When our good works are invested with the relation of gratitude towards God, it is a well ascertained fact, that men collect from this that they are now the heirs and proprietors of life eternal, and are in a state of grace and everlasting salvation, before they ever begin to perform good works. This delusion makes them think it expedient also to follow the hypothesis that the performance of good works is not absolutely necessary. In this case, it must be maintained from the Scriptures, that a true conversion and the performance of good works form a prerequisite condition before justification, according to this passage from St. John, "But if we walk in the light, as he is in the light, we have fellowship one with another, and the blood of Jesus Christ, his Son cleanseth us from all sin." (1 John i. 7) This is consonant with that celebrated passage in Isaiah, in which the Lord promises to the Jews the cleansing and the destruction of all their sins, even those which were of the most aggravated kind, after they turned themselves to him, and corrected their ways. (Isa. i. 15-20.) When the sacraments are considered only in the light of sealing to us the promises and the grace of God, but not as binding us to the performance of our duty and admonishing us of it, the discussion of them is not only defective, but it may also, through such defect, be accounted injurious to the work of personal piety. "Believers and the regenerate are still prone and inclined to every evil;" and "the most holy among them have only the small beginnings of the obedience which is required." These are phrases which describe, in a manner far too low and weak, the efficacy of the new creation, and they are, therefore, kata ton rhton in reality exceedingly dangerous. For the former of these phrases seems entirely to remove all distinction between the regenerate and the, while the latter seems to place such minutiae of obedience in the regenerate, as will induce a man, who has been accustomed to bless himself if he perceives even the slightest thought or motion about the performance of obedience, immediately to conclude himself to be a partaker of true regeneration. When the continued imperfection of the regenerate, and the impossibility of keeping the law in this life, are urged unseasonably and beyond measure, without the addition of what may be done by holy men through faith and the Spirit of Christ, the thought is apt to suggest itself to the mind even of the most pious of their hearers, that they can do nothing which is at all good. Through this erroneous view, it happens that sometimes far less is attributed to the regenerate than the unregenerate are themselves able to perform. The ancient church did not reckon the question about the impossibility of performing the law among those which are capital: This is apparent from St. Augustine himself, who expresses a wish that Pelagius would acknowledge it possible to be performed by the grace of Christ, and declares that peace would then be concluded. The apostles of Christ were themselves occupied in endeavouring to convince men, when placed out of the influence of grace, of their incapability to perform obedience. But about the imperfection and impotency of the regenerate, you will scarcely find them employing a single expression. On the contrary, they attribute to believers the crucifying of the flesh and the affections, the mortification of the works of the flesh, a resurrection to a new life, and walking according to the Spirit; and they are not afraid openly to protest, that by faith they overcome the world. The acknowledgment of their imperfection was but a small matter, because that was a thing previous to Christianity. But the glory of Christians lies in this--that they know the power of the resurrection of Christ, and, being led by the Spirit of God, they live according to the purest light of the gospel. The distribution of theology into God, and the acts of God, introduces to us a speculative religion, and is not sufficiently well calculated to urge men to the performance of their duty. To this may be added that too subtle disquisition, which is an invention unsanctioned by Scripture, about the relations of those acts which are performed by us. As unsuitable for the promotion of piety, seems likewise that deduction or dispensation of our religion, by which all things are directed to the assurance of special mercy as the principal part of our duty, and to the consolation which is elicited from it against the despair that is opposed to it, but in which all things are not directed to the necessary performance of obedience in opposition to security. It derives its origin from the idea that greater fear ought to be entertained respecting despair than respecting security, when the contrary to this is the truth. For in the whole history of the Old and New Testament, which comprises a period of so many thousand years, only a single instance occurs of a person in despair, and that was Judas Iscariot, the perfidious betrayer of his saviour--the case of Cain being entirely out of the question; while, on the contrary, as the world was formerly, so is it now, very full of persons in a state of security, and negligent of the duty divinely imposed on them; yet these men, in the mean time, sweetly bless their souls, and promise themselves grace and peace from God in full measure. To proceed further: To these and all other delusions of a similar nature, we ought to oppose a soul truly pious, and most firmly rooted in the faith of God and Christ, exercising much solicitous caution about this--not to be called off from the serious and solid study of piety, and not to yield ourselves up to sins or to take delight in them, either through the deceptive force of any conceits, such as have now been enumerated or any others, or by the incautious use of any phrases and the sinister distortion of particular subjects; but, on the contrary, denying all ungodliness, let us sedulously and constantly walk in the paths of virtue; and let us always bear in mind the very serious admonition which the apostle Paul propounds to the Ephesians; having dehorted them from indulging in impurity and other crimes, he says: "Let no man deceive you with vain words" or reasons; "for, because of these things cometh the wrath of God upon the children of disobedience." (Verse 6) It is worthy of observation, how significantly the hypothesis and arguments on which men depend when they bless themselves in their vices, are designated as "vain speeches;" For "vain" they truly are; that is, false and deceitful are those reasons with which men are deceived while they are in bondage to their lusts, and persuade themselves that they are in a state of grace and salvation, when, on the contrary, they are in a state of wrath and eternal perdition; than which, no other more capital imposture or deception can be produced. But, beside those things of which we have made previous mention, and which place obstructions to the progress of piety, another also occurs, which particularly belongs to the subject on which we are now treating; that is, the depraved and perverted interpretation of certain passages of Scripture, by which, in general, either all attention to good works is superseded, or in particular some part of it is weakened. This kind of hindrance ought undoubtedly to be reckoned among those which are the greatest; for thus either evil itself seems to be established by divine authority, or a more remiss pursuit of good, which, of the two, is without exception the greater evil. Wherefore, as all those persons deserve praise who endeavour to overturn every kind of hypothesis that is injurious to piety, so those among them are worthy of the highest commendation who try to give a correct interpretation, and such as is agreeable to "the form of sound words," of those passages which are, through common abuse, generally so explained as, by such exposition, either directly or indirectly to countenance a disorderly course of life--to free them from such a depraved interpretation, and to act as torch-bearers, in a thing so useful and necessary to Christian people and chiefly to the pastors of the church. Many are those passages which are usually distorted to the injury of godliness; and from which we shall in this place select only the three following. (1.) In the Proverbs of Solomon it is said, "A just man falleth seven times." This sentence is in the mouth of every one, with this gloss superadded, "in a day," which is an interpolation to be found in the Latin Vulgate. This passage ought to be understood of falling into misfortune; yet it is most perversely interpreted to signify a fall into sin, and thus contributes to nourish vices. (2.) In the prophecy of Isaiah, when the Jewish church, after having been defiled by manifold idolatries, by her defection from God, and by other innumerable crimes, was severely punished for all these her foul transgressions; in a tone of lamentation, complaining of the heaviness of her punishment, and at the same time making humble confession of her sins, she acknowledges, amongst other things, that "her righteousnesses are as the cloth of a menstruous woman," designating by this phrase the best of those works which she had performed during her public defection. This passage, by a pernicious contortion, is commonly corrupted; for it is very constantly quoted, as if the sense to be inferred from it was, that each of the excellent works of the most eminent Christians, and therefore that the most ardent prayers poured forth in the name of Christ, deeds of charity performed from a heart truly and inwardly moved with mercy, and the flowing of the blood of martyrs even unto death for the sake of Christ--that all these are as the cloth of a menstruous woman, filthy, detestable and horrid things, and thus mere abominations in the sight of God. And as this name is, in the Scriptures, bestowed only on flagitous crimes and the greatest transgressions, it further follows [from this mode of reasoning] that the best and most excellent works differ in no respect from the most dreadful wickedness. When a man has once thoroughly imbibed this conceit, will he not east away all care and regard for piety? Will he not consider it of no great consequence whether he leads a bad or a good life? And will he not, in the mean time, indulge in the persuasion, that he can, notwithstanding all this, be a true disciple of Christ Jesus? The reason, undoubtedly, seems to be evident, since, according to this hypothesis, the best works are equally filthy with the worst crimes in the sight of God. (3.) In this number of abused passages is included the seventh chapter of the epistle of Paul to the Romans, from the fourteenth verse to the end of the chapter; that is, if the apostle be understood, in that chapter, to be speaking about a man who is regenerated. For then it will follow that a renewed man is still "carnal, and sold under sin," that is, the slave of sin; that "he wills to do good, but does it not; but the evil which he wills not, that he does;" nay, that he is conquered, and "brought into captivity to the law of sin," that is, under the power and efficacy of sin. From this view it is further deduced, that, if any one be regenerate, it is sufficient for him "to will that which is good," though with a will that is incomplete, and that is not followed by action; and "not to will that which is evil," though he actually perpetrates it. If this view of that chapter be correct, then all attention to piety, the whole of new obedience, and thus the entire new creation, will be reduced to such narrow limits as to consist not in effects, but only in affections or feelings. Every man, at first sight, perceives how languid, cold and remiss such a belief will render all of us, both in our abstaining from evil, and in the performance of that which is good. Those, indeed, who defend this opinion, have their subterfuges and palliatives; but they are of such a kind, that the comment is generally repugnant to the text on which it is founded. With respect to the exercise of piety, it is dangerous for men to have this conceit previously impressed on their minds: "This chapter must be understood about regenerate persons;" for they who hold it as a foundation, in other things wander wherever they are led by their feelings, and never recollect the glosses proposed by their teachers. This effect was observed by St. Augustine, and being afraid of giving offense, in the more early period of his Christian career, he interpreted the passage as applicable to a man under the law, but in his latter days he applied it to a man under grace; but he held this opinion in a much milder form than it is now maintained, and almost without any injury to godliness. For "the good" which the apostle says "he willed but did not," St. Augustine interprets into "a refraining from concupiscence;" and "the evil" which the apostle declares "he willed not and yet did," he interprets as "an indulgence in concupiscence;"--though this novel interpretation involves a wonderful mixture of the preceptive and prohibitive parts of the law. Modern interpreters [among the Calvinists] understand it as relating to actual good and evil--a most notable distinction! But as our venerated father laboured with all diligence in removing the other hindrances of piety, so did he principally expend much toil and unwearied study in searching out the true meaning of such passages of Scripture as were imperfectly understood, particularly if they placed a stumbling-block in the way of those who were studious of piety. If, in that species of labour, he ever had eminent success, it must undoubtedly be confessed that it was in his attempts on this seventh chapter of the epistle to the Romans; for he wrote a commentary on it of great length, which, with the greatest accuracy, he prepared and finished, and which we now publish. When he returned from Geneva to his native country, he understood this very chapter as it is now commonly explained; having been instructed in that view of it by his teachers, whose authority was so great among the students, that not one of the latter durst even inquire about any thing which they uttered. But when, in the exercise of his ministry in the church of Amsterdam, he had afterwards taken epistle to the Romans as the subject of a series of discourses from the pulpit, and when he had come to the explication of the seventh chapter, concerning the received interpretation of which he had then begun to conceive scruples in his mind, because it seemed both to undervalue the grace of regeneration and to diminish all zeal and attention to piety; he diligently considered the chapter from the beginning to the conclusion with a good conscience, as it was proper that he should do, and as the nature of his public function required; he collated it with those passages which preceded it and followed; he revolved all of them, in their several particulars, as in the presence of God; he read all the various commentators upon it which he could procure, whether among the ancients, those of the middle ages, or among the moderns; and, at length, after having frequently invoked the name and aid of Almighty God, and having derived his chief human assistance from the commentaries of Bucer and Musculus on that part of Holy Writ, he discovered that the received interpretation could not bear the scrutiny of truth, but that the passage was to be entirely understood in reference to a man living under the law, in whom the law has discharged its office, and who, therefore, feeling true contrition in his soul on account of sins, and being convinced of the incapability of the law to save him, inquires after a deliverer, and is not, in fact, a regenerated man, but stands in the nearest grade to regeneration. This explanation of the chapter he publicly delivered from the pulpit; because he thought that such a course was allowable by the liberty of prophesying, which ought always to have a place in the church of Christ. Though this diligence in elucidating the Scriptures, and the candour which he displayed, deserved singular praise and commendation, especially from all persons of the ecclesiastical order, yet, by some zealots, in whom such a conduct was the least becoming, it was received in a manner which shewed that the author ranked no higher with them than as one who, instead of receiving a reward, ought to be charged with mischief and insanity. Such is the result of employing a sedulous care in the investigation of the Scriptures, and of cultivating the liberty of prophesying; and it is esteemed a preferable service, to render the servants of Christ the slaves of certain men who lived only a short time before ourselves, and almost to canonize their interpretation of the Scriptures as the only rule and guide for us in our interpretation. When our father perceived these things, he began to write this commentary, which at length he brought to a conclusion. If God had granted him longer life, he would have corrected his production with greater accuracy, as he had already begun to do; but as he was prevented by death, and thus rendered incapable of giving it a final polish, and yet as, in the judgment of many great men, it is a work that is worthy to see the light, we have now ventured to publish it. Here then, Firstly, the author proposes his own sentiments, and proves them by deductions from the entire chapter, as well as from the connection in which it stands with the preceding and following chapters. Secondly. He shows that this interpretation has never been condemned, but has always had the greatest number of supporters. Thirdly. He defends it from the black charge of Pelagianism, and demonstrates that it is directly opposed to that error. Fourthly. He contends that the interpretation now generally received is quite new, and was never embraced by any of the ancients, but rejected by many of them. Lastly. And that it is injurious to grace and hurtful to good morals. He then enters into a comparison of the opinion of St. Augustine, and of that which is now generally received with his own interpretation; and concludes the work with a friendly address to his fellow-ministers. It was our wish, most noble Bardesius, to dedicate and address this work to your mightiness; for this desire, we had several reasons. From the first entrance on his ministry, a sacred friendship subsisted between our revered father and that nobleman of honoured memory, your excellent father--a friendship which continued till our venerable parent came down to the grave, full of years and loaded with honours. You, as the lawful inheritor of your father's possessions, have also succeeded in his place as the heir of his friendships; and this is the reason why the closest intimacy was formed between you and our good father, immediately after your return from your travels, which you had undertaken for the purpose of prosecuting your studies and visiting foreign nations. You were accustomed to place a high estimate on his endowments, and frequently consulted him on questions of theology, and very often acted upon his advice--as he did, also, upon yours. But after he had reflected in his mind, that he was not the slave of men, but the servant of Jesus Christ, and that he was under an oath [to the observance of] his words alone, when, on this account, he had begun freely to inquire into the sentiments invented by men, and into their truth and necessity, and, after comparing them with the Scriptures, had also occasionally proposed, with great modesty, his doubts concerning them, and His animadversions on them--when for this reason, many of those who were formerly his acquaintances and intimate friends, became alienated from him as from one who had removed the ancient land-marks out of their places; and when some of them, by degrees, both in public and private, began either to take an occasion or to make one, to circulate sinister reports concerning him, while others, with sufficient plainness, openly renounced all friendship with him; and when the whole chorus of ecclesiastical zealots had excited each other to rise up against him; yet, amidst all these things, you took no offense, but, having weighed the matter in the just balance of your judgment, you persisted to cherish a constant love for him. When he was debilitated by a slow and constant malady, as soon as the mildness of the weather and the intervals in his disorder would permit his removal, you invited him to your house in a manner the most friendly, and, on his arrival, you received him as the angel of the Lord; and a friendship, thus pure and refined, you cultivated with him, until he departed out of this life, and ascended to Christ, his Lord and Master. Besides, after his decease, by your conduct to our afflicted family, you shewed yourself such a one as it became that man to be who was not a pretended friend to the survivors of his departed friend--affording, by words and deeds, such substantial proofs of your kindness and beneficence towards his sorrowing widow and distressed orphans, as far exceed the feebleness of our expressions. Therefore, unless we wished not only to be the most ungrateful of mortals, but likewise to be generally depicted as such, it was exceedingly proper in us, while the posthumous writings of our revered parent are occasionally issuing from the press, to inscribe some portion of them to your very honourable and most friendly name, and by this method, as by a public document, to testify at once before the whole world our gratitude to you as well as our vast obligations. To these considerations, we may add that our father had determined within himself, if God had granted him life and leisure, to write a system of the whole Christian religion, not drawing it out of the stagnant lakes of Egypt, but out of the pure fountains of Israel, and to inscribe it to your mightiness. As he was unable to execute his purpose, partly through the multiplicity of his engagements, and partly through the lingering nature of his disorder, you have here, in the place of the other world, the present commentary; for in no other way than this, can the design of our father now be fulfilled. We hope the subject itself, which is treated in this commentary, will not be disagreeable to you; for it is one which is excellently accordant with your genius and disposition. It is a fact which is well known to all those who are acquainted with you and which you do not wish to be regarded as a secret, but which you openly profess, as often as occasion demands, that you take no delight in those thorny disputations and discussions which contribute nothing to the practice of the Christian life; but that you place the chief part of religion in the pursuit of real and solid piety. As our honoured father also shows in this work that his wishes and purposes were in this respect similar to yours, we have thought that nothing could be more appropriate than to dedicate to a man of extensive learning, who is likewise deeply attached to the interests of religion, a work which is highly conducive to the promotion of piety. Accept, therefore, with a cheerful heart and a serene countenance, this small gift, which we and our dear mother are desirous to commit to posterity, that it may perpetually remain as an endless monument of that sacred friendship which subsisted between you and James Arminius, our venerated parent, and, at the same time, of our own great obligations to you. To you, who have been under the influence of mercy towards our afflicted family, may the Lord God in return shew mercy; and may he enrich you and your very honourable family with every kind of heavenly blessings, to the glory of his name and to the salvation of all of us! Amen. So pray those who are most attached to your mightiness,

THE NINE ORPHAN CHILDREN OF JAMES ARMINIUS, OF OUDEWATER. LEYDEN, 13th August, 1612. </div2>

A DISSERTATION ON THE TRUE AND GENUINE SENSE OF THE SEVENTH CHAPTER OF THE EPISTLE TO THE ROMANS

INTRODUCTION 1. What is the subject of inquiry concerning the meaning of this chapter? 2. The manner in which this question is made a subject of dispute; formerly, a latitude of sentiment respecting it, was permitted. 3. Those who explain this passage as relating to a man under the law, are rashly charged with having some affinity With the Pelagian heresy. 4. Distribution of the subjects to be discussed in this Commentary. 1. The subject of inquiry concerning the meaning of the seventh chapter of the epistle to the Romans, and particularly of the latter part of it, which is treated upon from the beginning of the fourteenth or fifteenth verse to the end of the chapter, is this: "Does the apostle there treat of himself, such as he then was?" Or, which is almost the same question, "Under his own person, does he treat about a man living in the possession of the grace of Christ, or does he there personate a man placed under the law?" This question is also usually proposed in other words, thus: "Does the apostle there treat about a man who is still unregenerate, or about one who is already regenerated through the Spirit of Christ?" The latter question differs a little in its meaning from the former, (1.) because the word "unregenerate" has a more extensive signification, embracing even those who are under the law, and at whose state the apostle has also briefly glanced in the ninth verse of this chapter, and (2.) because the same word, with some persons, denotes not only the mere absence of regeneration, but likewise of all those things which are necessarily previous to regeneration; and these previous things are so far from being excluded by the words, "under the law," that, on the contrary, a great part of them is necessarily comprehended in the ample compass of that state which these words describe. This ought not to be passed over without some animadversion; because this notion about the word "unregenerate" which many persons have previously formed, is no small cause why they think they must reject the opinion, which declares that this passage of Scripture relates to an unregenerate man, that is, to one not only devoid of regeneration, but likewise of all those things which usually precede regeneration; and why they suppose that they ought to approve of the one contrary to this, without any further attentive consideration of the words and of the things signified. 2. But this question has now become a subject of dispute, not as one of those about which the writers who treat on Catholic doctrine may be allowed to maintain different sentiments, but as if it was one of such importance and weight to the truth of faith, that, without great detriment to truth and manifest heresy, no determination can be made concerning it except in one way, which is the affirmation that the apostle is there treating about a man who lives under grace and is regenerate. This judgment about the question seems new to me, and is one which was never heard in the church before these our times. In those better days, liberty was granted to the divines of the church to maintain an opinion on the one part of this question or on the other, provided they did not produce an explanation of their meaning that was at variance with the articles and doctrines of faith. The thing itself will shew that it is possible to do so in this matter, and such was the persuasion which was entertained on the subject by those who granted this liberty of sentiment, because no man ever supposed that any opinion was to be tolerated in the church which could not admit of an explanation that was agreeable to the doctrines and articles of belief. 3. Those who explain this passage in reference to a man living under the law, are charged with holding a doctrine which has some affinity to the two-fold heresy of Pelagius, and are said to ascribe to man, without the grace of Christ, some true and saving good, and, taking away the contest between the flesh and the spirit which is carried on in the regenerate, are said to maintain a perfection of righteousness in the present life. But I ingenuously confess that I detest, from my heart, the consequences which are here deduced; in the mean time, I do not perceive how they can flow from such an opinion. If any one will deign to prove this, I will instantly abjure an opinion thus conducting to heresy; knowing that nothing can be true, from which a falsehood may, by good consequence, be concluded. But if this cannot be demonstrated, and if I can make it evident that neither these heresies, nor any other, are derived from this opinion when it is properly explained, then, under these circumstances, it seems that I may require, in my own right, that no molestation shall be offered to me, or to any one else, on account of this opinion. If I shall confirm this opinion by arguments which are not only probable, but likewise incapable of refutation, or which at least have a greater semblance of probability than those by which the contrary opinion is supported, then let me be allowed to request that, by at least an equal right, this sentiment may obtain a place with the other in the church. If, lastly, I shall prove that the other opinion as it is in these days explained by most divines, cannot, without the greatest difficulty, be reconciled to many of the plainest passages of Scripture, that it is in no small degree injurious to the grace of the indwelling Spirit, that it has a hurtful effect on good morals, and that it was never approved by any of the ancient fathers of the church, but, on the contrary, disapproved by some of them, and even to St. Augustine himself; then may I be permitted by a most deserved right to admonish the defenders of that other sentiment, that they reflect frequently and seriously, whether they be wishful to excite the wrath of God against themselves by an unjust condemnation of this better opinion and of those who are its defenders. 4. Having premised these things, let us now enter on the matter itself, which shall be treated by us after being distributed in the following parts: I. I will show that, in this passage, the apostle does not speak about himself, nor about a man living under grace, but that he has transferred to himself the person of a man placed under the law. II. I will make it evident that this opinion has never been condemned in the church as heretical, but that it has always had some defenders among the divines of the church. III. I will show that no heresy, neither that of Pelagius, nor any other, can be derived from this opinion, but that it is most evidently opposed to Pelagianism, and that in a most distinguished manner and designedly, it refutes the grand falsehood of Pelagius. Confining myself within the bounds of necessary defense, I might, after having explained these three heads, conclude this treatise, unless it might seem to some one advisable and useful to confute by equal arguments the contrary opinion, especially as it is explained in these days. This I will attempt in other two chapters, subjoined to the preceding three, which will then be analogous and appear as parallels to the last two. IV. Therefore, I will prove that the meaning which some of our modern divines attribute to the apostle in this was not approved by any of the ancient fathers of the church, not even by St. Augustine himself, but that it was repudiated and confuted by him and some others. V. And, lastly, I will demonstrate, that this opinion, as explained in these days by many persons, is not only injurious to grace, but likewise adverse to good morals. God grant that I may meditate and write nothing but what is agreeable to his sacred truth. If, however, any thing of a contrary kind should escape from me, which is a fault of easy occurrence to one who "knows but in part, and prophesies in part;" I wish that neither to be [considered as] spoken nor written. I make this previous protestation against any such thing; and will, in reality, declare those things which possess greater truth and certainty, when any one has taught them to me.

FIRST PART

I. THE THESIS TO BE PROVED

A description of the terms contained in the Thesis. 2. The reason why the description of the apostle is here omitted. 3. What is meant by "being under the law. 4. What it is to be "under grace." 5. What is meant by "a regenerate man?" 6. Who is "an unregenerate?" THE apostle, in this passage, is treating neither about himself, such as he then was, nor about a man living under grace; but he has transferred to himself the person of a man placed under the law. Or as some other persons express it : The apostle, in this passage, is not treating about a man who is already regenerate through the Spirit of Christ, but has assumed the person of a man who is not yet regenerate. 1. To the proof of the thesis, must be premised and prefixed definitions or descriptions of the subjects which it comprises. The subjects are--the apostle himself, a man placed under grace, a man placed under the law, a man regenerate by the Spirit of Christ, and a man not yet regenerate. 2. I have set the apostle apart from those who are regenerate and placed under grace, not because I would take him away from the number of regenerate persons, among whom he holds a conspicuous station, but because some people have thought proper to deduce, from the description of the apostolical perfection, arguments by which they prove, that the apostle could not, in this passage, be speaking concerning himself, as he then was; because those things which he here ascribes to himself are at variance with some things that, in other passages, he writes about himself, and because they are a disgrace to his eminent state of grace, and to his progress in faith and newness of life. But since it is certain, that the apostle has not, in this chapter, treated of himself personally, as distinguished from all other men of whatsoever condition or order they may be, but that he, under his own person, described a certain kind and order of men, whether they be those who are under the law and not yet regenerate, or those who are regenerate and placed under grace, omitting the description of the apostle, we will first see what is meant by being under grace and under the law, and what by being regenerate, and not yet regenerate or unregenerate; yet we will do this in such a man--that, in the subsequent establishment of our own opinion, we may produce arguments drawn from the description given by the apostle. 3. The expression, therefore, to be under the law, does not signify merely that the man is liable to perform it, or that he is bound to obey the commands of the law; in which sense all men generally, both those who are said in the ninth verse of this chapter to be "without law," are reckoned to be under the law by right of creation, and those also who are under grace, are considered to be under the law by the further fight of redemption and sanctification, and yet in such a manner as not to be under its rigor, because they are under the law to Christ, who makes his people free from the rigor of the law. But because the office of the law concerning sinners is two-fold-- the one, to conclude sinners under the guilt of that punishment which is denounced by the law against transgressors, and to condemn them by its sentence--the other, first to instruct sinners and to give them assurance about its equity, justice and holiness, and afterwards to accuse them of sin, to urge them to obedience, to convince them of their own weakness, to terrify them by a dread of punishment, to compel them to seek deliverance, and, generally, to lead, govern and actuate sinners according to its efficacy. Therefore, with regard to the first office of the law, all sinners universally are said to be under it, even those who are without law and have sinned without it; "for they shall also perish without law (Rom. ii. 12) yet they are not to be condemned without a just sentence of the law. In relation to the second office of the law, they are said to be under its dominion, government, lordship and (pedagogy) tutelage, who are ruled and actuated by the efficacy and guidance of the law, in whom it exerts its power, and exercises these its operations, whether some of them or all, whether more or less, in which respect there may be, and really are, different degrees and orders of those persons who are said, in this second view, to be under the law. But in this passage, we define a man under the law to be "one who is under its entire efficacy and all its operations;" the design of the apostle requiring this, as we shall afterwards perceive. 4. This phrase "to be under grace," answers in opposition to the other of being "under the law," since the effect of this grace is two-fold. The first is, to absolve a sinful man from the guilt of sin and from condemnation; the second is, to endow man with the Spirit of adoption and of regeneration, and by that Spirit to vivify or quicken, to lead, actuate and govern him. Hence, not only are they said to be "under grace" who are free from guilt and condemnation, but likewise they who are governed and actuated by the guidance of grace and of the Holy Spirit. But since we are in this place discussing, not properly the condemnation of sin, but the tyranny and dominion which it violently exercises over those who are its subjects, by compelling them with its own force to yield it complete obedience, and to which are opposed in vain the efficacy and power of the law; and since we are now treating, not about the remission of sins, but about that grace which inhibits or restrains the force of this tyrant and lord, and which leads men to yield it due obedience; therefore we must restrict the expressions, "to be under the law," and "to be under grace," to the latter signification--that he is "under the law" who is governed and actuated by the guidance of the law, and that he is "under grace" who is governed and actuated by the guidance of grace. This will be rendered evident from the fourteenth verse of the sixth chapter, when accurately compared with the preceding and following verses of the same chapter, and from the 17th and 18th verses of the fifth chapter of the epistle to the Galatians, when they are properly applied to this matter. Yet if any one be desirous of extending these passages to the two-fold signification of each of the expressions, he has my free permission for such extension; for it cannot prove the least hindrance in the inquiry and discovery of the truth of the matter which is the subject of our present discussion. 5. LET us now see about the regenerate and the unregenerate man. That we may define him with strictness, as it is proper to do in oppositions and distinctions, we say that a regenerate man is one who is so called, not from the commenced act or operation of the Holy Spirit, though this is regeneration, but from the same act or operation when it is perfected with respect to its essential parts, though not with respect to its quantity and degree; he is not one "who was once enlightened, and has tasted of the heavenly gift, and was made partaker of the Holy Ghost, and who has tasted the good word of God, and the powers of the world to come;" (Heb. vi. 4,5) because the explanation given by most of our divines to this passage, applies only to unregenerate persons. Neither is he one who "has escaped the pollutions of the world through the knowledge of the Lord and saviour Jesus Christ, and who has known the way of righteousness;" (2 Pet. ii. 20,21) or they explain this passage also as applicable solely to the unregenerate. Nor is it a man who "heareth the law, and has the work of the law written in his heart, whose thoughts mutually accuse or else excuse themselves, who rests in the law, makes his boast of God, knows his will, and approves the things that are more excellent, being instructed out of the law." (Rom. ii. 13-18.) Neither is he one who "has prophesied in the name of the Lord, and in his name cast out devils;" (Matt. vii. 22) and who "has all faith, so that he could remove mountains." (1 Cor. xiii. 2) Nor is he one who acknowledges himself to be a sinner, mourns on account of sin, and is affected with godly sorrow, and who is fatigued and "heavy laden" under the burden of his sins; (Matt. xi. 28) for such persons as these Christ came to call, and this call precedes justification and sanctification, that is, regeneration. (Rom. viii. 30.) Neither is it he who "knows himself to be wretched, and miserable, and poor, and blind, and naked;" for this is the man whom Christ "counsels to buy" of him the things necessary for himself. (Rev. iii. 17,18.) This interpretation is not invalidated by the fact that the church of Laodicea is said not to know herself; for the "counsel" or advice bestowed will never persuade her to buy those things of Christ, unless she have previously known herself to be such a one as is there described. Nor is he one who knows that a man cannot be justified by the works of the law, and who, from this very circumstance, is compelled to flee to Christ, that in him he may obtain justification. (Gal. ii. 16) Nor is he a man, who, acknowledging himself as being unworthy even to lift up his eyes to heaven, and who, smiting on his breast, has exclaimed, God be merciful to me a sinner! This has been well observed by Beza in his Refutation of the calumnies of Tilman Heshusius, where he makes a beautiful distinction between "the things which precede regeneration" and "regeneration itself" and thus expresses himself: "It is one thing to inquire by what methods God prepares for repentance or newness of life, and it is another to treat on repentance itself. Let, therefore, the acknowledgment of sin and godly sorrow be the beginning of repentance, but so far as God begins in this way to prepare us for newness of life, in which respect it was the practice of Calvin deservedly to call this fear initial. Besides, in the description of penitence we are not so accustomed as some people are, to call these dreadful qualms of conscience the mortification of the flesh or of the old man; though we know that the word of God is compared to a sword, which, in some manner, slays us, that we may offer ourselves for a sacrifice to God; and St. Paul somewhere calls afflictions the death of Christ which we carry about with us in the body. For it is very evident that, by the mortification or death of the flesh and of the old man, or of our members, St. Paul means something far different: He means not that efficacy of the Spirit of Christ which may terrify us, but that which may sanctify us, by destroying in us that corrupt nature which brought forth fruit unto death. Besides, we also differ from some persons on this point, not with respect to the thing itself, but in the method or form of teaching it, that they wish faith to be the second part of penitence, but we say that metanoia [a change of mind for the better,] by which term we understand, according to Scripture usage, renovation of life or newness of living, is the effect of faith," &c. (Opuscula, tom. I, fol. 328.) Such are the sentiments of Beza; but how exactly they agree with those things which I have advanced, will be rendered very apparent to any man who will compare the one with the other. Consonant with these is that which John Calvin says about initial fear, in the following words: "They have probably been deceived by this--that some persons are tamed by the qualms or terrors of conscience, or are prepared by them for obedience, before they have been imbued with the knowledge of grace, nay, before they have tasted it. And this is that initial fear which some persons reckon among the virtues, because they discern that it approaches nearly to a true and just obedience. But this is not the place for discussing the various ways by which Christ draws us to himself, or prepares us for the pursuit of piety," &c. But a regenerate man is one who comprises within himself all the particulars which I shall here enumerate: "has put off the old man with his deeds, and has put on the new man, who is renewed in knowledge, which agrees with the image of him who created him." (Col. iii. 9,10.) has received from God "the Spirit of wisdom and revelation through the knowledge of Him, the eyes of his understanding being illuminated" or opened. (Ephes. i. 18.) He has put off, "concerning the former conversation, the old man, which is corrupt according to the deceitful lusts; and he is renewed in the spirit of his mind, and has put on the new man, which, after God, is created in righteousness and true holiness." (Ephes. iv. 22- 24) He, "with open face, beholding, as in a glass, the glory of the Lord, is changed into the same image from glory to glory, even us by the Spirit of the Lord." (2 Cor. iii. 18) He is "dead to sin; his old man is crucified with Christ, that the body of sin might be destroyed, that henceforth he should not serve sin; he is freed from sin, and is alive unto God through Jesus Christ our Lord?" (Rom. vi. 2,6, 7,11) "he is crucified with Christ; nevertheless he lives, yet not he; but Christ liveth in him; and the life which he now lives in the flesh, he lives by the faith of the Son of God." (Gal. ii. 20.) Being one of Christ's followers, "he has crucified the flesh with its affections and lusts, and now lives in the Spirit." (v. 24,25) "By our Lord Jesus Christ, the world is crucified unto him, and he unto the world." (vi, 14) "In Christ Jesus the Lord, he is also circumcised with the circumcision made without hands, in putting off the body of the sins of the flesh by the circumcision of Christ." (Col. ii. 11.) "In him, God worketh both to will and to do." (Phil. ii. 13.) "He is not in the flesh, but in the Spirit; the Spirit of Christ dwelleth in him; through the Spirit, he mortifies the deeds of the body; he is led by the Spirit of God, and does not walk after the flesh, but after the Spirit." (Rom. viii. 4,9,13,14) Uniting in a brief manner, all the parts and fruits of generation into one summary--A regenerate man is he who has a mind freed from the darkness and vanity of the world, and illuminated with the true and saving knowledge of Christ, and with faith, who has affections that are mortified, and delivered from the dominion and slavery of sin, that are inflamed with such new desires as agree with the divine nature, and as are prepared and fitted for newness of living, who has a will reduced to order, and conformed to the will of God, who has powers and faculties able, through the assistance of the Holy Spirit, to contend against sin, the world and Satan, and to gain the victory over them, and to bring forth fruit unto God, such as is meet for repentance--who also actually fights against sin, and, having obtained the victory over it, no longer does those things which are pleasing to the flesh and to unlawful desires, but does those which are grateful to God; that is, he actually desists from evil and does good--not indeed perfectly, but according to the measure of faith and of the gift of Christ, according to the small degree of regeneration, which, begun in the present life, must be gradually improved or increased, till at length it is perfected after this short life is ended--not with respect to essential parts, but with respect to quantity, as we have already declared--not always without interruption, (for he sometimes stumbles, falls, wanders astray, commits sin, grieves the Holy Spirit, ac.,) but generally, and for the most part, he does good. 6. But an unregenerate man is, not only he who is entirely blind, ignorant of the will of God, knowingly and willingly contaminating himself by sins without any remorse of conscience, affected with no sense of the wrath of God, terrified with no compunctions visits of conscience, not oppressed with the burden of sin, and inflamed with no desire of deliverance--but it is also he who knows the will of God but does it not, who is acquainted with the way of righteousness, but departs from it--who has the law of God written in his heart, and has thoughts mutually accusing and excusing each other--who receives the word of the gospel with gladness, and for a season rejoices in its light--who comes to baptism, but either does not receive the word itself in a good heart, or, at least, does not bring forth fruit--who is affected with a painful sense of sin, is oppressed with its burden, and who sorrows after a godly sort--who knows that righteousness cannot be acquired by the law, and who is, therefore, compelled to flee to Christ. For all these particulars, in what manner soever they be taken, do not belong to the essence and the essential parts of regeneration, penitence, or repentance, which are mortification and vivification and quickening; but they are only things preceding, and may have some place among the beginnings, and, if such be the pleasure of any one, they may be reckoned the causes of penitence and regeneration, as Calvin has learnedly and nervously explained them in his Christian Institutes. (Lib. 3, cap. 3.) Besides, even true and living faith in Christ precedes regeneration strictly taken, and consisting of the mortification or death of the old man, and the vivification of the new man, as Calvin has, in the same passage of his Institutes, openly declared, and in a manner which agrees with the Scriptures and the nature of faith. For Christ becomes ours by faith, and we are engrafted into Christ, are made members of his body, of his flesh and of his bones, and, being thus planted with him, we coalesce or are united together, that we may draw from him the vivifying power of the Holy Spirit, by which power the old man is mortified and we rise again into a new life. All these things cohere together with each other in a certain order, and must thus also be considered, if any one be desirous of knowing them not confusedly but distinctly, and of explaining them well to others. But we are not, in this place, treating about all the unregenerate in general, but only about those in whom the law has exerted all its efficacy, and who are, on this account, reciprocally said to be under the law. II.

THE CONNECTION OF THE SEVENTH CHAPTER WITH THE SIXTH

1. The design of the Apostle in the sixth chapter. 2. A short disposition of this argument. 3. Four enunciations of it. 4. This distribution is treated in order [in the seventh chapter]. 5. The two former enunciations are contained in conjunction. 6. What therefore is proved by them. 7. The third and fourth enunciations are proposed in the fifth and sixth verses. 8. In the third enunciation lies the principal part of the controversy; its deduction consists of the proposition of the enunciation and of its method of being treated. 9. The proposition of the enunciation. 10. The investigation of the proposition, consisting of a larger explanation, and the rendering of the cause. 11. A larger explanation of the seventh chapter, from the seventh verse to the fourteenth. 12. The rendering of the cause, from the fourteenth verse to the end of the seventh chapter. 13. The fourteenth verse contains the rendering of a two-fold reason. 14. The proof of this is contained in the fifteenth verse. 15. And a more ample explanation of it. 16. From which two consectaries are deduced--the first in the sixteenth verse, and the second in the seventeenth. 17. From this, the apostle returns to the rendering of the cause, in the eighteenth verse, and to the proof of it. 18. Its more ample explanation follows in the nineteenth verse, from which is deduced the second consectary in the twentieth verse. 19. The conclusion of the thing intended, in the twenty-first verse, and the proof of it is given in the twenty-second and twenty-third verses. 20. A votive exclamation for the deliverance of a man who is under the law, occurs in the twenty-fourth verse. 21. An answer or a thanksgiving reference to that exclamation, is given in the former part of the twenty-fifth verse, and the conclusion of the whole investigation, in which the state of a man who is under the law is briefly defined in the latter part of the twenty-fifth verse. 22. A brief recapitulation of the second part. 1. Having, from necessity of the thing and of order, thus premised these things, let us now proceed to treat on the question and the thesis itself. But it will be useful, briefly to place before our eyes the sum of the whole chapter, its disposition and distribution; that, after having considered the design of the apostle, and those things which conduce to that design, and which have been brought forward by the apostle as subservient to his purpose, his mind and intention, may the more plainly be made known to us. That this may the more appropriately be done, the matter must be traced a little further backward. In the 12th and 13th verses, as well as in the preceding verses of the sixth chapter of the epistle to the Romans, the apostle had exhorted all the believers at Rome to contend strenuously against sin, and not to suffer sin to domineer or rule over them, or to exercise authority in their mortal body; but to devote themselves to God, and to yield their members as the instruments of righteousness unto God; and he demonstrated and confirmed the equity of his exhortation by many arguments, especially by those which are deduced from the communion of believers with Christ. But, in order to animate them the more powerfully to this spiritual contest--the persuasion to enter on which was to be wrought not only by a demonstration of its equity, but also by a promise of its felicitous and successful issue--in the 14th verse of the same chapter, he proposed to them the certain hope of victory, declaring "sin shall not have dominion over you." For nothing can so strongly incite men to engage manfully and with spirit in this warfare, as that certain confidence of obtaining the victory which the apostle promises in these words. But he grounds his promise, in the 14th verse, on a reason drawn from it, and on the power and ability of that [grace] under the guidance and auspices of which they were about to contend against sin, or from that state in which they were then placed it, and through Christ, when he says, "For ye are not under the law but under grace," thus extolling the powers of grace at the expense of the contrary weakness of the law, as though he had said, "I employ these continual exhortations to induce you strenuously to engage in the conflict against sin; and I do this, not only because I consider it most equitable that you should enter into that warfare, while I have regard to your communion with Christ, but also because I arrive at an assured hope, while I view your present condition, that you will at length enjoy the victory over sin, through that under whose auspices you fight; and it can by no means come to pass, that sin shall have dominion over you, as it formerly had; for you are under grace, under the government and guidance of the Spirit of Christ, and no longer under the law. if you were still in that state in which you were before faith in Christ, that is, if you were yet under the law, I might indulge in despair about declaring a victory for you, as placed under the dominion of sin. Such a victory over the power of sin contending within you, you would not be able to obtain by the strength or power of the law, which knows how to command, but affords no aid for the performance of the things commanded, how great soever might be the exertions which you made to gain the battle under the auspices of the law." But this reasoning, in the first place, possessed validity to prove the necessity of the grace which was offered and to be obtained in Christ

alone, in opposition to those who were the patrons of the cause of the law against the gospel, and who urged that covenant, the law of works, against the covenant of grace and the law of faith. This reasoning also contributed greatly to the design which the apostle proposed to himself in the principal part of this epistle. His design was to teach that, not the law, but "the gospel is the power of God to salvation to every one that believeth," both because by the law, and by the works of the law, no man can be justified from the sins which he has committed, and because, by the power and aid of the same law no one can oppose himself to the power of sin to shake off its yoke, and, alter having been freed from its yoke, to serve God, since he immediately falls in the conflict. But in Christ Jesus, as he is offered to us through the gospel, and apprehended by faith we can obtain both these blessings--the forgiveness of sins through faith in his blood, and the power of the Spirit of Christ, by which, being delivered from the dominion of sin, we may, through the same Spirit, be able to resist sin, to gain the victory over it, and to serve God "in newness of life." These things in the sixth chapter may be perceived at one glance when placed before the eyes in the following order:

THE PROPOSITION OF THE APOSTLE
Dehortatory.--"

Neither yield ye your members as instruments of unrighteousness unto sin." Hortatory.--"But yield your members as instruments of righteousness unto God." THE REASON "For sin shall not have dominion over you." Hence, an enthymeme, whose Antecedent is--"Sin shall not have dominion over you." Its consequent--"Therefore, neither yield your members as instruments of unrighteousness unto sin, but yield yourselves unto God," &c.

THE PROOF OF THE ANTECEDENT OR OF THE REASON "For ye are under grace; therefore, sin shall not have dominion over you." AN ILLUSTRATION CF THE PROOF FROM ITS CONTRARY For ye are not under the law." A BRIEF EXPLICATION OF THE PROOF, AND OF ITS ILLUSTRATION "If, indeed, you were yet under the law, as you formerly were, sin would have the dominion over you as it once had; and, having followed its commands and impulses, you would not be able to do any other than yield your members as instruments of unrighteousness unto sin. "But as you are now no longer under the law, but under grace, sin shall not in any wise have the dominion over you, but by the power of grace you shall easily resist sin, and yield your members as instruments of righteousness unto God." From the 14th verse, the apostle perseveres in the same exhortation throughout the remainder of the sixth chapter, with a slight intermission of this argument, yet having previously refuted the objection which might be deduced from it; being about to resume the same argument, and to treat it more at large, in the whole of the seventh chapter, and in the former part of the eighth, since, as we have already perceived, the prosecution of this argument contributes very materially to his design. 2. But the apostle treats this subject in the order and method which was demanded by reason itself, and by the necessity of its discussion. For he had said, "Sin shall not have dominion over you, for ye are not under the law, but under grace." 3. In these words, are contained the four following enunciations: (1.) Christians are not under the law. (2.) Christians are under grace. (3.) Sin shall have dominion over those who are under the law. (4.) Sin shall not have dominion over those who are under grace. Of these four enunciations, the second and the fourth are necessary and sufficient to persuade in favour of this exhortation; but the first and the third are adduced, both for the sake of illustration, and because they were required by the principal design of the entire epistle. The former of these [pairs of conjoint enunciations] is well known to all who understand the nature of a separated axiom and the mutual relation which exists between its parts; but the latter of them will he rendered very apparent by the deduction of the epistle itself, and on a diligent inspection of its conformation. 4. The apostle, therefore, thought that these four axioms ought to be treated by him in order, and indeed always with the mention of the conclusion which he was desirous to infer from them as from premises; and in which the sum of the exhortation consisted. 5. But the apostle treats those two former enunciations conjointly, such a course being required by their nature. For he gives one thing to those from which he takes another away, and this very properly; because there exists one and the same cause why the one should be attributed and the other taken away, why they are under grace and not under the law. This cause is expressed in the fourth verse of the seventh chapter, in the following words: "Ye, also, are become dead to the law in the body of Christ, that ye should be married to another." 6. But in the first four verses, the apostle proves that Christians or believers are not under the law, but under grace; which proof may be comprised in this syllogism: They who are dead to the law, and this in the body of Christ, that they may be married to another, even to Christ, are no longer under the law, but are now under grace; But Christians are dead to the law, that they should he married to another, even to Christ; Therefore, Christians are no longer under the law, but under grace. The first part of the proposition--"They who are dead to the law, are no longer under the law," is expressed in the first verse of the seventh chapter in these words: "The law hath dominion over a man as long as he liveth." The latter part of it, "They who are made Christ's are under grace, -- is included in the fourth verse, from which it may be deduced. But a confirmation of the first part of the proposition is added, in the first verse, from the testimony of the consciences of those who are expert in the knowledge of the law; and the same part of the proposition is illustrated, in the second and third verses, by a simile, that of marriage, in which the woman is no longer liable to the law of her husband than "so long as he liveth;" but when he is dead, she is free from the law of her husband, so that she may be allowed to transfer herself to another man without committing the crime of adultery. The application of this comparison is evident, the difference only being observed, that the apostle has declared, by a change in the mode of speaking, that Christians are become dead to the law, and not that the law is become dead to them. This change of speech is attributed by some persons to the prudence of the apostle, who wished to avoid the use of a phrase which he previously knew would be offensive to the Jews. By others it is transferred to the nature of the thing, in which they say that sin, and not the law, sustained the part or person of the husband, because in the sixth verse sin is said to be dead; but this makes nothing to our present purpose. The assumption, in the fourth verse, is in these words: "we also are become dead to the law in the body of Christ, that ye should be married to another, even to Christ." This assumption is illustrated, First, by the efficient cause of that mortification or death, which is the crucifixion and the resurrection of the body of Christ, and the communion of believers with Christ in that crucifixion and in the rising again of His body. Secondly. This assumption is illustrated by the final cause of deliverance, which contains the scope or design of the apostolical exhortation, that is, "to bring forth fruit unto God." But he perseveres in the same end in the two subsequent verses, the sixth and seventh, by treating it through a comparison of things similar, as he had also done in the nineteenth verse of the sixth chapter. The parallel is, that we serve God, and since we are not now in the oldness of the letter, but in the newness of Spirit, and are delivered from the law, that thing being dead in which we were held, it is equitable that we bring forth fruit unto God; because when we were in the flesh, the motion of sins, existing through the law, did work in our members to bring forth fruit unto death. The conclusion is not openly inferred, but is understood, which is a mode of frequent occurrence, because the proposition, or question to be treated, does not differ from the conclusion in the matter, but only in the mode of position. 7. But though these two verses, the fifth and sixth, have such a relation to those things which preceded as has been already explained, yet they are likewise to be referred to those which follow. For the third and fourth enunciations are proposed in these two verses--the third in the fifth verse, and the fourth in the sixth. For, this expression, "The motions of sins, which are by the law, are vigourous, or operate in the members of men who are yet in the flesh," (verse 5) is tantamount in meaning to these words: "Sin has the dominion over those who are under the law." These words likewise, "But now we are delivered from the law, that being dead wherein we were held, wse so that we should serve in newness of spirit, and not in the oldness of the letter," (verse sixth,) agree well with the following: "Sin shall not have the dominion over those who are under grace." This will be rendered evident if any one translates the particle wse as an ancient interpreter has done, by the words "so that," and understands it not of the end or intention, but of the issue or event, as the almost perpetual use of that particle requires. For the sense is this: "When we were yet in the oldness of the letter and under the law, then we were held under sin; and when we are now delivered from the law and placed in newness of spirit, we are able to serve God in righteousness and true holiness," agreeably to this state of our newness of living. 8. But let us now more closely inspect how this third enunciation is treated, since in it is laid the principal part of the controversy. The exposition of the whole matter consists of the proposing of the enunciation, and of its investigation, the latter of which is partly an explanation, and partly an application of the cause. Both of these are briefly joined to the proposition, as it is laid down in the fifth verse of this chapter; wherefore they are more copious, and better accommodated to the more prolix investigation, than as they are proposed from the fourteenth verse of the sixth chapter. 9. For that proposition is, "sin," or, as it is more energetically expressed, "The motions of sins have the dominion over those who are under the law." This attribute is likewise more nervously expressed by this method of speech, by which the motions of sins are said to have existence by the law itself. Two effects of this dominion, therefore, are added to the proposition for the sake of explication. One is, its vigour, and its working in the members; the other is, its bringing forth fruits unto death. The cause why, in men under the law, "the motions of sins work in their members to bring forth fruit unto death," is rendered in these words, "when we were in the flesh." For the reference to the time preceding is taken from the carnal state, which state comprises the cause why, in times past, "the motions of sins did work in our members." As if the apostle had said, "It is not wonderful that the motions of sins have had the dominion over us, and have worked in our members to bring forth fruit unto death; for we are in the flesh; and the law itself is so far from being able to hinder this dominion and to restrain the vigourous growth of sin, that these motions are by the law far more fervid and vehement, not through the fault of the law, but through the wickedness and obstinacy of sin that holds the dominion and abuses its power." 10. This proposition, therefore, is more largely explained, from the seventh verse to the fourteenth; and its cause is fully treated from the fourteenth verse inclusive, to the end of the chapter. The explanation is occupied about this two- fold effect--the working of sin, and its fructification by which it brings forth fruit unto death. The rendering of the cause is continually intent upon what is said in the fifth verse, "When we were in the flesh." But on both these points, we must carefully guard against bringing the law under the suspicion of blame, as though it were of itself the cause of depraved desires in us, and of death; when it is only the occasion, upon which sin violently seizes, and uses it to produce these effects in men who live under the law. In the explanation, both these effects are removed from the law, and they are attributed to sin as to their proper cause; yet this is done in such a way, that it is at the same time added, that sin abuses the law to produce these effects. 11. (i) The former of these effects is removed from the law, in the seventh verse, by these words: "What shall we say then? Is the law sin? God forbid." That is, as if he had said, "Can it, therefore, be attributed to the law that it is itself, or the cause of depraved desires in us, because it is called in the fifth verse, the motions of sin which are by the law?" The apostle replies, that it is very wrong to entertain even the bare thought of such a thing concerning the law. He subjoins a proof of this removal of the first effect, from the contrary effect which the law has; for the law is the index of sin, or that which points it out; therefore, it is neither sin nor the cause of sin. He then illustrates this proof by a special example: "For I should not have known concupiscence, unless the law had said, Thou shaft not desire or covet." But the same effect is, in the eighth verse, attributed to sin, in these words: "But sin wrought in me all manner of concupiscence," yet so that it abuses the law as an occasion to produce this effect. This is intimated in the words which immediately follow:. "Sin, taking occasion by the commandment, wrought in me," &c. The latter effect [the fructification of sin] is proved in the next verse, in these words: "For, without the law, sin was dead; but, on the approach of the law, sin revived," which is illustrated by its opposite privatives, "For I was alive when sin was dead; but when sin revived then I died;" but, as this was done by the law, it is evident that sin abused the law to produce this effect. But the apostle here joins the second effect to the first, (because they cohere together by nature, and the former is the cause of the latter,) and thus in the tenth and eleventh verses, ascribes death to sin, which abuses the law, yet so as to excuse the law also from the effect of death, as it is expressed in the tenth verse, "the commandment which was unto life;" the cause of death being transferred to sin, in the expression, "for sin, taking occasion by the commandment," &c. But he follows up his exculpation of the law, in the twelfth verse, by a description of the nature of the law, that it "is holy, and just, and good," and, therefore, by no means the cause of death--an insinuation against the law which he indignantly repels in the former part of the thirteenth verse, by saying, "God forbid that that which is good, should be made death unto me." But in the latter part of this verse, he ascribes the same effect to sin, with the addition of a two-fold end, both of them inclining to the disparagement of sin itself, in these words: "That sin might appear sin, working death in me by that which is good; that sin, by the commandment, might become exceedingly sinful." As though he had said--"Sin, by this abuse of the law to seduce and kill us, has produced the effect, that. in return, its own depravity and perverseness be made manifest by the law. This perverse depravity consists in sin working death by the law which is good, and in being made exceedingly sinful by the commandment which is just and holy, and that it might only become as it were a sinner above measure by its own wickedness, but also might be declared to be such by the indication of the law, which it has so shamefully abused to produce these effects." But it is apparent from the whole of this explanation, that the apostle has so attempered his style as to draw a conclusion of the necessity of the grace of Christ, from the efficacy of sin, and from the weakness of the law. This will be still more perspicuous, if we briefly comprise this explanation of the apostle in the following form: "Sin has the dominion over those who are under the law, by working in them all manner of concupiscence through the law itself, and also by killing them through it, yet so that the law is free from all blame in both cases, since, it is holy and good, the index of sin, and was given for life. But sin is so powerful in men who are still under the law, that it abuses the law to produce those effects in a man who is under subjection to it; by which abuse of the law, sin, on the other hand, takes away the reward from the law, that its own perverse and noxious disposition and tendency may be manifested by the indication of the law. From these circumstances a man who is under the law is compelled to flee to grace, that he may by its beneficent aid be delivered from the tyranny of such a wicked and injurious master." 12. The rendering of the cause follows from the fourteenth verse to the end of the chapter; in which, as we have already observed, the utmost care is evinced not to impose any ignominy on the law, or to ascribe any blame to it; and the entire mischief is attributed to the power of sin, and to the weakness of that man who is under the law. But the cause is briefly given in the fourteenth verse, in these words: "For we know that the law is spiritual; but I am carnal, sold under sin." But in order that this rendering of the cause may be accurately understood, we must again consider that proposition, the cause of which the apostle determines in this place to explain, and which is this: "Sin has dominion over those who are under the law;" or, "The motions of sins, which are by the law, work in men who are under the law." 13. That the cause of this may be fully and perfectly rendered, it must be shown why the law cannot weaken the force and tyranny of sin in those who are under the law, and why sin holds those who are under the law bound and obnoxious to itself as by some right of its own. Therefore, this rendering of the cause consists of two parts: The first is contained in these words: "For truly the law is spiritual; but I am carnal." That the particle "indeed" or "truly" must be added, is proved both by its relative de, "but," as well as by the very subject. The second is contained in these words: "For I am sold under sin;" that is, I am under the dominion of sin, as one who is constituted a purchased servant by the right of sale, and like one who becomes the bond-slave of sin. As though the apostle had said, "That the law is incapable of hindering the strength and operation of sin in men who are under the law, arises from this, that men under the law are carnal; in whom therefore the law, though it is spiritual, does not possess so much power as to enable it to restrain the strong inclination of the flesh to things which are evil and contrary to the law. And since sin, by a certain right of its own, exercises dominion over those men who are under the law, therefore it comes to pass that they have been made bond-slaves to sin, and are bound and "fettered like a purchased menial." 14. The apostle immediately subjoins a proof, in the fifteenth verse, not so much of the fact that a man under the law is carnal, as that he is the slave of sin. But the proof is taken from the peculiar adjunct or effect of a purchased servant, in these words: "For that which I do I allow not." For a servant does not do that which seems good to himself, but that which his master is pleased to prescribe to him; because thus is the word "I allow" used in this passage, for "I approve." But if any one thinks that it is here used in its proper signification, the argument will be the same, and equal its validity; "for," as Christ has told us, "the servant knoweth not what his Lord doeth;" (John xv. 15;) neither is his Lord bound, nor is he accustomed, to make known to his servant all his will, except so far as it seems proper to himself to employ the services of his menial through the knowledge of that will. 15. But the first signification of the word is better accommodated to this passage, and seems to be required by those things which follow; for a more ample explanation of this argument is produced in the following words: "For what I would, that do I not; but what I hate, that do I;" which is an evident token of a will that is subjugated, and subject to the will of another; that is, to the will of sin. Therefore he is the servant and the slave of sin. 16. The apostle now deduces two consectaries from this, by the first of which he excuses the law, and by the second, he throws on sin all the blame respecting this matter, as he had also done in a previous part of the chapter. The first consectary is, "if, then, I do that which I would not, I consent unto the law that it is good." (16.) That is, "if I unwillingly do that which sin prescribes to me, now, indeed, I consent unto the law that it is good, as being that against which sin is committed. I assent to the law that commands, though, while placed under the dominion of sin, I am unable to perform what it prescribes." The second consectary is, "Now then it is no more I that do it, but sin that dwelleth in me." (17.) That is, "therefore, because I reluctantly do what I do, not at my own option but at that of another, that Is, of my master, who is sin; it follows from this, that it is not I who do it, but sin which dwells in me, has the dominion over me, and impels me to do it." 17. Having treated upon these subjects in the manner now stated, the apostle returns to the same rendering of the cause and the proof of it. The eighteenth verse contains the rendering of the cause, in these words: "For I know that in me (that is, in my flesh) dwelleth no good thing:" Wherefore it is not surprising that the law, though it be spiritual, is not able to break the power of sin in a man who is under the law; for that which is good does not dwell, that is, has not the dominion, in a carnal man who is under the law. The proof of this is subjoined in the same verse: "For to will is present with me; but how to perform that which is good I find not." Or, "I do not find how I can perform any thing good." 18. The more ample explanation of it is given in the nineteenth verse, "For the good that I would, I do not; but the evil that I would not, that I do;" which is an evident token that no good thing dwelleth in my flesh. For if any good thing dwelt in my flesh, I should then be actually capable of performing that to which my mind and will are inclined. He then deduces once more the second consectary, in the twentieth verse: "Now if I do that I would not, it is no more I that do it, but sin that dwelleth in me." 19. But from all these arguments, in the twenty-first verse he concludes the thing intended: "I find then a law, [which is imposed in this way,] that, when I would do good, evil is present with me." That is, In reality, therefore, I find from the circumstance of "to will being present with me," but of not being capable of performing what is good, that evil or sin is present with me, and not only has it a place in me but it likewise prevails. This conclusion does not differ in meaning from the rendering of the cause which is comprised in the fourteenth verse, in this expression: "But I am carnal, sold under sin." But in the two subsequent verses, the twenty-second and twenty-third, the apostle proves the conclusion which immediately preceded; and, in proving it, he more clearly explains whence and how it happens, that a man who is under the law cannot have dominion over sin, and that, whether willing or unwilling, such a person is compelled to fulfill the lusts of sin; and he says, "for I delight in the law of God after the inward man; but I see another law in my members, warring against the law of my mind, and bringing me into captivity to the law of sin which is in my members." 20. At the close, from a consideration of the miserable state of those men who are under the law, a votive exclamation is raised for their deliverance from this tyranny and servitude of sin, in the following terms: "O wretched man that I am! who shall deliver (or snatch) me from the body of this death?" That is, not from this mortal body, but from the dominion of sin, which he here calls the body of death, as he calls it also in other passages the body of sin. 21. To this exclamation he subjoins a reply--"the grace of God, through Jesus Christ our Lord, will deliver thee"--or a thanksgiving, in which the apostle intimates, in his own person, whence deliverance must be sought and expected. In the last place, a conclusion is annexed to the whole investigation, in the latter part of the twenty-fifth verse, in which is briefly defined the entire condition of a man under the law, that had been previously and at great length described; "so then, with the mind, I myself, serve the law of God, but with the flesh, the law of sin." And in this manner is concluded the seventh chapter. 22. But in order that these arguments, after having been reduced to a small compass, may be perceived at a single glance, let us briefly recapitulate this second part likewise, in the following manner: "We have already declared, that sin has dominion over those men who are under the law: But the cause of this is, that, though the law itself is spiritual, and though the men who are under it consent unto it that it is good, and though they will what is good and delight in the law of God after the inward man; yet these very men who are under the law are carnal, sold under sin, have no good thing dwelling in their flesh, but have sin dwelling in them, and evil is present with them; they have likewise a law in their members which not only wars against the law of their mind, but which also renders them captives to the law of sin which is in their members. Of this matter it is a certain and evident token, that the good which such men would, they do not; but the evil which they hate, that they do; and that when they will to do good, they do not obtain the ability. Hence it is undoubtedly evident, that they are not themselves the masters of their own acts, but sin which dwelleth in them; to which is also chiefly to be ascribed the culpability of the evil which is committed by these men who are like the reluctant perpetrators of it. But on this account, these persons, from the shewing of the law, having become acquainted with their misery, are compelled to cry out, and to implore the grace of Jesus Christ."

VERSE THE FOURTEENTH 1

A closer investigation of this question and a demonstration taken from the text itself, that the apostle is here treating about a man paced under the law, and not under grace. 2. The manner in which Carnal and spiritual are opposed to each other in the scriptures. 3. An objection taken from 1 Corinthians iii. 1,2; and a reply to it. 4. The meaning of the phrase, sold under sin. The views of Calvin and Beza on this verse. 1. Having, in the preceding manner, considered the disposition and economy of the whole chapter, let us now somewhat more strictly investigate the question proposed by us, which is this: "Are those things which are recorded, from the fourteenth verse to the end of the seventh chapter, to be understood concerning a man who is under the law, or concerning one who is under grace?" First of all, let some attention be bestowed on the connection of the fourteenth verse with those which preceded it; for the rational particle gar "for," indicates its connection with the preceding. This connection shows, that the same subject is discussed in this verse, as in those before it; and the pronoun egw I, must be understood as relating to the same man, as had been signified in the previous verses by the same pronoun. But the investigation in the former part of the chapter was respecting a man who is under the law, and the pronoun "I" had previously denoted the man who was under the law: Therefore, in this fourteenth verse also, in which a, cause is given of that which had been before explained, a man under the law is still the subject. If it be otherwise, the whole of it is nothing less than loose reasoning; nor, in this case, have we ever been able to perceive even any probable connection, according to which these consequences that follow can be in coherence with the matters preceding, and which has been adduced by those who suppose that, in the first thirteen verses of this seventh chapter, the discourse refers to a man under the law, but that in the fourteenth verse and those which follow, the subject of the discourse is a man under grace. If any one denies this, let him attempt to make out the connection [between the two portions of the chapter which have just been specified]. Some of those who have entertained that opinion, perceiving the difficulty of such an undertaking, interpret this fourteenth verse as well as those which preceded it, as relating to a man under the law, but the fifteenth and following verses as applicable to a man under grace. This, also, we shall hereafter perceive. Secondly. In the same fourteenth verse, that man about whom the apostle treats under his own person, is said to be carnal; but a man who is regenerate and placed under grace is not carnal, but spiritual. Therefore, it is a matter of the greatest certainty, that the subject of the apostle in this verse is not a man placed under grace. But a man who is under the law is carnal; therefore, it is plain that the subject of discourse in this verse is a man under the law. I prove that a regenerate man, one who is placed under grace, is neither carnal, nor so designated in the Scriptures. In Romans viii. 9, it is said "but ye are not in the flesh, but in the Spirit." And in the verse preceding, it is said, "so then they that are in the flesh cannot please God:" But a regenerate man, one who is placed under grace, pleases God. In Romans viii. 5, it is said "They that are after the flesh do mind the things of the flesh," but [as it is expressed in the same verse] a man under grace "minds the things of the Spirit." In Gal. v. 24, it is said, "They that are Christ's have crucified the flesh, with the affections and lusts;" and they that "have crucified the flesh" are not carnal. But men who are regenerate and placed under grace "are Christ's and have crucified the flesh." Therefore, such men as answer this description are not carnal. In Romans viii. 14, it is said, "As many as are led by the Spirit of God, they are the sons of God." Therefore, they are "led by the Spirit of God;" but such persons are spiritual. 2. But it is here objected, "the same man may, in a different respect, be called carnal and spiritual--spiritual,' so far as he is regenerate through the Spirit--carnal' so far as he is unregenerate; for, as long as man is in this mortal body, he is not fully regenerate. From this arises a two-fold signification of the work carnal': one denotes a man purely carnal, in whom sin has the dominion; the other denotes a man partly carnal and partly spiritual." Answer: I grant, according to the Scriptures, that man is not fully and perfectly regenerate so long as he is in the present life. But this admission must be correctly apprehended, that is, that such perfection be understood as relating not to the essence and essential parts of regeneration itself, but to the degree and measure of the quantity. For the business of regeneration is not carried on in such a manner, that a man is regenerate or renewed with regard to some of his faculties, but remains with regard to others of them altogether in the oldness of depraved nature. But this second birth is ordered in the same manner as our first nativity, by which we are born human beings-- that is, partaking entirely of human nature, but not in the perfection of adult manhood. Thus also, does the power of regeneration pervade all the faculties of man, none of them excepted; but it does not pervade them perfectly at the first moment; for it is carried on gradually, and by daily advances, until it is expanded or drawn out to a full and mature age in Christ Hence, the whole man is said to be regenerated, according to all his faculties, mind, affections and will; and he is, therefore, with regard to these, his regenerated faculties, a spiritual person. But as in the Scripture, a spiritual man and a carnal man are opposed to each other in their entire definitions, [for the former of them is one who walks according to the Spirit, and the latter is he that walks after the flesh, and as the one is mentioned for the opposite of the other,) in this respect indeed, the same man cannot be said to be at once both spiritual and carnal. And thus I reject, according to the Scriptures, this distinction of carnal persons, by which some of them are called carnal, in whom sin has dominion on the predominant part, and by which others receive the appellation of carnal men, in whom the flesh contends against the Spirit on the part which is less powerful; for the rejection of this distinction, I have the permission of Scripture, which is not accustomed to reckon the latter of these two classes in the number of carnal persons. This is expressed in a very significant manner by Leo, on the resurrection of our Lord, in the following words: "Though we are saved by hope, and still bear about with us corruption and mortal flesh, yet we are correctly said not to be in the flesh if carnal affections have not dominion over us, and we deservedly lay aside and discard the name of that thing whose will we no longer follow."' But were this, their distinction, allowed, still, that is not yet proved which they attempt, unless it be demonstrated that this man is called carnal, not in the first of these respects or senses, but in the second--not because sin has the dominion in him, but because the flesh contends against the Spirit, which is a result that can never be deduced from the text itself: For It is evident that, in the man whom the apostle here calls carnal, sin has the dominion, and the party of the flesh is more powerful in him than that of the Spirit. Because "sin dwelleth in him, he does the evil that he would not, and he does not the good which he would; to perform what is good, finds not; but sin, which dwelleth in him, perpetrates that which is evil; he is brought into captivity to the law of sin, or he is a captive under the law of sin." All these are certain and manifest tokens of sin, which has the dominion. Nor is it any valid objection, that the man is compelled, though unwilling and reluctant, to obey sin; for the dominion of sin is two fold--either with the consent of him who sins, or against his conscience, and his consent arising from his conscience. For whether a servant obeys his Lord willingly or unwillingly, he is still the servant of him to whom he yields obedience. This is such a certain truth, that no one is able to come from the servitude of sin to liberty, except through this way-- the way of this hatred of servitude, and of this desire of obtaining deliverance. 3. But some one will say, "Even those who are under grace are called carnal in" 1 Corinthians iii. 1,2. I reply, The question does not relate to the word itself; but to its true meaning and the thing signified by it. We must try, therefore, whether this word has the same signification in this passage as it has in the seventh chapter of the epistle to the Romans. But they [at Corinth] are called carnal with respect to knowledge, and in reference to feeling or inclination. In this sense, being unskillful and inexperienced in the doctrine of piety, and the knowledge of the gospel, they are called carnal in opposition to those who are spiritual, who know how to "judge all things," (1 Cor. ii. 15,) and who are also called "who are perfect," in (1 Cor. ii. 6,) and, in this sense, "babes in Christ," and those who have need to be fed with milk are called carnal. But with respect to feeling or inclination, those men are called carnal in whom human and carnal affections have the dominion and prevail, and who are said, in other passages, to be in the flesh, and to walk according to the flesh, in opposition to those who are spiritual, who, "through the Spirit, have mortified the deeds of the flesh and have crucified the flesh with its affections and lusts." But the apostle seems here to bestow this appellation on the Corinthians, or on some of them, with this two-fold reference; for he says that, with respect to knowledge, they are "babes in Christ," that is, unskillful and inexperienced in the doctrine of piety, who had to be "fed with milk, and who were not able to bear solid food." But with respect to affections, he says that they "are carnal, and walk as men," on account of the contentions and divisions which prevailed among them, from which it was evident that, in them, the flesh had the predominance over the Spirit. But in whatever sense or manner the word is used in this passage, it brings no advantage to the cause of those who declare that the apostle calls himself a carnal man in

Romans vii. 14. For if the same word is not used in 1 Corinthians iii. 1, in a sense similar to that which it bears in Romans vii. 14, then it is adduced in an unlearned and useless manner in elucidation of this question; for equivocation is the fruitful parent of error. If the word is to be received in the same sense in both passages, then I am at liberty firmly to conclude from this, in favour of my opinion, that the apostle cannot be called carnal in Romans 7, for under that appellation he severely reprehends the Corinthians because he "was not able to speak unto them as unto spiritual persons," since they were such as were still carnal; which he would have done without any just cause, if he were himself also comprehended under that title when understood in the same signification. 4. Thirdly. The same man about whom the apostle is here treating, is also said, in this, the fourteenth verse, to be sold under sin, or, (which is the same thing,) the slave of sin, and become its servant by purchase, which title can, in no sense whatsoever, be adapted to men placed under grace--a misappropriation of epithet, against which the Scriptures openly reclaim in many passages: "If the Son, therefore, shall make you free, ye shall be free indeed." (John viii. 36.) "For he that is dead" is justified, that is, he "is freed from sin" (Rom. vi. 7.) "But God be thanked that ye were the servants of sin; being then made free from sin, ye became the servants of righteousness," or those who are completely subject to it. (Rom. vi. 17,18.) But that the two things here specified [the service of sin, and that of righteousness] are so opposed to each other, as not to be able to meet together at once in the same individual, is evident from the twentieth verse of the same chapter: "For when ye were the servants of sin, ye were free from righteousness." But that the same remark applies to a man who is under the law, is apparent from a comparison of 2 Corinthians iii. 17, "Where the Spirit of the Lord is, there is liberty," with Gal. v. 18, "But if ye be led of Spirit, ye are not under the law;" therefore, they who are of the Spirit are free. But such persons are not under the law; therefore, those who are under the law are not free, but are the servants of sin. For, whether any one unwillingly, and compelled by the force of sin, obeys it, or whether it willingly--whether anyone becomes the slave of sin by the deed of his first parents, or whether, in addition to this, "he has sold himself to work evil in the sight of the Lord," as it is related concerning Ahab in 1 Kings xxi. 20. In each of these cases is the man truly and deservedly called the servant of sin. "For of whom a man is overcome, of the same is he brought into bondage." (2 Pet. ii. 19.) And "whosoever committeth sin is the servant of sin." (John viii. 34.) "Know ye not that to whom ye yield yourselves servants to obey, his servants ye are to whom ye obey, whether of sin unto death, or of obedience unto righteousness?" (Rom. vi. 16.) For the different mode of servitude does not exempt or discharge [the subject of it] from servitude, but is conclusive that he is under it. Should any one reply, concerning the man mentioned in Romans vii. 14, "that he is not simply called the servant of sin, but that he is so denominated with this restriction--that he is the servant of sin with respect to the flesh, and not with respect to the mind, as is apparent from the last verse of the same chapter, which is an explanation of this verse," I rejoin that this man is simply called the servant of sin, but of the description of those who unwillingly and with a reluctant conscience serve sin. But with respect to the manner in which the last verse of the chapter is to be understood, we shall perceive what it is when we arrive at that part. But the greater part of the divines of our profession acknowledge that this fourteenth verse must be understood as relating to an unregenerate man, to one who is not placed under grace. Thus Calvin observes on verse, "The apostle now begins to bring the law and the nature of man a little more closely into hostile contact with each other." And on the subsequent verse he says, "He now descends to the more particular example of a man already regenerate." Thus also, Beza, against Castellio, in the refutation of the first argument to the thirteenth and fourteenth calumny, (fol. 413,) says, "St. Paul exclaims that he is not sufficient even to think that which is good; and in another passage, considering himself not within the boundaries of grace, he says, But I am carnal, sold under sin."

VERSE THE FIFTEENTH

1. He does not approve of that which he does, neither does he do that which he would, but he does that which he hates. 2. The nature of the contest carried on in man. 3. The opinion of St. Augustine and Peter Martyr, respecting the conflict in men who are not born again. 1. The fifteenth verse contains a proof of the affirmation in the preceding verse, which is, that the man about whom the apostle is treating, is "sold under sin" or is the bond-slave of sin. For the argument is taken from the office and proper effect of a purchased servant, and of one who has no legal control over himself, but who is subjected to the power of another. For it is the property of a servant, not to execute his own will, but that of his lord, whether he does this willingly and with full consent, or he does it with the judgment of his own mind exclaiming against it, and with his will resisting it. This is expressed in no unskillful manner by St. Augustine, in his Retractions (lib. I, cap. i,) "he who by the flesh that lusteth against the Spirit, does those things which he would not, lusteth indeed unwillingly; and in this he does not that which he would; but if he be overcome [by the flesh lusting against the Spirit] he willingly consents to his lusts-- and in this he does nothing but what he has willed, that is, devoid of righteousness and the servant of

sin." This is confirmed by Zanchius, on the works of Redemption: (lib. I, cap. iii,) "Undoubtedly Peter, therefore, denied Christ because he would, though he did not that with a full will, but reluctantly." But the proof [which the apostle adduces in the fifteenth verse] is accommodated to the condition of the man about whom he is treating, that is, of a man who is under the law, and who is the servant of sin just so far as to serve it not with full consent, but with a conscience crying out against it. For these are the words of the apostle: "For that which I do, I allow not," that is, I do not approve of it. This sentiment, he explains and proves more at large in the words which immediately follow in the same verse: "For what I would, that do I not; but what I hate, that I do," from which we frame this syllogism. He who approves not of that which he does, nor does that which he would, is the slave of another, that is, of sin; But the man about whom the apostle is treating, approves not of that which he does, nor does what he would, but he does that which he hates: Therefore, the man who is in this place the subject of discussion, is the slave of another, that is, of sin; and therefore the same man is unregenerate, and not placed under grace. 2. But perhaps you will say, "In this passage is described a contest in the man about whom the apostle is treating, which contest cannot take place in a man who is unregenerate." Answer. In this passage, the contest between this man and sin is not described; but the dominion of sin, and the servitude of the man himself under sin, are demonstrated from the proper effect of a servant by purchase, which effect, in reality, is not produced by this man without much reluctance of conscience and great mental struggles, which precede the very production of the act; but this deed is not committed except by a mind which is conquered and overcome by the force of sin. Then I deny the preceding affirmation that, in an unregenerate man, of what description soever he may be, there is discovered no contest of the mind or conscience with the inclinations and desires of the flesh and of sin. Nay, I further assert and affirm, that, in a man who is under the law, there is necessarily a conflict between the mind and conscience on the one part, that prescribe those things which are just and honest, and the inclinations or motions of sin, on the other, which impel the man to things that are unlawful and forbidden. For the Scriptures describe to us a two-fold conflict against sin--the First, that of the flesh, and of the mind or the conscience-the Second, that of the flesh, or sin, and of the Spirit. The former of these obtains in all those who have a knowledge of what is righteous and iniquitous, of what is just and unjust, "in whose hearts is written the work of the law, and whose thoughts, in the mean while, either accuse or excuse one another," as it is recorded in Romans ii. 15, "who hold the truth in unrighteousness," (i, 18) whose consciences are not yet seared as with a hot iron, who are not yet "past all feeling," (Ephes. iv. 19,) and who know the will of their Lord, but do it not. (Luke xii. 47) 3. This view of the matter is confirmed to us by St. Augustine, in his book "The Exposition of certain propositions in the Epistle to the Romans,"(cap. 3) in which he says, "Before the law, that is, in the state or degree before the law, we do not fight; because we not only lust and sin, but sins have also our approval. Under the law we fight, but are overcome; for we confess that those things which we do, are evil; and, by making such confession, we intimate that we would not do them. But, because we have not yet any grace we are conquered. In this condition it is shown to us, in what situation we be; and while we are desirous of rising up, and still fall down, we are the more grievously afflicted," &c. This is likewise acknowledged by Peter Martyr, who observes, on Romans v. 8, "We do not deny that there is occasionally some contest of this kind in unregenerate men; not because their minds are not carnal and inclined to vicious pursuits, but because in them are still engraven the laws of nature, and because in them shines some illumination of the Spirit of God, though it be not such as can justify them, or can produce a saving change." The latter contest, that between the flesh and the Spirit, obtains in the regenerate alone. For in that heart in which the Spirit of God neither is nor dwells, there can be no contest--though some persons are said to "resist the Holy Spirit," and, to "sin against the Holy Ghost," which expressions have another meaning. The difference between these two contests is very manifest from the diversity of the issue or consequence of each: For, in the first, the flesh overcomes; but, in the latter, the Spirit usually gains the victory and becomes the conqueror. This may be seen by a comparison of this passage with Gal. v. 16,17 -- a comparison which we will afterwards undertake. But from the proper effects of the law itself, it may be most certainly demonstrated that a contest against sin is carried on within a man who is so under the law as that it has discharged all its office towards him, and has exerted all its powers in him. For it is the effect of the law to convict a man, already convicted of sin, of the righteousness of God, to incite him to obedience, to convince him of his own weakness, to inflame him with a desire to be delivered, and to compel him to seek for deliverance. It is well known, however, that these effects cannot be completed without a contest against indwelling sin. But we have already said that about such a man as this the apostle treats in this passage - - one who is in this manner under the law. If any man will yet obstinately maintain, that all unregenerate persons in general perpetrate that to the commission of which, sin and the flesh persuade, with full consent and without any reluctance, let him not view it as a grievance if I demand proof for his assertion, since it is made against express testimonies of Scripture, and since many examples may be adduced in proof of the contrary, such as that of Balsam, who, against his own conscience, obeyed the king of Moab--that of Saul, who, against his own conscience, persecuted David--that of the Pharisees, who, through obstinate malice, resisted the Holy Spirit, &c. But even that very common distinction, which sins are distinguished into those of ignorance, infirmity and malice, is likewise by this method destroyed, if all unregenerate persons commit sin with full assent and without any struggle or reluctance. I am desirous also, on this occasion, to bring to the recollection of the adverse party, the steps or degrees by which God is accustomed to convert his children to himself from wickedness of life, and which, if they will diligently and without prejudice consider, they will perceive that the contest between the mind and the flesh, which is excited by the law, must of necessity be placed among the beginnings and the precursors of regeneration.

VERSE THE SIXTEENTH.

1. He consents to the law that it is good; a consectary deduced. 2. An objection answered. 3. A second objection. 1. From what has preceded, a consectary or consequence is deduced for the excuse of the law, in the following words: "If then, I do that which I would not, I consent unto the law that it is good." In this verse nothing is said, which may not, in the best possible manner and without any controversy, agree with one who is under the law. For unless a man under the law yields his assent to it that it is good, he is not at all under the law: For this is the first effect of the law in those whom it will subject to itself--to convince them of its equity and justice; and when this is done, such consent necessarily arises. It is also apparent from the first and second chapters of the epistle to the Romans, and from the tenth chapter, in which "a zeal of God touching the law" is attributed to the Jews, that this consent is not peculiar to a regenerate man, nor is it the proper effect of the regenerating Spirit. 2. If any one say, "The subject in this passage is that assent by which a man assents to the whole law of God, and which cannot be in those who do not understand the whole law, but none among the unregenerate understands the entire law of God," I reply, FIRST, it can never be affirmed with truth, that "none among the unregenerate understands the entire law" while the following passages exclaim against such an assertion: "That servant who knew his Lord's will and did not according to it, shall be beaten with many stripes." (Luke xii. 47) "Though I have the gift of prophecy, and understand all mysteries and all knowledge, and though I have all faith, so that I could remove mountains, and have not charity, it profiteth me nothing;" (1 Cor. xiii. 2) "Knowledge puffeth up, but charity edifieth;" (1 Cor. viii. 1) "For it had been better for them not to have known the way of righteousness, than, after they have known it, to turn from the holy commandment delivered unto them." (2 Pet. ii. 21.) Secondly. Neither can this affirmation be truly made in every case: "No man assents to the entire law unless he understands the whole of it;" for he assents to the whole law who knows it to be from God and to be good, though he may not particularly understand all things which are prescribed and forbidden in the law. And where, among the regenerate, is that man to be found who dares to claim for himself such a knowledge of the whole law? Thirdly. That which is appropriately subservient to this purpose, is, a denial that this passage has any reference to that consent by which a man assents to all the precepts Of the law as being specially understood; for neither do the words themselves indicate any such thing, nor does the analogy of the connection permit it. Because it is concluded from the circumstance of his doing what he would not, that he "consents unto the law that it is good "which conclusion cannot be deduced from this deed if it be said, that this expression relates to the consent which arises from a special acquaintance with and an understanding of all the precepts of the law. For that which this man here says that he does, is a particular deed; it is, therefore, prohibited by some special precept of the law, the knowledge and approval of which is the cause why he who does that deed does it with reluctance. Hence, as from a consequent, it is concluded from this deed thus performed, (that Is committed with a mind crying out and striving against it,) that he who commits the deed in this manner, consents to the law that it is good. 3. But some one will perhaps rejoin and say, "This passage does not relate to the consent of general estimation, which may be possessed, and is so, in reality, by many of the unregenerate. But it has reference to the consent of particular approbation, which is the peculiar act of the regenerating Spirit." Such an objector ought to know that those things which are confidently uttered without any attempt at proof, may, with equal freedom, be rejected without offering the smallest reason. The thing itself, however, evinces the contrary; for, to consent to the law that it is good, is not to approve in particular a deed which has been prescribed by the law; for this consent of particular approbation cannot consist with the perpetration of a deed which is particularly disapproved. But the commission of such an act agrees well with the consent about which the apostle here treats.

VERSE THE SEVENTEENTH

1. He no longer himself perpetrates this evil, but it is done by sin that dwelleth in him, a second Consectary deduced. 2. From this verse are drawn two arguments for the contrary opinion, both of which are refuted--the first argument, and a reply to it. 3. The second argument and a reply. 4. An argument from this verse in favour of true opinion. 5. On the word dwelling, or inhabiting, according to its signification, and the usage of Scripture, with quotations from Zanchius, Bucer, Peter Martyr, and Musculus. 1. From the preceding verses is deduced another consectary, by which this man transfers to sin all the blame of this matter--not to excuse himself, that be far from him, for the law has been given and written on his heart, that "his thoughts may accuse or else excuse one another, but to point out his servile condition under the dominion of sin. In this consectary, therefore, nothing can be contained which does not agree with a man who is under the law. If it were otherwise, the consectary would contain more than was to be found in the premises, which, it has been demonstrated, agree extremely well with a man who is under the law. 2. But let us see the words of the consectary: "Now then, it is no more I that do it, but sin that dwelleth in me," that is, sin that dwelleth in me, does this." From these words, the opposite party seem capable of eliciting two arguments in support of the opinion which affirms that the apostle is here treating about a regenerate man and one who is placed under grace. The First of these arguments is of this kind: -- "It cannot be said of unregenerate men when they sin, that they do not commit it themselves, but that it is committed by sin which dwells in them. But this is most appropriately said about the regenerate: Therefore, the man about whom the apostle here treats, is "not an unregenerate man, but one who is regenerate." Answer. The antecedent must be examined; for, when it is either granted or denied, the consequence is also granted or denied. (1.) It is evident, that it cannot simply be affirmed concerning any man, whatever his condition may be, that he does of himself commit the sin which he commits; for this is a contradiction in the adjunct; and the apostle declares, that this man "does evil." Therefore, if this can be said with truth, the expression must be understood relatively and in a certain respect. But this relation or respect ought to be founded either in the man himself who perpetrates the offense, or in the perpetration itself. (i.) If this respect be founded in the man himself, it must be thus generally explained and enunciated--"The sin which this man commits, he does as he is such a one; and he does not as he is such a one." (ii.) If the respect be founded in the perpetration and the effecting of the sin, then it must be taken from the varied relation of causes of the same kind to the effect. But in this passage, the apostle is treating on the efficient cause of sin, which is here allowed to be two-fold--The man, and sin dwelling in him, but so as this may be said to be effected by indwelling sin, and not by the man. Wherefore, this effect must be taken from the distribution of the efficient cause, by which it is distributed into that which is primary and principal, and that which is secondary and less principal. (2.) It can by no means be said by him who is inspired with a sincere love of truth, that this two-fold respect is applicable only to a man who is regenerate and placed under grace, but that it does not at all appertain to a man placed under the law or does not in the least agree with him. For as this respect or relation is two-fold in the regenerate, On account of the imperfection of regeneration in this life, and the remains of "the old man," according to which respect it may be said concerning a regenerate man, that "as he is regenerate he does this, and as he is not regenerate he does it not or does not do it perfectly;" so, likewise, in a man under the law, the respect is two-fold on account of the coming in of the law; for he is "carnal" and "the servant of sin," and is under the law, that is, "he consents to the law that it is good," which consent is neither of the flesh nor according to the flesh, that is, it is not from depraved nature. Wherefore, it may be said concerning a man under the law, that he commits sin, not as he is under the law, nor as he consents to the law that it is good, but as he is carnal and the servant of sin. (3.) The second respect (according to which the effect, that has simply proceeded from two concurrent causes, is taken away from one of them and ascribed to the other) seems to hold the chief place in this passage, as it does also in this saying of the apostle, "I laboured more abundantly than they all; yet not I, but the grace of God which was with me." (1 Cor. xv. 10.) For it is well known to be a very general practice to ascribe the effect to the principal and primary of two concurrent causes, at the same time taking away the same effect from the secondary cause; especially if by some means, either beyond nature, or against the will and by the force of the superior cause, the secondary one has been drawn forth to efficiency. Thus, an ambassador who manages the cause of his prince, is not said himself to act, but his prince, who makes use of his services. Thus, much more appropriately, if a servant, who is oppressed by a tyrannical lord, does something against his own will at the command and through the compulsion of his lord, he will not himself be said to do this, but his lord who has the dominion over him. And it is most manifest, to every one who will look upon these words of the apostle with unjaundiced eyes, that they convey this meaning; as is apparent from the epithet which is attributed to sin, the perpetrator of this evil, and by which the dominion of sin is denoted, that is, "sin that dwelleth in me does it." (4.) It is no matter of wonder, that "he does it not, but sin does it;" for "when the law came, sin revived and he died." (Rom. vii. 9) Therefore, the cause of actions, is that which lives, and not

that which is dead. It is apparent, then, that the first part of the antecedent in this argument is false, and on this account the second part is not reciprocal; therefore, the conclusion cannot be deduced from it by good consequence, which consequence concludes [that the apostle is here treating] about a regenerate man, to the exclusion of the unregenerate, 3. The second argument is drawn from the adverbs of time, "now," and "no more," which are used in this verse; and from which a conclusion is thus drawn in favour of the same opinion: "These adverbs have respect to time antecedent; but the time antecedent is the time when the man was not regenerate. As though he had said, Formerly, when I was not yet regenerated, I committed sin; but now I no longer do this, because I am regenerated. Therefore, it is apparent that this present time, which is signified by the adverb "now," must be understood concerning the state of regeneration, since it cannot be said concerning an unregenerate man, that "though he formerly committed sin, he commits it no more." Answer.--I grant it to be a great truth, that these adverbs denote relation to time antecedent, and that in fact the passage is thus commodiously explained: Formerly indeed perpetrated evil, but now I no longer do this. But I deny that the time antecedent embraces the entire state before regenerations; for the state of unregeneracy, or that which is prior to regeneration, is distinguished by our author, the apostle himself, into another twofold state--before or without the law, and under the law, as it is expressed in the ninth verse of this very chapter. And the antecedent time, in reference to which it is said "now" and "no more," comprises the state without the law; but the present time [described by the two adverbs] comprises the state under the law. As if he had said, "Formerly, when I was without the law, I committed sin, but now, when I am under the law, I no longer commit it, but sin that dwelleth in me." This is in unison with what is said in the ninth verse: "For I was alive without the law once," or formerly; "but when the commandment came, sin revived, and I died." For, while "he was alive without the law," he committed evil without any reluctance of mind or of will. Therefore, at that time, he did evil; but now, being placed under the law, he undoubtedly commits sin, but he does it against his conscience and not without resistance on the part of his will. Wherefore, the cause and culpability of sin must be ascribed, not so much to the man himself, as to the violent impulse of sin. 4. Thus far we have perceived, that this verse contains nothing which can afford support to the opposite opinion. Let us further see whether an argument may not be elicited from it, for establishing the truth of the other opinion, which declares that it must be understood concerning an unregenerate man, and one who is placed under the law: The apostle says that "sin dwelleth in this man." But sin does not dwell in those who are regenerate. Therefore, the apostle is not, in this passage, treating about the regenerate or those who are placed under grace, but about the unregenerate and those who are under the law. One of the premises of this syllogism is in the text: the other must be demonstrated by us. I am aware indeed, that this seems wonderful to those who are accustomed to the distinction of sin, by which one kind is called ruling or governing, and another receives the appellation of sin existing within us, or of indwelling and inhabiting sin, and who suppose that the former of these epithets is peculiar to the unregenerate, and the latter to the regenerate. But if any one require a proof of this distinction, those who ought to give it will evince a degree of hesitation. But is not one kind of sin ruling or reigning, and another existing within and not reigning, and is not the former peculiar to the unregenerate, and the latter to the regenerate? Who can deny, when the Scriptures affirm, that there are in us the remains of sin and of the old man as long as we survive in this mortal life? But what man, conversant with the Scriptures, shall distinguish reigning from indwelling or inhabiting sin, and will account indwelling sin to be the same as the sin existing within? Indeed, indwelling sin is reigning sin, and reigning is indwelling, and therefore sin does not dwell in the regenerate, because it does not domineer or rule in them. I prove the first part of this, both from the very signification of the word to inhabit or dwell, and from the familiar usage of the Scriptures. 5. Concerning the signification of the word, Zanchius observes, in his treatise On the Attributes of God, "God is not said to dwell in the wicked, but he dwells in the pious. For what is it to dwell in any place? It is not simply to be there, as people are at inns and places of entertainment during journeys; but it is to reign and have the dominion at his pleasure as if in his own residence." (Lib. 2, cap. 6, quest. 3.) On Ephes. iii. 17, the same Zanchius says, "In this proposition, Christ dwells in your heart by faith, the word to dwell is undoubtedly put metaphorically; the metaphor being taken, not from those persons who, as tenants or lodgers, and as strangers or travelers, tarry for a season in the house or inn belonging to another; but it is taken from masters of families, who, in their own proper dwelling houses live at liberty, work, govern the family, and exercise dominion." Bucer observes, on the very passage which is the subject of our meditation, "He says that this destructive force or power dwells in him, that is, it entirely occupies him and has the dominion, as is the manner of those who are at their own house, in their proper dwelling and domicile. The apostle Paul, and all Scripture, frequently employ this metaphor of inhabitation or residing; and by it they usually signify the dominion and the certain presence, almost perpetually, of that which is said to inhabit." And this is one of his subsequent remarks: "When, in this manner, sin resides in us, it completely and more powerfully besieges us and exercises dominion." Peter Martyr says, on Romans viii. 9, "The metaphor of habitation, or indwelling, is taken from this circumstance--that they who inhabit a house, not only occupy it, but also govern in it and order [all things in it] at their own option."

The subjoined remark is from Musculus on this passage: "And that he may evidently express this tyranny and violence of sin, he does not say, Sin exists in me,' but Sin dwells in me.' For by the word to dwell or inhabit, he shows that the dominion of sin is complete in him; and that sin has, as it were, fixed his seat, or taken up his residence, in him. Evil reigns in no place with greater power than in the place where it has fixed its seat; that is what we see in the case of tyrants. Thus, in a contrary manner, God is said to have dwelt in the midst of the children of Israel; because among no other people did he declare his goodness with such strong evidence, as he did among them, according to this expression of the Psalmist--He hath not dealt so with any nation. (cxlvii, 20) In this sense, the word to inhabit or to dwell, is very often used in the Scriptures. When, therefore, the apostle wished to declare the power and tyranny of sin in him, he said that it dwelt in him, as in its proper domicile, and thus fully reigned." Calvin, in his Institutes, says (lib. iv, cap. 6, sec. 11,) that we are circumcised in Christ, with a circumcision not made by hands, having laid aside the body of sin which dwelt in our flesh; which he calls the circumcision of Christ. (2.) What I have said, in accordance with Bucer, about the usage of Scripture, is plain from the following passages: "My Father and I will come unto him, and make our abode with him." (John xiv. 23.) "But if the Spirit of him that raised up Jesus from the dead dwell in you, he that raised up Christ from the dead shall also quicken your mortal bodies by his Spirit that dwelleth in you." (Rom. viii. 11.) "For ye are the temple of the living God; as God hath said, I will dwell in them, and walk in them; and I will be their God, and they shall be my people." (2 Cor. vi. 16.) "That Christ may dwell in your hearts by faith." (Ephes. iii. 17.) "When I call to remembrance the unfeigned faith that is in thee, which dwelt first in thy grand-mother Lois, and thy mother Eunice; and, I am persuaded, in thee also." (2 Thess. i. 5.) "That good thing which was committed unto thee, keep by the Holy Ghost which dwelleth in us." (i, 14.) "Do ye think that the Scripture saith in vain, The Spirit that dwelleth in us lusteth to envy? (James iv. 5.) "Nevertheless, we, according to his promise, look for new heavens and a new earth, wherein dwelleth righteousness?' (2 Pet. iii. 13.) "Thou has not denied my faith, even in those days wherein Antipas was my faithful martyr, who was slain among you where Satan dwelleth." (Rev. ii. 13.) According to this usage, the saints are said to be "a habitation of God through the Spirit." (Ephes. ii. 22.) It is manifest, therefore, from the signification of the word and its most frequent usage in the Holy Scriptures, that indwelling sin is exactly the same as reigning sin. But it is easy now, likewise, to demonstrate the second premise in the syllogism, (p. 53,) which is, "Sin does not dwell in those who are regenerate." For [according to the passages of Scripture quoted in the preceding paragraph] the Holy Spirit dwells in them. Christ, also, dwells in their hearts by faith; and they are said to be "a habitation of God through the Spirit;" therefore, sin does not dwell in them; because no man can be inhabited by both God and sin at the same time; and when Christ has "overcome the strong man armed," he binds him hand and foot and casts him out, and thus occupies his house and dwells in it. Sin does not dwell in those who are "dead to sin," and "in whom Christ liveth." But the regenerate "do not live in sin," but are "dead to it;"(Rom. vi. 2) and in them Christ dwelleth and liveth; (Gal. ii. 20) therefore, sin does not dwell in the regenerate. Let the two subjoined passages of Scripture be compared together: "Now then it is no more I that do it, but sin that dwelleth in me:" (Rom. vii. 17) "I live; yet no more I, but Christ liveth in me." (Gal. ii. 20.) We shall be able by this comparison most fully to demonstrate, that in this verse the apostle has not been speaking about himself, but has taken upon himself to personate the character of a man who lives to sin, and in whom sin lives, dwells and operates. Yet it does not follow from this, that no sin is in the regenerate; for it has already been shown, that to be in any place, and there to dwell, to have the dominion, and to reign, are two different things.

THE EIGHTEENTH AND NINETEENTH VERSES

1. "In this man, (that is, in his flesh,) dwelleth no good thing," &c. 2. An argument for the contrary opinion is proposed from the eighteenth verse--the answer to it. 3. A reply and its rejoinder. 4. Another reply and its rejoinder. 5. An argument from the same words in favour of the true opinion. 6. The second part of the eighteenth verse, "To will is present with this man, but how to perform that which is good, he finds not." 7. An argument for the contrary opinion from the second part of this verse--the answer to it, with distinctions between each kind of willing and nilling, with extracts from St. Augustine, Zanchius and Bucer. 8. An argument for the true opinion, from the eighteenth and nineteenth verses--the proof of the major proposition, which alone can be called in question. 9. An objection and the answer to it. 10. Another reply and its rejoinder--not only some other things, but likewise those which precede things, that are saving, have a place in some of the unregenerate, with extracts in confirmation from St. Augustine, and references to Calvin, Beza and Zanchius. 11. The dissimilar appellations by which the Scriptures distinguish those who are under constraint through the law, from those who are renewed or regenerated by the grace of the gospel. 1. Let the 18th verse now be brought under consideration, in which the apostle follows up the same rendering of a cause, and the proof of it. The rendering of the cause is, "For I know that in me, (that is, in my flesh,)dwelleth no good thing;" by

which words the same thing is signified, as by the following: "I am carnal." For he is carnal, in whom no good thing dwelleth. The proof is contained in these words: "For to will is present with me; but how to perform that which is good, I find not." 2. From this rendering of the cause, some persons have instituted an argument for the support of their opinion, in the following terms: "In this man, about whom the apostle is treating, are the flesh, and some other thing either distinct or differing from flesh; otherwise, the apostle would not have corrected himself by saying, In me, that is, in my flesh. "But in unregenerate persons, there is nothing else but the flesh; Therefore, the man about whom the apostle here treats, is a regenerate person. Answer. I grant, that, "in this man is some other thing diverse or distinct from the flesh;" for this is to be seen in the apostolical correction. But I deny, that "in unregenerate persons is nothing else beside the flesh"--in those unregenerate persons, I say, who are under the law, and about whom we are engaged in this controversy. I adduce this reason for the justness of my negation; because in men who are under the law is a mind which knows some truth concerning God and "that which may be known of God," (Rom. i. 18,19) which has a knowledge of that which is just and unjust, and whose "thoughts accuse or else excuse one another," (ii, 1-15,) which knows that the indulgence of carnal desires is sinful, (vii, 7) which says that "men must neither steal nor commit adultery," (2, 21,22)&c., &c. To certain of the unregenerate, also is attributed some illumination of the Holy Ghost, (Heb. vi. 4,) a "knowledge of the Lord and saviour Jesus Christ,", a "knowledge of the way of righteousness," (2 Pet. 2, 20,21) some acquaintance with the will of the Lord, (Luke xii. 47,) the gift of prophecy, &c., &c. (1 Cor. 13.) That man who is bold enough to style such things as these "the flesh," inflicts a signal injury on God and his Spirit. And indeed how, under the appellation of "the flesh" can be comprehended that which accuses sin, convinces men of sin, and compels them to seek deliverance? There is, then, in men who are under the law, "the flesh, and something beside the flesh," that Is a mind imbued with a knowledge of the law and consenting to it that it is good; and in some unregenerate persons there Is beside the flesh, a mind enlightened by a knowledge of the gospel. But to the "other thing which is distinct from the flesh," the apostle does not, in this chapter, give the title of the Spirit, but that of the mind. The remark of Musculus on this passage is as follows: "Behold how cautiously the apostle again employs the word to dwell. He does not say, "I know that in me is no good thing;' for, whence could he otherwise approve of good things and detest those which are evil, consenting to the law of God, that is holy, and just, and good,' if he had in himself nothing of good? But he say, I know that in me dwelleth no good thing;' that Is, it does not reign in me, does not possess the dominion, since it has seized upon sin for itself, and since the will earnestly desires that which is good, though it is not free, but weak and under restraint, enduring the power of a tyrant." 3. But some one will here reply, "Not only is something different from the flesh attributed to this man, but the inhabitation or residence of good is likewise attributed to that which is different from the flesh; for, otherwise, that part of the verse in which the apostle corrects himself, would not have been necessary; but in an unregenerate man, or one who is under the law, there is nothing in which good may reside. Therefore, this is a regenerate man," &c. Rejoinder. While I concede the first of these premises, I deny the second which affirms, "In an unregenerate man, or one who is under the law, there is nothing in which good may dwell or reside." For in the mind of such a man dwells some good thing, that is, some truth and knowledge of the law. The signs of habitation or residence are the works which this knowledge and truth in the mind unfold or disclose. For instance--a conscience not only accusing a man of sin, but also convincing him of it--the delivering of a sentence of condemnation against the man himself--the enacting of good laws--careful attention to public discipline--the punishment of crimes--the defense of good people--despair of obtaining righteousness by the law and by legal works the impelling necessity to desire deliverance and to seek for it. These works, indeed, are most certain signs of the law dwelling and reigning in the mind of such a man as has been described. On this point, I intreat, that no one will condemn as heresy that which he has yet either not heard, or not sufficiently considered. For I do not assert that good dwells and reigns in a man under the law, or in any of the unregenerate. For to reign in the mind, and, simply, to reign in the man, are not the same thing. Because, if this knowledge were simply to dwell and reign in the man, this very man would then live in a manner agreeable to his knowledge, the resistance of the flesh being repelled by that which would simply obtain the first and principal place in a man. If any one closely considers this rendering of the cause, and accommodates it to the design of the apostle, he will understand that the apostolical correction was both necessary and produced for this purpose--that, notwithstanding the indwelling of something good in the mind of a man who is under the law, a proper and adequate cause might be given why, in such a man as this, "the motions of sins" flourish, and work all concupiscence; which cause is this: In the flesh of this man dwelleth no good thing. For if any good thing dwelt in his flesh, he would then not only know and will what is good, but would also complete it in actual operation, his passions or desires being tamed and subdued, and subjected to the law of God. In reference to this, it is appositely observed by Thomas Aquinas on this very passage--"And by this, it is rendered manifest that the good thing [or blessing] of grace does not dwell in the flesh; because if it dwelt in the flesh, as I have the faculty of willing that which is good through the grace that dwells in my mind, so I should then that of perfecting or fulfilling what is good through the grace that would dwell in my mind." 4. But some one will object--"In the Scriptures, the whole unregenerate man is styled flesh. Thus, For that he also is flesh. (Gen. vi. 3.) That which is born of the fish, is flesh. (John iii. 6.)" REPLY.--First. This mode of speaking is metonymical, and the word carnal "flesh," is used instead of carnal, by a usage peculiar to the Hebrews, who employ the abstract for the concrete. This is clearly pointed out by Beza, on the passage just quoted, (John iii, 6,) on which he observes--"Flesh is here put for carnal, as, among the Hebrews, appellatives are frequently employed as adjectives. This was also a practice among the Greeks and Romans, as in the words, kaqarma &c. Secondly. Though the word flesh, in the abstract, be urged, yet the whole man may be called flesh, but not the whole of man; for the mind which condemns sin and justifies the law, is not flesh. But this very same mind may in some degree be called carnal, because it is in a man who is carnal, and because the flesh, which fights against the mind, brings the whole man into captivity to the law of sin, and by this means has the predominance in that man. 5. But from these remarks may be constructed an argument in confirmation of the true sentiment, in the following manner: In the flesh of a regenerate man dwells that which is good; therefore, the man about whom the apostle discourses is unregenerate. I prove the proposition from the proper effect of the indwelling Spirit; for the Holy Spirit crucifies the flesh with its affections and lusts, mortifies the flesh and its deeds, subdues the flesh to Himself, and weakens the body of the flesh of sin: And He performs all these operations by his indwelling. Therefore, good dwelleth in the flesh of a regenerate man. The assumption is in the text itself; therefore, the conclusion follows from it. 6. Let us now examine the proof of the affirmation--that in the flesh of this man "dwelleth no good thing." This is contained in the words subjoined: "For to will is present with me; but how to perform that which is good, I find not." From a comparison of the question to be proved, and the argument produced to prove it, it is apparent that the argument is contained in these words: "For I find not to perform that which is good," that is, I attain not to the performance of that which is good. This proof is taken from the effect; for as, from the indwelling in the flesh of that which is good, would follow the performance of good; so, from "no good thing dwelling in the flesh," arises the impossibility of performing that which is good. For these words, "for to will is present with me," are employed through a comparison of things that differ; which was necessary in this place, because the proof was to be accommodated to the man about whom the apostle was treating: And this is the way in which the proof is accommodated--"To will is indeed present" with a man who is under the law; but the same man "does not find to perform that which is good," because he is carnal. From this it is apparent, that "he is carnal," and that "in his flesh dwelleth no good thing." If any good thing resided in his flesh, it would in that case restrain the strong force and desires of the flesh, and prevent their being able to hinder the performance of the good which he might will. But let the whole proof be stated in the following syllogism: In the flesh of him who has the power to will, but who "does not find to perform that which is good," dwelleth no good thing; But the man about whom the apostle is treating, has indeed the power of willing, but "does not find to perform that which is good; " Therefore, in the flesh of such a man as this, "dwelleth no good thing." It will not be denied by any one who is in the least degree acquainted with logic, and who has accurately considered the eighteenth verse, that this is the syllogism of the apostle. But from this proposition I may conclude the proposition of the syllogism which I have already adduced for confirming my opinion, and which is, "In the flesh of a regenerate man dwelleth some good thing," by this argument, "Because a regenerate man finds to perform that which is good." For the contrary would be a consequence from things contrary. That this may the more plainly appear, let us now see this proposition, with others which are deduced from it by inversion. The proposition is, "No man who is incapable of performing that which is good, has any good thing dwelling in his flesh;" therefore, by inversion, "No man who has that which is good dwelling in his flesh, is incapable of performing what is good." To this, is equivalent the following: "Every man who has any thing good dwelling in his flesh, is capable of performing what is good; in fact he is capable, because he has good dwelling within him," therefore, by simple Inversion in a necessary and reciprocal matter, "Every one who is capable of performing what is good, has good dwelling in his flesh." This is the major, from which I assume, "But a regenerate man can perform that which is good." (Phil. 2.) "Therefore, a regenerate man has good dwelling in his flesh;" which was the major of the syllogism that I had previously adduced. 7. But the defenders of the contrary opinion seem to think, that, from this proof, they are able, for the confirmation of their own opinion, to deduce an argument, which they frame thus: He is a regenerate man, with whom to will that which is good is present: But to will that which is good, is present with this man; Therefore, this man is regenerate. Answer. Before I reply to each part of this syllogism, I must remove the ambiguity which is in this phrase, "to will that which is good," or the equivocation in the word "to will." For it is certain, that there are two kinds of this volition or willing; since it is here asserted of one and the same man, that he is occupied both in willing and in not willing that which is good, concerning one and the same object; in willing it, as he [merely] wills, it but in not willing it as he does not perform it; for this is the reason why he does not perform it, because he does not will it, though [he acts thus] with a will which is, as it were, the servant of sin and compelled not to will [that which is good]. Again, he is occupied both in not willing and in willing that which is evil concerning one and the same object--in not willing it, as he does not will it and hates it--in willing it, as he performs the very same [evil] thing; for he would not do it, unless he willed it, though [he acts thus] with a will which is impelled to will by sin that dwelleth in him. St. Augustine gives his testimony to the expressions which I have here employed, in his Retractions. (Lib. I, cap. 13.) The remarks of Bucer on this passage are: "Hence it came to pass that David did, not only that which he willed, but also that which he willed not. He did that which he willed not, not indeed when he committed the offense, but when the consideration of the divine law still remained, and when it was restored. He did that which he willed, just at the time when he actually concluded and determined about the woman presented to his view. So Peter," &c. (Fol. 368.) Zanchius, also, in his book, On the Works of Redemption, observes--"This was undoubtedly the reason why Peter denied Christ, because he willed so to do, though not with a full will, neither did he willingly deny Him." (Lib. I, cap. 3, fol. 25) Wherefore, since it is impossible that there should be only a single genus of volition and nolition, or one mode of willing and not willing, by which a man wills the good and does not will the same good, and by which he does not will the evil and wills the same evil; this phrase, "to will that which is good" and "not to will that which is evil," must have a twofold meaning, which we will endeavour now to explain. (1.) Because every volition and every nolition follows the judgment of the man respecting the thing presented as an object, each of them, therefore, is also different according to the diversity of the judgment. But the judgment itself, with reference to its cause, is two-fold: For it either proceeds from the mind and reason approving the law that it is good, and highly esteeming the good which the law prescribes, and hating the evil which it forbids; or, it proceeds from the senses and affections, and (as the expression is) from sensible knowledge, or that which is derived from the senses, and which approves of that which is useful, pleasant and delightful, though it be forbidden; but which disapproves of that which is hurtful, useless, and unpleasant, though it be prescribed. The former of these is called "' the judgment of general estimation," the latter "the judgment of particular approbation or operation." Hence, one volition is from the judgment of general estimation; the other is from the judgment of particular approbation, and thus becomes a nolition. On this account, the will which follows the judgment of general estimation wills that which the law prescribes, and does not will that which the law forbids. But the same will, when it follows the judgment of particular approbation, wills the delectable or useful evil which the law forbids, and does not will the troublesome and hurtful good which the law prescribes. (2.) This distinction, when considered with respect to one and the same object contemplated in various ways, will be still further illustrated. For that object which is presented to the will, is considered either under a general form, or under one that is particular. Thus adultery is considered either in general, or in particular; considered in general, adultery is condemned by reason as an evil and as that which has been forbidden by the law; considered in particular, it is approved, by the will which is derived from the senses, as something good and delectable. Bucer, when treating on this subject, in his remarks on the same verse, says: "But there is in man a two-fold will--one, that by which he consents to the law--another, that by which he does what he detests. The one follows the knowledge of the law by which it is known to be good; The other follows the knowledge which is derived from the senses, and which is concerning things present." (3.) This volition and nolition may likewise be distinguished in another manner. There is one volition and nolition which follow the last judgment formed concerning the object; and another volition and nolition which follow not the last but the antecedent judgment. In reference to the former of these, volition will be concerning good; in reference to the latter, volition will be concerning the evil opposed to it, and contrariwise. Thus, likewise, concerning nolition. And with respect to the former, it will be volition; in respect to the latter, it will be nolition, concerning the same object, and the contrary. But the volition and nolition which follow not the last judgment, cannot so well be simply and absolutely called "volition" and "nolition," as velicity and nolicity. Those, however, which follow the last judgment, are simply and absolutely called efficacious volition and nolition, to which the effect succeeds. (4.) Thomas Aquinas, on this very passage in Romans 7, says, that the former is not a full will, the latter is a complete will. But let this same distinction be considered as it is employed concerning God. For God is said to will some things approvingly as being good in themselves, but to will other things efficaciously, as simply conducing to his glory. We must now consider the kind of willing and nilling about which the apostle is here treating. He is treating, not about the volition and nolition of particular approbation, but about those of general estimation--not about the volition and nolition which are occupied concerning an object considered in particular, but concerning one generally considered--not about the volition and nolition which follow the last judgment, but about those which follow the antecedent judgment--not about simple, absolute and complete volition, but about that which is incomplete, and which rather deserves to be called velicity. "For the good that he would, he does not; but the evil which he would not, that he does." If he willed the good prescribed by the law, with the will of particular approbation, which follows the last judgment, he would then also perform the good which he had thus willed. If, in the same manner, he did not will the evil forbidden by the law, he would then abstain from it. This is explained, in a learned and prolix manner, by Bucer on this passage. (1.) I now come specially to each part of the syllogism, in which the Major Proposition seems to me to be reprehensible on two accounts: (1.) Because "to will that which is good, "which is here the subject of the apostle's argument, is not peculiar to the regenerate; for it also appertains to the unregenerate--for instance, to those who are under the law, and who have in themselves all those things which God usually effects by the law; (2.) Because, even when used in that other sense, [as applicable to the regenerate,] it does not contain a full definition of a regenerate man; for a regenerate man not only wills that which is good, but he also performs it; because "it is God who worketh in" the regenerate "both to will and to do." (Phil. ii. 13.) And "God hath prepared good works," that the regenerate "might walk in them;" or, "he hath created them in Christ Jesus unto good works." (Ephes. ii. 10.) They are "new creatures;" (2 Cor. v. 17) are endued with that "faith which worketh by love;" (Gal. v. 6) and to them is attributed the observance, or "keeping of the commandments of God;" (1 Cor. vii. 19;) they "do the will of God from the heart;" (Ephes. vi. 6) "have obeyed from the heart that form of doctrine to which they were delivered." (Rom. vi. 17) etc, &c. From these observations, it is apparent that the particle "only" must be added to the proposition; for when this is appended, it will, at first sight, betray the falsehood and insufficiency of the proposition in this manner: "He is a regenerate man, with whom only to will that which is good is present." (2.) To the assumption, I reply that it is proposed in a mutilated form. For this, "to will is present with me," is not the entire sentence of the apostle; but it is one part separated from another. without which it is not consistent. For this is a single discrete axiom: "To will is present with me; but how to perform that which is good, I find not." But nothing can be solidly concluded from a passage of Scripture proposed in a form that is mutilated. I add that, when this latter part of the apostle's sentence is omitted, the reader is left in doubt concerning the kind of volition and nolition which is here the subject of investigation. But when the omission is supplied from the text of the apostle, it plainly signifies that the subject of discussion is inefficacious volition and that of general estimation, but, as has already been observed, this kind of volition is not peculiar to the regenerate. But the assumption may be simply denied, as not having been constructed from the context of the apostle. For St. Paul does not attribute to the man about whom he is treating, that he wills that which is good and does not will that which is evil, but that he does that which is evil, and does not perform that which is good, to which attributes, something tantamount to a description is added--"That which I would not," and "that which I would." This description is added in accommodation to the state of the man about whom the apostle is treating, and it is required by the method of demonstrative investigation. For he had determined to produce the proper and reciprocal cause, why the man about whom he is treating "does not find to perform that which is good;" and therefore all other causes were to be removed, among which were the nolition of good and the volition of evil, also ignorance of that which is good and that which is evil, &c. Thus, in that other disjunctive axiom, "to will is present with me; but how to perform that which is good I find not," the principal thing which is attributed to the man about whom the apostle is treating, or that which is predicated concerning him, is that "he does not find to perform that which is good;" for the illustration of which, is produced that differing attribute, "to will indeed is present with me." This is a remark which must be diligently observed by every one who engages in the inquiry, about the most correct manner in which this very difficult passage is to be understood. 8. But the preceding observations make it evident that a contrary conclusion may be drawn from these two verses in the following manner: He is not a regenerate man, with whom to will is indeed present, but not to perform, and who does not perform the good which he would, but who commits the evil which he would not; (this is from the description of regeneration and its parts;) But to will is present with this man, but not to perform; and the same man does not perform the good which he would, but commits the evil which he would not; Therefore, the man about whom the apostle is treating, is unregenerate. The assumption is in the text of the apostle; the proposition alone, therefore, remains to be proved. Regeneration not only illuminates the mind and conforms the will, but it likewise restrains and regulates the affections, and directs the external and the internal members to obedience to the divine law. It is not he who wills, but he who performs the will of the Father, that enters into the kingdom of heaven. (Matt. vii. 21.) And, at the close of the same chapter, he is called a wise or prudent man "who doeth the sayings of Christ," not he who only wills them. Consult what has already been remarked in the negation of the proposition in that syllogism which was produced for the establishment of the contrary opinion; And, Those persons who fulfill the will of the flesh in its desires, are unregenerate; But this man fulfills the will of the flesh; Therefore, he is unregenerate. But these [attributes] agree most appropriately with a man who is under the law--to will that which is good and not to will evil, as agreeing with one who "consents to the law that it is good," but not to do that which is good and to do evil, as agreeing with one who is "carnal and the servant of sin." 9. But perhaps some one will here reply, "From this man is not simply taken away the performing of that which is good, but the completion of it, that is, the perfect performance of it--a view of the matter which has the sanction of St. Augustine, who gives this explanation of the word." Answer. Omitting all reference to the manner in which the opinion of these persons agrees with that of St. Augustine, which we shall afterwards examine, I affirm that this is a mere evasion. For the Greek verb katergazomai does not signify to do any thing perfectly, but simply to do, to perform, to dispatch, as is very evident from the verb poiw "to do," which follows, and from this word itself as it is used in the fifteenth verse, where, according to their opinion, this verb cannot signify completion or perfect performance--for the regenerate, to whom, as they understand it, this clause in the fifteenth verse applies, do not perfectly perform that which is evil. Let those passages of the sacred writings be consulted in which this word occurs, and its true meaning will be easily understood from Scripture usage. I add that, in this sense, "the completion," that is, "the perfect performance" of that which is good, can no more be taken away from a regenerate man, than "the willing" of that which is good. For while the regenerate continue in this state of mortality, they do not "perfectly will" that which is good. 10. But some one will further insist, that "to will good" and "not to will evil," in what mode and sense soever these expressions are taken, is "some good thing;" and that, to an unregenerate man can be attributed nothing at all which can be called GOOD, without bringing contumely on grace and the Holy Spirit. To this I reply, We have already understood the quality and the quantity of this "good thing." But I am desirous to have proof given to me, that nothing at all which is good can be attributed to an unregenerate man, of what description soever he may be. According to the judgment which I have formed, the Scriptures in no passage, openly affirm this; neither do I think that, by good consequence from them, it can be asserted. But the contrary assertion may be most evidently proved: "The truth" which is mentioned in Romans i. 18, is good, as being opposed to "unrighteousness;" but this "truth" is in some unregenerate persons. "The work of the law," which is mentioned in Romans ii. 15, is a good thing; but it is: written in the hearts" of heathens, and that by God. "The taste of the heavenly gift, of the good word of God, and of the powers of the world to come," (Heb. vi. 4,5,) is good; and yet it is in the unregenerate. "To have escaped the pollutions of the world through the knowledge of the Lord and saviour Jesus Christ, and to have known the way of righteousness," (2 Pet. ii. 20,21) are good things; yet they belong to the unregenerate. "To receive the word of God with joy," (Matt. xiii. 20, is good; and it appertains to the unregenerate. And, in general, all those gifts of the Holy Spirit which are for the edification of the church, and which are attributed to several of the reprobate, are good things. (1 Cor. 12 & 13.) To acknowledge themselves to be sinners, to mourn and lament on account of personal transgressions, and to seek deliverance from sin, are good things; and they belong to some who are unregenerate. Nay, no man can be made partaker of regeneration, unless he have previously had within him such things as these. From these passages, it is evident that it cannot be said with truth, that nothing of good can be attributed to the unregenerate, what kind of men soever they may be. If any one reply, "But these good things are not saving in their nature, neither are they such as they ought to be "I acknowledge the justness of the remark. Yet some of them are necessarily previous to those which are of a saving nature; besides, they are themselves in a certain degree saving. That which has not yet come up to the point toward which it aims, does not immediately lose the name of "a good thing" The dread of punishment, and slavish fear are not that dread and fear which are required from the children of God; yet they are, in the mean time, reckoned by St. Augustine among those good things which precede conversion. In his thirteenth sermon on these words of the apostle, have not received the spirit of bondage again unto fear, (Rom. viii. 15) he says, "What is this word again? It is the manner in which this most troublesome schoolmaster terrifies. What is this word again? It is as ye received the spirit of bondage in Mount Sinai. Some man will say, The Spirit of Bondage is one, the spirit of liberty another. If they were not the same, the apostle would not use the word again. Therefore, the spirit [in both cases] is the same; but, in the one case, it is on tables of stone in fear, in the other, it is on the fleshly tables of the heart in love," &c. In a subsequent passage he says, "You are now, therefore, not in fear, but in love, that you may be sons, and not servants. For that man whose reason for still doing well is his fear of punishment, and who does not love God, is not yet among the children of God. My wish, however, is that he may continue even to fear punishment. Fear is a bond-servant, love is a free man; and, if we may thus express ourselves, fear is the servant of love. Therefore, lest the devil take possession of the heart, let this servant have the precedence in it, and preserve a place within for his Lord and Master, who will soon arrive. Do this, act thus, even from fear of punishment, if you are not yet able to do it from a love of righteousness. The master will come and the servant will depart; because, when love is perfected, it casts out fear." Calvin likewise numbers initial fear among good things; and Beza, from the meaning attached to it by Calvin and himself, makes it to be preliminary to regeneration, as we have already perceived. But these things, and others, (if any such there be,) are attributed to the unregenerate, without any injury to grace and the Holy Spirit; because they are believed to be, in those in whom they are found, through the operation of grace and of the Holy Spirit. For there are certain acts which precede conversion, and they proceed from the Holy Spirit, who prepares the will; as it is said by Zanchius, in his Judgment on the First and Second Tome of the objections and answers of Pezelius, which judgment is subjoined to the second tome. Consult likewise what we have cited in a preceding page from Beza against Tilman. Heshusius. 11. What man is there who possesses but a moderate acquaintance with theological matters, and does not know, that the Holy Spirit employs the preaching of the word in this order, that he may first convict us of sin, by the law, of whose equity and righteousness he convinces the mind--may accuse us of being obnoxious to condemnation--may place before our eyes our own impotency and weakness--may teach us that it is impossible to be justified through the law, (Rom. iii. 19-21) -- that he may compel us to flee to Christ, using "the law as a schoolmaster, to lead us by the hand to Christ," who is "the end of the law for righteousness to every one that believeth"? (Gal. ii. 16-21; iii, 1-29.) On this account, also, the unregenerate receive certain names or appellations, in the Scriptures: They are called sinners, as they are contra-distinguished from the righteous that boasted themselves of their righteousness, which sinners Christ came to call--labouring and Heavy-Laden, to whom Christ came to afford refreshment and rest-- sick and infirm, and such as stand in need of a Physician's aid, that they may be distinguished from those who supposed themselves to be "whole," and not to require the services of a Physician--poor and needy, to whom Christ came to preach the gospel--captives and prisoners in bonds, who acknowledge their sad condition, and whom Christ came to deliver--contrite in spirit and broken hearted, whom Christ came to bind up, &c. Secondly. Having completed these effects by the law, the same Spirit begins to use the preaching of the gospel, by which he manifests and reveals Christ, infuses faith, unites believers together into one body with Christ, leads them to a participation of the blessings of Christ, that, remission of sins being solicited and obtained through his name, they may begin further to live in him and from him. On this account likewise, the very same persons are distinguished by certain other appellations in the Scriptures. They are called believers, justified, redeemed, sanctified, regenerated, and liberated persons, grafted into Christ, concorporate with him, bones of his bones, flesh of his flesh, &c. From this order, it appears that some acts of the Holy Spirit are occupied concerning those who are unregenerate, but who are to be born again, and that some operations arise from them in the minds of those who are not yet regenerate, but who are to be born again. But I do not attempt to determine whether these be the operations of the Spirit as He is the regenerator. I know that, in Romans viii. 15-17, the apostle distinguishes between the Spirit of adoption and the spirit of bondage. I know that, in 2 Corinthians iii. 6-11, he distinguishes between the ministration of the law and of death, and the ministration of the gospel and of the Spirit. I know the apostle said, when he was writing to the Galatians, that the Spirit is not received by the works of the law, but by the faith of the gospel of Christ. And I think that we must make a distinction between the Spirit as he prepares a temple for himself, and the same Spirit as He inhabits that temple when it is sanctified. Yet I am unwilling to contend with any earnestness about this point--whether these acts and operations may be attributed to the Spirit, the regenerator, not as He regenerates, but as He prepares the hearts of men to admit the efficiency of regeneration and renovation. Hence, I think it is once generally clear, that this opinion is not contumelious to the Holy Spirit, nor can it take away from the Spirit any thing which is attributed to Him in the Scriptures; but that it only indicates the order according to which the Holy Spirit disposes and distributes his acts. I am not certain whether, on the contrary, it be not contumelious to the Spirit of adoption who dwells in the hearts of the regenerate, if he be said to effect in them a volition of this description from which no effect follows, but which fails or becomes defective in the very attempt, being conquered by the tyranny of sin that dwelleth within--and this in opposition to the declaration in 1 John iv. 4, "Greater is HE that is in you, than he that is in the world." Neither do I think it to flow as a consequence from this, that in Romans vii. 18,19, the subject under investigation is a man faced under grace; for it is one thing to feel or perceive some effect of preparing grace; and it is another to be under grace, or to be ruled, led and influenced by grace.

VERSE THE TWENTIETH

If he does that which he would not, then it is no more he that does it, but sin that dwelleth in him. We have already taken the twentieth verse into consideration. But I here briefly remind the reader, that in this passage, likewise, is manifestly discovered the truth of our exposition which has been adduced; because, in this verse, he says, both that he does what he would not, and yet that he does not do it himself, but sin that dwelleth in him. He does it, therefore, and he does it not; because he does it as a servant who is under compulsion by his master, and who does not execute his own will so much as that of his master, though it is also his own, otherwise he would not perform it; for he consents to the will of his master before he performs it, because he does it without co-action or force; for the will cannot be forced.

VERSE THE TWENTY-FIRST

He finds that, where he would do good, evil is present with him. The twenty-first verse contains a conclusion from the preceding, accommodated to the purpose of the apostle upon which he is here treating. For, from the circumstance of this man knowing that "to will is present with him" but not to perform it, he concludes, that "when he would do good, evil is present with him." But it must be observed, that, in the eighteenth verse, the apostle employs the same phrase about willing, as he here uses about evil; and thus he says, that both to will good, and to will evil, are present with him, or lie close to him. And as "to will that which is good is present with him" through his inclination for the law, and through his mind which approves of it as "just and good," so "to will evil is likewise present with him" through a certain law of sin, that is, by the force and tyranny of sin, assuming to itself the power, and usurping the right or jurisdiction over this man. We must now consider whether the essence and adjacency of each (if I may employ such a word) are of equal power; or whether the one prevails over the other, and which of them it is that acquires this ascendancy. It is manifest that the two are not equally potent, but that the one prevails over the other, and that, in fact, "evil is present" in a more powerful and vehement manner: For that obtains and prevails in a man, through the command, instigation and impulse of which he is found to act and to cease from acting. But I wish to see it explained from the Scriptures, how such an assertion as this can be made with truth concerning a regenerate man who is placed under grace; for, in every passage, the sacred records seem to me to affirm the contrary.

THE TWENTY-SECOND AND TWENTY-THIRD VERSES

1. HE delights in the law of God, or he finds a kind of con, delectation with it, after the inward man; but he sees another law in his members, warring against the law of his mind, &c. 2. An argument, from the twenty-second verse, for the contrary opinion. 3. An answer to the PROPOSITION in this argument. The inward man signifies the MIND, as the OUTWARD Man signifies the BODY. (1.) This is shown from the etymology of the word, and from the usage of Scriptures, especially in 2 Corinthians iv. 16, and in Ephes. iii. 16,17. (2.) Proofs of this are given at great length from the ancient Christian fathers. (3.) Similar proofs are adduced from modern divines 4. The meaning of the phrase, "to delight in the law of God after the inward man." 5. An answer to the assumption, which is shown to be proposed in a mutilated form, by the omission of those things which are mentioned in the twenty-third verse. 6. An argument, from the twenty-third verse, for the contrary opinion. (1.) An answer to the proposition in it. (2.) And to the assumption. 7. A most irrefragable argument deduced from these two verses. (1.) To the refutation of the contrary opinion. (2.) To the establishment of the true one, which at first is proposed in an ample manner, and afterwards in an abridged form. (3.) The proposition is proved by three reasons, which are confirmed against all objections. (4.) It is proved from the Scriptures, that, in the conflict against sin, the regenerate usually obtain the conquest 8. A special consideration of the text, Gal. v. 16-18, and a collation of it with this passage. 9. An objection, and a reply to it. 10. An objection to the third reason, and a reply. 11. A consideration of Isaiah lxiv. 10. 1. In the twenty-second and twenty-third verses is adduced a clearer explanation and proof of the conclusion which had been drawn in the twenty-first verse, and which agrees with the very topic that the apostle had, in this part, proposed to himself for investigation. But the proof is, properly, contained in the twenty-third verse; because that verse corresponds with these words, "When I would do good, evil is present with me," an affirmation which was to be proved. The proof is taken from the effect of the evil which is present with the man, and it is the warfare against the law of his mind, the victory obtained over him, and, after such victory, the captivity of the man to the law of sin. The twenty-second verse has reference to these words, "When I would do good;" and it contains a more ample explanation of this willing, from the proper cause, and an illustration of the following verse from things diverse and disjunctive. But in these two verses is contained one axiom, which is appropriately called a discrete or disjunctive axiom; as is apparent from the use of the particle, de "but," in the twenty-third verse, which is the relative of men though the latter is omitted in the twenty-third verse. It is likewise apparent from the very form of opposition. The antecedent and less principal part of this axiom is contained in the twenty-second verse; the consequent and principal part, in the twenty-third. For the antecedent is employed for the illustration of the consequent, as is very manifest in all axioms. Thus, as in many similar instances, "I indeed baptize you with water unto repentance; but He that cometh after me, shall baptize you with the Holy Ghost and with life." (Matt. ii. 11.) "Though our outward man perish, yet the inward man is renewed day by day." (2 Cor. iv. 16.) For the particles, indeed, though, since, when, &c., denote the antecedent

and less principal part of the axiom; while the particles, but, yet, then, &c., denote the consequent and principal part. "To delight in the law of God," or, "to find a sort of condelectation in it," "after the inward man," is the cause that to will is present with this man. "The evil which is present with him," is "the law of sin in his members." The effect, by which the presence of this evil is proved, is contained in these words, "Warring against the law of my mind, and bringing me into captivity to the law of sin which is in my members." I have considered it proper to offer these remarks to assist in forming a right judgment about a discrete or disjunctive axiom, lest any one should separate the one part from the other, and should account the less principal to be the principal one. Let us now further see what conclusion can be drawn from these two verses, in proof of the one opinion or of the other. 2. Those who hold sentiments contrary to mine, draw the following conclusion, from the twenty-second verse, for the establishment of their view of the subject: He who delights in the law of God after the inward man, is regenerate and placed under grace; But this man about whom the apostle is treating delights in the law of God after the inward man; Therefore, this man is regenerate and placed under grace. They suppose that, in the proposition, they have a two-fold foundation for their opinion: (1.) Because "the inward man" is attributed to this person. (2.) Because that same individual is said "to delight in the law of God after the inward man? For, they say, both these adjuncts can appertain to regenerate persons alone. The First agrees with them only, because, in the Scriptures, "the inward man" has the same signification as that of "the new man and the regenerate;" the Second, because it is declared concerning the pious, that "they meditate in the law of the Lord, and that their delight is in it, day and night? 3. To the proposition, I reply, first, that the inward man is not the same as the new man or the regenerate, either from the etymology of the word, or from the usage of Scripture; and the inward man is not peculiar to the regenerate, but that it also belongs to the unregenerate. Secondly, that to delight in the law of God, or, rather, to find a sort of condelectation in the law of God after the inward man, is not a property peculiar to the regenerate and to those who are placed under grace, but that it appertains to a man placed under the law. (1.) With regard to the first, I say, from the etymology of the epithet, he is called the inward man, relatively and oppositely to the outward man. For there are two men in the same individual, the one existing within the other, and the one having the other first within himself. The first of these is the hidden man of the heart, (1 Peter iii. 4,) the second is the outward man of the body; the former is he who inhabits or dwells in, the latter, he who is inhabited; the former is calculated or adapted to invisible and incorporeal blessings, the latter, to those which are earthly and visible; the former is immortal, the latter is mortal and liable to death. In these two words, not a single syllable occurs which can afford even the least indication of regeneration, and of the newness arising from regeneration. But these three epithets, the inward man, the regenerate Man, and the new man, hold the following order among each other, which the words themselves indicate at the first sight of them. The inward man denotes the subject, the regenerate man denotes the act, of the Holy Spirit who regenerates; and the new man denotes the quality which exists in the inward man through the act of regeneration. (2.) The sense and usage of Scripture are not adverse to this signification, but, on the contrary, are very consentaneous to it. This will be apparent from a diligent consideration of those passages in which mention is made of "the inward man." One of them is the text now under discussion; the second is 2 Corinthians iv. 16; and the third is Ephes. iii. 16,17. Let us at present take into consideration the last two passages. 2 CORINTHIANS iv, 16. The former of the two is thus expressed: "for which cause we faint not; but though our outward man perish, yet the inward man is renewed day by day." From this verse itself, I shew that the inward and the outward man are not in this passage taken for the new and the old man; but that the inward man is to be understood as that which is incorporeal and inhabiting, so denominated from the interior of man, that is, his mind or soul; and that the outward man is here taken for that which is corporeal and inhibited, so denominated from the body, the exterior part of man. This I shew, First. Because, if the outward and the inward man were to be taken for the old and the new man, then this disjunctive mode of speech could not attain in this verse. For these two could not then be distinguished in this following manner from each other: "Though our old man perish, yet the new man is renewed day by day;" for [as there stated] they are necessarily cohering, and mutually consequent on each other; because whatever is taken away from the old man, is so much added to the new. The absurdity of such a distinction will be still more manifest, if the same thing be thus proposed: "Though our old man be crucified, destroyed and buried, yet the new man rises again, is quickened or vivified, and is renewed still more and more." And, "Though we lay aside our former oldness, yet we make greater and still greater proficiency in newness of life." Let any one that pleases render himself ridiculous by employing the following language: "Though this youth unlearns and lays aside his ignorance, yet he daily makes a greater proficiency in the knowledge of necessary things." Secondly. The solace which the apostle produces, in opposition to those oppressions and distresses to which holy people are liable, while they remain in this world, consists in the following words: "The inward man is renewed day by day;" and not in these, "though our outward man perish." This is shown by the mode of speech adopted by the apostle, indicating that this very "perishing of the outward man," which is effected through oppressions and distresses, is that against which the consolation, comprehended in the following words, is produced by the apostle. The afflicted person says, "But our outward man is perishing." The apostle replies to him, "Do not grieve on this account; for our inward man is renewed day by day, in the renewal of which consists our salvation. For we must not have regard to external and visible blessings, which conduce to the life of the outward man; because they are liable to perish. But we must highly estimate and regard internal and invisible things, which appertain to the life of the inward man; because these are eternal, and will never perish." But if, by this word, "the outward man" were to be understood "the old man," then the apostle must have produced this in the place of consolation, in the following manner: "Do not lament that you are liable to many afflictions and oppressions, for those are the very things by which your old man perishes, and by which the inward man is the more renewed." But that the perishing of the outward man, and that of the old man, are not the same, is evident from this circumstance, that the former of these is against the very nature of man and the good of natural life, but that the latter is against depraved nature, and is contrary to the life of sin in man. Thirdly. From the word "renewed," it is apparent that "the inward man" is the subject of renovation or renewal, and of the act of the Holy Spirit. I confess indeed, that it may be correctly said, "The new man is daily renewed more and more," both because it is needful that this newness, which has been produced in a man by the act of the regenerating Spirit, should increase and be augmented day by day, and because the remains of the old man ought by degrees to be taken away and weakened yet more and more. But even in this case the subject is the inward man, that is called new from the newness which now begins to be effected in him by the regenerating Spirit; for the subject of increasing and progressive renovation, and that of commencing renovation, are the same. But the subject of incipient or commencing renovation is not the new man, (for he is not called new before the act of renovation, and prior to the quality impressed by that act,) but it is the inward man. Therefore, though the new man be said to be renewed, (a phrase which I am not aware that the Scriptures employ,) yet the subject is the inward man, which subject may receive the appellation of the new man from the quality impressed. As we say that a white man becomes whiter every day, whiteness being communicated to a white man as he is white, but as he is a man who has still some dark shades remaining, and who has not yet attained to that degree of whiteness which he desires. Consonantly with this view, the Scriptures themselves use these words: "Be renewed in the spirit of your mind, and put on the new man, which after God is created in righteousness and true holiness," (Ephes. iv. 23,24.) In this passage the subject of renovation is called "the spirit of our mind," that is, the inward man, or the mind; and "the new man," in the same passage, is not the subject itself, but it is the quality which the subject ought to induce: This quality is there called "righteousness and true holiness." I have said that I am not quite certain whether the Scriptures use this phrase in any passage: I have felt this hesitation on account of Col. iii. 10, in which it seems to be so used; the apostle saying, "and ye have put on the new man, which is renewed in knowledge after the image of Him who created him." But it will be obvious to every one who consider, the passage with diligence, that these words, "which is renewed," or ton anakainoumenon must be joined with what preceded, "and ye have put on the new man," that is, "that which is renewed," or, "the renewed," "in knowledge," &c., so as to be a description of the new man, not some new attribute of this new man. But to this criticism no great importance is attached; and I have said, I do not deny that the new man is renewed more and more. The same thing is manifest from the rest of this passage. (2 Cor. iv. 16.) For, "the outward man," (16,) "an earthen vessel," (7,) "our body," (10,) "our mortal flesh," (11,) are all synonymous terms; as are also, "troubled," "perplexed," "persecuted," "bearing about in the body the dying of the Lord Jesus," "delivered unto death," and "perishing." This may be rendered very clear to the studious inquirer after the truth, who will compare the preceding and the succeeding verses with the 16th. EPHESIANS iii, 16,17. The latter of the two passages is thus expressed: "That he would grant you, according to the riches of his glory, to be strengthened with might by his Spirit in the inner man; that Christ may dwell in your hearts by faith." From these verses, it is plain, that by the inner man is denoted the subject about which the Holy Spirit is occupied in his act and operation; and this operation is here denominated "a corroboration," or "a being strengthened." This is also plain from the synonym mentioned in the following verse, "that Christ may dwell in your hearts by faith;" for "the heart," and "the inner man," are taken from the same thing. In this view of the subject I am supported by the very learned Zanchius, who writes in the following manner upon this passage: "We have asserted, and from 2 Corinthians iv. 16, we have demonstrated, that by the term inner man is signified the principal part of man, that is, the mind, which consists of the understanding and the will, and which is usually denoted by the word heart, in which the affections or passions flourish; as, on the contrary, by the term outward man, no other thing can be understood than the corporeal part of man, which grows, possesses senses, locomotion," &c. And in a subsequent passage, he says, "Therefore, by this particle, in the inner man, the apostle teaches, that as the gift of might or strength, so likewise the other virtues of the Spirit, have not their seat in the vegetative or growing part Of man, but in his mind, heart, spirit," &c. (2.) Because it is not only held for a certainty by some persons, that "the inward man" is the same with the new and the regenerate man, from which they venture to assert, "that the regenerate alone possess the inward man;" but because this is also urged as an article of belief, let us therefore see what a great portion of the divines of the Christian church here understood by the epithet, "the inward man."

THE ANCIENT FATHERS CLEMENT OF ALEXANDRIA

The apostle gives two appellations to the man--his person and his mind. (Strom. lib. 3, fol. 194.) TERTULLIAN "BUT," says the apostle, "though our outward man be destroyed," that is, the flesh, by the force of persecutions, "yet the inward man is renewed day by day," that is, the mind, by the hope of the promises. (Against the Gnostics, cap. 15.) Having, therefore, obtained the two men mentioned by the apostle--the inward man, that is, the mind, and the outward man, that is, the flesh--the heretics have in fact adjudged salvation to the mind, that is, to the inward man, but destruction to the flesh, that is, to the outward man; because it is recorded 2 Corinthians iv. 16, "for though our outward man perish," &c. (On the resurrection of the Body, cap. 40.) From without, wars that overcome the body; inwardly, fear that afflicts the mind. So, "though our outward man perish," perishing will not be understood as losing our resurrection, but as sustaining vexation; and this, not without the inward man. Thus it will be the part of both of them to be glorified together, as well as to be fellow-sufferers. (Ibid.) For though the apostle calls the flesh "an earthen vessel," which he commands to be honourably treated; yet it is also called, by the same apostle, "the outward man," that is, the clay which was first impressed and engraved under the title of man, not of a cup, of a sword, or of any small vessel; for it was called "a vessel" on account of its capacity, which holds and contains the mind. But this flesh is called "man," from community of nature, which renders it not an instrument in operations, but a minister or assistant, (Ibid. cap. 16.) AMBROSE. "For I delight in the law of God after the inward man." he says that his mind delights in those things which are delivered by the law; and thus it is the inward man. (On Rom. vii. 22.) "Though our outward man perish, yet the inward man is renewed day by day." The flesh perishes or wastes away by afflictions, stripes, famine, thirst, cold and nakedness; but the mind is renewed by the hope of a future reward, because it is purified by incessant tribulations. For the mind is profited in afflictions, and does not perish; so that when additional temptations occur, it makes daily advances in worthiness; because this "perishing" is profitable also to the body for its immortality through the excellence of the mind. (On 2 Corinthians iv. 16.) "I delight in the law of God after the inward man." Our inward man is that which was made after the image and likeness of God; the outward man is that which was formed and shaped from clay. As therefore there are two men, there is likewise a two-fold course of conduct--one is that of the inward man, the other that of the outward man. And, indeed, most of the acts of the inward man extend to the outward man. As the chasteness of the inward man also passes to the chastity of the body. For he who is ignorant of the adultery of the heart, is likewise unacquainted with the adultery of the body, &c. It is, therefore, the circumcision of the inward man; for he who is circumcised has stripped off the enticements of his whole flesh, as his foreskin, that he may be in the Spirit, and not in the flesh; and that in the Spirit he may mortify the deeds of his body, &c., &c. When our inward man is in the flesh, he is in the foreskin. (Letter 77th, to Constantius.) BASIL THE GREAT "Let us make man according to our image." He means the inward man, when he says, "Let us make man," &c., &c. Listen to the apostle, who says, "Though our outward man perish, yet the inward man is renewed day by day." How do I know the two men? One of them is apparent; the other is hidden in him who appears, it is the invisible, the inward man. We have then a man within us; and we are twofold; and what is said is very true, that we are inward. (Homily 10th, on the six days of Creation.) "Thy hands have made me, and fashioned me." God made the inward man, and fashioned the outward man. For "the fashioning" belongs to clay; but "the making" appertains to that which is after his own image. Wherefore the thing which was fashioned is the flesh, but that which was made is the mind. (Ibid. Homily 11.) Since there are, indeed, two men, as the apostle declares, the one outward and the other inward, we must also, in like manner, receive the age in both, according to him whom we behold, and according to him whom we understand in secret. (Discourse on the beginning of the Proverbs of Solomon.) CYRIL OF ALEXANDRIA "But though our outward man perish, yet the inward man is renewed day by day." If any one, therefore, says that our inward man dwells in the outward man, he repeats an important truth; yet he will not on this account seem to divide the unity of man. (On the incarnation, of the only begotten Son, cap. 12.) MACARIUS The true death consists in the heart, and is hidden, when our inward man is dead. If therefore any one has passed over from death to the hidden life, he in reality lives forever, and dies no more, &c., &c. Sin acts secretly upon the inward man and the mind, and commences a conflict with the thoughts. (Homily 15.) The members of the soul are many: such as the mind, the conscience, the will, the thoughts which accuse or else defend. But all these have been collected together into one reason; yet they are the members of the soul. But the soul is single, that is, the inward man. (Homily 7.) "The inward man" and "the soul" are taken for the same thing, in his 27th Homily. CHRYSOSTOM "But though our outward man perish," &c. How does it perish? While it is beaten with stripes, is driven away, and endures innumerable evils. "Yet the inward man is renewed day by day." How is it renewed? By faith, hope and alacrity, that it may have the courage to oppose itself to evils. For, the more the evils which the body endures, the greater is the hope which the inward man entertains, and the more bright and resplendent does it become, as gold which is examined or tested by much fire. (On 2 Corinthians iv. 16.) Let us now see what is said by one who stands higher than many: AUGUSTINE But who, except the greatest mad man, will say that in the body we are, or shall afterwards be, like God, That likeness, therefore, exists in the inward man, "which is renewed in the knowledge of God, after the image of him that created him." (Tom. 2, Epist. 6.) By this grace, righteousness is written in the inward man, when renewed, which transgression had destroyed. (On the Spirit and the Letter, cap. 27.) As he called him the inward man when coming into this world, because the outward man is corporeal as this world is. (On the Demerits and Remission of Sin, lib.1, cap. 25; Tom. 7.) As the eyes of the body derive no aid from the light, that they may depart from it with eyelids closed and turned in another direction, but in order to see, they are assisted by the light, (nor can this be done at all, unless the light lends its aid,) so God, who is the light of the inward man, assists the drowsiness of our mind, that we may perform something that is good, not according to our righteousness, but according to his own. (Ibid. lib. 2, cap. 5.) If, in the mind itself, which is "the inward man," perfect newness were formed in baptism, the apostle would not declare, "Though our outward man perish, yet the inward man is renewed day by day." (Ibid. cap. 7.) As that tree of life was placed in the corporeal Paradise, so this wisdom is in the spiritual Paradise, the former of them affording vital vigour to the senses of the outward man, the latter to those of the inward man, without any change of time for the worse. (Ibid. cap. 21.) Behold, then, of how many things are we ignorant--not only such as are past, but also of those which are present, concerning our nature, and not only in reference to the body, but likewise I, reference to the inward man; yet we are not compared to the beasts. (Tom. 7. 0n the Soul and its Origin, lib. 4, cap. 8.) Because the thing is either the foot itself, the body, or the man, who hobbles along with a lame foot; yet the man cannot avoid a lame foot, unless he have it healed. This can also be done in the inward man, but it must be by the grace of God through Jesus Christ. (On Perfection against Caelestius, fol. I, letter f.) Thus also the mind is the thing of the inward man, robbery is an act, avarice is a vice, that is, a quality, according to which the mind is evil, even when it does nothing by which it can render any service to avarice or robbery. (Ibid.) Beside the inward and the outward man, I do not indeed perceive that the apostle makes another inward of the inward man, that is, the innermost of the whole man. (On the Mind and its Origins, lib. 4, cap. 4.) He confesses in the same passage, that the mind is the inward man to the body, but he denies that the spirit is the inward man to the mind. Some persons have also made this supposition, that now the inward man was made, but the body of the man afterwards, when the Scripture says, "And God formed man of the dust of the ground." (Tom. 3. On Genesis according to the letter, l. 3, c. 22.) The apostle Paul wishes "the inward man" to be understood by the spirit of the mind, "the outward man" in the body and this mortal life. Yet it is sometimes read in his epistles, that he has not called both of these together "two men," but one entire man whom God made, that is, both that which is the inward man, and that which is the outward. But he does not make him after his own image, except with regard to that which is inward, not only what is incorporeal, but also what is rational, and which is not within beasts. (Tom. 6. Against Faustus the Manichee, lib. 24, cap. 1.) Behold God is likewise proclaimed, by the same apostle, as former of the outward man. "But now hath God set the members every one in the body as it hath pleased him."(Ibid.) The apostle says that "the old man" is nothing more than the old [course of] life, which is in sin, and in which men live according to the first Adam, concerning whom he declares, "By one man sin entered into the world, and death by sin, and so death passed upon all men, for that all have sinned." Therefore, the whole of that man, both in his outward and inward part; has become old on account of sin, and is sentenced to the punishment of mortality, &c. (Ibid.) And therefore, by such a cross, the body of sin is emptied, that we may "not now yield our members as instruments of unrighteousness unto sin;" because this inward man also, if he be really renewed day by day, is certainly old before he is renewed. For that is an inward act of which the apostle speaks thus: "Put off the old man, and put on the new man." (Tom. 3. On the Trinity, lib. 4, cap. 3.) But now the death of the flesh of our Lord belongs to the example of the death of our outward man, &c. And the resurrection of the body of the Lord is found to appertain to the example of the resurrection of our outward man." (Ibid.) Come now, let us see where is that which bears some resemblance to the confines of the man, both the outward and the inward; for, whatever we have in the mind in common with the beasts, is correctly said still to belong to the outward man; For not only will the body be accounted as "the outward man," but likewise certain things united to its life, by which the joints of the body and all the senses flourish and grow, and with which it is furnished for entering upon outward things. When the images of these perceptions, infixed in the memory, are revisited by recollection, the matter is still a transaction which belongs to the outward man. And in all these things we are at no great distance from the cattle, except that in the shape of our bodies we are not bending downwards, but erect. (On the Trinity, lib. 12, cap. 1.) While ascending, therefore, inwardly by certain degrees of consideration through the parts of the mind, another thing begins from this to occur to us, which is not common to us with the beasts; thence reason has its commencement, that the inward man may not be known. (Ibid. cap. 8.) Both believers and unbelievers are well acquainted with the nature of man, whose outward part, that is, the body, they have learned the lights of the body; but they have learned the inward part, that is, the mind, within themselves. (Ibid. lib. 13, cap. 1.) Besides, the Scriptures thus attest it to us in this that, when these two things also are joined together and the man lives, and when likewise they bestow on each of them the appellation of man, calling the mind "the inward man," but the body "the outward man," as though they were two men, while both of them together are only one man. (Tom. 5. On the City of God, lib. 13, cap. 24. See also lib. 11, cap. 27 & 3.) As this outward and visible world nourishes and contains the outward man, so that invisible world contains the inward man. (Tom. 8. On the First Psalm.) He who believes in Him, eats and is invisibly fattened, because he is also invisibly born again. The infant is within, the new man is within; where young and tender vines are planted, there are they filled and satiated. (On John, Tract 26.) THEOPHYLACT Moreover, "the outward man," that is, the body, "perishes." How is this? While it is beaten with stripes, while it is driven about. "But the inward man," that is, the spirit and the mind, "is renewed." By what means? When it hopes well, and freely acts, as though suffering and rejoicing on account of God. (On 2 Corinthians iv. 16.) VIGILIUS Let us spiritually advert to the spiritual expressions of the apostle, by which he testifies, that he has seen and handled the word of God, not with his bodily eyes and hands, but with the members of the inner man. (Against Eutychus, lib. 4.) PROCOPIUS OF GAZA The substance of man, if you consider his inward man, is this image of God; if you take his outward man into consideration, his substance will be the earth, or the dust of the ground. Yet one and the same is the man in the composition which is completed from both of them. (0n Genesis, cap. 1.) BERNARD As the outward man is recognized by his countenance, so is the inward man pointed out by his will. (Sermon 3, On Ascension Day.) LEO THE GREAT When the outward man is slightly afflicted, let the inward man be refreshed; and withdrawing corporeal fullness from the flesh, let the mind be strengthened by spiritual delights. (Sermon 4, On Quadragesima Sunday.) GREGORY NAZIANZEN But in this, our nature, every care is towards the inward man of the heart, and every desire is directed to it. (Apology for his flight.) GREGORY NYSSEN Let us make man in our image, after our likeness. God speaks thus respecting the inward man. "But," you will say, "you are giving a dissertation upon reason. Shew us man after the image of God. Is reason the man?" Listen to the apostle: Though your outward man perish, yet the inward man is renewed day by day. By what means? I own that man is two-fold, one who is seen, another who is hidden, and whom he that is seen does not perceive. We have, therefore, an inward man, and in some degree are two-fold. For I am that man who is inward; but I am not those things which are outward; but they are mine. Neither am I the hand, but I am the reason which is in the mind; but the hand is a part of the outward man. (On Genesis, i, 26.) Thus, when the inward man, whom God denominates the heart, has wiped off the rusty filth which, on account of his depraved thirst, had grown up with his form; he will once more recover the likeness [of God] with his original and principal form, when he will become good. (On the Beatitudes.) (3.) MODERN DIVINES Let us now see the opinions of certain divines of our own age and religious profession, on the inward man. CALVIN Though the reprobate do not proceed so far with the children of God, as, after the casting down of the flesh, to be renewed in the inner man, and to flourish again. (Instit. lib. 2, cap. 7, sect. 9.) But the reprobate are terrified, not because their inward mind is moved or affected, but because, as by a bridle cast upon them, they refrain less from outward work, and inwardly curb their own depravity, which they would otherwise have shed abroad. (Ibid. sect. 10.) Besides, since we have already laid down a two-fold regimen in man, and as we have, in another place, said enough about the other, which is placed in the mind, or the inward man, and which has reference to life eternal, &c. (Ibid. lib. 4, cap. 20, sect. 1.) Though the glory of God shines forth in the outward man, yet the proper seat of it is undoubtedly in the mind. (Ibid. lib. I, cap. 15, sect. 3.) Some persons perversely and unskillfully confound the outward man with the old man. For the old man, about whom the apostle treats in Romans vi. 6, is something far different. In the reprobate, also, the outward man perishes, but without any counterbalancing compensation. (On 2 Corinthians iv. 16.) BEZA - Is renewed, that is, acquires fresh strength, lest the outward man, who is sustained by the strength of the inward man, should be broken when assaulted with fresh evils, for which reason, the apostle said, in the 12th verse, "So, then, death worketh in us." (On 2 Corinthians iv. 16.) BUCER In holy persons, likewise, there are two men, an inward and an outward one. St. Paul says, "Though our outward man perish, yet the inward man is renewed day by day." As, therefore, man is two-fold, so, likewise, are his judgment and his will two-fold--a fact which our Lord himself was not ashamed to confess, when he said to his Father, "nevertheless, not my will, but thine, be done." By saying this, "not what I will, but what thou willest, be done," he undoubtedly shewed that he willed what the Father willed; and yet, at the same time, he acknowledges that this was his will: "Remove this cup from me." Our Lord, therefore, acknowledges the existence within himself of two wills, one of which was apparently at variance with the other. (On Romans 5. Fol. 261.) FRANCIS JUNIUS The outward man hears the word of God outwardly, but the inward man hears it inwardly. (On the Three Verities, lib. 3, cap. 2. fol. 182.) But then, as in ecclesiastical administration, not only the inward man is informed in the knowledge of God, but as aids and services are also sought by the outward man, so far as the external signs of the communion of saints are required to feed and promote the inward communion, in this cause, likewise, we acknowledge that God has delegated his authority to the magistrate. (On Ecclesiast. lib. 3, cap. 5.) PISCATOR The outward man, that is, the body, as he had previously called it. The inward man, that is, the soul or mind. (On 2 Corinthians iv. 16.) THE CHURCH OF HOLLAND When, indeed, from the depraved heart, and from the inward man, evil fruits do proceed, a necessary consequence of this is that he who is desirous of boasting that he is pure, must demonstrate the truth of his assertion by a spontaneous approval of the commands of Christ, and by a willing obedience to them. (A pamphlet, in which they give a reason for the excommunication of Koolhaes. Fol. 93.) JOHN DRIEDO The inward man is the rational mind unfolded in its powers, which never perishes. But the body, adorned with its senses, is called "the outward man," or "our man who is outward and corruptible," as the apostle says in 2 Corinthians iv. 16," though our outward man perish, yet the inward man is renewed day by day." Again, he says, in Romans vii. 22, "I delight in the law of God after the inward man." (On Grace and Free Will. Fol. 262.) The apostle Paul frequently does not understand the same thing by "the old man" and by "the outward man," nor has he signified the same thing by "the new man" and by "the inward man;" but in the inward man are found both the old and the new man. For, in the mind, oldness of this kind is formed at the same time as newness. In it, the likeness is either heavenly or earthly, that is, either a carnal will, living according to the exciting feel of Sin, or a Spiritual will, living according to the Spirit of God. (Ibid.) I AM aware that the divines of our profession frequently take "the inward man" for the regenerate and this new man; but then they do not consider "the inward man," except with a certain quality infused into it by the Holy and Regenerating Spirit, with which quality, when the inward man is considered, he is then correctly called regenerate and a new man. If any one urges that the very designation of "the inward man" possesses, of itself, as great a value with those divines as do the titles of "the regenerate" and "the new man," I shall desire him to demonstrate, by sure and stable arguments, that the meaning adopted by those divines is conformable to truth. 4. Let us now approach to the other foundation, which is that this man, to whom it is attributed that "he delights in the law of God," is regenerate; and that this attribute can agree with no other than a regenerate person. That we may be able to clear up this matter in a satisfactory manner, we must see what is meant by this phrase, "to delight in the law of God;" or "to feel a joint delight with the law of God," as it appears the Greek text is capable of being rendered, and as an ancient version has it; for the verb, sunhdomai seems to signify the mutual pleasure which subsists between this man and the law, and by which not only this man feels a joint delight in the law, but the law also feels a similar delight in him. "I feel a joint delight with the law of God," that is, I delight with the law: the same things are pleasing to me as are pleasing to the law. This interpretation may be illustrated and confirmed by a comparison of similar phrases, which frequently occur in other passages of the New Testament; Sunagwnisasqai moi "that ye strive together with me in your prayers to God for me"--Sunanapauswmai umin "that I may with you be refreshed, (Rom. xv. 30,32) -- Sunhqlhsan moi "those women who laboured with me in the gospel," (Phil. iv. 3) -- Summarturei tw pneumati umwn "the Spirit itself beareth witness with our spirit that we are the children of God," (Rom. viii. 16,) from which St. Chrysostom not inappropriately explains, "I feel a joint delight with the law," by this paraphrase, "I assent to the law that it is well applied, as the law, also, in return, assents to me, that it is a good thing for a man to will to do it." He takes this explanation of the phrase from the text itself, which kind of interpretation not only may obtain, but likewise ought to be employed, in this passage, since there is no other in the whole of the Scriptures in which this same phrase is used. If any one wishes to attach the same meaning to the phrase as to that which is used in Psalm i. 2, "But his delight is in the law of the Lord;" let him who says this, know that it is incumbent on him to produce proof for his assertion. This is not unreasonably required of him, because the antecedents and the consequences which are attributed to the man who is denoted in the first Psalm and described as being blessed, are not only vastly different from those things which are attributed to the man on whom we are now treating, but are likewise quite contrary to them. Conceding, however, this for the sake of argument, but by no means absolutely granting it, (which I am far from doing,) we must observe, that this man [in Romans vii. 22] is said, not simply "to delight in the law of God," or "to feel a joint delight with the law of God," but he does so with restriction and relatively, that is "according to the inward man." This restriction intimates that "the inward man" has not obtained the pre-eminence in this man, but that it is weaker than the flesh; as the latter is that which hinders it from being able, in operation and reality, to perform the law, to which it consents, and in which it delights. He who will compare the following verse with this will perceive that the cause of that restriction is the one which we have here assigned. For in the subsequent verse, (the 23rd,) it is not said, "But I see another law in my members, according to which I do not delight in the law of God," such as the opposition ought to have been, it, by that restriction, the apostle wished only to ascribe this "delighting" to the man according to one part of him, and to take it away according to the other part of him. But since the apostle not only takes this "delighting" from the other part of him, but likewise attributes it to the power of warring against that inward man and overcoming him, it is evident that the restriction has been added on this account - - to shew that, in the man who is now the subject of discussion, "the inward man" has not the dominion, but is, in fact, the inferior. Let him who is desirous to contradict these remarks, shew us, in any passage in which regenerate persons are made the subject of investigation, a similar restriction employed, and adduced for another purpose. From these observations, therefore, it appears that the proposition is most deservedly denied. Let us now attend to the assumption. 5. I say that the assumption is proposed in a mutilated form, as it was previously in the argument produced from the eighteenth verse. For with it, the apostle joins the following verse, in such a manner that the twenty-third verse may be the principal part of a compound and discrete axiom, employed for the purpose of proving what the apostle intended. But that which is now placed in the assumption, is a less principal part, conducing to the illustration of the other by separation. From this, it follows that the conclusion cannot be deduced From the premises, because the proposition is destitute of truth, the assumption mutilated, and the conclusion itself, beyond the purpose of the apostle and contrary to his design. 6. Let us see whether any thing further can be brought from the twenty-third verse for the demonstration of the contrary opinion. The man who has within him, beside the law of his members, the law of his mind, which is contrary to the other, is a regenerate man. Such a man is the one mentioned in this passage; Therefore, he is a regenerate man. (1.) The defenders of the contrary opinion believe the proposition in this syllogism to be true, because "the law of the mind" is opposed to "the law of the members," as it consents to the law of God--a quality which they suppose to belong only to the regenerate. This, they think, is confirmed from the circumstance that the same apostle expressly calls a certain mind, in Col. ii. 18, "a fleshly mind," which he likewise calls in Romans viii. 7, "the carnal mind." But the proposition cannot be supported by these passages; for it is simply false, and those arguments which are produced in proof of it are inappropriate. For to some of the regenerate also, (that is, to those who are under the law, who have some knowledge of the law, who have thoughts accusing or else excusing them, and who know that concupiscence is sin,) belongs something beside "the law of the members," "a fleshly mind," and one that is "carnal," which is opposite and repugnant to these: And this is "the work of the law written in their hearts;" which is neither "the law of the members," "a fleshly mind," nor one that is "carnal," but it contends with them. For a conscience or consciousness of good and evil, which compels a man, though in vain, to good, and deters him from evil, is directly opposed to "the law of the members" impelling to evil, and "to the carnal affections which cannot be subject to the law of God." For this conscience consents to the law of God, and is the instrument of the same law even in an unregenerate man to accuse and convict him. We may, therefore, be permitted to deny that proposition, and to demand stronger proofs for it. (2.) With regard to the assumption, we may say the same as we did about the assumption in the previous syllogism--that it is not fully proposed, as it ought to have been, and it omits those things which were joined together in the text of the apostle. But those things are of such a description, as, when added to the assumption, will easily point out the falsity of the proposition; that is, such is the opposition in this man between this law of the members and that of the mind, that the former not only "wars against" the latter, but likewise obtains the conquest in the fight; that is, "it brings man into captivity under the law of sin." From these observations also it is evident, that no good consequence can ensue from the assumption. 7. But let us now try, whether something cannot be deduced from these two verses for the establishment of our opinion. It appeals indeed to me, that I can from them deduce an invincible argument for the refutation of the contrary opinion, and for the confirmation of my own. (1.) The argument in refutation of the contrary opinion may be stated in the following manner: The law of the mind which wars against the law of the members, is conquered by the law of the members, so that the man "is brought into captivity to the law of sin which is in his members;" (as it occurs in this very passage;) But the law of the Spirit of life in Christ Jesus, when warring against the law of the members, overcomes the latter; so that it liberates the man, who had been brought into captivity under the law of sin, from the law of sin and death: (Rom. viii. 2.) Therefore, the law of the Spirit is not the law of the mind; neither is the law of the mind, the law of the Spirit. This is evident from simple inversion, and from this very syllogism, the premises being so transposed, as for the assumption to take the place of the proposition, and vice versa: and, therefore, the word "mind" is not used in this passage for "the Spirit." This argument is irrefragable. Let him who is desirous of proving the contrary, make the experiment, and he will find this to be the result. But its peculiar force will be more correctly understood towards the close of this investigation, in which is more fully explained the whole of the matter about which the apostle is here treating. (2.) For the confirmation of my own opinion, I deduce the following argument from these verses: That man, who delights indeed in the law of God after the inward man, but who, with the law of his mind warring against the law of his members, not only cannot prevail against the latter, but is also conquered by it and brought into captivity under the law of sin, while the law of his mind fruitlessly contends against it, is an unregenerate man, and placed, not under grace, but under the law; But though this man delights in the law of God after the inward man, and though with the law of his mind he wars against the law of His members; yet not only is he unable to prevail against the law of his members, but he is likewise brought into captivity under the law of sin by the law of his members, the law of his mind maintaining a strong but useless contest; Therefore, the man [described] in this passage is unregenerate, and placed, not under grace, but under the law; Or, to state the argument in a shorter form, omitting whatever it is possible to omit--That man in whom the law of the members so wages war against the law of the mind, as, when the latter is overcome, or at least while it offers a vain resistance, to bring the man himself into captivity under the law of sin, is unregenerate, and placed under the law; But in this man, about whom the apostle is treating, the law of the members so wages war with the law of the mind, as, when the latter is overcome, or at least while it offers a vain resistance, to bring the man himself into captivity under the law of sin; Therefore, this man is unregenerate and placed under the law. (3.) The truth of the proposition rests on these three reasons: I. Because a regenerate man not only with the law of his mind wages war against the law of his members, but he does this principally with the law of the Spirit, that is, by the strength and power of the Holy Spirit; for it is said in Gal. v. 17: "The flesh lusteth against the Spirit, and the Spirit against the flesh." II. Because far different is the result of that contest which, by the strength and power of the Spirit, or by "the law of the Spirit," a regenerate man maintains against the law of the members and against the flesh. For the law of the Spirit always obtains the victory, except when the man ceases from employing it in the battle, and from defending himself with it against the invading temptations of the flesh, Satan, and the world. III. Because it is not an attribute of a regenerate man, of one who is placed under grace, to be brought into captivity under the law of sin; but that, rather, is his which is ascribed to him in the second verse of the following chapter--"The law of the Spirit of life in Christ Jesus hath made me free from the law of sin and death." For when he was formerly placed under the law, he was in captivity under the strength and power of sin. I will now confirm these reasons against the objections which are, or which can be, made against them. Against the first it may be objected--"Since the law of the mind,' and the law of the Spirit,' are one, they are in this argument unskillfully distinguished; both because no one lights against the law of the members except by the law of the Spirit, or by the strength and power of the Holy Spirit; and therefore the law of the mind is the law of the Spirit." To this I reply, it has already been proved, that the law of the mind, and the law of the Spirit, are not the same, and that the conscience also wages war against the law of the members in those men who are under the law. Against the Second reason it may be objected, "Even the regenerate themselves offend in many things.' (James iii. 2.) There is on earth no man that sinneth not.' (1 Kings viii. 46.) The regenerate cannot say with truth that they have no sin.' (1 John i. 8.)" With other objections similar in their import. To these, I reply, that I heartily acknowledge all these things, but that I do not perceive how by means of them the second reason can be weakened. For these expressions are not repugnant to each other--"In many things the regenerate offend," and "The regenerate most generally gain the victory in the contest against sin," that is, when they use the arms with which they are furnished by the Holy Spirit. (4.), any one says, "In this contest, the regenerate are more frequently the conquered than the conquerors," I shall request him to explain how then it can be declared concerning the regenerate, "that they walk not after the flesh, but after the Spirit;" for, "to be the conquered" is "to fulfill the desires of the flesh;" and he who usually does this, "walks after the flesh." But many passages of Scripture teach that this contest, which the regenerate maintain against sin by the strength and power of the Holy Spirit, has generally a felicitous and successful termination; "for whatsoever is born of God overcometh the world; and this is the victory that overcometh the world, even our faith. Who is he that overcometh the world, but he that believeth Jesus to be the Son of God," (1 John v. 4,5.) "Submit yourselves therefore to God; resist the devil, and he will flee from you." (James iv. 7.) Greater is He that is in you, than he that is in the world." (1 John iv. 4.) "Put on the whole armour of God, that ye may be able to stand against the wiles of the devil. Wherefore, take unto you the whole armour of God, that ye may be able to withstand in the evil day, and, having done all, to stand." (Ephes. vi. 11,13.) "I can do all things through Christ which strengtheneth me." (Phil. iv. 13.) "All things are possible to him that believeth." (Mark ix. 23.) This truth also is proved, by various examples, through the whole of Hebrews 11. "Now unto him that is able to do exceeding abundantly above all that we ask or think, according to the power that worketh in us, unto him be glory," &c. (Ephes. iii. 20,21.) "Now unto Him that is able to keep you from falling," "and to present you, faultless, before the presence of his glory with exceeding joy, to the only wise God our saviour, be glory," &c. (Jude 24, 25.) "They that are after the Spirit, do mind the things of the Spirit. If ye, through the Spirit, do mortify the deeds of the body, ye shall live. Nay, in all these things we are more than conquerors through Him that loved us." (Rom. viii. 5,13,37.) By many other passages of Scripture, this may also be proved. GALATIANS v, 16-1 8. But let us now consider Gal. v. 16-18, and let us compare it with Romans vii. 22,23, the passage at present under investigation, that it may also clearly appear, from such consideration and comparison, that the result of the contest between the Spirit and the flesh is generally this: the Spirit departs from the combat the conqueror of the flesh, especially as, in this seventh chapter to the Romans, we perceive an entirely contrary issue or result is described and deplored. The passage may be thus rendered: "This I say then, Walk in the Spirit and fulfill not that after which the flesh lusteth," or "ye shall not fulfill the lusts of the flesh." "For the flesh lusteth against the Spirit, and the Spirit against the flesh; and these are contrary the one to the other; that ye may not do the things that ye would. But if ye be led of the Spirit, ye are not under the law? The exhortation of the apostle occurs in the sixteenth verse; and, on account of the ambiguity of the Greek word, it may be read in two different ways, "fulfill not," or "ye shall not fulfill." If the former rendering be adopted, then the exhortation consists of two parts, of which the one teaches what must be done, and the other what must be omitted; that is, we must walk in the Spirit, and the desires of the flesh must not be fulfilled." But if the clause be rendered in the second manner, then the sixteenth verse contains an exhortation in these words: "Walk in the Spirit;" and a consectary subjoined to the exhortation in these words: "And ye shall not fulfill the desires or lusts of the flesh." The latter mode of reading the passage seems to be more agreeable to the mind of the apostle; for he had previously, in the thirteenth verse, exhorted the Galatians not to abuse their Christian liberty for carnal licentiousness and lasciviousness. But now, in the sixteenth verse, he produces a remedy, by which they will be able to restrain and curb the assaults and the power of the flesh, and which is, if they walk in the Spirit, it shall then come to pass, that they shall not fulfill the lusts of the flesh. In the seventeenth verse a reason is added, that is deduced from the contrariety or contest which subsists between the flesh and the Spirit, and from either the end or the result of this contest. (1.) The contrariety or contest is described in these words: "For the flesh lusteth against the Spirit, and the Spirit against the flesh." From which is manifest the necessity both of the exhortation, not to abuse their Christian liberty to carnal licentiousness, and not to fulfill the lusts of the flesh; and of the remedy, by which alone the lusts of the flesh can be curbed and restrained, and which is this: "if they walk in the Spirit, that lusteth against the flesh." For it is from this enmity and contrariety which subsists between the flesh and the Spirit that the conclusion is drawn, "If ye walk in the Spirit, ye shall not fulfill the lusts of the flesh." From this it is also manifest, that this latter mode of rendering is better adapted to the meaning of the apostle. (2.) The end or result of this contest is described in these words: "And these are contrary the one to the other, that ye may not do the things that ye would." I have said that the end or the issue of the contest is here described; because some persons suppose that its issue, and not its end, is pointed out in this passage. (i.)But the particle, ina "that," which is used by the apostle, signifies the end or intention, and not the result or issue; and this interpretation is entirely agreeable to the mind of the apostle. "For the Spirit lusteth against the flesh" for this purpose, "that we may not do those things" which we lust according to the flesh, and "which we would," the consequence of which is, "if we walk in the Spirit, we shall not fulfill the desires of the flesh." And, on the contrary, since "the flesh also lusteth against the Spirit" for this purpose, "that we may not do those things which we lust according to the Spirit," it follows that if we walk in the flesh or according to the flesh, we shall not fulfill the desires of the Spirit. But this rendering is agreeable to the scope or design of the apostle, "that ye may not do what things soever ye would according to the flesh." (ii.) If we assert that the result or issue is here signified, then the meaning will likewise be two-fold. For it will be possible for it to be as follows: "The flesh and the Spirit are contrary the one to the other, so that ye cannot do those things which according to the Spirit ye would." It may likewise be this: "So that ye cannot do these things which, according to the flesh ye would." That is, this contest obtains the following result, "that ye cannot do those things which, according to the Spirit, ye would;" or, "that ye cannot do those things, which, according to the flesh, ye would." But let us see which of these two meanings is the more suitable: Truly, the latter of them is. It is not only more suitable, but likewise necessary, if the apostle is here treating about the issue or result. This will be still more apparent from the absurdity of the admonition, if the passage be explained in the other sense: The apostle admonishes the Galatians, "to walk in the Spirit, and not to fulfill the desires of the flesh;" (for we will now retain this rendering of the latter clause, as that which is more consentaneous with the meaning that explains the passage concerning this issue or result;) and the persuasion to this will then be: "For the flesh and the Spirit are contrary the one to the other, by this result, that ye cannot do those things which, according to the Spirit, ye would." This indeed is not to exhort, but to dissuade and dehort by a forewarning of the unhappy result. Besides, reason itself requires, according to [logical] scientific usage, that what has been proposed be drawn out in the conclusion; otherwise the parts of connection will be broken. But the proposition was either this--"Walk in the Spirit, and ye shall not fulfill the lusts of the flesh," or it was this: "Walk in the Spirit, and fulfill not the lusts of the flesh." I am desirous to have it demonstrated to me, by what means this proposition can be concluded from the eighteenth verse understood about the issue or result, by which the flesh hinders the Galatians from doing that which, according to the Spirit, they would. But it has been already shown, that each of these propositions may be fairly concluded from the passage, when understood as relating to the end or intention of the conflict, nay, when also understood as referring to the issue or result when the Spirit is the conqueror. It is apparent, therefore, not only that this is the end or design of the contest which is here mentioned from the lusting of the Spirit, but that this is likewise its issue or result from the strength and power of the Spirit--that, when the flesh is subdued, the Spirit comes off as the conqueror; and that the man who, by the Spirit, wages war against the flesh, and who walks in the Spirit, does not fulfill the lusts of the flesh. From these is inferred a consectary in the eighteenth verse: "But if ye be led of the Spirit, ye are not under the law;" that is, if ye walk in the Spirit, if under the guidance of the Spirit ye contend against the lusts of the flesh, and contend so as not to fulfill them, from these circumstances you may assuredly conclude that ye are not under the law. In this consectary, we see, that the phrases, "to be under the law," and "not to fulfill the lusts of the flesh," are opposed to each other; for the latter of them is descriptive of the proper effect of the guidance of the Spirit. Wherefore, the phrases, "to be under the law," and "to fulfill the lusts of the flesh," are consentaneous and of the same import. But this is the very thing which is asserted in Romans vi. 14: "For sin shall not have dominion over you; for ye are not under the law, but under grace." From this, it is apparent, that the dominion of sin, which is the cause why the lusts of the flesh are fulfilled, prevails in those persons who are under the law. But since the dominion of sin does not obtain in those who are under grace, (and, in fact, on this account, because they are under grace,) it is therefore evident that these phrases, "to be under grace," and "to be led by the Spirit," are consentaneous, nay, that they are exactly the same. For the effect of each of them is one and alike, and that is, to prevent sin from having dominion over a man, and to hinder man from fulfilling the lusts of the flesh, which is also explained at great length in Romans 8, in a manner agreeable to that which is briefly laid down in this seventeenth verse, that is, "The Spirit is contrary to the flesh for this purpose--that men may not do those things which, according to the flesh, they would." But, from Romans 7 it is very plain, that the result of that contest is different from the one upon which the apostle is here treating: For, in that chapter, the man does that which, after the flesh, he would, and does not what he is said to will after the inward man; the law of God, the law of the mind, and the inward man, vainly attempting to restrain the power of sin and to hinder the lusts of the flesh, because all these [strive as they may] are debilitated through the flesh. 9. If any one urge this as an objection, "It likewise befalls the best of the regenerate, that they do not the things which, according to the Spirit, they would, but that they fulfill the lusts of the flesh;" I perfectly assent to the truth of this, if the small addition be made, that "this sometimes happens to the regenerate." For if such be their general practice, they do not now walk in the Spirit; though this is a property of the regenerate. I say, that Romans 7 does not describe what sometimes befalls the pious, and that it contains a description of the state of that man about whom the apostle is there treating, that is, of a man who is under the law, before he is led by the guidance of grace, and is governed by the motions of the Holy Spirit. This is confirmed by the passage in Gal. v. 16-18. Then I reply, such a case as this does not occur from the circumstance of the Spirit, who has for a long time maintained a strenuous contest with the desires of the flesh, being at length conquered, and yielding on account of impotence or weakness: But it happens, because the man is either overtaken with temptation and overcome, before he begins to oppose to it the arms of the Spirit and of grace; or, in the progress of the conflict, he throws out of his hands those arms which, at the commencement, he began to use; or he uses them no longer, having begun the battle in the Spirit, but ending in the flesh. In no other way than in this can it happen, that the flesh, the world and Satan can overcome us; because "greater is He who is in us, than he that is in the world "as has already been pointed out in several passages. Without manifest ignomy and contumely poured on divine grace and on the Spirit of Christ, no other cause can be assigned why the pious, and those who are placed under grace, should sometimes be conquered by the flesh, the world and Satan; for either the Spirit that is in us is not the stronger of the two; or, while lusting and fighting against the flesh, He overcomes. And how can it possibly come to pass, that He who has conquered the flesh while it was still in its full strength, and has thus subjected us to Himself, should not be able to gain the victory over the flesh when it is crucified and dead in the body of Christ? 10. To the Third reason it is objected, "Even the regenerate may in some degree and relatively be said to be captives under sin, that is, so far as they are not yet fully regenerated, and still feel within themselves the motions of the flesh lusting against the Spirit, from which they are not completely delivered while they continue in this mortal body." I grant the antecedent, but I deny the consequence; for so far are the scriptures from ascribing the detention of the regenerate as captives under sin, to the imperfection of regeneration and to the remains of the flesh, that they are said with respect to this very regeneration to be freed from the yoke and slavery of sin and from the tyranny of the devil. "The remains of sin survive in the regenerate," and, "The regenerate are detained as captives by the remains of sin," are contradictory affirmations: For the former of the two is a token of sin conquered and overcome; the latter attributes victory and triumph to sin. After the Holy Spirit has commenced the mortification and death of sin, what is the act of the same Spirit respecting sin? Undoubtedly it is the persecution of the remains of sin, that He may subdue and extinguish them until they no longer exist; "and when their place is sought after, it is no more to be found," as St. Augustine has elegantly observed, when treating on this matter in a passage of his works. But the cause why such an opinion as this is entertained, is because "deliverance from sin" and "slavery under its tyrannical power," "a being loosed from the chains of Satan" and "captivity under his tyranny," are so accounted as if they can concur together, as the phrase is, in remiss degrees, and meet together in one subject, in much the same manner as the colour of white and that of black meet together in green, and heat and cold meet together in lukewarmness. Yet this matter stands in a situation vastly different; for liberty cannot consist with even the smallest portion of servitude or captivity; though it may labour under great difficulties in resisting its assaulting foes, and though it may occasionally come out of the conflict with something like a defeat. But if the matter stood in the relation of similes which have been adduced, yet even then it could not be said, "This man is partly free from sin, and partly its slave and captive;" but a necessity would then arise for the existence of a third thing from these two, which might obtain the name of "a medium between the extremes," belonging neither to this nor to that. But I am desirous to see some passage of Scripture adduced, where that is said about the regenerate, and about those who are placed under grace, which is ascribed to the man about whom the apostle is treating, or what is equivalent to it. ISAIAH LXIV, 6 11. But a passage is produced from the prophet Isaiah to prove that pious persons, and those who are placed under grace are, by the law of their members, brought into captivity under the law of sin. The degree of correctness with such an affirmation is made, will be very manifest from a comparison of the two passages. That in Isaiah (lxiv, 6) says, "But we are all as an unclean thing, and all our righteousness are as filthy rags; and we all do fade as a leaf; and our iniquities, like the wind, have taken us away." The passage in Romans, (vii, 23,) now under investigation, is this. "But I see another law in my members, warring against the law of my mind, and bringing me into captivity to the law of sin which is in my members." Let us now approach and institute a comparison. The subject of the first of these passages is, the captivity by which the children of Israel were led away into exile on account of their sins; the subject of the latter is, captivity under sin; therefore, this is to pass over to a different genus, contrary to the method observed in every approved discussion. In the former of these passages, the subject is the punishments which that people deservedly suffered on account of the actual sins which they had committed against God; but, in the latter, the subject is the cause whence it arises that the man who consents to the law of God, and who, with the law of his mind, wages war against the law of his members, is conquered and overcome, so that he actually commits sin, to which he is instigated and impelled by sin which dwelleth in him. Wherefore, the latter passage treats upon the CAUSE of actual sin, and the former upon the PUNISHMENTS of actual sins. For this phrase, "We all do fade as a leaf, and our iniquities, like the wind, have taken us away," does not signify that those men were impelled to some kind of sin through the depraved lusts of the flesh, as by a vehement wind, or that they melted away, as it were, into sins; but it signifies, that, on account of actual sins, which are distinguished by the appellation of "our iniquities," they are driven away into banishment as by a wind, and were scattered about as leaves. Let this passage be compared with the first Psalm, in which similar declarations are made concerning the wicked. Consult our interpreters of holy writ, such as Calvin, Musculus, Gualther, &c., and it will be evident, even with respect to the things which precede it, that the whole of this passage is unaptly cited by many persons to prove what they are desirous to establish. For the plainer and more obvious explanation of this matter we must observe, that there is a two-fold captivity under the tyranny of sin--the one, that of our primeval origin from Adam, according to which we are all born "children of wrath" and the servants of sin--the other, that of our own particular act, when, by actual transgressions, we subject and bind ourselves still more to sin, and engage in its service. Some persons will have this two-fold servitude to have been allegorically typified by the Egyptian and Babylonian captivities. For the Israelites, in their parents, entered into Egypt; and while there, after a lapse of years, they began to be oppressed and to be regarded as servants. The same people, on account of their sins, were led away, by the violence of their enemies, into captivity in Babylon. But the captivity about which the apostle is here treating, is posterior to the first of these two kinds; for the law of the members, which we have from our primeval origin, waging war with the law of the mind, when the latter is overcome, brings a man who is under the law into captivity to the law of sin, that very man who was formerly conceived in sin and born in iniquity. And, to express the whole in one word, he who was born in sin and originally under captivity to it, is brought into captivity under the law of sin by means of actual sins. From these observations, therefore, it is apparent, that the proposition of our syllogism is true, and stands unshaken against all these objections. The assumption stands in the very text of the apostle, from which the conclusion follows, that the man about whom the apostle treats in this passage, is an unregenerate man, and not placed under grace, but under the law.

VERSE THE TWENTY-FOURTH

The lamentable exclamation, O wretched man that I am! -- a two-fold reading of it. 2. The body of death is the body of sin. 3. By four reasons it is proved that the body of death is not our mortal body. 4. This is confirmed by the testimonies of St. Augustine and Epiphanius. 5. An argument in favour of the true opinion. 6. Another argument in its favour. 1. From the condition of this man, when accurately considered by himself, follows the mournful lament and exclamation, "O wretched man that I am! who shall deliver me from the body of this death, or from this body of death?" Of this, a two-fold explanation is produced, according to the double meaning of the words--either "from the body of this death," or "from this body of death," which some people interpret by "this mortal body that we bear about with us," and others, by "that body of sin which has the dominion in a man who is under the law, and which renders him liable to death." The latter interpretation, however, is more agreeable both to the phrase and to the context; for the pronoun, toutou must not be referred to Swmatov "the body," but to

Qanatou "death," to which it is most nearly conjoined; and the clause ought to be rendered thus: "Who shall deliver me from the body of this death," [which is sin not only existing within me, but dwelling and reigning]? as it is expressed in the 17th and 20th verses. 2. For the apostle attributes a body to sin in the sixth verse of the sixth chapter of this epistle: "Our old man is crucified with him, that The Body of Sin might be destroyed," the destruction of which is followed by a deliverance from the servitude of sin, as it is expressed in the same verse. The phrase also occurs in Col. ii. 11: "In putting off the Body of the Sins of the flesh by the circumcision of Christ." Wherefore, according to this mode of reading it, the meaning of the exclamation is, "Who shall deliver me from this tyranny of sin, which, reigning in me and dwelling in my flesh, bringing me into captivity and subjecting me to itself, brings certain death to me?" 3. Some other persons are urgent about a different rendering, and give this meaning to the words, "Who shall deliver me from this mortal body?" That is, as the apostle speaks in another passage, "I desire to be dissolved, and to be with Christ." But this meaning does not agree with the exclamation, (1.) On account of the construction, which declares that the pronoun, toutou "this," must not be referred to the body, but to death. (2.) Because the preceding verses do not permit this meaning to be entertained. For the force and tyranny of sin, dwelling in this man, and impelling him to fulfill his desires, is the subject on which the apostle is here treating. But "the deliverance" which is earnestly sought in this 24th verse, opposed to "the captivity" which is the subject of the verse. (3.) On account of the thanksgiving which is appended to it, and which ought not to be subjoined to a desire which was not then fulfilled [if the meaning of the phrase were, this mortal body]. (4.) Because the grace of Christ is not simply to deliver out of this mortal body, but to free us from the body of sin and from its dominion. It is true indeed, that, through the blessed analusin "dissolution" or "departure," for which we are waiting in the faith and hope of Christ, rest is granted to us from all our labours, and from the conflict of lusts with which we are inwardly attacked. But in this passage the apostle is treating, not about the conflict and impulse of lusts which exist within us, but about the fulfilling of those lusts by that impulse to which "the law of the mind" opposes itself in vain. 4. St. Augustine is one of my supporters, who says, in his treatise On Nature and Grace (cap. 53,) "The saints most certainly do not pray to be delivered from the substance of the body, which is good, but from carnal vices; from which no man is delivered without the grace of the saviour, nor at the time of his departure from the body, when it dies." It is no injury to my interpretation, that St. Augustine here says, that, according to his interpretation, "Saints or holy persons pray for deliverance from carnal vices" &c.; I only point out what he understood by "the body of death? On the Perfection of Justice, against Celestius, St. Augustine also says, "It is one thing, therefore, to depart out of this body, which the last day of the present life compels all men to do; but it is another thing to be delivered from the body of this death, which divine grace alone, through Jesus Christ, imparts to his saints and believers? Epiphanius, On the 64th Heresy, (lib. 2, tom. I,) from Methodius, says, "Wherefore, O Aglaophon, he does not call this body death, but sin which dwells in the body through the lust of the flesh, and from which God has delivered him by his coming? 5. Wherefore, from the 24th verse, when rightly understood, I argue thus for the establishment of my own opinion: Those men who are placed under grace are not wretched; But this man is wretched; Therefore, this man is not placed under grace. The assumption is in the text, and thus placed beyond all controversy. In reference to the proposition, perhaps some one will say, "Men, placed under grace, are partly blessed, and partly wretched--blessed, as they are regenerate and partakers of the grace of Christ--wretched, as they still have within them the remains of sin, with which they ought to maintain a constant warfare. This is a sure sign of a felicity which is not yet full and perfect." I confess that, while the regenerate continue as sojourners in this mortal life, they do not attain to a felicity that is full, complete in all its parts, and perfect. But I do not recollect ever to have read [in the Scriptures] that they are, on this account, called "wretched" with regard to the "spiritual life which they live by faith of the Son of God," though, in reference to this natural life, "they be of all men most miserable." (1 Cor. xv. 19.) The opposite to this may be easily proved from the Scriptures: "Blessed are the poor in spirit--they that mourn--that hunger and thirst after righteousness," &c. (Matt. v. 3-12.) "But," some one will rejoin, "Is it not wretched to contend with the remains of sin, to be buffeted by the messenger of Satan, sometimes to be overcome, and to be grievously injured?" It is undoubtedly desirable that this were not necessary, that it never occurred, that they might be delivered from the messenger of Satan; but the contenders, and those who are thus buffeted, cannot be called "wretched" on account of that contest and buffeting. But it is wretched indeed, to be overcome; yet neither are they called "wretched," who, though they be sometimes conquered, more frequently obtain the victory over the world, sin and Satan. 6. He who desires to be delivered from the body of this death, that is, from the dominion and tyranny of sin, is not placed under grace, but under the law. But this man desires to be delivered from the dominion and tyranny of sin; therefore, this man is not placed under grace, but under the law. The proposition is true, because regenerate men, and those who are placed under grace, are free from the servitude and tyranny of sin--not indeed perfectly free, but yet so far as to render it impossible for them to be said to be under the dominion and servitude of sin, if the person who speaks concerning them be desirous of talking in accordance with the Scriptures. But it has been already proved, that this man is desirous of being freed from the body of sin which dwells and reigns within him; therefore, the conclusion regularly follows.

VERSE THE TWENTY-FIFTH

1. Various readings of the first clause, from the ancient fathers. 2. In the latter clause, this man is said "to serve the law of God with his mind, but with his flesh, the law of sin." 3. "To serve God," and "to serve the law of God," are not the same thing. 4. The various kinds of law mentioned in this chapter, with a diagram, and the explanation of it. 5. From this verse nothing can be obtained in confirmation of the contrary opinion. 1. St. Chrysostom reads the former part of this verse thus: "I thank," &c., which is also the reading of Theophylact. This is the reading of St. Ambrose: "The grace of God through Jesus Christ." St. Jerome, also, against Pelagius, adopts the same reading. St. Augustine renders the clause thus: "By the grace of God through Jesus Christ." (Discourse 5. On the Words of the Apostle. Tom. 10.) Epiphanius renders it, "The grace of God through Jesus Christ." (From Methodius against Origen, Heresy 64. Lib. 2, tom. 1.) But this clause contains a thanksgiving, in which St. Paul returns thanks to God that he, in his own person, has been delivered from this body of sin, about which he had been treating, and to which that man was liable whose character he was then personating. In this, thanksgiving is contained, by implication, an answer to the preceding interrogatory exclamation; that is, "The grace of God will deliver this man from the body of this death, from which he could not be delivered by the law." This is directly and openly explained by some copies of the Greek original, in which this verse is thus read: "The grace of God, through our Lord Jesus Christ," that is, "This grace will deliver me, or the man whose character I have been personating, from the body of this death"--a thing which it was the chief purpose of the apostle to prove in this investigation. 2. In the latter part of the same verse, is something resembling a brief recapitulation of all that had been previously spoken, in which the state of the man about whom the apostle is here treating, is briefly defined and described in the following words: "So then, with the mind, I myself serve the law of God; but with the flesh, the law of sin." In the correct explanation of these phrases, lies an important key for the clear exposition and dilucidation of the whole matter; these phrases must, therefore, be subjected to a diligent examination. 3. Those persons who interpret this passage as relating to a regenerate man and to one placed under grace, are desirous to intimate, by these phrases, that St. Paul, so far as he was regenerate, "served God," but that so far as he was unregenerate, and still partly carnal, "he served sin." They also take "the mind" in the acceptation of the regenerated portion of man, and "the flesh" for that portion of him which is not yet regenerate; and they suppose that "to serve the law of God" is the same thing as "to serve God," and that "to serve the law of sin" is the same thing as "to serve sin." But neither of these suppositions can be proved by this text or by other passages of Scripture. (1.) For the apostle is not accustomed to bestow on man, as he is regenerate, the epithet of "the mind," but that of "the Spirit." And this he does for a very just reason; for "the mind" is the subject of regeneration, "the Holy Spirit" is the effector of it, from communion with whom a participation also with his name arises. Besides, "the mind" is attributed to the flesh:" Vainly puffed up by his fleshly mind." (Col. ii. 18.) The gentiles are said to have "walked in the vanity of their mind." (Ephes. ii. 17.) Idolaters are "given over to a reprobate mind;" (Rom. i. 28;) and the apostle mentions "men of corrupt minds." (1 Thess. vi. 5; 2 Tim. iii. 8.) (2.) But that "to serve God" is not the same as "to serve the law of God," and "to serve sin" is not the same as "to serve the law of sin," is evident, First. From the difference of the words themselves. For it is very probable, that different phrases denote different meaning. If any one denies this, the proof of his position is incumbent on himself. Secondly. From the words of Christ, who denied the possibility of any man serving two masters, God and Mammon, God and sin. If any one say that "it is possible for this to be done in a different respect, that is, to serve God with the mind, and to serve sin with the flesh," I reply that, by such a petty distinction as this, the general affirmation of Christ is evaded, to the great detriment of piety and divine worship, and that a wide door will thus be opened for libertines and Pseudo-Nicodemites. But some one will say, "The apostle expressly affirms this, which I deny, and my denial will be supported by the phrases themselves, when correctly explained, as they will soon be; for this man serves sin, and not God. Thirdly. From the perpetual usage of the Scriptures, which are not accustomed to employ these restrictions when any man is said to serve God, or to serve sin. Wherefore, since they are employed in this passage, it is exceedingly probable that the same thing is not signified by these different phrases. 4. But the subject itself, upon which the apostle here treats, when placed plainly before the eyes, may disclose to us the true meaning of these phrases; so that the man who will inspect it with honest eyes, and with eyes desirous to investigate and ascertain the truth alone, may have that with which to satisfy himself. The apostle, therefore, here makes mention of four laws. (1.) The law of God. (2.) The law of sin. (3.) The law of the mind. (4.) The law of the members. They are opposed to each other and agree together in the following manner: "The law of God," and "the law of sin," are directly opposed; as are likewise "the law of the mind," and "that of the members." "The law of God," and "the law of the mind," agree together; as do likewise "the law of sin," and "the law of the members.

From this, it follows that "the law of God," and "the law of the members," are indirectly opposed; as are also "the law of sin," and "that of the mind." But it will be possible to render these things more intelligible by the subjoined diagram: "The law of God" and "the law of sin," obtain in this place the principal dignity. "The law of the mind" and "that of the members" are placed as hand-maids or assistants to them, rendering due service to their superiors; for "the mind delights in the law of God," and "the law of the members brings a man into captivity to the law of sin." (Rom. vii. 22,23.) These things being premised, I proceed to the explanation. The apostle here lays down two lords, who are completely contrary to each other, and directly opposed, God and sin--the former of these, the lawful lord; the latter, a tyrant, and, by violent means, usurping dominion over man, by the fault indeed of man himself, and by the just judgment of God. Both of them impose a law on man. God imposes his law, that man may obey him in those things which it prescribes; and sin Imposes its law, that man may obey it in "the lusts thereof," which it proposes by a certain law of its own. The former is called "the law of God;" the latter, "the law of sin." By the former, God endeavours to lead the man, who is placed under the law, to yield obedience to him; by the latter, sin strives and attempts, by every kind of violence, to compel the man to obey him. By his law, God prescribes those things which are "holy, and just, and good;" by its law, sin proposes those things which are useful, pleasant, and agreeable to the flesh. Now both of them, God and sin, have, in this man who is under the law, something which favours their several causes and purposes, and which assents to each of these laws. God has the mind, or "the law of the mind;" sin has the flesh, or the. law of the flesh, or "of the members." The mind, consenting to the law of God, that it "is holy, and just, and good;" the flesh, assenting to the law of sin, that it is useful, pleasant and agreeable; "the law of the mind," which is the knowledge of the divine law, and an assent to it; "the law of the members," which is an inclination and propension towards those things which are useful, pleasant, and agreeable to the flesh, that is, towards these mundane, earthly and visible objects. In the 23rd verse of this chapter, these two laws are said to be, antisrateuomenoi "waging war together," like soldier, who are in the field of battle, and drawn up in hostile array against each other, that the one army may overcome that which is opposed to it, and may gain the victory for its lord and general. "The law of the mind" fights for "the law of God," and "the law of the members" marches under the banner of "the law of sin;" the former, that, after having conquered the flesh and the law of the members, it may bring man into subjection to the law of God, with this design--that man may serve God; the latter, that, after having overcome the law of the mind, it may sentence man to bondage, and "bring him into captivity to the law of sin," with this design--that man may serve sin. The conflict between these two contending parties, is about man, whom God wishes to bring into subjection to himself; and sin eagerly indulges the same wish. The former of these prescribes his own law to him; the latter also prescribes its law; and both of them employ their own military forces, that they severally have in the man, each to obtain the victory for himself. From these explanations it will now appear what the phrases signify; "With the mind to serve the law of God," is, with a mind consenting to the law of God, to perform its military services to that law, for the purpose of bringing man into subjection to God; "With the flesh, to serve the law of sin," is with the flesh assenting to the desires of sin, to render its military services to the law of sin, in order to bring man into captivity to that law and to subject him to sin. The end, therefore, or the intention of the battle is, that man may be brought into subjection either to the law of God, or to the law of sin; that is, that he may walk either according to the flesh, or according to the mind. The act tending to this end, is the waging of war, which is indeed actual hostility, and an inimical encounter between the parties; but it is also the employment of persuasion towards man, without whose assent neither party can obtain this its end. The mind, adverse to the flesh, persuades the will of man to do that which is holy, and just, and good, and to reject what is merely delectable. The flesh, repugnant to the mind, persuades the same human will to set aside and disregard that which is holy, and just, and good, and to embrace that which is capable of affording present delight and usefulness. The effect produced by the mind on the will, is the volition of good and the hatred of evil; the effect which the flesh produces on the same will, is the volition of evil and the nolition of good. This is a change of the will, first to one party, and then to the other. But the issue or result declares which of the parties in this man has produced the stronger and more powerful effect. But this is the result of the conflict, [as it is described in the twenty-third verse,] the nonperformance of good, the nonomission of evil, a token of the impotence of the mind, which commanded good to be done, and forbade the commission of evil, which approved of the performance of good, but disapproved of the perpetration of evil; and it is the commission of what is evil, the omission of what is good, the captivity of man under the law of sin, plainly demonstrating that, in this man, the party of sin and of the flesh is the more powerful of the two, the law of the mind fruitlessly striving against it. The cause of this result is the weakness of the law, which has been debilitated by the flesh, (Rom. viii. 3,) and the force and pertinacious power of the flesh in this man, the effect of which is, that the man does not walk according to the law but according to the flesh, and does not march according to the law of the mind but according to that of the members. But if to this conflict be added a stronger force of the Spirit of Christ, who does not write the letter of the law on tables of stone, but impresses the love and fear of God on the fleshly tables of the heart--then are we permitted not only to hope for a different result, but it is also given us assuredly to obtain a successful issue. This is indicated by the apostle in Romans viii. 2: "For the law of the Spirit of life in Christ Jesus hath made me tree from the law of sin and death." For it comes to pass, by means of the power of this Spirit, that the man, who had previously been "brought into captivity to the law of sin," is delivered from it, and "no longer walks after the flesh, but after the Spirit;" that is, in his life, he follows the motion, the influence, and the guidance of the Holy Spirit, which motion, influence and guidance tend indeed to the same end as that to which the law of God, and the law of the mind, endeavoured to lead the man, but with an energy not equal; as not being able to complete their attempt, on account of the hindrance of the law of sin and of the members. This is likewise the cause why this man is said to walk not according to the law of the mind, but according to the Spirit, [a phrase frequently employed by the apostle in Romans 8,] and "to be led of the Spirit, and not to be under the law," (Gal. v. 18.) Not indeed because the man who lives according to the Spirit, does not live according to the law of God; but because the Spirit of Christ, and not the law, is the cause why the man regulates his life according to the law of God. For the law knows how to command, but cannot afford any assistance--a doctrine which St. Augustine frequently inculcates. 5. From these observations, it may now be evident, that even from this (25th) verse, nothing can be adduced in proof of the contrary opinion; but that the opinion which explains the passage as referring to a man under the law, is also established by this verse. For this man, as he is under the law, "with his mind serves the law of God;" but, as he is carnal, "with his flesh he serves the law of sin," and he serves it so as to bring himself into captivity to the law of sin--his mind and conscience vainly struggling against it. Nor is it of the least service for the establishment of the other opinion, that the apostle says, "I myself;" for he had previously used the word "I" in many instances in this chapter, even when he said, "Sin wrought in me all manner of concupiscence;" (verse 8) "for I lived," or I was alive, "without the law once; but, when the commandment came, I died;" (9) "I found the commandment to be unto death to me;" (10;) "Sin, taking occasion by the commandment, deceived me, and by it slew me," (11) and other passages. But the pronoun, autov [in our English version, translated "myself,"] which is an adjunct to the pronoun "I," indicates that this pronoun "I" must be referred to the person about whom he had been previously treating. For it is the demonstrative [pronoun] of the nearest antecedent; as though he had said, "I am he about whom I have already been discoursing." This is likewise evident, because he concludes from the preceding verses, that the man whose character he took on him self to personate, (the prudence of [him who was under the influence of] the Holy Spirit requiring such personation,) "with his mind serves the law of God, but with his flesh the law of sin." Let those things be taken into consideration which, in his epistle, the apostles writes concerning himself, and let them be compared with the particulars of the description here given; and it will then clearly appear, that the apostle, in this passage, was by no means treating about himself, such as he was at that time. III. RECAPITULATION 1. What distinctly belongs to the man described in this chapter, both as he is under the law, and as he is carnal and the slave of sin. 2. The inconsistent state of a man who is under the law. 3. The manner in which God leads a sinner to penitence, faith in Christ, and the obedience of faith. 4. This representation of it confirmed by St. Augustine and Musculus--How far this is the work of the regenerating Spirit. 5. To this it is objected that a three-fold state of man is thus laid down--A reply to this objection. 1. But now, if not disagreeable, let all these things be collected together, and in a compendious form be exhibited before the eyes, that they may at one glance be examined, and a judgment formed concerning them.

THE MAN ABOUT WHOM THE APOSTLE IS HERE TREATING, DO FAR AS HE IS: UNDER THE LAW

He allows not, or approves not of, that which he does; He wills indeed that which is good; He hates evil; He consents to the law of God that it is good; He has it [in him] to will that which is good; It is no longer himself that does evil; He truly delights in the law of God after the inward man; According to the law of his mind he wages war with the law of his members; This causes him to exclaim, Who shall deliver me With his mind, therefore, he serves the law of God; CARNAL AND THE SLAVE OF SIN. He does that which he allows not, or of which he disapproves. But he does not what is good. And yet he does that which is evil. Yet he does that which he would not. But he finds evil present with him, and he finds not [how] to perform what is good. But the evil is done by sin which dwelleth in him.. But he has another law in his members. But the law of his members wages war against the law of his mind, so as to bring the man into captivity to the law of sin. From this misery, and the body of this death? But with his flesh he serves the law of sin. The things which are thus opposed to each other must not be disjoined, while they are attributed to the man about whom the apostle here treats; but they ought both to be united together, and jointly attributed to him. For this is required by the analogy of the subject itself that is under the law and the dominion of sin--as he is under the law, the particulars enumerated in the first column belong to him--as he is under the dominion of sin, those in the second column are his attributes. But the mode by which the apostle joins these things with each other, and attributes them to this man in a conjoint form, is that of a disjunctive enunciation. This is indicated by the frequent use of the particle, de which is the post- positive of men itself, or what immediately follows it. The one without the other does not render a sentence complete; but men "indeed, truly," denotes that something will follow, and de "but, yet, then," that something has preceded, with which the former or the latter part of the sentence ought to be joined. This remark must be diligently observed in the consideration of Romans 7, as must likewise the following--that both parts are not of the same order and dignity, but that the latter clause [in which de is used as the connecting word] is the chief and principal one, for whose explanation, illustration and amplification, the former clause [in which men occurs] is employed; as a proposition, or the first part of a sentence, is for its rendition or concluding part. Those latter particulars, therefore, [which are here inserted in the second column,] belong to the more ample explanation and proof of the proper cause, on account of which a man who is under the law cannot resist sin, but sin has the dominion over him. But the former particulars [enumerated in the first column] belong or conduce to the excusing of the law, lest the blame of this crime could be justly ascribed to it. From all which things united together the conclusion may be drawn that the man about whom the apostle is treating, must, on account of the predominant flesh and of sin which dwells in his flesh, be still reckoned in the number of carnal persons. But, because he is under the law, and so under it that it has effected in him whatever is usually effected by the law in transferring and conducting man as a sinner to the grace of Christ, he must, [almost at any hour], speedily be taken out from the number of carnal persons, and placed in a state of grace; in which higher state, he will no longer be put to the necessity of fighting, under the auspices and guidance of the law, against the vigourous and lively "motions of sins;" but, by the power of grace and under the guidance and influence of the Holy Spirit, he will contend against his crucified and mortified inclinations, till he obtain over them, when they are nearly dead and buried, a complete victory. 2. The man who will reflect upon this inconsistent state, if I may so denominate it, will easily perceive, that the things which the apostle has here written, must be referred to this state. For, diligently, and as if purposely, he exercises caution over himself not to employ the word "Spirit" in any passage in his description of this state; yet this word, the use of which he here so carefully avoids, is that which he employs in almost every verse of the next chapter, (Rom. 8) and which is so familiar to this apostle in all his epistles, as to seem to be perpetually before his eyes and his mind, especially when he is treating about the regenerate and their duty to God and their neighbour, and also when he treats upon the contest which the pious still have with the flesh and the remains of sin. The thoughtful consideration of this single matter is able and ought to cause doubts in the minds of those who interpret this portion of holy writ as applicable to regenerate persons and those who are placed under grace, if they only be animated with a sincere desire of ascertaining the truth, and love the truth for its own sake, even when it does not agree with their own preconceived opinions. 3. I am also desirous that all men seriously consider how God leads us to faith, in his Son, and to the obedience of faith, and what means he uses to convert a sinner. We know that God employs his holy word to produce this effect; we know that this word consists of two essential and integral parts, the law and the gospel; we know, also, that the law must first be preached to a sinner, that he may understand and approve it, that he may explore and examine his life by it when it is known and approved, that, when such examination is completed, he may acknowledge himself to be a sinner, and by his demerits, deserving of damnation, that he may mourn and be sorrowful on account of sin, and may detest it, that he may understand himself to be in urgent need of a deliverer, and that he may be instigated and compelled to seek him. To a man who is thus prepared by the law, the grace of the gospel must be announced, which, being manifested to the mind by the Holy Spirit, and by the same Spirit sealed on the heart, produces faith within us, by which we are united to Christ; that, holding communion with him, we may obtain remission of sins in his name, and may draw from him the vivifying power of his Spirit. By this quickening power, the flesh is mortified with its affections and lusts, and we are regenerated to a new life, in which we not only will or resolve to bring forth the fruits of gratitude to God, but we are likewise capable to bring them forth, and actually do so by this same Spirit, "who worketh in us both to will and to do." Let any man now describe to me out of the Scriptures the proper effects which flow from the preaching of the law, in the minds of those whom God has decreed to convert to a better life; and I will instantly present to him a man, such as he who is described to us by the apostle, under his own person, in this chapter, (Rom. 7.) "But are these effects through the preaching of the law produced in this man, without the grace of Christ, and the operation of the Holy Spirit?" What man can have the audacity to affirm this, unless he be one of the prime defenders of Pelagian doctrine, He who, by the preaching of the law, (the Holy Spirit blessing such preaching, and co-operating with it,) is compelled to flee to the grace of Christ, is not instantly, or at once, under grace, or under the influence, guidance and government of the Spirit. For, "the law is our schoolmaster [to bring us] unto Christ." (Gal. iii. 24.) "Christ is the end of the law for righteousness to every one that believeth." (Rom. x. 4.) "By the law is the knowledge of sin." (iii, 20.) 4. St. Augustine, when treating upon the use of the law, says, in his Reply to the two epistles of the Pelagians to

Boniface, "The law, as a schoolmaster, leads and conducts a man to this grace of God, by terrifying him concerning his transgressions of the law, that something may be conferred on him which it was not able to bestow." And in a subsequent passage, "We do not, therefore, make void the law through faith, but we establish the law,' which, by terrifying men, leads them to faith. Therefore, because the law worketh wrath,' that grace may bestow, on the man who is thus terrified and turned to fulfill the righteousness of the law, the mercy of God through Jesus Christ our Lord, who is the wisdom of God, and concerning whom it is written, He beareth in his tongue law and mercy. Law, by which he may terrify--Mercy, by which he may afford relief; law by a servant--mercy, by himself" &c., &c. (Lib. 4, cap. 5.) Let St. Augustine also be consulted, in his treatise on corruption and grace, in the first chapter of which he speaks thus appropriately to the matter under discussion: "The Lord himself has not only shown us from what evil we may turn aside, and what good we may perform, which the letter of the law alone is able to shew; but he also assists us, that we may turn aside from evil and may do good, which no one can do without the Spirit of grace. If this grace be wanting, the law is present for this purpose--to bring us in guilty and to kill us, on which account, the apostle says, The letter killeth, but the Spirit giveth life. (2 Cor. iii. 6.) He, therefore, who lawfully uses the law, learns in it evil and good; and, not confiding in his own strength, he flees to grace, by the aid of which he ceases from evil and does good. But what man thus flees to grace, except when his steps are directed by the Lord, and he delighteth in his way? (Psalm xxxvii. 23.) And by this also, the act of desiring the assistance of grace is the beginning of grace." Consult also the fifth chapter of the same treatise, in which the following passage occurs: "You are not willing to have your faults pointed out. You are unwilling that they should be smitten, and that you should feel useful grief, which may induce you to seek a physician. You are not desirous to have yourself shown to yourself, that when you perceive your own [mental] deformity you may be very importunate for a reformation of yourself, and may supplicate God not to suffer you to remain in this foul and deformed condition." And in the sixth chapter, he says: "Therefore, let the damnable origin be reprehended, that a willingness for regeneration may arise out of the sorrow consequent on such reprehension; yet, if he who is thus chastised be a son of the promise, that, when the noise of the correction sounds outwardly and the strokes of the whip are heard, God may work inwardly in him also to will by his secret inspiration." Musculus says, in his Common Places, in the chapter On Laws, (fol. 124,) "The law causes me not only to understand, but likewise with anguish and remorse of conscience to feel and experience that sin is in me. The proper effect of the law is, that it convicts us of being inexcusably guilty of sin, subjects us to the curse, and condemns us, (Gal. 3,) and when we are deeply affected with the smart of sin and condemnation, it renders us, anxious and earnest in our desires for the grace of God. Hence, arises that of the apostle, which is the subject of his investigation in Romans 7, and at the close of which he exclaims, O wretched man that I am! who shall deliver me from the body of this death?

THE GRACE OF GOD THROUGH JESUS CHRIST

"But is this, therefore, the work of the regenerating Spirit?" With regard to the END, I confess that it is; but with regard to the EFFECT itself, I dare not make any assertion. For mortification and vivification, which, as integral parts, contain the whole of regeneration, are completed in us by our participation of the death and resurrection of Christ. (Rom. 6.) In Romans viii. 15, the apostle distinguishes between "the Spirit of bondage to fear," and "the Spirit of adoption." Many persons denominate the former of these, "a legal Spirit," and the latter "the Spirit of the gospel of Christ." I, therefore, make the service of the Spirit of bondage to precede that of the Spirit of adoption, though both of them tend to one design. Whence, it appears that this my explanation of the seventh chapter is not contrary to the true doctrine concerning the law and its use, and the necessity of the grace of Christ; but that the doctors of the church, who give a different interpretation of it, have not reflected on this matter when they entered on an explanation of the chapter. For, since they teach, from the Scriptures, the very same thing as I suppose the apostle here to make the subject of his investigation, we do not differ from each other in our opinion of doctrines, but only in this single circumstance--that they do not think this passage relates to that head of doctrine, which, I affirm, is professedly treated in it: Yet, in this opinion, I do not stand alone, but I have many others with me, as we shall afterwards perceive. 5. Some one may here object, "that by this, my explanation, a three-fold state of man is laid down, when the Scriptures acknowledge but a two-fold state; and that three kinds of men are introduced, when no more than two are known to the Scriptures--that is, the state of regeneration and that which precedes regeneration, believers and unbelievers, regenerate and unregenerate men," &c. To this I reply, (1.) that in my explanation three consistent states of men are not laid down, neither are there three distinct and perfectly opposite kinds of men; but that it teaches how much the law has the power of effecting in a man, and how the same individual is compelled by the law to flee to the grace of Christ. (2.) I say that the state of the man described in this chapter is not a consistent one, but is rather a grade or step from the one to the other--from a state of impiety and infidelity to a state of regeneration and grace--from the old state in Adam to the new state in Christ. According to this grade or step, the man is denominated by some persons renascent, [or in the article of being born again]. And, truly, the distance of the one of these states from the other is far too great, for a man to be able to pass from one to the other without some intermediate steps. (3.) I deny that there is any absurdity in laying down a three-fold state of man, regard being had to the different times; that is, a state before or without the law, one under the law, and another under grace. For the apostolical Scriptures make mention of such a three-fold state in the two chapters now under consideration, and in Romans 6 and 7, and Galatians 4 and 5. St. Augustine says, in his book, The Exposition of certain Propositions in the Epistle to the Romans, (Cap. 3) "Therefore we distinguish the four conditions of man, into that BEFORE the law, UNDER the law, under grace, and in peace. In the state before the law, we follow the lusts of the flesh; under the law, we are drawn along with them; under grace, we neither follow those lusts, nor are drawn by them; in peace, there is no lusting of the flesh. Before the law, therefore, we do not fight; under the law, we fight," &c., &c. Consult also Bucer, in his commentary on this passage. For he lays down a three-fold man, (1.) a profane man who does not yet believe in God, (2.) a holy man who loves God, but who is weak to prevail against sin, and (3.) lastly, a man furnished with a stronger portion of the Spirit of Christ, so that he is able, not only to repress and condemn the flesh, but likewise to live, in reality, the life of God, with pleasure, and with confirmed and perpetual diligence. Let, therefore, the whole of his commentary on this passage be perused, and it will appear that, with respect to the substance of the matter, the difference is very slight between his explanation of it, and that which I have now given. This I shall also clearly prove in the following chapter, by passages cited from the same commentary. But let us see whether the Scriptures themselves do not, in many places, propose three kinds of men, and give us a description of a three-fold state. In Rev. iii. 15,16, some persons are described, as being neither hot nor cold, but lukewarm. Christ says that he came not to call to repentance "the righteous," that is, those who esteemed themselves as such, but "sinners," that is, those who owned themselves, or who, on his preaching, would own themselves to be of that description. (Matt. ix. 13.) Christ calls to himself those who are fatigued, weary, heavy-laden, and oppressed with the burden of their sins, (Matt. xi. 28,)but drives away from him those who are proud and puffed up with arrogance on account of their own righteousness. (Luke xviii. 9.) "Jesus said unto them, If ye were blind, ye should have no sin; but now ye say, We see; therefore, your sin remaineth." (John ix. 41.) In the parable of the Pharisee and the Publican, is intimated to us a three-fold description of men--one kind in the Pharisee, two kinds in the Publican, one before his justification, the other after it. But who can enumerate all the similar instances, Indeed, such enumeration is unnecessary. It is rather a matter of surprise, that, as the books of our divines are filled with such distinctions, they did not occur to their minds when meditating on this passage, in which this matter [of the different conditions or states of man] is professedly treated. IV.

THE CONNECTION BETWEEN THE SEVENTH AND THE EIGHTH CHAPTERS

The truth of the interpretation of the seventh chapter, as it has been so far deduced by the author, is proved from some of the early verses of the eighth chapter when compared with those which precede them. 2. The first verse. 3. The second verse, and an explanation of the phrases used in it. 4. The third verse. A comparison of the former part of it with Romans vii. 5 and 14, and of the latter part of it with the sixth verse of the same chapter. 5. The fourth verse, and a comparison of it with Romans vii. 4. A paraphrastical recapitulation of those things which are taught in the first four verses of the eighth chapter, and their connection with the preceding chapter. 1. But I may now be permitted to confirm this my interpretation from some of the first of the verses of the next chapter, provided they be diligently compared with those in the seventh chapter. 2. For, in the first verse, a conclusion is inferred from verses of the preceding chapter, which is agreeable and accommodated to the principal design proposed by the apostle through the whole of this epistle. The words are these: "There is, therefore, now no condemnation to them who are in Christ Jesus, who walk not after the flesh, but after the Spirit." That this verse contains a conclusion, is evident from the illative particle "therefore," and indeed a conclusion not deduced from the former part of the last verse in the seventh chapter, but from the entire investigation, which consists of these two parts: "Men do not obtain righteousness, and power to conquer sin and to live in a holy manner, by means either of the law of nature or that of Moses; but, through the faith of the gospel of Jesus Christ, those very blessings are gratuitously bestowed on them who work not, but believe on Christ." But these two things, JUSTIFICATION which consists of remission of sins, and The Spirit of Holiness by which believers are enabled to overcome sin and to live in a holy manner, are parts of the gracious covenant into which God has entered with us in Christ: "I will put my laws into their minds, and write them in their hearts, &c.; for I will be merciful to their unrighteousness, and their sins and their iniquities will I remember no more." (Heb. viii. 10,12.) Therefore, when the apostle had proceeded so far with the proof of this thesis, (having in the first five chapters treated on righteousness and remission of sins, and in the sixth and seventh chapters, on the power to conquer sin and live in a holy manner,) he now infers this conclusion: "There is, therefore, now no condemnation to them who are in Christ Jesus, who walk not after the flesh, but after the Spirit." The emphasis of the conclusion lies in these words: "Who are in Christ Jesus, who walk, not after the flesh, but after the Spirit," to the exclusion of those who are under the law, and for whom is prepared certain condemnation, as being persons out of Christ, and subjected to the dominion of sin--as if the apostle had said, "From all these things, therefore, it is apparent that condemnation impends over all those who are under the law, because they neither perform the law, nor are able to perform it; but that freedom from condemnation granted only to those who are in Christ, and who walk according to the Spirit." But that the emphasis lies in these words: "Those who are in Christ Jesus," to the exclusion of the others, is apparent, (1.) From the fact, that this very part is repeated. though in other words, which are these, "who walk after the Spirit." (2.) Because the exclusion of other persons is openly placed in the repetition, "who walk not after the flesh." (3.) From the subject, itself, of the apostle's investigation, which is this: "The gospel and not the law, is the power of God to salvation to those who believe and do not work." Wherefore, in order that the conclusion may correspond with the proposition, it ought to be read and understood with the opposition here produced. (4.) From other conclusions in this epistle, inferred in similar cases--"therefore, we conclude that a man is justified by faith without the deeds of the law," (Rom. iii. 28) also, in the twenty-seventh verse of the same chapter, "Where is boasting then, It is excluded. By what law? By that of works? No; but by the law of faith." "But it was written for us also, to whom it shall be imputed," that is, to those who "believe on him that raised up Jesus our Lord from the dead." (iv, 24) And it appears that these things are spoken in opposition, to the complete exclusion of another opposite, thus: "But to him that worketh not, but believeth on Him that justifieth the ungodly, his faith is accounted for righteousness." (iv, 5.) "For the promise was not made to Abraham through the law, but through the righteousness of faith." (13.) "Ye are become dead to the law, that ye should be married to Christ." (vii, 4.) As, likewise, in the passage at present under consideration, "There is, therefore, now no condemnation to them who are in Christ Jesus, who walk not after the flesh, but after the Spirit," From these remarks, it is apparent that the words after the flesh, but after the Spirit," do not belong to the description either of the subject or of the attribute of the preceding conclusion, as if they were described who are in Christ, but that they are the consequent or the antecedent itself of the same conclusion, though enunciated in a form somewhat different. This is likewise evident from the very words; for the pronoun, τοιv "those," which is properly subservient to this matter, is not used in this clause. 3. The same thing is taught in the second verse, in which these two things are united, "the law of the Spirit of life in Christ Jesus," that have reference to these two things in the preceding verse, "Those in Christ Jesus," and walking after the Spirit." But let us inspect the verse itself, which reads thus: "For the law of the Spirit of life in Christ Jesus hath made me free from the law of sin and death." Before we compare this verse with that which preceded it, we must give a preliminary explanation of the phrases used in it. "The law of the Spirit" is, therefore, called the right, the power, and the force or virtue of the Holy Spirit; for the apostle continues in the mode of speaking which he had previously adopted in the seventh chapter, where he attributes a law to sin, to the mind and to the members, that is, the power and force of commanding and impelling. The Spirit is here called that "of life," that is, "the vivifying Spirit" by a phrase familiar to the Hebrews, who employ the genitive cases of substantives instead of adjectives; as "the city of God," "the man of God," "the God of justice," &c. But the Spirit is thus designated in opposition or distinction to the law of the letter, or the letter of the law, which is weak for the work of vivification, and knows nothing more than to kill--according to this passage, "The letter killeth, but the Spirit giveth life," (2 Cor. iii. 6) and according to this: "for if there had been a law given which could have given life, verily righteousness should have been by the law." (Gal. iii. 21.) But this "law of the Spirit of life" is said to be "in Christ Jesus," not because it is only in the person of Christ Jesus, but because it can be obtained in Jesus Christ alone; according to this declaration: "Believers receive the Spirit, not by the works of the law, but by the hearing of faith." (Gal. iii. 2,5.) This phrase, "in Christ," is very often used in the same manner in the apostolical writings. But that the phrase is to be received in this sense also in the present passage, is manifest, (1.) From the scope or design of the apostle, which is to teach, that not through the law, but through the grace of Christ, believers obtain righteousness and the Holy Spirit, by whose power they may be enabled to have dominion over sin, and to yield their members instruments of righteousness unto God. (2.) From comparing this passage with the first verse. For, "to those who are in Christ Jesus," is attributed freedom from condemnation, because "the vivifying Spirit in Christ Jesus has made them free from the law of sin and death." (3.) Because this "vivifying Spirit" does not "deliver from the law of sin and death," except as it is communicated "to those who are in Christ Jesus." But to this "Spirit of life" is attributed that "it makes those who are in Christ Jesus free from the law of sin and death;" that is, from the power and tyranny of sin reigning, and killing by means of the law. This deliverance or emancipation is opposed to the captivity unto the law of sin," of which mention is made in Romans vii. 23, and to "the body of death" which is mentioned in verse the twenty-fourth. From this "law of sin," and from this "body of death," a man who is under the law could be delivered neither through the law of Moses, nor through "the law of the mind" which "consents to the law of God." But from this is also most admirably proved the conclusion deduced in the first verse from those which preceded it [in the seventh chapter]. For "deliverance from the law of sin and death" is opposed to "condemnation;" and, therefore, when the former of those is laid down, the latter is removed. This deliverance is attributed "to those who are in Christ Jesus," and "who walk according to the Spirit," from which it follows, that they are made free from condemnation. But the reason why this deliverance is attributed to that subject, arises from the cause of deliverance, that is, the vivifying Spirit, which Spirit, as it exists in Christ and is to be obtained in him, is likewise in "those who are in Christ Jesus." Wherefore, it is not at all wonderful, that this Spirit exercises his own proper force and efficacy in those persons in whom he dwells; and since this force or virtue is so peculiar to him, that he has it not in common with the law of Moses, it follows from this, that those only "who are in Christ Jesus" and are partakers of his Spirit, or that those who, being in Christ Jesus, are partakers of his Spirit, are delivered from condemnation, while those who are under the law remain under condemnation, as being those who are overcome by "the law of the members," and have been "brought into captivity under the law of sin," no successful resistance being offered by "the law of the mind," which "consents to the law of God." We have already said that, from a comparison of this verse with the twenty-third verse of the preceding chapter, an unanswerable argument is deducible in proof--that, in the two verses now specified, the apostle is not treating about the same man; but that, in the twenty-third verse of the seventh chapter, he treats about a man who is under the law, and in this second verse, about one who is under grace; because the man described in the former of these verses is "brought into captivity under the law of sin and death," and this by "the law of the members," "the law of the mind" offering fruitless resistance; but the man who is mentioned in the second verse, by the power of the life-giving Spirit, whom he has obtained in Christ Jesus, is "made free from the same law of sin and death." 4. Let us consider the third verse, in which the same thing may appear still more plainly to us; for in it the cause is explained why men who are under the law, cannot be made free from the dominion and condemnation of sin; but it is shown that this is obtained for them and effected by Christ. But the cause is this, because deliverance from the law of sin and death, or freedom from condemnation, could not be obtained except by the condemnation of sin, that is, except sin had been previously despoiled of the [assumed] right which it possessed, and of its power which it exercised over men who were subject to it. But it possessed the right and power of exercising dominion and of killing. But sin could not be despoiled of its right, and deprived of its power, by the law; for the law was rendered "weak, through the flesh," for the performance of such an arduous service. When God saw this state of things, and was unwilling the unhappy race of men should be perpetually detained under the tyranny and condemnation of sin, "he sent his own Son in the likeness of sinful flesh, and indeed for sin," that is, for destroying it, and he condemned sin in the flesh of his Son, who bore sin in his own body [on the tree] and took away from it that authority over us which it possessed, and weakened its powers. From these remarks it appears that this passage, which has hitherto been accounted one of great difficulty, is plain and perspicuous, provided each part of it be arranged aright, in the following manner: "For God, having sent his own Son in the likeness of sinful flesh and for sin, condemned sin in the flesh; which was a thing impossible to the law, because it was weakened through the flesh." For "that which the law could not do" is, "the condemnation of sin in the flesh?' Hence it is manifest, that this verse briefly explains the whole cause why sin reigns unto death over men who are under the law, and why it possesses neither the authority nor the power of reigning over "those who are in Christ Jesus" and under grace. This may be briefly shown from a comparison of those things which had been previously said, with this verse. For these words, "what was impossible to the law because it was weakened by the flesh," agree with the following declaration, contained in the fifth verse of the preceding chapter: "When we were in the flesh, the motions of sing, which are by the law, did work in our members;" and with these words in the fourteenth verse, "We know that the law is spiritual, but I am carnal;" they also agree with the eighteenth verse, "I know that in me, [that is, in my flesh,] dwelleth no good thing." But these words, "God, in the flesh of his Son, condemned sin," agree with what is said in the sixth verse, of the preceding chapter: "But now we are delivered from the law, that being dead wherein we were held;" that is, sin being condemned which held us bound and in subjection to it. But, in this passage, the cause is more fully explained, that in the flesh of Christ such condemnation was effected. 5. From these observations is deduced the meaning of the fourth verse, plainly agreeing with those which preceded. It is this, after it had come to pass, that sin was condemned in the flesh of the Son of God, the right or authority of the law was completed and consummated in those who are in Christ Jesus, and who walk after the Spirit; so that they are no longer under the guidance and government of the law, but under the guidance of Him who has delivered us from sin, and who has claimed us for his own people. This is plainly expressed by the apostle, in the fourth verse of the preceding chapter, in these words: "Ye also are become dead to the law in the body of Christ, that ye should be married to another, even to Him who is raised from the dead, that we should bring forth fruit unto God." For these phrases agree with each other: "Ye are become dead to the law," and, "the right or authority of the law is fulfilled or completed in you." And, "in the body of Christ ye are become dead to the law," is the same as, "sin was condemned in the flesh of Christ, that the right or authority of the law might be fulfilled in us." But when the right of the law is completed and consummated by the condemnation of sin which was effected in the flesh of Christ, we belong or are married to another, that is, the right is transferred from the law to Christ, that we may be no longer under the law, but under Christ, and may live under grace and the guidance of his Spirit. For these words, "that the right or authority of the law might or may be fulfilled in us," must not be understood as if, when sin had been condemned in the flesh of Christ, the right or authority of the law was still to be completed; but that after the condemnation of sin in the flesh of Christ, the right of the law was actually fulfilled. Several forms of speech, similar to this, are used in this manner in the Scriptures. For instance: "All this was done, that it might be fulfilled which was spoken of the Lord by the prophet: (Matt. i. 22) "He came and dwelt in a city called Nazareth, that it might be fulfilled which was spoken by the prophets, He shall be called a Nazarene." (ii, 23.) "He came and dwelt in Capernaum, which is upon the sea coast, in the borders of Zabulon and Nephthalim, that it might be fulfilled which was spoken by Esaias the prophet, saying, The land of Zabulon, and the land of Nepthalim, &c., light is sprung up to them who sat in the region and shadow of death." (iv, 13-16.) "He cast out the spirits With His word, and healed all that were sick, that it might be fulfilled which was spoken by Esaias the prophet, saying, Himself took our infirmities," &c. (viii, 16,17.) See also Matt. xii. 17; xiii, 35; xxvi, 56. In all these examples, the phrase, "that it might be fulfilled," evidently means that the prediction was actually fulfilled by those acts which are mentioned in the several passages. This is also signified by a phrase different from the preceding, in Matt. xxvii. 9, "Then was fulfilled that which was spoken by Jeremy the prophet." It is lawful also to change the mode of speech in this verse, (Rom. viii, 4,) into another exactly of the same import: "Then was fulfilled the right or authority of the law in us." In addition to these, consult Matt. xxvii. 35; Luke xxi. 22; John xiii. 18; xvii, 12; xviii, 9; and innumerable other passages. From this explication it is apparent, that this portion of holy writ, (Rom. viii. 1-4,) is plain and perspicuous, though, without this interpretation, it is encompassed with much obscurity, as almost all interpreters have confessed, while they have laboured hard to explain it. We will now, by permission, compress all these remarks into a small compass, and briefly recapitulate them; what I have advanced will then become far more evident. Let us do this in the following manner: "Since, therefore, we have already seen, that men under the law are held captive under the dominion and tyranny of sin, we may easily conclude from this, that those only who are in Christ Jesus, and who walk after the Spirit and not after the flesh, are free from all condemnation; because the law, the right, the power, the force or virtue of the vivifying Spirit, which is and can be obtained in Jesus Christ alone, has liberated persons of this description from the law, the power and this force of sin and death, from the empire and dominion of sin, and of its condemnation. Christ Jesus could lawfully do this by his Spirit, as being the person in whose flesh sin was condemned, that it has no longer any right, neither can have any, over those who are Christ's; in which flesh, indeed, He was sent by his Father, because this very thing was impossible to the law, weakened as it was through the flesh. And thus it has come to pass, that the right of the law, which it had over us when we were still under the law, is completed or fulfilled in persons of this description, who have become Christ's people through faith, that they might hereafter live, be influenced, and governed by his grace and according to the guidance of the Holy Spirit. From these things we may certainly conclude that sin cannot have dominion over them, and therefore, that they are able to yield their members instruments of righteousness to God, as those who have been translated from the death of sin to the life of the Spirit." But these topics the apostle pursues as far as the sixteenth verse of this eighth chapter, in a manner accommodated to the same scope or design as we have hitherto pointed out; and he seems always mindful of the exhortation which he had given in Romans vi, 12,13; from the conjoint reason in which he descends into the succeeding long investigation. These observations, however, may suffice, lest we be too operose in demonstrating a matter that is so plain and perspicuous.

SECOND PART

I. THE OPINION WHICH IS TO BE CORROBORATED BY TESTIMONIES

This opinion, which explains Romans 7, as relating not to a man under grace, but to one who is placed under the law, and to one who is not yet regenerated by the Spirit of Christ, was never yet condemned in the church of Christ, as heretical, but has always had some defenders among the doctors of the church. We will now approach to the second part of our proposition, which we have judged it right to treat for the purpose of making it evident to all men, that the opinion which I defend is not of recent growth, neither has it been fabricated by my brain, nor borrowed from some heretic, but that it is very ancient, and approved by a great part of the doctors of the primitive church, and that, besides, it has never been so far rejected, by those who have given a different interpretation to the passage, as to induce them to judge it worthy of being branded with the black mark of heresy.

II. THE MOST ANCIENT AND MOST RESPECTABLE OF THE CHRISTIAN FATHERS APPROVE OF THE INTERPRETATION WHICH WE GIVE TO THIS CHAPTER

Irenaeus. 2. Tertullian. 3. Origen. 4. Cyprian. 5. Chrysostom. 6. Basil the Great. 7. Theodouret. 8. Cyril. 9. Macarius the Egyptian. 10. Damascenus. 11. Theophylact. 12. Ambrose. 13. Jerome. 1. IRENAEUS Irenaeus thus cites part of this chapter in lib. 3, cap. xx, "On this account, therefore, he, who through the virgin is Emmanuel, God with us, the Lord himself, is the sign of our salvation; because he was the Lord who saved them, as through themselves, they possessed not the means of being saved. On account of this also, when St. Paul is shewing the weakness of man, he says, I know that in me, (that is, in my flesh,) dwelleth no good thing, thus intimating that the blessing of salvation is not from us, but from God. And again, O wretched man that I am, who shall deliver me from the body of this death? He then infers a deliverer, the grace of Jesus Christ our Lord." In this quotation, [when referring to St. Paul's declaration,] he does not say, "a regenerate Man," "a believer," or Christian," but simply "a man," under which appellation, neither the Scriptures nor the fathers are accustomed to speak of one who is a Christian, a believer, and a regenerate man. 2. TERTULLIAN For though he denied that in His flesh dwelt any good thing, yet it was according to the law of the letter in which he was; but according to the law of the Spirit, with which he connects us, he delivers from the weakness of the flesh. He says, "For the law of the Spirit of life hath manumitted thee from the law of sin and death." For though he seems to dispute on the part of Judaism, yet he directs to us the integrity and plenitude of instructions, on account of whom, as labouring "in the law through the flesh, God sent his own Son in the likeness of sinful flesh, and for sin, condemned sin in the flesh." (On Chastity, cap. 17.) In this sentence, Tertullian openly affirms, that the passage must be explained concerning "a man who is under the law of the letter." Nor is it a very great objection if any one assert, that this book was written by him while he was in a heresy; for on this point he was not heretical, and the opinion, it is apparent, had then obtained, that this chapter was to be understood in this manner. 3. ORIGEN But with respect to what he says, "but I am carnal, sold under sin," on this occasion, as a teacher of the church, he takes upon himself the personation of the weak, on which account he has also said in another passage, "to the weak became I also as weak." Therefore, in this passage St. Paul is made "a carnal man and sold under sin," to those who are the weak, (that is, to the carnal,) and who are sold-under sin, and he speaks those things which it is their practice to utter under the pretext either of excuse or of accusation. Speaking, therefore, as in their person, he says, "but I am carnal, sold under sin," that is, living according to the flesh, and reduced, [as a servant] by purchase, to the power of sin, lust and concupiscence; "for that which I do, I allow not," &c. And he (that is, Paul the carnal man) here says, "now then it is no more I that do it, but sin that dwelleth in me." But in other passages Paul the spiritual man says, "I laboured more abundantly than they all, yet not I, but the grace of God which was with me." Therefore, as he thus ascribes his labours, not to himself, but to the grace of God which worked in him; so does that carnal man attribute the evil works, not to himself, but to sin that dwelleth and worketh in him. On this account he says, "now then it is no more I that do it, but sin that dwelleth in me; for in me, (that is, in my flesh,) dwelleth no good thing." For Christ does not yet dwell in him, neither in his body yet the temple of the Holy Spirit. Nevertheless, this man whose character is personated is not in every respect averse from good things, but in purpose and in will he begins to seek after good things. But he cannot yet obtain such things in reality and in works. For there is a certain infirmity of this kind in those who receive the beginnings of conversion, that when they truly will instantly to do every thing that is good, the effect does not immediately follow the will. (On Romans 7.) 4. CYPRIAN When treating upon the contest between the flesh and the Spirit, in his sixth Discourse On the Lord's Prayer, as well as in his pamphlet On the Celibacy of the Clergy, Cyprian does not cite Romans 7, but he quotes Gal. v. 17, "The flesh lusteth against the Spirit, and the Spirit against the flesh," &c. But that he understood Romans 7, to relate not only to the indwelling of sin, but also to its dominion, is evident from his Prologue concerning the Cardinal Works of Christ, in which, among other remarks, the following occurs - - "If I do not know who it is that inscribed this law in my members that it may, with such violent domination, oppress the Spirit, and that the better and more worthy nature may succumb to the worse, I must patiently endure it if I do not understand the Almighty Operator of the universe." He adds, in a subsequent passage of the same prologue: It is difficult to understand wherefore this law of sin, in this and in similar individuals, oppresses the law of righteousness, and wherefore weak and enervated reason so miserably falls, when it is able to stand; especially when this defect depends on the sentence of damnation, and the ancient transgression has obtained this inevitable punishment." 5. CHRYSOSTOM When treating professedly on this portion of holy writ and explaining it, in his comment on Romans 7, Chrysostom, after confirming what he had advanced in the preceding verses, expresses himself in the following manner: Therefore, Paul subjoined this assertion, "but I am carnal, sold under sin." Thus describing a man who lives under the law and before it. Therefore, sin itself is adverse to the law of nature. For this is what he says, "Warring against the law of my mind." It also imposes on the law of nature a universal contest and warfare, when it afterwards draws up in battle array the forces of sin. For the Mosaic law was lastly added beyond what was necessary. But, though the former law teaches indeed those things which ought to be done, and though the latter unites in extolling them; yet neither the one nor the other has performed any execution in this battle against sin. So great is the tyranny of sin, so wonderfully prevailing and overcoming! This is likewise intimated by St. Paul, when, after announcing the conflict of opposing and predominant sin, he says: "But I see another law in my members, warring against the law of my mind, and bringing me into captivity to the law of sin." For he does not simply say, "conquering me," but "rendering me a captive to the law of sin." Neither does he say, "bringing me into captivity to the impulse of the flesh or of carnal nature," but "bringing me into captivity to the law of sin," that is, to the tyranny and power of sin. O wretched man that I am! who shall deliver me from the body of this death? Do you here behold how amazingly great is the tyranny of wickedness, and how it also overcomes the mind which "finds a condelectation, or joint delight, in the law of God?" For he says, "It is not that any one says I hate the law of God "or am averse to it, and am brought into captivity to sin. For "I find a condelectation in the law, I consent to it, and flee to it." Yet it was not able to save him when he fled to it. But Christ has saved him, when he was fleeing, from it. Here you acknowledge the great excellence of grace. And in his Commentary on Romans viii. 9, he says: After sin has been destroyed, this difficult warfare is terminated by the grace of the Holy Spirit, through which the contest is now become easy to us. For this grace first Crowns us [as Victors], and then leads us forth to battle honourably attended by numerous auxiliary forces. 6. BASIL THE GREAT But we will now adduce what he has said in another passage, when delivering the same doctrine, in a manner far more objurgatory: "For we know that the law is spiritual; but I am carnal, sold under sin. For that which I do I allow not," &c. And, prosecuting this speculation in more particulars, that it is impossible for him who is held captive by sin to serve the Lord, he manifestly points out to us our Deliverer from this tyranny, while he says, "O wretched man that I am I who shall deliver me from this body of death, I give thanks to God through Jesus Christ our Lord," &c. (On Baptism, lib. 1 fol. 409.) It is, therefore quite necessary, both from the things already related, and from others of a similar kind, (if we have not received the blessing of God in vain,) that we be first delivered from the power of the devil, who leads the man that is detained in captivity by sin to [the commission of] those evils which he would not, and then, having denied all things present, and our own self, and having left all kindred feeling for this life, that we become the Lord's disciples, as he hath himself said, "If any man will come to me, let him deny himself," &c. (Ibid.) This is what he who is unwillingly drawn by sin ought to know, that he is governed by another sin pre-existing in himself, which while he willingly serves, with regard to other things he is led by it even to those which he does not will. As it is said in Romans 7, "For we know that the law is spiritual; but I am carnal, sold under sin," &c., quoted as far as the seventeenth verse, "but sin that dwelleth in me. (Summary of Morals, Sum. 23, cap. I, fol. 477.) The spirit or mind, which is the patient bearer of the dominion of the affections or inclinations, is not permitted by them to be free to [do] those things which it wills, according to the speculation of the apostle already related, who said, "but I am carnal, sold under sin. For what I would, that do I not; but what I hate, that do I." (Compendium of Questions explained, Quest. 16, fol. 563.) "Now then it is no more I that do it, but sin that dwelleth in me," God himself permitting even this to befall us for our good, if by any means the mind, through those things which it reluctantly suffers, may be brought to understand that which has the dominion over it; and if, knowing itself, that it unwillingly serves sin, it recover from the snare of the devil, and seek for the mercy of God which is prepared to receive those who are legitimately penitent. (Ibid.) 7. THEODORET But I am carnal. He introduces a man before [he has obtained] grace, who is beset with motions and perturbations of mind. For he denominates that man carnal who has not yet obtained spiritual grace. (On Romans 7.) For what I would, that do I not; but what I hate, that do I. The law beautifully effects one thing, that is, it teaches what is evil, and induces a hatred of it on the mind. But these words, "I would not," and "I hate," signify weakness, and not necessity. For we do not sin, as being impelled by necessity or by some force; but, being enticed by pleasure, we do those things which we abhor as wicked and flagitious deeds. (Ibid.) I delight in the law of God after the inward man. He has called the mind "the inward man" (Ibid.) But I see another law in my members, warring, &c. He bestows on sin the appellation of "the law of sin." It exerts its operation when the corporeal perturbations of the mind are in lively motion; but, on account of that supineness with which the mind has invested itself from the beginning, it is unable to restrain them. Though the mind has cast away its own liberty, yet it has patience enough to serve them. But though the mind thus serves them, yet it hates servitude; and commends him who brings an accusation against servitude. After the apostle had discoursed on all these topics, that he might show what sort of people we were before grace, and our condition after grace, and having taken on himself the personation of those who, before grace, had been besieged and encompassed by sin; therefore, as though he was completely surrounded by a mass of enemies, and led away into captivity and compelled to become a slave, and seeing no aid from any other quarter, he grievously groans and laments; he shows that help could not be afforded by the law, and he cries out, "O wretched man that I am!" (Ibid.) There is therefore now no condemnation, &c. For the perturbations of our mind do not overcome us who are now unwilling, because we have accepted the grace of the divine Spirit. (On Romans 8.) For the law of the Spirit of life in Christ Jesus, &c. As he called sin "the law of sin," so does he call the vivifying Spirit "the law of the Spirit." he says, that the grace of this Spirit, through faith in Jesus Christ, has endowed thee with a two-fold liberty; for it has not only broken the power of sin, but it has also destroyed the tyranny of death. (Ibid.) 8. CYRIL For what the law could not do, in that it was weak through the flesh, &c. Therefore, when the only Begotten became man for us, the law of sin was indeed abolished in the flesh; and our affairs were brought back again that they may return to their first origin. For death, corruption, pleasures and other lusts prevailed, which, having corruption as their assistant, committed depredations on the weak and infirm mind. (Against Julian, lib. 3, fol. 184.) So then with the mind I myself serve the law of God, but with the flesh,, the law of sin. There is, therefore, now no condemnation to them who are in Christ Jesus, &c., quoting the whole passage down to the 5th verse. For the flesh and the spirit manifestly fight the one against the other; that is, carnal prudence and the motions of innate lusts war against the power of life according to the Spirit. Though the divine law urges us that we ought to choose the good, yet the desire of the flesh is born, towards that which is contrary. But now that is loosened which hindered, and the law of sin is weakened; but the law of the Spirit has prevailed. On what account, "For God hath sent his own Son in the likeness of the flesh of sin, that he might condemn sin in the flesh." Now, in what manner was not the incarnation of the Word exceedingly useful, For even "our sin is here condemned in the flesh." But if the Word had not been made flesh, our affairs would have remained without any amendment, and we should now be serving in the flesh the law of sin, no one having abolished it within us. (On the True Faith, to the Queens, lib. I, fol. 283.) We confess, therefore, that, by Adam's personal transgression of the law, the human substance has been corrupted; and that, by the pleasures of the flesh, and those motions which are so pleasing to our nature, our understanding is oppressed as by the domination of a tyrant. Wherefore it was necessary for our salvation, who are sojourners on earth, that the WORD OF GOD should become man, and he should take human flesh upon himself as his own, given up though it was to corruption, and sickly through the allurements of pleasure; and that, as he is the life of all, he should indeed destroy its corruption, but restrain its innate motions, that is, those which impelled us headlong to vices and pleasures; for in this manner it was necessary that offenses should be mortified in our flesh. But we recollect that the blessed Paul denominates the voluptuous motions which art planted within us, "the law of sin." Wherefore, because human flesh became a property of the WORD, it has now ceased to yield to corruption. And because he knew no sin, as God who united him to himself, and, as I have already said, who made [human nature] a property [of the WORD], it has now ceased to be sick with vices and pleasures. Neither did the only begotten Son of God perform this for himself, (for he is the Word which always exists,) but he undoubtedly did it for us. For if we are alike brought into captivity through Adam's transgression of the law, therefore the blessings which are in Christ will descend upon us, and which are incorruption and the destruction of sins. (First Epistle to Successus.) 9. MACARIUS THE EGYPTIAN Adam having transgressed the command of God, and having obeyed the impious serpent, sold himself to the devil; and thus wickedness invested his mind, that excellent creature, which God had formed after his own image, as the apostle likewise says: "Having spoiled principalities and powers, and triumphed over them in his cross." For the Lord came on this account, that he might expel them, [the principalities and powers,] and might receive his own house and his proper temple, which is MAN. The mind, therefore, is called "the body of darkness and of wickedness," so long as it has within itself the darkness of sin; because it lives there in a wicked world of darkness, and is there detained captive. As Paul likewise, when giving it the appellation of "the body of sin and death," says "that the body of sin might be destroyed." And again, "Who shall deliver me from the body of this death?" On the contrary, the mind that has believed in God, is both delivered from the mortified sin of a life of darkness, and has received the light of the Holy Spirit as its life; living in which, from that time it perseveres; because it is there governed by the light divine. (Homily 1.) From this, it is evident, that Macarius understood this passage, as referring to a man who was subjected to the spirit of darkness, the slave of sin, and the captive of Satan, and who, not being yet dead to sin, has not received the light of the Holy Spirit, that is, who is not yet regenerated by the Spirit of Christ. 10. DAMASCENUS In the fourth book of his Orthodox Faith, (cap. 23,) he explains this matter very satisfactorily; wherefore, it will not be considered irksome, if at greater length we transcribe his opinion in his own words, as they have been rendered by his Latin translator: The law of God, when coming to our mind, attracts it to itself, and stimulates our consciences. But our conscience is also called "the Law of our mind." But the suggestion of the devil, that is, the law of sin, when coming to the members of the flesh, also commits itself, through the flesh, to us. For, after we have once voluntarily transgressed the law of God, and have admitted the suggestion of the devil, we have granted entrance to him, being brought into captivity by our own selves to sin: Whence our body is promptly led on to commit sin. Therefore, the odour and feeling of sin is said to be inherent to our body, that is, the lust and pleasure of the body, "the law in the members of our flesh." Therefore, "the law of the mind," that is, the conscience, feels a sort of condelectation in the law of God, that is, in the commandment which it really wills. But "the law of sin," that is, the suggestion through. the law which is in the members, that is, the concupiscence, the inclination and motion of the body, by means of the irrational part of the soul also "wars against the law of my mind," that is, my conscience, and brings me, consenting to the law of God and not fulfilling it, yet not desiring sin, into captivity, according to contradiction through the enticement of pleasure and the lust of the body, and the brute part of the soul which is devoid of reason--as I have before said, it causes me to err, and persuades me to serve sin. "But what was impossible to the law, in that the law was rendered weak through the flesh, God, sending his own Son in the likeness of the flesh of sin," (for he assumed flesh, but by no means sin,) "condemned sin in the flesh, that the righteousness of the law might be fulfilled in us, who walk not after the flesh, but after the Spirit." For "the Spirit strives with our infirmity," and affords strength to "the law of the mind" in our souls, against "the law which is in our members." 11. THEOPHYLACT He says, "I am carnal," that is, human nature universally--both that part of it in existence before the enactment of the law, and that at the time of the giving of the law--had a numerous multitude of passions associated with it. For we not only became mortal through Adam's transgression of the law, but human nature, being "sold under sin," receives likewise corrupt inclinations, being evidently subjected to the authority and domination of sin, so that it cannot raise its head. (On Romans 7.) This weakness, therefore, the law could not cure, though it dictated what ought to be done, but when Christ came, he healed it. This then is the scope or design of those things which the apostle has said, or will yet say--to shew that human nature has endured those things which are immedicable, and that it cannot be restored to soundness by any other than by Christ, and by him alone. (ibid.) O wretched man that I am! who shall deliver me from the body of this death? The law of nature was not able, the written law could not; but the tyranny of sin conquered both of them. Whence, therefore, is the hope of salvation, &c. (Ibid.) I yield thanks to God through Jesus Christ. For he has performed those things which the law was unable to do. For he has delivered me from weakness of body, inspiring into it strength and consolation, that it may no longer be oppressed by the tyranny of sin. 12. AMBROSE Whether St. Ambrose, or some other person, was the author or the interpolator of those Commentaries on the Epistle to the Romans, which generally pass under his name, the following are some of his remarks on the seventh chapter: That he is sold under sin, is that he derives his origin from Adam, who first sinned, and by his own transgression rendered himself subject to sin, as Isaiah says, "For your iniquities have ye sold yourselves." (i, 1.) For Adam first sold himself; and by this act, all his seed was subjected to sin. Wherefore man is too full of weakness to observe the precepts of the law, unless he be strengthened by divine aids. Hence arises that which he says, "The law is spiritual, but I am carnal," &c.; that is, the law is strong, and just, and faultless; but man is frail, and subjugated by the offense of his progenitor, that he is unable to use his power with regard to yielding obedience to the law. He must therefore flee to the mercy of God, that he may avoid the severity of the law, and being exonerated from his transgressions, may, with regard to other things, resist his enemy under the favour of heaven. But to perform that which is good I find not. Therefore, that which is commanded by the law is pleasing to him, and his will is to do it; but, in order to its completion, power and virtue are wanting; because he is so oppressed by the power of sin, that he cannot go where he would; neither is he able to contradict, because another is the lord and master of his power. (Ibid.) That he may extol the grace of God, the apostle expounds these words, concerning the great evils from which it has delivered man; that he might point out what destructive materials he derives from Adam, but what blessings through Christ have been obtained for him whom the law could neither succour nor relieve. (Ibid.) Let the whole [of the rest of the] passage be perused. 13. JEROME We have sinned, and have committed iniquity, and have done wickedly, and have rebelled, &c. Undoubtedly the three Hebrew children had not sinned, neither were they of that [accountable] age when they were led away to Babylon, so as to be punished for their vices. Therefore, as they here speak in the person of their nation at large, so we must read and apply that passage of the apostle, "for what I would, that do I not," &c. (On Daniel 9.)

III. THE OPINION OF ST. AUGUSTINE

Quotations from his writings. 2. These passages confirm the interpretation of the author. It is objected, that St. Augustine afterwards gave a different explanation, and retracted his former opinion; to this the reply is, it appears that his interpretation of this chapter was free from any such change. 3. What St. Augustine properly retracted is shown by quotations from his writings. 4. His modesty in the explanation of this chapter. He understands this passage to refer, not to actual sins, but to the internal motions of concupiscence. 1. But let us approach to St. Augustine, and see what was his opinion concerning this passage, since my opinion is loaded and oppressed with the weight of his authority: If then I do that which I would not, I consent unto the law that it is good. The law is indeed sufficiently defended from all crimination. But we must be on our guard to prevent any one from supposing, that, by these words, the free exercise or choice of the will is taken away from us; which is not the fact. For now is described a man placed under the law, before [the arrival of] grace. (Exposition of certain Propositions from the Epistle to the Romans, cap. 7.) But I see another law in my members, warring against the law of my mind, &c. He calls that "the law of sin" by which every one is bound who is entangled in the habit or nature of the flesh. He says that this wars against "the law of the mind," and "brings it into captivity to the law of sin." From this, the man is understood to be described who is not yet under grace. For, if the carnal habit or nature were only to maintain a warfare, and not to bring into captivity, there would not be condemnation. For in this consists condemnation--that we obey and serve corrupt and carnal desires. But, if such desires still exist and do not all disappear, yet in this case we do not yield obedience to them, we are not brought into captivity, and we are now under grace, concerning which he speaks when he cries out for the aid of the Deliverer, that this might be possible through the grace, of love, which fear was not able to do through the law. For he has said, "O wretched man that I am! who shall deliver me from the body of this death," And he added, "the grace of God through Jesus Christ our Lord." He then begins to describe man placed under grace, which is the third degree of those four into which we have distinguished mankind. (Ibid.) But not being yet content with the past inquiry and explanation, lest I had, with too much negligence, passed by any thing in it, (Rom. 7,) I have still more cautiously and attentively examined the very same words of the apostle, and the tenor of their meanings. For you would not consider it proper to ask such things, if the manner in which they may be understood were easy and devoid of difficulties. For, from the passage in which it is written--"What shall we say then? Is the law sin? God forbid," unto that in which the apostle says, "I find then a law, that, when I would do good," &c., and, I believe, as far the verse in which, it is said, "O wretched man that I am! who shall deliver me from the body of this death, The grace of God through Jesus Christ our Lord"--you wished me to elucidate or resolve the question first from these passages, in which the apostle seems to me to have transfigured unto himself, a man placed under the law, with whose words he speaks from his own person. (To Simplicianus, the Bishop of the Church of Milan.) Hence it is evident, FIRST, that the church had at that period prescribed nothing definite concerning the meaning of this passage: For Simplicianus, the bishop of Milan, indeed, officiating in the very Church in which St. Ambrose had formerly discharged the Episcopal functions, would not have earnestly requested to have the opinion of St. Augustine, if the opinion to be maintained concerning it had been prescribed. Secondly. After St. Augustine had diligently considered the matter, he openly declares, that the whole passage must be understood as referring to a man under the law. "For," he says, "I was without the law once." By this he plainly shows that he was not speaking properly in his own person, but generally in the person of "the old man." (Ibid.) He afterwards subjoins the cause why it is so, and says, "For we know that the law is spiritual, but I am carnal," in which he shows, that the law cannot be fulfilled except by spiritual persons, who do not become such without the aid of grace. (Ibid.) Indeed, when he had said--"but I am carnal," he also subjoined the kind of carnal man that he was. For even those who are now placed under grace, and who are now redeemed by the blood of Christ, and born again through faith, are called "carnal" after a certain manner; to whom the same apostle says, "And I, brethren, could not speak unto you as unto spiritual, but as unto carnal," &c. (1 Cor. iii. 1.) But that man who is still under the law and not under grace, is so very carnal as not yet to be born again from sin, but to be sold under the law by sin; because the price of deadly pleasure embraces that sweetness by which a man is deceived and delighted to act even contrary to the law, since the pleasure is greater in proportion to its unlawfulness, &c. "He consents, therefore, to the law of God," inasmuch as he does not what it prohibits, but chiefly by not willing that which he does. For, not being yet liberated by grace, he is conquered [by sin], although through the law he is both conscious that he is acting improperly, and is reluctant. But with regard to that which follows, where he says, "Now then it is no more I that do it, but sin that dwelleth in me;" he does not, therefore, say it, because he does not consent to commit sin, though he consents to the law by disapproving of the sin which he commits. But he is still speaking in the person of a man placed under the law, who is not yet under grace, and who is indeed drawn, by reigning concupiscence and by the deceitful sweetness of prohibited sin, to perpetrate evil, though, through his knowledge of the law, he partly disapproves of such bad actions. But this is the reason why he says, "It is no more I that do it," because, being conquered, he does it, since it is done by evil desires, to whose conquering power he yields. But grace causes him no longer thus to yield, and strengthens the mind of man against lusts, of which grace the apostle is now about to treat. (Ibid.) SEE ALSO WHAT IMMEDIATELY FOLLOWS THIS QUOTATION. "To will is present with me." He says this with respect to facility. For what can be more easy, to a man placed under the law, than to will that which is good, and to do what is evil, &c. (Ibid.) But the whole of this is said for the purpose of shewing to man, while yet a captive, that he must not presume on his own strength or power. On this account he reproved the Jews as proudly boasting about the works of the law, when they were attracted by concupiscence to whatsoever was unlawful, though the law, of which they boasted, declared "Thou shalt not covet," or indulge in concupiscence. Therefore, a man who is conquered, condemned and captivated, must humbly declare--a man who, after having received the law, is not as one that lives according to the law, but is rather a transgressor of it, must humbly exclaim, "O wretched man that I am," &c. (Ibid.) 2. That man who will compare these passages from St. Augustine with my arguments concerning Romans 7, will perceive that we entirely agree in sentiment, and that I subscribe to this opinion of St. Augustine. From these extracts, it likewise appears that nothing had, at that period, been prescribed by the church concerning this portion of the apostolical writing,, but nothing towards that part especially--that it was to be understood about a man who is regenerate and placed under grace. But I am here met with this objection: "St. Augustine, in subsequent years, gave a different explanation to this chapter, that is, as being applicable to a regenerate man placed under grace, as he has done in the 43rd, 45th, and 47th of his discourses On Time, and in several other passages." I confess, that the fact was as it is here stated; and we will afterwards examine those passages; we shall perceive how much they are able to contribute towards the establishment of the opinion that is opposed to mine. "But," the same objectors say, "St. Augustine retracted and condemned that very opinion which he had first explained in his treatise, entitled, An Exposition of certain Propositions in the Epistle to the Romans, and in his book addressed to Simplicianus, bishop of Milan; his authority, therefore, cannot be adduced in confirmation of that opinion." To this I might reply, First, from the fact of St. Augustine having first entertained the same opinion about this passage as I do, and afterwards a different one, it is evident that neither of these opinions had been considered by the church in the light of a catholic or universally admitted doctrine. Secondly. It is possible that St. Augustine may, in the beginning, have held a more correct opinion than that which he subsequently maintained, especially when, in the first instant, he followed his own judgment, which had been formed from an accurate inspection of the entire chapter, and from a diligent comparison of different sentiments on the subject; but he was afterwards influenced by the authority of certain interpreters of holy writ, as he informs us in his Retractions, (lib. I, cap. 23,) though he adds, that he had with much diligence considered the subject; for he did not consider it without some of that prejudice which he had imbibed from the authority of those expositors. 3. But though I might make those preliminary replies, yet the answer which I will give is this: St. Augustine never trusted or condemned that opinion by which he had explained this chapter as applicable to a man placed under the law; but he only retracted this part of his early opinion "These words must not be received as uttered in the person of the apostle himself, who was then spiritual, but in that of a man placed under the law and not yet under grace." For he had made two assertions, First, that this chapter must be understood as relating to a man placed under the law. Secondly, that it must neither be understood as relating to a man placed under grace, nor as relating to the apostle himself who was then spiritual. The former of these assertions was never retracted by St. Augustine; the latter he has retracted, as will most clearly appear to any one who will examine the passage, which it will be no trouble to transcribe on this occasion, since the works of this father are not in the hands of every one. In the first book of his "Retractions," (cap. 23,) he says: "While I was yet a priest, it happened that the Epistle of the apostle to the Romans was read among us who were at that time together at Carthage, and my brethren made inquiries of me about some passages in it, to which when I had given as proper replies as I was able, it was the wish of my brethren that what I spoke on this subject should be written out, rather than be uttered in an extemporaneous manner; when, on this point I had acceded to their request, another book was added to my Opuscula. In that book I say, But when the apostle asserts, For we know that the law is spiritual; but I am carnal, sold under sin, he shows in a manner sufficiently plain, that it is impossible for the law to be fulfilled by any persons, except by those who are spiritual, and are made such by the grace of God.' This I wished not to be received in the person of the apostle, who was at that time spiritual, but in that of a man placed under the law, and who was not yet under grace. For that was the manner in which I first understood these words; which I afterwards considered with more diligence, after having perused the productions of certain commentators on the divine oracles, by whose authority I was moved; and I perceived that, when he says for we know that the law is spiritual; but I am carnal, sold under sin, the words may also be understood as referring to the apostle himself. This I have shown, with as much diligence as I was able, in those books which I have lately written against the Pelagians. "In this book, therefore, I have said that, by the words but I am carnal, sold under sin, through the remainder of the chapter to the verse in which he says, O wretched man that I am! a man is described who is still under the law, but not yet placed under grace, who wills to do that which is good, but who, conquered by the desires of the flesh, does that which is evil. From the dominion of this concupiscence the man is not delivered, except by the grace of God through Jesus Christ our Lord, by the gift of the Holy Ghost, through whom love being diffused, or shed abroad, in our hearts, overcomes all the desires of the flesh, that we may not consent to those desires to do evil, but rather that we may do good. By this, indeed, is now overturned the Pelagian heresy, that will not admit that the love by which we live good and pious lives is from God to us, but that asserts it to be from ourselves. "But in those books which we have published against the Pelagians, we have shown, that the words of the apostle in Romans 7, are better understood as those of a spiritual man who is now placed under grace on account of the body of flesh which is not yet spiritual, but which will be so in the resurrection of the dead, and on account of carnal concupiscence itself, with which the saints maintain such a conflict, not consenting to it for evil, as not to be without its opposing motions in this life which yet they resist. But the saints will not have such motions to evil in that world in which death will be swallowed up in victory. Therefore, on account of this concupiscence and those motions to which such a resistance is given as they may still be in us, [or as suffers them yet to be in us,] every holy person who is now placed under grace can utter all those words which I have here said are the expressions of a man who is not yet placed under grace, but under the law. To show this, would require much time; and I have mentioned the place where I have shown it." (Ibid.) "Of the books which I wrote when a bishop, the first two were addressed to Simplicianus, bishop of the church of Milan, who was successor to the blessed Ambrose--in them I discussed diverse questions. Two of the questions on which I treated in the first book, were from St. Paul's Epistle to the Romans. The first of them was on what is written in vii, 7 -- What shall we say then? Is the law sin? God forbid! -- down to the 25th verse in which it is said, Who shall deliver me from the body of this death? The grace of God though Jesus Christ our Lord. In that book, I have expounded these words of the apostle, The law is spiritual, but I am carnal, and the other expressions by which the flesh is shown to contend against the Spirit. In it I have explained them in such a manner as that in which a man is described who is still under the law, but not yet placed under grace. For a long time afterwards elapsed, before I discerned that they could also be the words of a spiritual man, and this with a stronger semblance of probability." (Retractations, lib. 2, cap. 1.) 4. These are the passages transcribed with verbal accuracy, in which St. Augustine retracts the opinion which he had previously explained, from which it is apparent that he neither rejected his former opinion, nor convicted it of falsehood, error or heresy; but that he only said, "This passage in the apostle's writings may also be understood as referring to a man who is regenerate, spiritual, and placed under grace, and this much better and with more probability than concerning a man placed under the law;" yet he says that this [his first] opinion is opposed to the Pelagian heresy. But the very words which he employs in his Retractations teach us, that this chapter in the apostolical writings may likewise be understood concerning a man who is placed under the law, but [according to his latest judgment] not so well, and with less probability. We see therefore, that the modesty of St. Augustine was at an immense distance from the vehemence of those who assert, that "this part of holy writ must be understood concerning a man who is placed under grace, nor can it by any means be explained as referring to a man placed under the law without incurring the charge of Pelagian heresy." Let the reader examine, if he pleases, the works of St. Augustine, (tom. 10,) concerning the words of the apostle, (Sermon 5, on Romans vii. 7, fol. 59, col. 3,) "Speak to me, holy apostle, about thyself, when no one doubts that thou art speaking about thyself." And in the same sermon, (col. 4,), If, therefore, I say that the apostle speaks of himself, I do not affirm it." But it is improper for this last, whether it be an explanation or a retractation of St. Augustine, to be urged by those who reject the cause of this change, by which, he openly declares, he was moved to suppose that this passage might likewise be explained in reference to a man under grace, and this much better and with greater probability. He says that the cause of it was, because he perceived that this man might be called "carnal" on account of the body of flesh which is not yet spiritual, and because he has yet within him the desires of the flesh, though he does not consent to them. This is also the opinion of those expounders whom St. Augustine says he followed. But our divines who oppose themselves to me on Romans 7, do not explain that chapter in this manner, as, -- to will that which is good, is to will not to lust or indulge in unlawful desires, and to do evil, is to lust; but they explain it, actually to do or to commit that which is evil. The authority, therefore, of St. Augustine ought not to be produced by them; because, as we shall afterwards more clearly demonstrate, his judgment was this: If this chapter be explained as referring to actual sins, it cannot be explained concerning a regenerate man. But if it be explained respecting a regenerate man, it must necessarily be understood only concerning the inward motions of concupiscence or lust. Wherefore, I have St. Augustine in his first opinion, fully agreeing with me, and in his latter not differing greatly from me; but those who are opposed to me have St. Augustine contrary and adverse to them in both these his opinions. IV.

OUR OPINION IS SUPPORTED BY SEVERAL WRITERS OF THE MIDDLE AGES

Venerable Bede. 2. St. Paulinus. 3. Nicholas De Lyra. 4. Ordinary Gloss. 5. Interlineary Gloss. 6. Hugh the cardinal. 7. Thomas Aquinas, who thinks that Romans vii. 14, may be explained in both ways, but he refers its application to a regenerate man. 8. He is of opinion, that the 17th and 18th verses can only be considered by a forced construction to relate to a man under sin. His reasons for advancing this last assertion are examined and answered. 9. An abbreviation of the comments which Thomas has given on these two verses; with a conclusion deduced from them, that they may be appropriately understood to relate to a man under the law, but in no other than a forced manner to a man under grace. 1. VENERABLE BEDE For we know that the law is spiritual, but I am carnal. Perhaps, therefore, it is some other person, or perhaps thyself. Either thou art the person, or I am. If, therefore, it be some one of us, let us listen to him as if concerning himself, and, divesting our minds of angry feelings, let us correct ourselves. But if it be he, [the apostle,] let us not thus understand what he has said, "What I would, that do I not; but what I hate, that do I." (On Romans 7.) Therefore, because he thrice intreated the Lord, that this thorn might be taken away from him; and because he who was, not heard according to his wishes, was heard according to that which was for his healing; he perhaps does not speak in a manner that is unbecoming when he says, The law is spiritual, but I am carnal." (Ibid.) 2. ST. PAULINUS And I am perfectly aware that this blessed man prefers to employ my weakness; and, lamenting concerning my afflictions, he cries out, instead of me, "O wretched man that I am" (Second Epistle to Severus Sulpicius, Priest at Tours.) 3. NICHOLAS DE LYRA For we know that the law is spiritual and placing men in right order to follow the instigation of the Spirit or of reason. (On Romans 7.) But I am carnal, that is, I follow the impulse of the flesh or of sensuality; and the apostle speaks, as was before observed, in the person of the fallen human race, in which there are more persons who follow the impulse of sensuality than that of reason. After the inward man that is according to the natural dictates of reason; because reason is called "the inward man," and sensuality "the outward man." O wretched man that I am! In this passage, he consequently begs to be delivered, speaking in the person of all mankind, "O wretched man that I am" through the corruption of nature! So then, with the mind, I serve the law of God that is, according to the inclination of reason. But with the flesh, the law of sin by following the inclination of the flesh. 4. ORDINARY GLOSS "For we know that the law is spiritual," &c., quoted to the end of the chapter. It is not perfectly clear whether these things are better understood as spoken in his own person, or in that of all mankind. (On Romans 7.) 5. INTERLINEARY GLOSS But I am carnal unable to resist the corruption of my mind or the devil. (On Romans 7.) Sold under sin in my first parent, that I may be really under sin as a servant. Now then it is no more I that do it under the law before the times of grace. Evil is present with me with my reason; it is near to my inward man. I see another law the fuel or flame, which reigns. Warring against the law of my mind, the law and my reason united together in one. Bringing me into captivity through consent and working, because it governs by habit or custom. To the law of sin for sin is the law, because it has the dominion. The grace of God, not that the law, nor my own powers, but that the grace of God delivers. So then with the mind the rational and inward man, having, as before, fuel. 6. HUGH THE CARDINAL For we know that the law is spiritual. This is the third part of the chapter, in which he shows, that those things which were commanded in the law of Moses, cannot be fulfilled without the law of the Spirit, that is, without grace. But I am carnal that is, frail and weak to resist the devil and the lust of the flesh. For what I would according to reason, that is, I approve. but what I hate that is, evil. But from this it is inferred that he wants the spiritual law, by which he may do that which he wills according to reason. There is, therefore, now no condemnation. The preceding things have been expounded concerning the captivity of mortal sin under which man was carnally living, and concerning the captivity of the venial sin of the man who is in grace; and that the law of the Spirit, or grace, delivers from the captivity of death; and he draws this inference: "There is, therefore, now no condemnation," that is, no mortal sin through which is condemnation. 7. THOMAS AQUINAS But I am carnal. He shows the condition of the man: And this expression may be expounded in two ways. In one way, that the apostle is speaking in the person of a man who is in sin. And St. Augustine expounds it thus in the 83d hook of his Questions. But, afterwards, in his book against Julian, he expounds it, that the apostle may be understood to speak in his own person, that is, of a man placed under grace. Let us proceed, therefore, in declaring what kind of words these are, and those which follow them, and how they may be differently expounded in either manner, though the second mode of exposition is the best. (On Romans 7.) I am fully aware that the same Thomas has marked out two passages in this chapter, which he asserts it to be impossible to explain concerning an unregenerate man except by a distorted interpretation. But it will repay our labour if we inspect those passages, and examine those reasons which moved Thomas to hold this sentiment. The first passage is the 17th verse: "Now then it is no more I that do it, but sin that dwelleth in me." The second passage is the 18th verse: "For I know that in me (that is, in my flesh) dwelleth no good thing." (1.) He says "that the first of these passages cannot, except by a distorted interpretation, be understood concerning a man who is under sin; because the sinner himself perpetrates that din, while he is one who, according to the principal part of himself, that is, according to his reason and mind, consents to the perpetration of sin. But this must properly be attributed to a man, which belongs to him according to what is man; but he is a man by his mind and his reason." But I answer, First, It is said, not only respecting a man who is under sin, that he does not perpetrate sin except with his mind and reason, which dictate, that sin is forbidden by the law, which yet are conquered through the lust of the flesh, and by the consent of the will, but it is likewise said respecting the regenerate and those who are under grace; for these persons do not actually commit sin except with a mind that is conquered, and through consent of the will; and, therefore, it is a vain attempt to be desirous to distinguish, in this manner, between him, who is under sin and him who is under grace. Secondly. I deny that all those who are under sin commit iniquity with the consent of their mind, that is, without any resistance of conscience. For when those persons who are under the law, sin, they do this against conscience and with a mind that is reluctant, because they are overcome by the tyranny of sin and carnal concupiscence. Thirdly. Though the matter really were as he has stated it, yet it would not follow that it cannot be said of this man by any interpretation, except a distorted one: "It is no more he that commits this sin, but it is sin." A reason is produced by Thomas himself; for the man does this through the motion and compulsion of sin which dwelleth in him and has the dominion. But effects are usually ascribed to the principal causes; therefore, this verse may be understood, without any distorted meaning, to relate to a man who is under the law. If any one, according to the judgment of St. Augustine, declare--"It cannot be attributed to a man who actually gives his consent to sin, that he does not himself commit it, but sin, and, therefore, the perpetration of it must be understood as relating not to the consent to evil and the commission of it, but to concupiscence or evil desire, and thus this act belongs to a man under grace," to this objection, I reply that I deny the antecedent, as I have previously observed; but I confess that if it be understood concerning concupiscence alone, and not concerning the consent to sin and the actual perpetration of it, the expression contained in this verse can by no means, not even distortedly, be employed concerning a man who is under the law and under sin. (2.) Thomas says "that the latter of these passages, the 18th verse, cannot be explained, except in a distorted manner, concerning a man under sin, on account of the correction which is added, and which it was unnecessary to adduce if the discourse were about a man under sin, as being one who has no good thing dwelling either in his flesh or in his mind. To this, I reply that the antecedent is false; for we have already demonstrated, in the remarks on this 18th verse, that, in the mind of a man who is under the law, some good exists and dwells, as Thomas here employs the word to dwell - - nay, that it also reigns and has the dominion, as the word ought properly to be received. Therefore, the ignorance of Thomas about this matter, caused him thus to think and to write. 9. But let the entire comment of Thomas on this passage be perused, and it will then appear, that all these things in the two verses may be explained in the plainest manner concerning a man under the law, but with much perversion and contortion about a regenerate man who is placed under grace, I show this in the following brief manner, having united together, in a compendious summary, those things which he has treated with greater prolixity, as any one may perceive on referring to his pages: "If the man or the reason be called fleshly or carnal because he is attacked by the flesh--if to do signifies the same as to lust or desire--if to will good, and not to will evil, be taken for a complete volition and nolition, which continue in the election or choice of a particular operation; -- but if to commit evil, and not to do good, be understood according to an incomplete act, which consists only in the sensitive appetite, not reaching so far as to the consent of reason--if this captivity be produced solely at the motion of concupiscence--if deliverance from the body of this death be desired, that the corruption of the body may be totally removed, then the expression in this passage of Scripture must be understood concerning a regenerate and just man, who is placed under grace. "But if this man or reason be called fleshly or carnal because he is in subjection to the flesh, consenting to those things to which he is instigated by the flesh--if to do be the same thing as to execute by actual operation--if to will that which is good, and not to will what is evil, be taken in the acceptation of an incomplete volition and nolition, by which men will good in general and do not will what is evil, and if they do neither of these in particular; -- but if to commit evil, and not to do good, be understood according to a complete act, which is exercised in external operation through the consent of reason--if this captivity be produced through consent and operation or doing, and, lastly, if deliverance from the body of this death be desired or asked, that the corruption of the body may not have dominion over the mind, drawing it to commit sin, then the expressions in this passage must be understood concerning a man who is a sinner, and who is placed under the law." But let us now subjoin--A man who is attacked by the flesh, yet who conquers it in the conflict, is not called fleshly or carnal; but this appellation is bestowed on the man who, by yielding his consent, is brought into subjection to the flesh. The apostle is here treating about a volition and a nolition that are incomplete and imperfect, and about the actual perpetration of evil and the omission of good, and not solely about the act or motion of lusting or desiring; (for this is declared by the matter itself, for the man wills and does not, therefore the volition is imperfect.) This captivity is not at the motion of concupiscence alone, but it is by consent and operation; for either concupiscence itself, or the law of the members, brings a man into captivity through the waging of war against the law of the mind; and the deliverance which is required is from the corruption of the body, that it may not have dominion over the mind, and not that it may be totally removed; for the apostle presents a thanksgiving to God for having obtained that which he had desired. Therefore, this passage must be understood, not about a man under grace, but about one who is under the law; not about a man who is already restored by grace, but about one who is yet to be restored. Our proposition is taken from Thomas Aquinas. We have added the assumption from the text itself.

V. THE FAVOURABLE TESTIMONIES OF MORE RECENT DIVINES

is good, and I hate evil. To will, is present with me. With the mind, I myself serve the law of God." These undoubtedly are not the traits of a wicked or profane man, and of one who is not yet approaching to God; but they are those of a holy man who loves God and who trembles at his words. For God rescues us by certain degrees from that death into which we are all born. First, he suffers us, for some time, to live in ignorance, disregarding his judgments. At this period, "sin is dead," &c. But when it has pleased God to terminate this ignorance, he sends forth his law, and gives us to see that it is "holy, and just, and good." From this, it necessarily arises that "we consent to the law," that we will what it commends, and that we are abhorrent from those things which it condemns. But if the Spirit of Christ do not afford unto us powerful succour, this love of God and consent to his law remain so weak, and the force of sin which is still within us prevails so strongly, that, through the correction and command of the law, the depraved lusts become the more inflamed, and we occasionally do, not only by lusting or desiring, but also by actually committing, that which we ourselves detest, and we neglect those things of which we are not capable of doing otherwise than approving and willing. But these things cause the dread of the divine judgment to increase within us, by which we are completely unnerved, and deprived of sensation. All these effects are produced by the law, but through the corruption of our depraved nature; and it is the condition of the period now mentioned, which the apostle describes in himself in the present chapter. But whilst God, who is the Father of mercies, resolves more fully to impart himself to us, and vouchsafes more bountifully to bestow the Spirit of his Son upon us, by this, his Spirit, he represses and subdues that power of sin which otherwise impels us against the law and authority, how much soever we may consent to the law itself; he implants within us a true judgment concerning things, and a solid love, [honest, for that which is upright and honourable, so that now, with pleasure, and with a confirmed and perpetual inclination or purpose, we live the life of God. This condition of holy people is described by the apostle in the subsequent chapter, in which he declares that "the law of the Spirit of life in Christ Jesus had made him free from the law of sin and death." (Rom. viii, 2.) As, therefore, the apostle in this place begins to declare what the law, of itself, effects in holy people, and from this begins to commend it when it is so exceedingly beneficial, yet he asserts that it cannot render a man just before God, but that it drives him to Christ who alone can justify. And he brings forward in this place, and points out, the condition of a man of God, which is that of the middle age of holy people, in which the law is indeed already known, but not yet fully inscribed on the heart; that is, when the mind of man consents to the law of God, but the appetite of nature still offers resistance, and impels to act in opposition to the precepts of the law. I repeat it, in this condition, the apostle has proposed himself for an example, that he might point out in himself what power the law possessed, and how all things are death, until the Spirit of Christ obtains greater influence within us. But St. Paul did not still contend with his nature after the manner which is described in this passage, for he soon afterwards declares that "the law of the Spirit of life in Christ Jesus had made him free from the law of sin and death," and that through the Spirit of Christ, "the righteousness of the law was now fulfilled in him, as he walked, not after the, flesh, but after the Spirit." (On Romans 7.) 7. WOLFGANG MUSCULUS The law, indeed, has righteousness and justification, by commanding those things which are just. But it is impossible that it should have that by which to justify; for it is hindered and rendered inefficacious through the flesh, that is, through the corrupt and depraved inclinations of the flesh, through which it comes to pass that a man who is carnal, and the slave of sin, is incapable of obeying those commands which are holy, and just, and good. (Common Places in the chapter on the laws, under the title of The Power and efficacy of the law.) We say that the power and efficacy of the law, which is called "the letter," is two-fold. The one is that which it produces of its own, and may be called proper. The other is improper, which it does not bring from itself, but which it performs through the corruption of our flesh. The first is proper, because it produces the knowledge of sin. On this subject, the apostle speaks thus: "I had not known sin but by the law; for I had not known lust except the law had said, Thou shalt not covet." (Rom. vii. 7.) He also says, "By the law is the knowledge of sin." (iii, 20.) (Ibid.) He afterwards not only speaks about "the knowledge of sin," which consists of the understanding, but he also speaks principally about that knowledge of it which is received by a lively feeling of sin in our flesh; that is, the law causes me not only to understand, but likewise with gnawing remorse of conscience to feel and to experience that sin is within me. It is proper, because it convinces us that we are inexcusably guilty of sin, subjects and condemns us to malediction, (Gal. iii, 10,) and, through a feeling of sin, and when terrified of condemnation, it renders us anxious, and desirous of the grace of God. Hence, arises that which is the subject of the apostle's investigation in Romans 7, when at length he cries out, "O wretched man that I am! who shall deliver me from the body of this death? The grace of God through Jesus Christ."(Ibid.) After the apostle, in Romans 7, has disputed about the power and efficacy of the law, which works in carnal and natural men, speaking in the next chapter of the grace of the Holy Spirit, which is bestowed on those who believe in Christ, he subjoins--"for the law of the Spirit of life in Christ Jesus hath made me free from the law of sin and death," &c. under the title of the Law of the Spirit.) St. Paul understands "the law of sin" to be the power and tyranny of sin reigning in our flesh, by which we are violently dragged and impelled to commit sin. "The law of death" is that by which sinners are adjudged to death eternal. Therefore "the law of the Spirit of life" not only produces this effect in us, that we are not condemned on account of the imputation of righteousness which is through faith in Christ; but it likewise extinguishes the power of sin in us, that sin may now no longer reign in us, but the strength and grace of Christ, and that we may no more serve sin, but righteousness, nor be obnoxious to death, but challenged and claimed for the true life. (Ibid.) For the more lucid explanation of this matter, we must observe the three degrees of the saints, by which they are divinely led to the perfection of piety: The first is of those who resemble drunken men, and who, having for some time lulled to sleep all judgment and every good inclination, live in sins, the law of God not having yet produced its effect in them; the second degree is of those who, by what way soever they may have returned to themselves, the judgment of their reason being now illuminated, and their inclinations changed, desire that which is good, and thus consent to the law of God and delight in it, and really abhor that which is evil; but the tyranny of sin still prevailing, they are reluctantly drawn to evil things; and, therefore, the good of which they approve, and which they desire and will, they perform not; but the evil which they hate and avoid, they perpetrate, though their consciences exclaim against it, and though the judgment of their minds dictate something far different, &c. To this second degree must be referred those things of which St. Paul here treats in his own example. The Third Degree is of those who have been rescued into the liberty of righteousness, after having, through the Spirit, subdued and conquered the power and wickedness of sin, that they do not now obey the law of sin, but the law of the Spirit that reigns in their members, and possesses the double faculty of willing and doing. About this degree, the apostle will treat in the subsequent chapter. (Comment on Romans 7.) I thank God through Jesus Christ our Lord. A most wonderful and sudden turn of the affections. He had just before deplored himself as a wretched man and a captive, and almost immediately he gratefully returns thanks. From this, we perceive that St. Paul now uses his own person, not that which he sustained when he wrote these things, but that which he had formerly represented. (Ibid.) There is, therefore, now no condemnation. As he had previously described the condition of the man who was living in a legal spirit, so now he describes and points out the condition of him who is endued with the evangelical Spirit. (On Romans 8.) The mutual and unanimous agreement of the witnesses whom I have here produced, will, according to my judgment, very easily liberate my opinion from all surmise and suspicion of novelty.

THIRD PART

I. THIS OPINION IS NEITHER HERETICAL NOR ALLIED TO ANY HERESY

.In this third part, two things are contained: the first is a negative--that this, my interpretation of Romans 7 is not favourable to the Pelagian heresy. The principal dogmas of the Pelagian heresy are recounted from St. Augustine. 2. It is proved by induction and by comparison that this interpretation agrees with none of these dogmas. 3. Two rejoinders to the contrary. An answer to the first of them, that every good thing must not be taken away from the regenerate. 4. An answer to the second. The truth must be confirmed, and falsehood refitted, by solid arguments. 5. It is proved from St. Augustine that the doctrine which relates to the necessity of the grace of Christ, and to the impossibility of the law for the conquest of sin, was accounted by the ancients to be of far more importance than that which proves the perpetual imperfections of the regenerate in this life. 6. To this, the fathers of the Council of Carthage seem to give their assent, in their epistle to Pope Innocent. Thesis.--No heresy, neither that of Pelagius nor any other, can be derived or confirmed from this opinion. But this opinion is, in the most obvious manner, adverse to Pelagianism, and affords a signal and professed confutation of its grand and leading falsehood. 1. This thesis contains two parts. The First is, that this opinion is neither heretical, nor allied to heresy. The Second that it is directly contrary to the Pelagian heresy, and professedly refutes it. With regard to the First of these parts, because it consists of a negation, those who maintain the affirmative of it must destroy it by the proof of the contrary. I am desirous, therefore, to hear from them what heresy it is which this opinion advocates and favours. They will undoubtedly announce it to be that of Pelagius. But I require a proof of the particular point in which there is the least agreement between this opinion and Pelagianism. Let us shew, however, ex abundanti, that this opinion is not favourable to Pelagianism. The following heads of doctrine are those which St. Augustine has laid down in his book on Heresies and his Hypognosticon, as belonging to Pelagianism: (i.) Whether Adam had sinned, or had not sinned, he would have died. (ii.) The sin of Adam was injurious to no one except to himself; and therefore, (iii.) Little children do not contract original sin from Adam; neither will they perish from life eternal, if they depart out of the present life without the sacrament of baptism. (iv.) Lust or concupiscence in man is a natural good; neither is there any thing in it of which man may be ashamed. (v.) Through his free will, as per se, man is sufficient for himself, and is able to will what is good, and to fulfill or perfect that which he wills. Or even, for the merits of works, God bestows grace on every one. (vi.) The life of the just or the righteous in this life has in it no sin whatsoever; and from these persons, the church of Christ in this state of mortality are completed, that it may be altogether without spot or wrinkle. (vii.) Pelagius, being compelled to confess grace, says that it is a gift conferred in creation, is the preaching of the law, and the illumination of the mind, to know those things which are good and those which are evil, as well as the remission of sins if any one has sinned, excluding from this [definition of grace] love and the gift and assistance of the Holy Spirit, without which, he says, the good which is known may be performed, though he acknowledges that this grace has also been given for this purpose--that the thing may be the more easily done, which can indeed be otherwise done by the power of nature, but yet with greater difficulty. 2. These are the principal dogmas of the Pelagian heresy, to which others, if any such there be, may be referred. But none of these dogmas are patronized by the opinion which explains Romans 7, as applicable to a man placed under the law, and in the manner in which we have explained it, and as St. Augustine has declared it in his book entitled "The Exposition of certain Propositions from the epistle to the Romans," and in his first book to Simplicianus. This will be proved thus by induction: (i.) Our opinion openly professes that sin is the only and sole meritorious cause of death, and that man would not have died, had he not sinned. (ii.) By the commission of sin, Adam corrupted himself and all his posterity, and rendered them obnoxious to the wrath of God. (iii.) All who are born in the ordinary way from Adam, contract from him original sin and the penalty of death eternal. Our opinion lays this down as the foundation of further explanation; for this original sin is called, in Romans 7, "the sin," "the sin exceedingly sinful," "the indwelling sin," "the sin which is adjacent to a man, or present with him," or "the evil which is present with a man and" the law in the members." (iv.) Our opinion openly declares that concupiscence, under which is also comprehended lust, is an evil. (v.) The fifth of the enumerated Pelagian dogmas is professedly refuted by our opinion; for, in Romans 7, the apostle teaches, according to our opinion, that the natural man cannot will what is good, except he be under the law, and unless the legal spirit have produced this willing in him by the law; and though he wills what is good, yet it is by no means through free will, even though it be impelled and assisted by the law to be capable of performing that very thing. But it also teaches that the grace of Christ, that is, the gift of the Holy Spirit and of love, is absolutely necessary for this purpose, which grace is not bestowed according to merits, (which are nothing at all,) but is purely gratuitous. (vi.) The sixth of the enumerated dogmas of Pelagius is neither taught nor refuted by our opinion, because it maintain, that Romans 7 does not treat about the regenerate. But, in the mean time, the patrons and advocates of our opinion do not deny that what is said respecting the imperfection of believers in the present life, is true. (vii.) The seventh of the enumerated dogmas of Pelagius is refuted by our opinion; for it not only grants, that good can with difficulty be done by the man who is under the law, and who is not yet placed under grace; but it also unreservedly denies that it is possible for such a man by any means to resist sin and to perform what is good. 3. But some one will perhaps rejoin, and say "Your interpretation of this chapter is favourable to Pelagianism, on two accounts. First, because it attributes something of good to a man who is not yet regenerated and placed under grace. Secondly, because it takes away from the church a passage of Scripture, by which she is accustomed to prove the imperfection of the regenerate in the present life, and the conflict which is maintained between the flesh and the Spirit as long as man lives upon earth." With regard to the First of these objections, I reply that we must see, First, what kind of good it is that our interpretation attributes to a man who is unregenerate. For, it is certain that every good, of what kind soever it may be, must not be entirely taken away from an unregenerate man and one who is not yet placed under grace; because the knowledge of the truth, (Rom. i. 18,19,) the work of the law written in his heart, his thoughts accusing or else excusing one another, the discernment of what is just and unjust, (ii, 15,18,) the knowledge of sin, grief on account of sin, anxiety of conscience, desire of deliverance, &c., (vii, 7,9,13,24) are all good things, and yet they are attributed to a man who is unregenerate. Secondly. We must know that this, our opinion, which explains Romans 7 as relating to a man under the law, does not bring forth these good things from the storehouse of nature, but it deduces them from the operation of the Spirit, who employs the preaching of the law and blesses it. Thirdly. We must also consider that this was not a subject of controversy between the church and the Pelagians: "May something of good be attributed to an unregenerate man who is not yet under grace, but who is placed under the law; or may it not?" But the question between them was "Can something of good be attributed to man, without grace and its operation?" He who receives some operation of grace is not instantly under grace or regenerate; for grace prepares the will of man for itself, that it may dwell in it. Grace knocks at the door of our hearts; but that which has occasion to knock does not yet reside in the heart nor has it the dominion, though it may knock so as to cause the door to be opened to it on account of its persuasion. But we have frequently treated on topics similar to this in the first part of this our treatise. 4. With respect to the Second of these objections, I reply, First. This passage of Holy Writ was not produced by the church, in her earliest days, for establishing the imperfection of the regenerate in this life, and the conflict between the flesh and the Spirit such as that which is maintained in regenerate persons; for we have already shown that the most ancient of the Christian fathers did not explain Romans 7 in reference to the regenerate, or those who are placed under grace; though it subsequently began to be employed, by some divines, to establish this dogma. Secondly. It is inconsequent argumentation to say that "the opinion by which some passage is otherwise explained than it is by the many, nay which has been quoted by the church herself to destroy some heresy, is therefore or can be judged to be allied to heresy, because it takes away from the church a passage which has been usually employed to prove a true doctrine, and to refute a heresy." For if this be not inconsequent reasoning, there will scarcely be one of our divines who will not thus be deservedly judged to be allied to some heresy or other, and sometimes indeed to a very enormous one. By such a law [of criticism] as this, Calvin is called "an Aryan" by the Lutherans, because he openly avows in his writings, that "many passages of Scripture, which have been adduced by the ancient church (both Greek and Latin) to establish the doctrine of the trinity, do not contribute in the least to that purpose," and because he gives to them such a different interpretation. Thirdly. No detriment will accrue to the church by the removal of this passage, from the support of the imperfection of the regenerate in this life as she is furnished with a number (which is sufficiently copious) of other passages to prove the same doctrine, and to weaken the contrary one. This is abundantly demonstrated by St. Augustine, when be professedly treats upon, the Perfection of Righteousness in this life in opposition to Coelestius. Fourthly. We must well and carefully examine by what passages of Scripture, and by what arguments, the truth may be proved, and falsehood refuted, lest, if weak and less valid, and in some degree doubtful, passages and arguments be adduced, the hopes of heretics should be elevated, after they have demolished such weak bulwarks as those, and they should suppose it possible to disprove and confute the remaining [more suitable and valid] arguments on the same subject. For that man inflicts no slight injury on the truth who props it up by weak arguments; and the rules of art teach us, that a necessary conclusion must be verified or proved by necessary arguments; for the conclusion, follows that part [of a syllogism] which is the weakest. But it has been already shown, that this portion of Scripture has not been devoid of controversy even among the catholic commentators on the Holy Scriptures. Fifthly,. In what manner soever this chapter, as thus explained according to my mind, may not be able to serve the church to prove the imperfection of the regenerate in the present life, yet it serves her for the confirmation of another doctrine, and one of a far greater importance, against the Pelagians--that is, the necessity of the grace of Christ. and the incapability of the law to conquer or to avoid sin, and to order or direct the life of a man according to its rule. 5. But we may discover, from various passages in the writings of St. Augustine, the vast difference which the ancient church put between the necessity of the former of the two questions or doctrines, [specified in the preceding paragraph,] and the latter. For instance: But in that which Pelagius argues against those who say, "And who would be unwilling to be without sin, if this were placed in the power of man?" he in fact disputes correctly, that by this very question they own that it is not impossible, because either many persons or all men wish to be without sin. But let Pelagius only confess [from what source this is possible, and peace is instantly established. For the origin of it is the grace of God through Jesus Christ, &c. (On Nature and Grace, against the Pelagians, cap. 59.) There may be some question among real and pious Christians, whether there has ever been in this world, is now, or can possibly be, any man who lives so righteously as to have no sin whatsoever. Yet he is assuredly void of understanding who entertains any doubt whether it is possible for a man to be without sin after this life. But I do not wish to enter into a contest about this question. Though it seems to me that in no other sense can be understood what is written in the Psalms, and in similar passages, if any such there be: "In thy sight shall No man living be justified;" (cxliii, 2) yet it may be shown that even these expressions may be better understood in another sense, and that even perfect and complete righteousness, to which there may be no addition, was yesterday in an individual, while he lived in the body, is in him to-day, and will be in him to-morrow while there are still far more persons, who, while they do not doubt that it is necessary for them truly to say, even to the last day of [their continuance in] this life, "Forgive us our trespasses, as we forgive them that trespass against us," yet are firmly persuaded that their hope in Christ and in his promises is real, certain and firm, yet in no way except by the aid of the grace, of the saviour, Christ the crucified, and by the gift of his Spirit. I do not know whether that man can be correctly reckoned in the number of Christians of any description, who denies either that any persons attain to the most complete perfection, or that some arrive at any degree whatever of proficiency in true piety and righteousness. (Ibid. cap. 60.) Besides, though I am more inclined to believe that there is not now, has not been, and will not be, any one who is perfect with such a purity as this; and yet when it is defended and supposed, that there is, has been, or will be such a perfect man, as far as I am able to form a judgment, they who hold this opinion do not greatly or perniciously err, &c. But those persons are most strenuously and vehemently to be resisted, who suppose it possible either to fulfill or to perfect the righteousness of the human will, by its own power, without the aid of God, or by aiming at it to make some proficiency. (On the Spirit and the Letter, cap. 2.) Consult likewise his treatise On Nature and Grace, cap. 42, 43, 58, & 63; in which he briefly says--"It is no question at all, or not a great one, what man is perfected, or the time. when he becomes so, as long as no doubt is entertained that it is impossible for this to be done without the grace of Christ." See also his treatise On the Demerit and Remission of Sin, lib. 2, cap. 6,14; and lib. 3, cap. 13. 6. But in order that we may know this to have been the opinion not only of St. Augustine, but also of the church universal, let us listen to the bishops assembled together in the Council of Carthage, who write in the following manner to Pope Innocent: "But in what manner soever this question turns itself, because though a man is not found in this life without sin, yet it may be said to be possible by the adoption of grace and of the Spirit of God; and that [such perfection] may be attained we must urge most importunate intreaties and use our best endeavours. Whosoever is deceived on this point, ought to be tolerated. It is not a diabolical impiety, but it is a human error, to affirm that it must be MOST diligently pursued and desired, though it cannot shew that which it affirms; for it believes it possible for that to be done which it is undoubtedly laudable to will." We perceive, therefore, that Romans 7, when explained according to my mind, is serviceable to the church in establishing a doctrine of far greater importance than that which is declared from the other opinion. "But," some one will say, "it is possible to establish both these doctrines, [the imperfection and the perfection of the regenerate,] From that opinion which explains the chapter as relating to a man who is under grace." I reply, granting this, yet I deny that it is possible to establish both in a direct manner; for, one doctrine, that of the imperfection of the regenerate in this life, will be directly proved from this passage, and the other will be deduced from it by consequence. But it is a matter of much importance, whether a doctrine be confirmed by a passage of Scripture properly explained and according to the intention of the Scriptures, or whether it be deduced from them by the deduction of a consequence. For some passages of Scripture are like certain seats, out of which controversies ought to be determined; and those which are of this kind are usually employed in a very stable and safe manner for the decision of controversies. II.

OUR OPINION IS DIRECTLY OPPOSED TO THE PELAGIAN HERESY

THE Second thing contained in this third part is an affirmation, that our interpretation of Romans 7 is professedly adverse to the Pelagian heresy. 2. This is proved from the fact, that the principal dogma of that heresy is professedly confuted through this very interpretation. 3. In some passages of his works, which are here cited, St. Augustine confesses with sufficient plainness that this is true. 4.Objection and an Answer to it. 5. Another Objection--that Prosper Dysidaeus, the Samosatenian, explains this chapter in the same manner. Answer--no heretic is in error on every point. The Jesuits, those myrmidons of the pope, explain this chapter as referring to a man placed under grace. 6. A third objection--that his interpretation differs from the confessions of the reformed churches, which have been framed and established by the blood of martyrs. Answer--no article of any confession is contrary to this interpretation: No man ever shed his blood for the contrary interpretation. Numbers of martyrs were not even interrogated about this article on the perfection of righteousness. 1. I now come to the second part of the thesis, in which I said, that this chapter, when explained as referring to a man who is under the law, is directly and professedly contrary to the Pelagian heresy. Though I have already proved this in part, on the occasion of replying to the preceding objection, yet I will now at somewhat greater length teach and confirm it. 2. We have just seen that the article of the Pelagian heresy which is by no means either the last or the least, is that in which it is asserted that a man is able through his own free will, as being of itself sufficient for him, to fulfill the precept of God, if he be only instructed in the doctrine of the law, so as to be capable of knowing what he ought to perform and what to omit. It appears that this dogma is not only firmly refuted, but that it is also plucked up as if by the roots and extirpated, according to the very design and purpose of the apostle, by means of this chapter, when it is understood as referring to a man under the law. This is apparent from the opposition of the dogma to the context of the apostle. The former says, "Man, instructed by the teaching of the law, is capable, by the powers of his free will alone, to overcome sin and to obey the law of God." But the apostle declares that this cannot be effected by the powers of free will and of the law. he says, "sin shall not have dominion over you; for ye are not under the law, but under grace," (Rom. vi. 14,) from which it is manifest that, if they were under the law, sin would have the dominion over them--a consequence upon which he treats more copiously in the seventh chapter. Pelagius says, "Man is able, without the grace of Christ, and instructed solely by the teaching of the law, to perform the good which he wills, through his free will, and to omit the evil which he does not will;" but the apostle declares that this man "consents indeed to the law that it is good, but that to perform what is good he finds not in himself; he omits the good which he wills, and he performs the evil which he wills not." Therefore, the doctrine of the apostle is, independently of its consequence, directly repugnant to the Pelagian dogma, and this, indeed, from the scope and end which the apostle had, in the same chapter, proposed to himself. But, from passages of this description, heresies are far more powerfully convicted and destroyed, than they are from passages accommodated to their refutation beyond the scope and intention of the writer, though this also be done according to the correct meaning of the same passages. 3. St. Augustine himself confesses that, when this chapter is explained in reference to a man under the law, it is adverse to the Pelagian heresy: "But," says Pelagius, "why should I thus exclaim, who am now baptized in Christ? Let them make such an exclamation who have not yet perceived such a benefit, and whose expressions the apostle transferred to himself, if indeed this is said by them? But this defense of nature does not permit them to cry out with this voice. For nature does not exist in those who are baptized; and, in those who are not baptized, nature has no existence. Or, if nature is granted to be vitiated even in baptized persons, so that they exclaim, not without sufficient reason--O wretched man that I am! who shall deliver me from the body of this death? -- and if succour is afforded to them in that which immediately follows, The Grace of God through Jesus Christ our Lord, let it now at length be granted, that human nature requires the aid of a physician. (On Nature and Grace, cap. 54.) From these remarks it is apparent, according to the mind of St. Augustine, that this passage, even when it is understood in reference to a natural man, is destructive to that dogma of Pelagius, in which he asserts that the natural man is able, by the powers of nature, to perform the law of God. Thus also in a passage upon which we have already made some observations from his Retractations, lib. I, cap. 23, St. Augustine openly affirms that this chapter, when explained as relating to a man under the law, confutes the Pelagian heresy. These are his words: "By this, indeed, is now overturned the Pelagian heresy, that will not admit that the love, by which we live good and pious lives, is from God to us, but that asserts it to be from ourselves." Besides, if we can obtain from them even this admission, that those who are not yet baptized implore the aid of the saviour's grace, this will indeed be no small matter against that false defense of nature, as being sufficient for itself, and of the power of free will. For he is not sufficient for himself who says, O wretched man that I am! who shall deliver me? or else he must be said to possess full liberty, who still requires to be liberated. (On nature and Grace, cap. 55.) But at this point, on account of which we have undertaken the consideration of these things, the apostle begins to introduce his own person, and to speak as if concerning himself. In this passage the Pelagians are unwilling that the apostle himself should be understood, but assert that he has transferred to himself another man who is yet placed under the law, and not delivered through grace, in which passage they ought indeed to concede "that by the law no man is justified." as the same apostle has declared in another part of his writings, but that the law is of force for the knowledge of sin and the transgression of the law itself; that, after sin has been known and increased, grace may be required through faith. (Against the two Epistles of the Pelagians to Boniface, lib. I, cap. 8) 4. "But," some man will say, "the Pelagians have interpreted that chapter as applicable to a man who is unregenerate, not without good reason. They undoubtedly knew that such an interpretation was peculiarly favourable to their sentiments which they defended against the church." To this I reply, First. It has already been shown, both in reality, and by the testimony of St. Augustine, that this chapter, even when understood as applicable to a man under the law, and not yet regenerate, is adverse to the Pelagian doctrine. Secondly. It may have happened that the Pelagians supposed the chapter might be explained in reference to a man placed under the law, and not under grace, without any consideration of the controversy in which they were engaged with the orthodox. Thirdly. It cannot favour the sentiments of the Pelagians, that the apostle is said in this chapter to be treating about a man under the law; but this might be favourable, that they adduced such a description of a man who is under the law, as they knew was accommodated to strengthen their sentiments. For they said that "a man under this law is he who, by the power and instinct of nature, (which was not corrupted in Adam,) is able to will that which is good, and not to will what is evil; but who, through a depraved habit, was so bound to the service of sin, as in reality, and actually he was not able to perform the good which he would," &c. This false description of the man might also be met, not by denying that the subject of this chapter is a man under the law, but by refuting that description. For heretics are not heretical on all subjects and in every point; and it is their usual practice to intermix true things with those which are false, and frequently on true foundations to erect a superstructure of falsehoods--I repeat it, on true foundations, which, by some artifice, or by manifest violence are perverted to the support of falsehoods. 5. It is objected, besides, "It is impossible for this opinion not to be heretical or allied to heresy, when we see one Prosper Dysidaeus. a Samosatenian, who is deeply polluted by a multitude of heresies, interpreting Romans 7 in reference to a man who is not yet under grace, but under the law, which he undoubtedly would not have done, had he not understood that through it he had a mighty support for his own heresies." REPLY.--This objection is truly ridiculous--as if he who is a heretic ought to err in all things, and can speak nothing that is true, or if he does utter any truth, the whole of it must be referred to the confirmation of his heresy. Even the very worst of heretics have, in some articles, held the same sentiments as those of the church. It is a well known fact that the ancient heretics endeavoured, and indeed were accustomed, to interpret many passages of Scripture against the orthodox, in such a way as they could not injure their several heresies. Yet these very passages are, even at the present time, explained by our theologians against the sense of the ancient orthodox, and in accordance with the interpretation of those heretics. But such persons are not, on this account, to be denominated "the favourers of heresies." But I am desirous to have it demonstrated to me what affinity my explanation of Romans 7 has with Aryanism or Samosatenianism. If the same person, who is either an Aryan or a Samosatenian, is likewise earnest about the perfection of righteousness in this life, he will deny that this chapter ought to he understood as relating to the regenerate, not as he is either a Samosatenian or an Aryan, but as he is a Pelagian or a follower of Celestius. If it be allowable to reason in this manner, then the opinion which explains this chapter as referring to a man under grace, will itself labour under great prejudices, from the fact that it is generally so interpreted by the Jesuits, and by their leaders, who are the sworn enemies of the church of Christ, and of the truth, and, at the same time, the most able retainers of the popish church, that is, of a church which is idolatrous, tyrannical, and most polluted with innumerable heresies. Away, then, with such a mode of argumentation as this, about the explanation of any portion of Scripture! Let it never proceed from the mind or the lips of those persons who, with a good conscience, have undertaken the defense of the truth. Who does not perceive that arguments of this kind are employed for the purpose of abashing and unsettling the minds of ignorant and inexperienced hearers; that, being blinded by a certain fear and stupor, they may not be able to form a judgment on the truth, nay, that they may not dare to touch the matter under controversy, through a vain fear of heresy! Such artifices as these are notorious; and all men of learning and moderation are aware of them. Nor are they capable of proving injurious to any persons except to the unlearned and the simple, or to those who have spontaneously determined to wander into error. For we have shewn that this chapter has been understood in the same sense as we interpret it, by many doctors of the church, who declared and proved themselves to be the most eminent adversaries of Aryanism, Samosatenianism, and other heresies, and the most strenuous defendants of the true doctrine concerning the Father, the Son, and the Holy Spirit. Gracious Lord! What a wide and ample plain is here opened for those persons who feel a pleasure in thrusting out the most able and efficient assertors of catholic doctrine into the camp of heretics, under this pretext, that they Interpret certain passages of Scripture which have been usually adduced for the refutation of heresy, in such a manner as not to enable other persons to attack heresies with those passages so interpreted. 6. Lastly. This, my explanation is burdened with another objection--that "it differs from the confessions of all the reformed churches in Europe, for the establishment of which such a multitude of martyrs have shed their blood." This argument likewise, I assert, is employed, not for teaching the truth, but to inflame and blind the minds of those who listen to it, through the indignation which they conceive. For I deny that--in any confession, whether that of the French, the Dutch, the Swiss, the Savoy, the English, the Scotch, the Bohemian, or the Lutheran churches, or of any other--there is extant a single article that is contrary to this interpretation, or that is in the least weakened by this interpretation of Romans 7. It may, indeed, possibly have happened that some portion of this chapter has been used in some confession for the establishment of a doctrine which cannot be confirmed from it, unless it be explained as relating to a regenerate man who is under grace. But how does this circumstance militate against him who approves of the very same doctrine, and defends it in an earnest and accurate manner, by adducing several other passages of Scripture in its support, Such a man affirms this alone--that the true doctrine, in whose defense it has been cited, is not sufficiently well defended by this passage of holy writ. And what man ever shed his blood, or was compelled to shed it, because he was of opinion that this chapter ought to be explained in reference to a regenerate man, and not to a man who is under the law? I speak with freedom, and frankly declare that, while I am listening to such reasons, I am scarcely able to govern and restrain myself from openly crying out, through grief, that God would have mercy on those who teach these things, and would put within them a good mind and a sincere conscience, lest, while rushing headlong against conscience, they at length receive due punishment for the demerit of malignant ignorance, or that he would be pleased to hinder their attempts, or at least, that he would render them abortive, lest they should injure the truth which has been divinely manifested, and the church of Christ! For I cannot put any milder construction on such expressions, when they proceed from men that are endued with knowledge and understanding. All those matters contained in confessions are not equally necessary. All the particulars in any confession are not confirmed by the blood of those who are dragged away to the stake not for the whole of that confession, but on account of some part of it. And we know that many thousands of martyrs have sealed the truth of the gospel with their blood, who were never questioned respecting this article of the perfection or imperfection of righteousness, and who never expended any thoughts upon it. I refer now to this question: "Are those who, through Christ, are justified and sanctified, able in this life to fulfill the law of God without any defect, through the assistance of Christ and the Spirit of grace?" For all Christians are well assured, that, without the grace of Christ, they are not able to do any good whatsoever. Wherefore, the use of this kind of argument must be laid aside by those who are good and conscientious inquirers after the truth, and who endeavour to preserve her when she is discovered.

FOURTH PART

THE OPPOSITE OPINION IS APPROVED BY NONE OF THE ANCIENT DOCTORS OF THE CHURCH

THE ancients who have interpreted this chapter as relating to a man under grace, and the moderns who give it a similar interpretation, differ very materially from each other; because, by the good which the apostle says he wills and does not, and by the evil which he says he wills not and does, the ancients understand only the not-indulging in concupiscence, and the indulging in it; while the moderns understand GOOD and EVIL actually performed. 2. That such was the opinion of the ancients is proved by citations from Epiphanius, Augustine, Bede, and Thomas Aquinas. 3. The difference between these two diverse explanations of good and evil is so great, in the judgment of the ancients, that, according to both explanations, they cannot agree with a regenerate man. This is proved by citations from Augustine, Bede, Thomas Aquinas, and Hugh the cardinal. Thesis.--The meaning which the greater part of our modern divines ascribe to the apostle in this chapter, is not approved by any of the ancient doctors of the church, not even by Augustine himself; but by many of them, it was repudiated and rejected. In this thesis, I do not assert that none of the ancient doctors has interpreted this chapter as relating to a man who is regenerate and placed under grace; for I have already confessed that St. Augustine and some others give it that interpretation. But I affirm that the interpretation of our divines differs from the explanation of those ancients in a point of great moment; and so great is this difference, that, except by a forced construction and a meaning contrary to the mind of those old authors themselves, the moderns are unable to confirm their opinion on this subject by the authority of the ancients. This will, I think, be proved with sufficient accuracy, if it be shewn that those things which the apostle attributes to this man, are received by our divines in a widely different acceptation from that in which they were understood by those among the ancients who explained the chapter as relating to a man under grace. Indeed the moderns receive it in a sense so far different and dissenting from this explanation of some of the ancients, that these very ancients have entertained the opinion that these attributes, when received according to their modern construction by our divines, do not agree with a man who is regenerate and under grace, but with one who is placed under the law. The truth of this affirmation I will now proceed to point out in the following manner: That Good which the apostle says he indeed wills but does not, and that EVIL which, he says, he wills not and yet does, are interpreted by most of our divines as referring to ACTUAL GOOD AND EVIL. And they explain the evil by that very deed which is committed, with the consent of the will, through the lusting of the flesh against the lusting of the Spirit; in like manner, they explain the GOOD by that very deed which a man indeed lusts or desires to do according to the Spirit, but which he does not actually perform, being hindered by the lusting of the flesh. let the commentaries of our divines be examined, and it will at once be evident that this is their interpretation of the chapter; and this is openly declared by those who, on this subject, are opposed to me in opinion. But when St. Augustine, and all those ancients whom I have had an opportunity of perusing, interpret this chapter as referring to a man who is regenerate and placed under grace, they assert that the evil which the apostle says he would not, but did, is to lust or desire; but they interpret the GOOD which he says he would, but did not, by not lusting or coveting; yet they make a distinction between these two--lusting and going after their lusts--and not lusting and not going after their lusts. In a manner nearly similar, the apostle St., James denotes this difference in his epistle, i, 14, xv, "But every man is tempted, when he is drawn away of his own lust, and enticed. Then when lust hath conceived, it bringeth forth sin," that is, actual sin; "and sin, when it is finished, bringeth forth death." That this was the meaning of the ancients, is proved by 1. EPIPHANIUS For, that which is said, "What I do I allow not, but what I hate that I do," must not be received concerning that evil which we have performed and completed, but concerning that about which we have only thought. (Heresy 64th, against Origen, lib. 2, tom. 2.) Otherwise, how should the apostle have indeed chiefly done the evil which displeased him, but not the good which was pleasing, if he had not spoken about extraneous thoughts, which we have occasionally thought, and not willing them, not knowing from what cause they arise? (Ibid.) For this good is perfect, not only to abstain from doing, but likewise from thinking; and the good is not done which we will, but the evil which we will not. (Ibid.) Wherefore, this is placed within us: to will, that we will not think about these things. Yet this is not placed within us: to gain our end, that they be dispersed so as not to return again to our minds, but only that we may in some degree use them, or not use them--as is the sentiment in the subsequent passage: "For the good that I would I do not;" for I will not to think on those things which hurt me, because this is a good and immaculate employment, and devoid of reprehension, according to the common saying, [in reference to another affair.] "a square may be formed either in the mind, or by the hands, without any blame." Therefore, "the good that I would, I do not; but the evil which I would not, that I do;" I will not to think, and yet I think on those things which I will not.(Ibid.) In a subsequent passage, when refuting those who interpreted this passage as descriptive of the deeds performed by the apostle himself, his words are: But now, if any venture to dispute these words by objecting, "The apostle teaches us this, by these words--For the good that I would, I do not; but the evil which I would not, that I do that they are to be referred not only to our thinking evil in our minds from which we are averse and which we avoid, but likewise to our actually doing and performing evil," we therefore request the man who reasons thus, if what he says be correct, to explain to us what that evil was which, though the apostle hated and nilled to do, yet he did it. Or, on the contrary, let him inform us what good that was which he willed greatly to perform, but which he was not able to do, &c. (Ibid.) Consult the remaining portion of this passage. 2. AUGUSTINE And it follows, "I find then a law, that when I would do good, evil is present with me;" that is, I find a law to be within me when I will to do the good which the law wills; because "evil is present," not with the law itself which says, "Thou shalt not covet" or lust, but "evil is present with me," because I likewise unwillingly lust. (On Marriage and Concupiscence, cap. 30, ten,. 7.) To "the body of this death," therefore, is understood to belong, that "another law in the members wages war indeed against the law of the mind;" while the flesh lusteth against the Spirit, although it does not subjugate the mind, because the Spirit also lusteth against the flesh; and thus, though the law of sin itself holds some part of the flesh in captivity, by which it may resist the law of the mind, yet it does not reign in our body, though it be mortal, if we do not obey it in the lusts thereof (Ibid. cap. 31.) But the apostle subjoins this expression: "So, then, with the mind I myself serve the law of God; but with the flesh, the law of sin," which must be understood in this manner: "With my mind I serve the law of God, by not consenting to the law of sin; but with the flesh, I serve the law of sin by having desires of sin, to which, though I do not yield my consent, yet I am not totally free from them." (Ibid.) Or perhaps we are afraid of those words which follow: "For that which I do, I allow not; for what I would that do I not; but what I hate, that do 1." Are we afraid that, from these words, any one should suspect the apostle of consenting to the concupiscence of the flesh to evil works, But we must take into our consideration that which the apostle immediately subjoins: "If, then, I do that which I would not, I consent unto the law that it is good." For he here says that he consents to the law more than to the concupiscence of the flesh because he bestows on this latter the appellation of "sin." Therefore, he said that he does and performs not with an inclination of consenting and fulfilling, but with the very motion of lusting or coveting. Hence, therefore, he says, "I consent to the law that it is good." "I consent," because I will what it does not will. He afterwards says, "Now it is no more I that do it, but sin that dwelleth in me." What does this mean--"Now then,"--except that he is now under grace, which has delivered the delighting of the will from consenting with lust, Neither is the other part of the clause any better understood: "It is no more I that do it," than that he does not now consent to "yield his members as instruments of unrighteousness to sin." For if he both lusts, and consents, and performs, how is it "no more he that does it," though he is grieved at his doing it, and grievously groans on account of having been conquered? (Against the two Epistles of the Pelagians, cap. 10.) For this is "to perform that which is good," that a man do not indulge in concupiscence or lust. But this good is imperfect when the man lusts, though he does not consent to concupiscence for evil. (Ibid.) And from these things he afterwards concludes--"So, then, with the mind, I myself serve the law of God, but with the flesh, the law of sin," that is, "with the flesh, the law of sin" by indulging in concupiscence, "but with the mind, the law of God" by not consenting to such concupiscence. (Ibid.) He does not say, how to do or to perform, but "how to fulfill or complete that which is good;" because to perform or to do what is good, is, not to go after lusts; but to fulfill or to perfect what is good, is not to lust or to indulge in concupiscence. That, therefore, which is said to the Galatians, (v, 16,) "ye shall not fulfill or perfect the lusts of the flesh," is said about a contrary object in this passage of the epistle to the Romans--"but how to fulfill or perfect that which is good, I find not." Because those lusts are not perfected or fulfilled in evil, when the assent of our will is not added to them; nor is our will perfected or fulfilled in good, so long as the motion of those lusts continues, though we do not consent to such motion. But this conflict, in which even those who are baptized struggle as in an agony, when "the flesh lusteth against the Spirit, and the Spirit against the flesh," in which the Spirit also does or performs a good work, by not consenting to evil concupiscence; but it does not fulfill or perfect such work, because it does not consume or remove those evil desires or lusts. The flesh, likewise, does or performs an evil desire; but it does not fulfill or perfect it, because, the Spirit not consenting to it, the flesh also does not come so far as to the condemned works. This conflict, therefore, is not that of the Jews nor of any other description of men whatsoever, but it is evidently that of Christian believers, and of those who live good lives and labour hard in this contest, as is briefly shewn by the apostle, in Romans vii. 25, where he says, "then, with the mind, I myself serve the law of God; but with the flesh the law of sin." (Against Julian the Pelagian, lib. I, cap. 26.) Be unwilling, therefore, to do that which you are not willing to suffer; and do not say, that we allure you to sweet deeds, about which we cite the apostle as thus declaring himself: "For I know that in me, (that is, in my flesh,) dwelleth no good thing." For, though "they do not perfect or fulfill the good which they would" in not indulging in concupiscence; yet they do or perform good, in not going after their lusts. (Ibid. lib. 5, cap. 5.) Be it far from us, therefore, to assert what you pretend, that we affirm that, "the apostle spake these words as though he was desirous to be understood by them, that he was in the act of fornication, struggling hard against it, whilst he was led away by some hand of a pestiferous voluptuousness," when the apostle himself says, It is no more I that do it; thus shewing that the lusts of the flesh did work only a libidinous impulse without a consent to the sin. (Ibid. lib. 6. cap 11.) He likewise refrains himself from every evil thing, who has sin which he does not suffer to reign within him, and into whom secretly creeps a reprehensible thought which he does not permit to arrive at the end [intended] of a deed or performance. But it is one thing not to have sin, and it is another not to obey its desires or lusts. it is one thing to fulfill that which is commanded, "Thou shalt not covet or lust," and it is another at least, by a certain attempt at abstinence, to do that which is also written: "Thou shalt not go after thy lusts." Yet it is impossible for us to know any of these things correctly, without the grace of the saviour. To do or perform righteousness, therefore, in the true worship of God, is to fight by an internal conflict against the inward evil of concupiscence, and not at all to have, to perfect, or fulfill that which is its opposite. For he who fights, is still not only in great peril, but is also sometimes smitten, though he is not utterly cast down. But he who has no adversary, rejoices in full peace and tranquillity. He also is most truly said to be without sin, in whom no sin dwells, but not he, who, through abstaining from an evil work, says, "It is no more I that do it, but sin that dwelleth in me." (On Nature and Grace, cap. 62.) Therefore, the apostle "does that which he would not," because he wills not to lust or indulge in concupiscence, and yet he lusts; therefore, "he does that which he would not." Did that evil concupiscence draw the apostle into subjection to concupiscence to commit fornication? Far from it. Let not such a thought as this arise in our hearts. He struggled hard, and was not subdued. But because he was unwilling also to have this against which he was struggling, therefore, he said, "I do that which I would not;" I am unwilling to indulge in concupiscence, and yet I lust. Therefore, "I do that which I would not," but yet I no not consent to concupiscence. For otherwise he would not have said, "Ye shall not fulfill the lusts of the flesh," if he himself fulfilled them. (On Time, Sermon 55, tom. 10.) How do I perform that which is good, and not perfect what is good, I do or perform good, when I do not consent to evil concupiscence; but I do not perfect or fulfill what is good, in not entirely refraining from concupiscence. Again, therefore, how does my enemy perform that which is evil, and not perfect what is evil? He does or performs evil, because he moves an evil desire; and he does not perfect what is evil, because he does not draw me to evil.(Ibid.) "With the mind, I myself serve the law of God," by not consenting, "but with the flesh, the law of sin," by not indulging in concupiscence. (Ibid.) Hence, also this expression, "I do that which I would not;" "for the flesh lusteth against the Spirit" and I am unwilling that it should lust. I account it a great matter if I do not consent, for I wish to abstain from it; therefore, "I do that which I would not." For I will that the flesh lust not against the Spirit, and I am unable; this is what I have said, "I do that which I would not." (Sermon 13th, on the Words of the Apostle.) If, therefore, "the flesh lusteth against the Spirit," that in this very thing you do not what you would, because you will not to indulge in concupiscence and are not able, [to refrain from such indulgence,] at least hold thy will in the grace of the Lord, and persevere by its assistance. Repeat before him that which you have sung, "Direct my steps according to thy word; and let not any iniquity have dominion over me." (Psalm cxix. 133.) What is this, "Let not any iniquity have dominion over me"? Listen to the apostle: "Let not sin reign in your mortal body." What is this reigning, "By obeying it in the lusts thereof." He has not said, Do not have evil desires. For how have I not evil desires "in this mortal body," in which "the flesh lusts against the Spirit, and the Spirit against the flesh"? This thing, therefore, "Let not sin reign," &c. (Ibid.) 3. VENERABLE BEDE But if it be himself, (that is, the apostle,) let us not so understand that which he has said: "What I would, that do I not, but what I hate, that I do;" as if he willed to be chaste and yet was an adulterer, or willed to be merciful and was cruel, or willed to be pious and was impious. But what are we to understand, I will not to indulge in concupiscence, and yet I do indulge in it. (On Romans 7.) Though I do not consent to concupiscence, and though I do not go after my lusts, yet I still indulge in concupiscence. (Ibid.) What is it that I hate? To indulge in concupiscence: I hate to indulge in concupiscence, and yet I do so from my flesh and not from my mind. (Ibid.) But that which I do, is to indulge in concupiscence, not to consent to it; that no one may now seek in the apostle an example for himself of sinning, and afford a bad example. "What I would, that do I not." For what says the law? "Thou shalt not lust or covet." And I would not lust, and yet I do lust, although I do not yield up my consent to concupiscence, and though I do not go after it. For I offer resistance, I turn away my mind, I give a denial to the instruments, I repress my members; and yet that is done within me which I will not. That which the law likewise wills not, I nill with the law. What it would not, that I would not. Therefore, "I consent to the law." I am in the flesh, I am in the mind; but I am more in the mind than in the flesh. Because, when I am in the mind, I am in that which governs; for the mind governs; the flesh is governed. And I am more in that by which I rule or govern, than in that by which I am governed. Therefore, I rule more in the mind. (Ibid.) 4. THOMAS AQUINAS To will is present with me, that is, to me who am now recovered by grace. It is through the operation of divine grace, by which indeed I not only will that which is good, but I also perform something that is good, because I offer resistance to concupiscence, and under the guidance of the Spirit, I act against it. But I do not find in my power the manner in which I may perform that which is good, that is, in order entirely to exclude concupiscence. (On Romans 7.) 3. But these two explanations of those attributes are, in the judgment of those very ancients who have explained this chapter as relating to a regenerate man, so vastly diverse and dissentient, that the same things cannot agree with a regenerate man according to both these explanations; nay, that, according to the first of these explanations, they can agree with a regenerate man, but according to the second they can agree only with a man who is under sin and under the law. This I will now proceed to prove from the testimonies of those ancients themselves: 1. AUGUSTINE For in no better manner is this understood-- "It is no more I that do it" - than that he does not consent "to yield his members as instruments of unrighteousness unto sin." For if he both lusts, and consents, and does, how is it "no more he that does it," though he is grieved that he does it, and groans grievously at being conquered, (Against the two Epistles of the Pelagians, lib. I, cap. 10.) On two of these three passages we have before disputed, and which say, "But I am carnal, sold under sin:" And this is the third: "- bringing me into captivity to the law of sin which is in my members." On account of all the three, the apostle may seem to be describing him who is still living under the law, and not yet under grace. But as we have already expounded the two former of them to be spoken in reference to the flesh which is corruptible, so may this third passage likewise be understood; as if it said that I was brought into captivity by the flesh not by the mind, by motion not by consent; and that it therefore brought me into captivity, because in my flesh itself there is no other than our common [sinful] nature. (Ibid.) He is spiritual because he lives according to the Spirit; but still, on the part of mortal flesh, the same man is spiritual and carnal. Behold the spiritual man: "With the mind I myself serve the law of God.", Behold the carnal man: "But with the flesh I serve the law of sin." Is, then, this same man both spiritual and carnal? He is evidently so, as long as he is a dweller on earth. Whosoever thou art, be not surprised if thou yieldest and consentest to any lusts whatsoever, since thou either supposest them to be good for fulfilling libidinous excess, or thou undoubtedly seest them now to be so evil, that yet by yielding to them thou consentest, and followest whither they lead, and dost perpetrate those things which they wickedly suggest; thou art entirely carnal, whosoever thou art that dost correspond with this description--thou art totally carnal. But if indeed thou lustest or desirest that which the law forbids when it says: "Thou shaft not covet," yet if thou dost also observe that other thing which the law likewise says, "Thou shalt not go after thy lusts," in thy mind thou art spiritual, and in thy flesh carnal. For it is one thing, not to lust or not to indulge in concupiscence; and it is another, not to go after its lusts. The non-indulgence in concupiscence is the property of one who is entirely perfect; not to go after his lusts, is that of one who is fighting, engaged in a struggle, and labouring. Let me be allowed, likewise, to add what the thing itself requires, that it is also the property of him who does not walk after his lusts; it is the property of a man who is conquering and overcoming. For the first of these [the non- indulgence in concupiscence] is obtained by the battle, the struggle and the labour, but not till after the victory has been secured. (On the Words of the Apostle, Sermon 5.) It is apparent, therefore, from the mind of St. Augustine, that, if this chapter be explained as relating to consent and to the actual perpetration of evil, it can by no means be understood concerning a regenerate man, but concerning a man who is under the law, and "is merely carnal," as he expresses himself. 2. VENERABLE BEDE We know that the law is spiritual. There is, therefore, perhaps, some other; probably thou art the man; either thou art he, or I am. If, then, he be some one of us, let us listen to him about himself, and, not being offended, let us correct ourselves. But if it be himself, (that is, the apostle,) let us not so understand that which he has said: "What I would, that do I not; but what I hate, that I do;" as if it was his will to be chaste and yet he was an adulterer, or to be merciful and yet was cruel, or to be pious and yet was impious. But what are we to understand? My will is, not to indulge in concupiscence; and yet I do indulge in it. (On Romans 7.) 3. THOMAS AQUINAS Of all these writers, Thomas Aquinas most plainly places the two explanations in opposition to each other; and he declares that the things which are in this chapter attributed by the apostle to the man about whom he is treating, according to one of these explanations agree with a regenerate man, but, according to the other they agree with a man who is under sin: Man, therefore, is said to be carnal, because his reason is carnal. It is called "carnal" on two accounts: On the First, because when the reason consents to those things to which it is instigated by the flesh, it is brought into subjection to the flesh, according to the declaration in 1 Corinthians iii. 3: "For, whereas there is among you envying, and strife, and divisions, are ye not carnal?" In this manner, it is also understood about a man not yet restored by grace. On the Second account, reason is said to be carnal from the circumstance of its being attacked by the flesh; according to that declaration in Gal. v. 17, "The flesh lusteth against the Spirit." And, in this manner, the reason even of a man who is placed under grace is understood to be carnal. But both these carnalities proceed from sin, &c. Hence he says, "For that which I do I understand not," [or "allow not,"] that is, that it ought to be performed. This may indeed be understood in two ways: In the ONE mode, it may be understood concerning him who is subjected to sin, who knows in general that sin must not be committed, yet, being conquered, by the suggestion of the devil, or by passion, or by the inclination of a perverse habit, he commits it, and is, therefore, said to perform that which he understands ought not to be performed, doing this against his conscience, as it is said in Luke xii. 47, "That servant, who knew his Lord's will, and did not according to his will, shall deservedly be beaten with many stripes." In the other mode, it may be understood concerning him who is placed in grace, who indeed does that which is evil; not indeed by executing it in operation or with a consenting mind, but only by indulging in concupiscence according to the feeling of the sensual appetite. And that concupiscence is on account of the reason and the understanding, because it precedes his judgment, at this approach of which such an actual operation is hindered, &c. First, therefore, he says, in reference to the omission of good, "for the good which it is my will to do, I do not." This may indeed be understood, in one mode, about a man who is placed under sin; and thus that which he says in this place, "I do," must be received according to a complete act, which is exercised externally, through the consent of reason. But when he says, "It is my will," it must be understood not indeed in reference to a complete will which is preceptive of a work or operation, but in reference to a certain incomplete will, by which men will in general that which is good, as they also have in general a correct judgment concerning one thing; and such a will is corrupted in particular because it does not what it understands in general ought to be done, and that which it wills to do. But according to its being understood respecting a man recovered by grace, we must, on the contrary, understand by this which he says, "It is my will," a complete will continuing throughout in the election or choice of a particular operation, that by this which he says, "I do," may be understood an incomplete act which consists only in the sensual appetite, and does not extend to the consent of reason. For a man who is placed under grace, wills indeed to preserve his mind from corrupt lusts; but he does not perform this good, because of the inordinate motions of concupiscence which rise up in his sensual appetite. Similar to this is what he says in Gal. v. 17, "so that ye do not the things which ye would." Secondly, he subjoins, in reference to the perpetration of evil, "But the evil which I hate, that I do." If this be indeed understood concerning a man who is a sinner, then by this which is said, "I hate," is understood a certain imperfect hatred, according to which every man naturally hates evil. But by this which he says, "I do," is understood an act perfected by the execution of a work according to the consent of reason; for that hatred in general is taken away in a particular which is eligible through the inclination of a habit or passion. But if it be understood concerning a man placed under grace, then by this which he says, "I do," is, on the contrary, understood an imperfect act, which consists solely in the concupiscence of the sensual appetite; and by this which he says, "I hate," is understood a perfect hatred, by which any one perseveres in the detestation of evil, until the final reprobation of it, &c. But the law of sin brings a man into captivity in two ways: By the one mode, through consent and operation, it captivates a man who is a sinner; by the other mode, it captivates a man placed under grace, with respect to the motion of concupiscence. Grace delivers from the body of this death in two ways: By the ONE mode, that the corruption of the body may not have the dominion over the mind, drawing it to summit sin; by the OTHER mode, that the corruption of the body may be totally removed. Therefore, with respect to the First, it appertains to the sinner to say, "Grace has delivered me from the body of this death, that is, it has delivered me from sin, into which my soul was led through the corruption of the body." But from sin a righteous man has been already delivered; wherefore it belong, to him to say, "The grace of God hath made me free from the body of this death, that is, that there may not be in my body the corruption of sin or of death," which will occur in the resurrection. Afterwards when he says "so then with the mind I myself serve the law of God," &c., he infers a conclusion, which is inferred according to these two premised expositions, in different ways, from the premises. For, according to the exposition of the preceding words in the person of a sinner, the conclusion must be inferred thus: "It has been said that the grace of God hath made me free from the body of this death, that I may not be led away by it to sin. Therefore, since I shall now be free, with the mind I serve the law of God; but with the flesh I serve the law of sin, which indeed remains in the flesh with respect to the fuel, by which the flesh lusts against the Spirit." But if the preceding words be understood [as proceeding] from the person of a righteous man, then the conclusion must be thus inferred: "The grace of God through Jesus Christ hath made me free from the body of this death; that is, so that the corruption of sin and death may not be in me." 4. HUGH THE CARDINAL There is, therefore, now no condemnation. The preceding words have been expounded concerning the captivity of mortal sin, under which the man was carnally living; and concerning the captivity of venial sin, of the man who is in grace. But he gives the appellation of "mortal sin" to that which is exercised in operation itself, and "venial" to that which consists in the act and motion of lusting or indulging in concupiscence, without the consent of the will.

FIFTH PART

I. THE OPPOSITE OPINION IS INJURIOUS TO GRACE AND HURTFUL TO GOOD MORALS

It is First shewn, that the interpretation of Romans 7, which prevails in the present day is injurious to grace, by attributing to it less than is proper. (1.) The contest which is described in that chapter, cannot be attributed to the Holy Spirit dwelling in a man, without manifest contumely to the Holy Ghost. (2.) An objection and reply. 2. It is Secondly shewn, that the modern interpretation is hurtful to good morals; because it draws along with it, as a consequence, that a man flatters and encourages himself in his sins, provided only that he commits them with a reluctant conscience. This is illustrated by some instances. 3. It is likewise confirmed by St. Augustine and by the Venerable Bede. Thesis.-- The opinion which affirms, that this chapter treats about a man who is regenerate and placed under grace; and which also interprets the good which this man would and does not, and the evil which he would not but does, as referring to actual good and evil; is injurious to grace, and inimical to good morals. 1. That this modern opinion is injurious to divine grace, I demonstrate in the following manner: An injury is inflicted on grace, not only by him who attributes to nature or to free will that which belongs to grace, that is, having taken it away from grace; but likewise by him who attributes to it less than is its due, and than ought truly to be ascribed to grace. In the last of these modes, this modern opinion is inimical to grace: For it attributes less than, according to the Scriptures, ought to be ascribed to grace. The Scriptures ascribe to divine grace, that, in the regenerate, it worketh not only to will but also to do; (Phil. ii. 13) that, by its power, our old man is crucified, and the body of sin is destroyed or enervated, so that henceforth we should not obey it in the lusts thereof; that, through grace, the regenerate are dead indeed unto sin, and are raised up again to walk in newness of life, in which they serve not sin but God, neither do they yield their members as instruments of unrighteousness unto sin, but as instruments of righteousness to God; (Rom. vi. 2-13) that, through the efficacy of the Spirit, they mortify the deeds of the body; (viii, 13) and that grace not only supplies to the regenerate strength to resist the world, Satan, and the flesh, but, likewise, power to gain the victory over them. (Ephes. vi. 11-18; James iv. 4-8; 1 John iv. 4; v, 4; &c., &c.) But this modern opinion attributes to grace, that its only effect in the regenerate is to will and not to do, that it is too weak to crucify the old man, to destroy the body of sin, or to conquer the flesh, the world and Satan. For the regenerate man, according to this opinion, is said to obey sin in its lusts, and to walk after the desires of the flesh; though he is said to do this, compelled by the violence of sin, in opposition to conscience, and with a reluctant will. For the interpretation and addition alter the mode of obedience by which men obey sin; it does not deny obedience itself. This was also the cause why St. Augustine interpreted the chapter in reference to concupiscence; for he perceived that if he interpreted it concerning actual sins, he would be inflicting an injury on grace. (1.) I am desirous that it should be made the subject of diligent consideration, and that it should be frequently and deliberately pondered, whether the contest which is said to be described in this chapter can be ascribed to the indwelling Holy Spirit, without manifest contumely and dishonour to the grace of Christ and of His Spirit, if this be laid down as the issue of the contest, that the man works from the will of the flesh, not from concupiscence of the Spirit. This is the result of the battle, which is laid down by those who interpret the chapter concerning actual good and evil. To any who earnestly peruses the passage, it will indeed appear evident that such a contest cannot be ascribed to the Holy Spirit, without enormous disgrace to Him. For, what is it? It is said to be a contest, and a waging of war between "the law of the mind," that is, the Holy Spirit dwelling within, and "the law of the members;" and the victory is assigned to the law of the members against the law of the mind; for it leads the man away, as a captive, to the law of sin, the Holy Spirit, who dwells within vainly resisting and warring against it. Under these circumstances, is not the Holy Spirit represented as being much weaker than the law in the members, that is, than the lust of the flesh and indwelling sin, The man who denies this, will deny that the sun shines when he is to be seen in all his meridian splendour. For, in this place, no mention is made of his spontaneous yielding or surrender, of desisting from the combat, or the casting away of his weapons, which we have declared to be the cause why he who begins to fight in the Spirit is conquered by the flesh. But no mention of such circumstances can here be made; for it is said to be a battle, and a waging of war not between "the law of the members" and a man who uses "the law of the mind," but to be between "the law of the mind" and "the law of the members;" to which law of the mind the casting away of its weapons cannot be attributed, for it is itself engaged in the battle and not by proxy. Neither can a desisting from the combat be ascribed to the law of the mind before it has actually been conquered and overcome. Much less can a spontaneous surrender be attributed to it, because this can by no means occur between these two combatants. For "the law of the mind" must necessarily lose its life, and cease to have any existence, before it willingly and spontaneously yields to the rebellious flesh. (2.) Some one, however, may reply, "This is a metaphorical kind of speaking or discourse, and through a Prosopopoeia, a person and the properties of a person are attributed to the law of the mind and to that of the members. But, properly and without any trope or figure, this man is said to fight with himself; that is, the man, as he is regenerate, fights with himself as he is unregenerate." My answer to this is, there is nothing to prevent the thing from being done in the manner now specified; for a regenerate man, as such, fights in the power and strength of the grace and the Spirit of Christ. Therefore, if while fighting he is conquered, the grace and the Spirit of Christ are overcome, which would be a fact most ignominious to the grace and Spirit of Christ. But if he be conquered while in a state of nonresistance, and not during the conflict, but after he has cast away his weapons or has desisted from the combat, then this is not the case which is the subject of the present investigation; for, in the case stated by the apostle, the man is made prisoner while in actual combat, not after he has ceased to be a belligerent; because the effect and accomplishment of this bringing into captivity is joined to the act of waging war and that indeed immediately. But these two are properly joined together, and in a manner that is agreeable to the nature of parties fighting against each other, if "the law of the mind," that is, the conscience, convinced of the equity and justice of the law, be said to contend with "the law of the members;" for the former is conquered while fighting and in the very midst of the conflict, because it is too weak to be capable of withstanding the impetuosity of the shock against "the law of the members," that is, the lusts of the flesh and the desires of sin, though it earnestly strives to bear away, by every exertion and with all its powers, the palm of victory from the field of battle. 2. But matter of fact teaches that this opinion is inimical and hurtful to good morals. For nothing can be imagined more noxious to true morality than to assert that" it is a property of the regenerate not to do the good which they would, and to do the evil which they would not;" because it necessarily follows from this that those persons flatter themselves in their sins, who, while sinning, feel that they do so with a reluctant conscience and with a will that offered some resistance. For they conclude themselves to be regenerate from this circumstance--because it is not one of the properties of the unregenerate to do the evil which they would not, and to omit the performance of the good which they would; the unregenerate being those who omit the good, and perpetrate the evil, with a full consent of the will, and without any resistance. I truly and sacredly affirm that this has, in more instances than one, fallen within the range of my experience: When I have admonished certain persons to exercise a degree of caution over themselves and to guard against the commission of some wickedness which they knew to be prohibited by the law, they have replied "that it was indeed their will so to refrain, but that they must declare, with the apostle, We are unable to perform the good which we would." "I speak the truth in Christ and lie not, my conscience also bearing me witness in the Holy Ghost," that I have received this very answer from a certain individual, not after he had perpetrated the crime, but when he was previously admonished not to commit it. I am also acquainted with a lady, who on being admonished and blamed for a certain deed which she knew she had perpetrated against the law of God and her own conscience, coolly replied "that as she had done that deed with a reluctant will and not with a full consent, in this she experienced something similar to what the apostle Paul endured when he said, The evil that I would not, that I do." I have known both men and women, young persons and old, who, when I have explained this seventh chapter of the epistle to the Romans in the sense in which I defend it in this treatise, have openly confessed to me "that they had always previously entertained the opinion that, if they had actually perpetrated any evil with a reluctant mind, or had omitted the performance of any good when their conscience exclaimed against such omission, it was not necessary for them to care much about the matter or deeply to lament it, since they considered themselves in this respect to be similar to St. Paul." These persons, therefore, have returned me hearty thanks, as they have declared, because, by my interpretation, I had delivered them from that false opinion. 3. But, lest it might appear that I alone make this assertion, and, without any witness or supporter, declare that "the opinion which interprets this chapter as referring to actual good and evil, is adverse to good morals arid to piety," let us now see what judgment some of the ancients have formed about this matter. AUGUSTINE When discussing these words of the apostle--"for the good that I would, I do not; but the evil which I would not, that I do"--this father makes the following remarks: As often as the divine words which have just been recited from the epistle of the apostle Paul, are read, it is to be feared that, when they arc incorrectly understood, they furnish an occasion to men who are seeking one; because they are inclined to the commission of sin, and with difficulty restrain themselves. Therefore, when they have heard the apostle declaring, "For the good that I would, I do not; but the evil which I hate, that I do," they commit evil; and, as if displeased with themselves because they thus do evil, they suppose that they resemble the apostle, who said, "For the good that I would, I do not; but the evil which I would not, that I do." For this passage is sometimes read, and at present imposes on us the necessity of admonishing, that, when men take it in a wrong acceptation, they convert salutary food into poison. (0n Time, Sermons 43 a 45, tom. 10.) But lest, in this battle, these divine words when read should seem, to those who have not a good understanding of them, as the trumpet of the enemy's army and not that of our own ranks, by which we may be incited, and not by which we may be conquered, pay attention, I beseech you, my brethren, and, you who are in the contest, contend manfully. For, you who have not yet begun the combat, will not understand what I say; but you who are now contending, will easily understand my meaning. I speak openly; your words will be in silence. Recollect, in the first place, what the apostle has written to the Galatians, from which this passage may be well expounded; for, speaking to believers who had been baptized, he says-- speaking to them as those to whom all sins had been remitted in the sacred laver; but speaking to them as to those who are still fighting, he says, "This I say then: Walk in the Spirit and ye shall not fulfill the lusts of the flesh." He has not said, Ye shall not do or perform, but, Ye shall not fulfill or perfect. And why does he say this, He proceeds to say "for the flesh lusteth against the Spirit, and the Spirit against the flesh; for these are contrary, the one to the other, that ye may not do the things that ye would. But if ye be led of the Spirit, ye are not under the law." If ye be led of the Spirit--What is "to be led of the Spirit"? To consent to the Spirit of God which commands, and not to the flesh which lusteth. Yet it lusts, and resists, and wills something, and thou wiliest not. Persevere in not willing [that which the flesh wills]. And yet thy desire to God should be of this description, that there may not be any concupiscence for thee to resist. Consider what I have said. I repeat it: Thy request unto God should be of this kind, that no concupiscence whatever may remain which it may be necessary for thee to resist. For thou dost resist; and, by not consenting, thou dost overcome; but it is far better to have no enemy than to conquer one. The time will arrive when that enemy will have no existence. Apply thy mind to the notes of triumph, and see if it will be "O death, where is thy contest?" It will not be "O death, where is thy sting?" Thou shalt seek its place, and shalt not find it. (Ibid.) In a subsequent passage on the same treatise, when explaining still more plainly the meaning of the apostle, lest his words should prove hurtful to those who seek occasion, St. Augustine writes in the following manner: The apostle, therefore, does not what he would, because he wills not to lust or indulge in concupiscence; yet he lusts; therefore he does the evil which he wills not. Did this evil concupiscence draw the apostle into subjection to lust for fornication? By no means. Let not such thoughts as these arise in thy heart. He contended against it; he was not subdued. But because he willed not, and had this against which he might contend, therefore he said "What I would, that do I not;" I will not to lust, or to indulge in concupiscence, and yet I do lust. "Therefore, what I would, that do I not;" but yet I consent not to concupiscence. For, otherwise, he would not have said, "Ye shall not fulfill the lusts of the flesh:" if he fulfilled them himself. But he has placed for thee, before thy eyes, the combat in which he was engaged, that thou mayest not be afraid concerning thine own. For, if the blessed apostle had not said this, when thou hast perceived concupiscence in motion within thy members to which thou wouldst not yield thy consent, yet, since thou hast perceived it to be in motion, perhaps thou mightest despair concerning thyself, and say--if I belonged unto God, I should not have such motions. Look at the apostle engaged in the battle, and be unwilling to fill thyself with despair. He says, "But I see another law in my members, warring against the law of my mind; and because I am unwilling that it should wage ware for it is my own flesh, I am myself the person, it is a part of myself--"that which I would, I do not; but the evil which I hate, that do I," because I lust. Therefore, the good which I do in not giving consent to my evil concupiscence, I perform it, but I do not perfect it. And concupiscence, which is my enemy, performs evil, and does not perfect it. In what way do I perform good and not perfect it? I perform good when I do not consent to evil concupiscence, but I do not perfect good so as not to indulge the least concupiscence. Again, therefore, in what way does my enemy perform evil, and not perfect evil? It performs evil, because it puts evil desires in motion. It does not perfect evil, because it does not draw me to evil.(Ibid.) VENERABLE BEDE But the thing which I do or perform is to lust, not to consent to lust; lest any one should now seek in the apostle an example for himself, and should himself afford a bad one. "That which I would, I do not." For what saith the law, "Thou shalt not covet." And it is not my will to lust, and yet I lust, though I give no consent to my lust, and though I go not after it. (On Romans 7.) II.

VARIOUS OBJECTIONS IN FAVOUR OF THE COMMON INTERPRETATION ANSWERED

An objection for the common interpretation; it is possible for this to be the meaning of Romans 7, "that the regenerate do not so frequently and so perfectly perform what is good, and omit what is evil as they wish." Reply: The gloss is contrary to the text, because this chapter describes the continuous state of the man about whom it treats. 2. The manner in which St. Paul would have spoken, if had intended to convey the meaning that generally obtains, and this in conformity with the style and modes of speaking which he usually adopts in other passages when writing concerning himself. An argument against the usually received opinion, taken from those things which have been previously spoken, and which are here reduced into the form of a syllogism. 3. Another objection in favour of the common interpretation, and this in two members. An answer to the first member. An answer to the second, "that when the regenerate sin, they sin with reluctance." Every inward struggle against sin is not a sign that the man is regenerate. 4. Another objection, and a reply to it. Remarks on a complete and an incomplete will. The regenerate will not, with a complete will, more good than they perform, neither perpetrate more evil than they will. 5. Each of us must institute a serious examination into self and into all the motions of his will. 1. But some one will say, in defense of this modern opinion, and in order to wipe away this double stain, "By this interpretation, no injury is inflicted on divine grace, and no harm is done to good morals." Some other man, possessed of still greater vehemence in defending the opinion which he has once conceived, will bring against me the charge of calumny, [and will say,] "It is a well known fact that they who give this interpretation to the chapter, do not take away from the regenerate the performance of all actual good, and the omission of what is evil, and consequently, [the work of] the grace of regeneration; but this is all that they affirm: Sometimes, nay, very often, those men who are regenerated by the Spirit of Christ do the evil which. they would not, and, far more frequently, omit or do not perform the good which they would; and the same regenerate persons never perform so perfectly the good which they do as they will to perform it, and they never omit evil so perfectly as they will to omit it. But neither of these assertions can be denied by those who acknowledge the imperfection of righteousness in this life, and who accurately consider the examples of the most holy of mortals which are depicted in the Holy Scriptures." I reply, this subterfuge affords no defense or excuse for the modern explanation of Romans 7. For, (as the phrase is,) in this instance the gloss is contrary to the text. For that chapter does not treat about that which occasionally befalls the man who is the subject of discussion, but about what generally and for the most part is accustomed to happen to him; and it contains a description of the continuous state of the man about whom it treats. This is openly declared by the words themselves and by the mode of speech employed. The apostle says, "The good that I would, I do not; but the evil which I would not, that I do." This is said without any distinction or contraction of the general saying to its being specially understood as though he sometimes did not the good which he would, and sometimes did the evil which he would not, or as though he many times abstained from the evil which he hates, and performed the good which he would. But the apostle simply and indefinitely enunciates concerning the detested evil that he perpetrates it, and concerning the good which he willed that he performs it not. But if this indefinite enunciation be said to mean "that the good which has been willed is more frequently performed than omitted, and that the detested evil has been more frequently avoided than committed," which must necessarily be affirmed by those who explain the chapter in reference to a regenerate man, for a regenerate man walks not according to the flesh, but according to the Spirit--then I say, the apostle did not know how to enunciate his own meaning. For indefinite enunciations possess equal force with those which are universal, or they approach as near as possible to them; they enunciate, concerning objects, those attributes which are in every one of them and at all times, or most usually and according to the more excellent part. Thus it is said concerning the Cretians, that they are liars. (Tit. i. 12.) The Athenians are said to be light and frivolous, and to take pleasure in "hearing some new thing;" and the Carthaginians are called perfidious. The Scriptures speak thus, that the Jews have been rejected on account of the greater part, (for "God doth not cast away his people whom he foreknew,") and that the gentiles were received into their place. For power was given, and a command enjoined on the apostles, to preach the gospel to all nations, and most of them have now long since been converted to Christ, or will yet be converted. Neither in this chapter is the apostle treating about a perfect and, in every respect, complete performance of good and omission of evil, but simply about the performance of the one and the omission of the other. For he says that the man commits evil, but not perfectly, if he is regenerate; otherwise, he would sin with an entire and full will. But this will be subsequently treated at greater length. 2. But if St. Paul intended in this chapter to convey such a meaning as those interpreters ascribe to him, then he must have spoken in the following manner, if he was desirous of saying thing, in accordance with himself: "We know that the law is spiritual, and requires from us an obedience perfect in all its parts, and continuous without any intermission or interruption. But I have not yet so far conquered the flesh, I have not yet such a complete dominion over sin, neither have I broken or subdued the lusts of the flesh so much, as to be able to perform that perfect and uninterrupted obedience to the law. For it occasionally happens to me, that I do the evil which I would not, and omit the good which I would; nay, I perceive that I never perform what is good in such perfection and with so much zeal as it is in my will to perform; nor have I omitted what is evil in such perfection as I have wished. For in both cases, even while I am performing what is good and omitting what is evil, I feel the concupiscence of the flesh struggling and resisting; and I consider myself to have experienced admirable success if I come victorious out of the combat, that is, if I do that which the Spirit lusteth, and not what the flesh lusteth." Such a declaration as this would have been suitable to the sense which they attribute to the apostle, and this is properly the index and interpreter of that meaning. But many passages of Scripture, in which the apostle treats about himself, teach us that he ought to have spoken thus, if he had spoken things that were consistent with himself: "For I am conscious to myself of nothing; yet am I not hereby justified." (1 Cor. iv. 4.) "I therefore so run, not as uncertainly; so perform I my part as a combatant, not as one who beateth the air; but I beat down and keep my body under, and bring it into subjection; lest that by any means, when I have preached to others, I myself should become a reprobate." (vi, 26,27.) "Be ye followers of me, even as I also am of Christ." (xi, 1.) "- While we look not at the things which are seen, but at the things which are not seen; for the things which are seen are temporary, but those which are not seen are eternal." (2 Cor. iv. 18.) "- Giving no offense in any thing, that the ministry be not blamed; but in all things approving ourselves as the ministers of God, in much patience," &c. (vi, 3-10.) "For I through the law am dead to the law, that I may live unto God. I am crucified with Christ; nevertheless I live; yet not I, but Christ liveth in me; and the life which I now live in the flesh, I live by the faith of the Son of God, who loved me, and gave himself for me." (Gal. ii. 19, 20.) "But God forbid that I should glory, save in the cross of our Lord Jesus Christ, through whom the world is crucified unto me, and I unto the world." (vi, 14.) Many other passages of a similar import might be cited. Since, therefore, this interpretation does not agree with the chapter, it cannot, by this opinion, be excused from the two crimes which are objected against it, [as being injurious to divine grace, and noxious to good morals]. Wherefore I persist in preferring the same accusation, and I declare, The opinion which attributes to a regenerate man "that he generally does the evil which he would not, and that he most commonly omits the good which he would," is injurious to the grace of regeneration and hurtful to good morals; But the opinion which explains Romans 7 as referring to a regenerate man, attributes these things to one who is regenerate; Therefore, this opinion is injurious to the grace of regeneration, and hurtful to good morals. The light of the major proposition is so great as not to require either proof or illustration. The minor is in the text. For, as has already been shewn, to the man about whom the apostle is treating it is attributed, that he most commonly commits what is evil and omits what is good; therefore, the conclusion properly follows. It appears, therefore, that I have not through calumny affixed this objection to the opinion which is opposed to my own; and I can sacredly affirm, now, that prior to the act of taking the pen into my hands, I had made a vow before God that [in the discussion of this subject] I would indulge in no calumny. Wherefore, though the objection were false, it would in that case have escaped from me through ignorance and not through malice. 3. Some one, however, who is desirous of pertinaciously keeping and retaining the thesis which has been once laid down, will here reply--"Let it be granted, that this explanation is deficient in those things which the apostle attributes to this man; let it likewise be granted, that the interpretation produced by other persons is not suitable to the passage; yet it does not become disadvantageous to good morals, nor is any injury inflicted on grace through this opinion, provided that the whole together be excepted, as it equitably should be, and that one part be not separated from another--this also being granted, that, though this interpretation be unsuitable for Romans 7, yet it is agreeable to the rest of the Scriptures and to the analogy of faith." (1.) That I may not seem to be too rigid, I am willing to grant the former of these; about the latter we shall see something further. For I own, that the opinion of St. Augustine, which interprets the chapter as relating only to the act and motion of concupiscence, neither proves to be detrimental to grace, nor injurious to good morals, though he explains the passage concerning a regenerate man. But I say that, after it has been impressed and inculcated on the minds of hearers or readers that the apostle is treating about a regenerate man in Romans 7, it is not in our power to hinder such persons from understanding the rest of those things which are attributed to this man in a different manner from that in which they ought to be understood, that is, from receiving them in an acceptation which is not agreeable to the text and design of the apostle, and as they are not received when they are explained as relating to a man who is under sin, and under the law, especially when the inclination is a persuasive to such an interpretation, and when the concupiscence of the flesh gives a similar impulse. This, as I have already related, has been actually done by many people, and certainly not without blame attached to the opinion itself, though "the whole of it be received together." For this is not the only thing declared by that opinion, "The regenerate sometimes commit sin; and they never perfectly perform what is good, and omit what is evil, while they continue in the present life;" but this is likewise added: "It is a property of the regenerate, to commit sin not with a full consent of the will, and while in the act of sinning to will not to sin; since the unregenerate sin with a full consent of the will, and without any reluctance on its part." Those persons who wish to excuse themselves by this chapter, and who, while engaged in sin, feel some resistance of the will and remorse of conscience in the act of sinning, conclude from the preceding assertion, that they commit sin not with a full consent of the will, and, therefore, that the very fact itself of their thus committing sin is a sign of their regeneration. Such a conclusion as this is both injurious to grace and inimical to good morals. (i.) It is injurious to grace, because it lays that down, as a sign of regeneration, which is alike common to the regenerate and to the unregenerate, that is, to those who are under the law. (ii.) It is inimical to good morals, because sin is neither so much avoided by that man who holds such an opinion as this, nor does its perpetration produce deep sorrow in him who is its author, because from the mode of the deed he still concludes that he is regenerate. (2.) But let us now consider, whether those things which have been adduced to liberate their opinion from this two-fold criminal charge, be conformable to the rest of the Scriptures and to the analogy of faith, or not. I confess it indeed to be a very great truth, that, while the regenerate pass their lives in this mortal body, they neither perfectly perform what is good, nor omit what is evil. But I add, that, while in the present life, they never perfectly will what is good, or perfectly hate what is evil. I likewise confess, that even the best of the regenerate offend in many things, and sometimes actually sin, by doing what is evil and omitting what is good; for the regenerate do not always act from the principle of regeneration. But I deny that, when they sin, they sin unwillingly, though they may do so with a struggle in their mind and conscience. For, while the contest and struggle continued between the mind and the flesh, how much soever they might nill the evil to which the flesh incited them, and will the good from which it dehorted them; yet they do not proceed onward to the deed itself except when the battle is terminated, the mind or conscience is overcome, and after the will has yielded consent to the flesh--though such consent be not without stinging remorse of conscience. Then I deny, that it can be concluded from this opposition of the mind, that he is a regenerate man who sins in this manner. For, as we have often previously shewn, the commission of sin with a reluctant mind and conscience belongs to many of the unregenerate. Besides, as we have also previously taught, that resistance which immediately preceded the perpetration of sin, was not from the Holy Spirit who regenerated and inhabited, but from the mind which was convinced of the righteousness and equity of the law. For the life of the conscience continues; and from its life, action and motion remain, when the Holy Spirit is either wholly departed, or is so grieved as to employ no motion and act for the hindrance of sin. It is a well known fact, that the soul in man which is vegetative, performs the first and the last offices of life, while the rational soul ceases its operations as in the case of lunatics and maniacs, and the sensitive soul desists from acting in lethargic persons. I wish these observations to receive a diligent consideration; for they have a great tendency to induce a man to enter upon a serious and sure examination respecting himself, to attain a correct knowledge of the state of regeneration, and sedulously to distinguish between it and the state BEFORE the law, and chiefly between it and that UNDER the law. 4. Yet some person will here rejoin, and, for the sake of excusing or defending his opinion, will say, "It cannot be denied that the regenerate will more good than they actually perform, and perpetrate more evil than they will." My answer is, this, when correctly understood, may be conceded; for it is stated with some ambiguity. "To will and not to will this thing," may be understood concerning either a complete or an incomplete volition and nolition, (to use the words of Thomas Aquinas,) though in a sense a little different. (1.) I give the appellation of a complete will to that which is borne to a particular object that is particularly considered, approving or disapproving of that object according to the prescript or direction of the last judgment of the reason that is formed concerning it. (2.) I give the appellation of an incomplete will to that which is borne towards the same object generally considered, approving or disapproving of it according to the prescript or direction not of the last judgment of the reason which is formed concerning it. The former of these, which is indeed complete, may be called simply a volition and a nolition. But the latter, which is incomplete, is otherwise expressed by the words, desire and wishing, and ought to be called vellcity rather than will. Having premised these things, I now say, It cannot be affirmed with truth, "that a regenerate man wills more good with a complete will than he actually performs," unless without any fault of his own, he be hindered by necessity or by some greater force, or "that he actually does more evil than it is his will to do." For he does it not through coaction. A merchant who, for the sake of avoiding shipwreck, throws his heavy bales into the sea, willingly performs that act, having followed this last judgment of his reason--that it is better for his bales of goods to be destroyed, than for himself to perish with them. Thus, with a complete (I do not say with a full) volition, David willed his adulterous intercourse with Bathsheba. Willingly, and with a complete volition, Peter denied Christ. But if this be understood concerning an incomplete will, then I grant it may be said "that the regenerate will to perform more good than they really execute, and to omit more evil than they omit." This, however, is not an exclusive property of the regenerate; for it belongs to all those who are so under the law, that in them the law has discharged all its functions, and (the Holy Spirit employing it for this purpose) in them has produced all those effects which it is possible and usual for the law to produce. Both the regenerate, and those who are under the law, might indeed will, that there was not in them such a vast force and efficacy of sin yet existing and reigning in them; and might wish, that they were not solicited and impelled to evil deeds through concupiscence and the temptation of sin; nay, they might also will that they did not lust or indulge in concupiscence; but those evil acts to which they are solicited by sin which either is in them, or dwells in them and reigns, they do not perform, except through the intervention of the consent of the will that has been obtained by this temptation of sin. For lust does not bring forth sin, unless it has conceived; but it conceives through the consent of the will tanquam ex marito. But as long as the will remains in a state of suspense, inclining to neither part, so long no act is produced--as we behold in a just balance, or true scales, of which neither part verges upward or downward prior to one of them receiving an accession of weight which depresses that scale and elevates the opposite one. All motion reclines or depends on rest as on a foundation. Thus, the will does not move towards the part of sin unless when acquiescing in its temptation. 5. These remarks are exceedingly plain, and capable of being fully confirmed by experience itself, if any one will only accurately ponder within himself all the motions of his own will. But the greatest part of us avoid this duty; for it cannot be performed without [inducing] sorrow and sickness of mind, which no man willingly brings upon himself. But it is by no means probable, that sin should obtain a full consent from the will of that man who is generally well instructed in the righteousness and unrighteousness of actions, before he has ceased to feel any sorrow or regret: Wherefore, the difference between a regenerate and an unregenerate man must not be placed in this particular when both of them commit sin. For, in that particular deed, they equally yield to the temptation of sin, both of them sin from the same principle of depraved nature, and in both instances the resistance is one and the same when sin is perpetrated, that is, on the part of the mind and conscience convicted of the justice or the injustice of the deed. For if the Spirit were itself that resistance, then sin would not be perpetrated in the very act. "Is there then no difference between the regenerate and the unregenerate, when they commit sin?" That I may not deny this, I say that such difference must be brought forward from plain passages in the Holy Scriptures; otherwise, that man will deceive himself to his great peril, who follows some other rule of judging.

THE CONCLUSION AN Examination and comparison of each of the three Interpretations of this chapter

The FIRST, which is the latest of the two opinions embraced by St. Augustine, and which interprets this chapter concerning a man under grace, has various disadvantages: (1.) in the meaning of the word CARNAL, and that of the phrase, "sold under sin." (2.) In the explanation of the evil which, the apostle says, he did; and of the good which he omitted. (3.) In the explanation of the word To Do or To PERFORM. (4.) In the interpretation of "indwelling sin." (5.) In the explanation of "the law of the mind." (6.) In explaining the captivity of man under the law of sin. (7.) In the distorted meaning given to the votive exclamation. (8.) In assigning to a regenerate man a double servitude, and in interpreting "the mind" for "the spirit." These eight inconveniences are sufficient to induce a rejection of this First Interpretation. 2. The SECOND, which is that of modern divines, and which also explains the chapter concerning a man under grace, in addition to the inconveniences that it has in common with the First, has likewise some which are peculiar to itself. (1.) In saying, what permanently belongs to the continuous state of this man, sometimes only happens to him. (2.) In giving a rash explication of "performing that which is good." (3.) In asserting, that the regenerate commit sin unwillingly. (4.) In predicating contradictory things concerning this man. (5.) In predicating with restriction those things concerning the regenerate, which the Scriptures simply attribute to them. 3. The THIRD, which is St. Augustine's first opinion, as well as that of Arminius, and which understands this chapter as relating to a man who is under the law, is plain and perspicuous, and not at disagreement either with apostolical phraseology or with other passages of Scripture; this fact is rendered obvious even from this circumstance--that this man is said at once to be "placed under the law" and "under the dominion of sin." 4. This treatise is closed with an address, by Arminius, to his brethren in the ministry, in which the author offers himself for examination, with a most serious intreaty for them to admonish him, in a fraternal manner, if he has erred; but to yield their assent to the truth, if he has in this work written such things as are in accordance with the scriptures and with the meaning of the apostle. Let us now briefly compare these three expositions of Romans vii, FIRST, that which St. Augustine gave not long before his death; Secondly, that which he taught in early life, which is likewise my interpretation, and that of many doctors of the primitive church, as I have already proved, and that of some even among our own divines; and, LASTLY, the exposition of those persons who assent to St. Augustine in this particular-- that in common with him they explain it as relating to a regenerate man, but who dissent from him on another particular--that they interpret GOOD and EVIL, not as relating to the act of

CONCUPISCENCE, but as referring to ACTUAL GOOD AND EVIL. 1. That St. Augustine might be able to interpret this chapter as relating to a regenerate man and one placed under grace, (which he supposed would be serviceable to him in his disputes with the Pelagians,) he was compelled to put a forced construction on the apostolical phraseology, and to interpret many things in opposition to the express meaning and intention of the apostle. (1.) He has interpreted a carnal man to mean one who yet bears about with him mortal flesh, who is not yet become spiritual in the flesh, and who still has and feels within himself the lusts of the flesh. But about the first of these two descriptions of men the apostle is not here treating: It is, therefore, quite beyond the purpose; and I beseech St. Augustine to point out to me a single passage of Scripture, in which the regenerate are called carnal because they still have within them the lusts of the flesh. If they are called spiritual in the Scriptures, "because by the Spirit they mortify the deeds of the flesh" and do not go after carnal lusts, but walk according to the Spirit, then indeed they cannot be called carnal from the fact of their still having those lusts. They may be called "those who are not perfectly spiritual" on account of the presence of sinful lusts; but they can by no means be styled carnal, because the dominion of sin is taken away from them. In a similar manner he was under the necessity of distorting another attribute of this man, sold under sin, when this phrase properly signifies "one who is the slave of sin, and who serves sin," whether he does this willingly without any resistance of conscience, or in opposition to his mind and so far unwillingly. It is not allowed to us to frame petty distinctions, and, according to these, to attribute to persons certain words, which the Scriptures do not employ, in that sense, and which are not usually ascribed to those persons in holy writ. (2.) Then he interprets the evil which the apostle says he did, by the word to lust or to indulge in concupiscence; and the good which he says he omitted, by the word not to lust--a most absurd and distorted application of those terms! First. Because the words, Katergazesqai, Prassein and Poiein "to do," cannot have the same signification as concupisco, "to lust." At least, so far as I know, the Scriptures have in no passage, explained "to lust" by any of those three words. And St. Augustine himself, in the definition of sin, when distinguishing between these things, says, "Sin is every thing which is spoken, done, and lusted or desired against the law of God." Bucer, in his "Comment on Romans 7," says, "Some persons receive the three verbs here rendered to do,' in the acceptation, to lust,' but that is not St. Paul's mode of speaking. He understands by the word, the deed itself which is actually committed at the impulse of concupiscence, in opposition to that which the law dictates, and which the mind, consenting to that law, approves. Concupitio, to lust' or desire, is in reality, an internal act of concupiscence in the mind, which indulges in such concupiscence. But these verbs to do,' in this chapter do not signify an internal act of lusting, but, properly, the external act of doing those things which have been lusted or desired." (Fol. 369.) Secondly. "Sin is said to do this evil, and, by the perpetration of the evil, to slay the man himself." Sin does not slay him through concupiscence. St. James speaks thus: "Then when lust hath conceived, it bringeth forth sin; and sin, when it is finished [or completed by action], bringeth forth death." (i, 15.) But it slays the man through actual sin. This is declared by the apostle in the fifth verse of this very chapter, when he says, "for when we were in the flesh, the motions of sin, which were by the law, did work in our members to bring forth fruit unto death." I am now speaking, not according to the rigor of the law, but according to the grace of the gospel in Jesus Christ. Thirdly. The evil and the good, the former of which, he says, he perpetrates, but the latter he omits, are so opposed to each other, that evil is what is forbidden by a prohibitive law, which law is usually proposed by a negative; but Good is what is commanded by a preceptive law, which is usually propounded by an affirmative. A sin is perpetrated against a prohibitive law by commission, but against a preceptive law by omission. On this account they are called sins of omission and of commission. If a prohibitive law be observed, evil is said to be omitted, but if a preceptive law be observed, good is said to be performed. Now, to lust, and not to lust, are not thus opposed to each other. For though to lust be forbidden by a prohibitive law, yet not to lust is not commanded by a preceptive law; neither can it be commanded by such a law; for not to lust consists of a negative or the omission of an act; but by omission, an offense is committed against a preceptive law. But, by the omission of concupiscence, no offense is committed against a positive or preceptive law, but a prohibitive law is fulfilled; and by obedience, which consists in not lusting, good is not performed, but evil is omitted. That we may point out this absurdity [of St. Augustine's exposition], we will invert in the following manner what the apostle has said: "The good that I would, I do," that is, I do not lust; "but the evil which I would not, I do not," that is, I do not lust. For I will not to lust, and I do not lust; I nill to lust, and I do not lust. Therefore, in this case, the very same act is the performance of good and the omission of evil--a complete absurdity. And that is called the performance of a good action which is the omission of an evil one--an equal absurdity! O Augustine, where was thy usual acumen? Let the expression be pardoned; for a good philosopher is not always a philosopher, and our Homer himself will sometimes nod. Fourthly. It is an illogical mode of expression to say, "I will to lust," and "I will not to lust," because actual concupiscence is prior to volition and nolition, and the act of concupiscence does not depend upon the choice or determination of the will. According to the trite and true saying, "first motions are not in our power, unless they be occasioned by some act of the will," as the schoolmen express themselves. But we must say, "I could wish not to lust," that is, "I could wish to be free from the impulse of concupiscence." And this is an expression of desire, not tending to or going out towards the performance or omission of our act, but earnestly demanding the act of another person for our liberation from that evil which impels us to an evil act, and which hinders us from a good act--we approving of the good act and disapproving of the bad one. (3.) He was compelled, when expounding what the apostle says in the 18th verse, "But to perform that which is good I find not," to interpret it by "completing what is good," that is, "I find not perfectly to do what is good," as is evident from those passages which we have cited from St. Augustine. This interpretation is absurd, distorted, and contradictory to the sentiments and meaning of the author; for, First. The word, Katergazesqai does not signify "to perfect," that is, "perfectly to do any thing;" but it signifies "to operate, to perform, to effect, or to do," as this word is most commonly used, not for "doing any thing perfectly," but for "producing an effect." My observations on this point are evident from the text itself; for the same Greek word is employed in the first clause of the 15th verse, when the apostle says, "For that which I do, I allow not," yet he does not perfectly perform the evil of which he disapproves. It is also used in the latter clause of the 20th verse, "Now then it is no more I that do it, but sin that dwelleth in me." But sin does not perfectly perpetrate evil in this man, especially if he be regenerate, as St. Augustine supposes; and he openly says himself the contrary to this, as is evident from the passages which we have already cited in the fourth part of this treatise. Secondly. The synonyms of this verb which are promiscuously used in the seventh chapter, prassein and poiein prove the same thing. For the apostle says that he does and performs the evil which he would not, (verses 15, 16, 19,) yet he does not perfectly perform that evil; this is obvious from what he adds, "which I would not." Therefore he performs it not with a full consent of his will. For this is confessed by St. Augustine, when he explains the passage about the regenerate; but he does it not with a full consent of the will, that is, he does it not perfectly. Thirdly. "The GOOD which the apostle would, but which he does not," (19,) is, according to St. Augustine, not to lust. But how is it that the apostle indeed does this "good," [by willing it, but does not perfect it, Therefore, a two-fold omission of concupiscence must be laid down [by those who adopt St. Augustine's argumentation,] one, under the term to do, is called an imperfect omission; the other, under the word to complete, receives the appellation of perfect. According to St. Augustine's sense, the apostle says in this verse, (19,) "I will not to lust, and this good I indeed do, but I do not perfect it." From this remark, the absurdity which I have mentioned is most manifest. Fourthly. More good is attributed to the will of this man, than to its capability and powers or efficacy. But the perfect volition of good is not attributed to his will, neither can it be attributed. Therefore, from its capability and efficacy not only can the perfect performance of good be taken away, but the imperfect performance is likewise taken away from them. That is, it is denied respecting this man, not only that he perfects good, but that he even performs it. Wherefore, this passage must not be understood concerning perfection, that is, the perfect performance of good. (4.) He was forced to interpret "sin that dwelleth or inhabiteth within me," by "sin existing within," and to create a distinction between it and "sin reigning and exercising the dominion over a man," while the phrase, "dwelling within me," denotes dominion, and the full and supreme power of him who is the resident, as we have previously shewn in its proper place. But it is apparent that sin reigns in this man; for it commits that sin in him which he himself would not, and leads him away as a captive under its power. (5.) He was under the necessity of interpreting "the law of the mind" by "the law of the Spirit," though in contradiction to the great contrariety subsisting between the attribute which is given to "the law of the mind," and that which is ascribed to "the law of the Spirit." For, in Romans vii. 23, "the law of the mind" is said to be overcome in combat by "the law of the members," from which event, the man "is brought into captivity to the law of sin." And in Romans viii. 2, "the law of the Spirit" is said to make the man "free from the law of sin and death;" that is, it is stronger and superior in the conflict against "the law of the members;" and, when the latter is conquered and overcome, "the law of the Spirit" delivers the man from the captivity into which he had been brought by the force of "the law of the members." (6.) St. Augustine was compelled to pervert the phrase, "captivity to the law of sin," and to give it the meaning of our primeval state in Adam, from whom we are born corrupt and under the captivity of sin and Satan, when, in this passage, the apostle is not treating on that captivity, but on another, which is produced from it, that is, by "the law of the members" which we have contracted from Adam, waging war against "the law of the mind," overcoming it, and bringing man, by his own act, under captivity to the law of sin. For we have the former captivity originally from Adam, but we bring down the latter upon ourselves by our own act. Even if the discourse of the apostle had referred to our primeval state, yet, because the regenerate have received remission of sin and are endowed with the spirit of the grace of Christ, they cannot be said to be captives under sin. For, though the fuel has not been extinguished, yet the power of commanding, and of subjecting us to itself, is taken away from sin by the power of regeneration. (7.) He is forced to torture the votive exclamation in the 24th verse, to a desire different from that on which the apostle is here treating, and with which the thanksgiving in the 25th verse does not correspond. For, in this passage, St. Paul treats upon the desire by which the man requests to be delivered from the dominion of sin, which he calls "the body of death;" and St. Augustine is compelled [by the scheme of interpretation which he had adopted] to explain in reference to the desire by which he desires to be liberated from this mortal body, and when that event occurs, he will at once be free from the concupiscence of sin. A thanksgiving, however, seems [in this case] to be most unadvisedly subjoined to the votive desire, before the fruition of the thing which is said to be wished; yet this is done in this passage, according to the interpretation of St. Augustine. (8.) Lastly, St. Augustine is forced to assign a double servitude to a regenerate man--the one, as he serves God--the other, as he serves sin; and this in contradiction to the express declaration of Christ--"No man can at one time serve two masters." It is objected, "that in a different respect, and according to his different parts, man is said to serve God, and to serve sin;" but this remark does not clear this opinion from the stain with which it is aspersed. (i.) Because the Scriptures are unacquainted with that distinction, when they are speaking about regenerate persons; let a passage to the contrary be produced. (ii.) Because, if even the flesh war against the Spirit or the mind by lusting; yet a man cannot be said, solely on account of this resistance and warfare, "with his flesh to serve" sin, or "the law of sin;" for, with St. Augustine, these two are the same things. He is likewise compelled to use the word, "the mind," for the regenerated part of man, for the man so far as he is regenerate, in opposition to Scripture usage and phraseology, as we have explained in the first part of this treatise. These appear to me most equitable reasons for rejecting the latter opinion of St. Augustine, and for appealing from him when asleep to St. Augustine in his waking moments. I have no doubt that he would also have abandoned this his second opinion, had he taken into his consideration the arguments which are now adduced, especially when he had perceived the explication of the whole chapter to be so suitable and proper, and impossible to be wrested in any point by the Pelagians for proving their doctrine. 2. Our divines have fallen into some of these errors with which we have charged the opinion of St. Augustine, such as the following: They are forced to interpret "to be carnal," and "to be sold under sin," in a manner very different from that which the meaning of the apostle will allow; they call "sin that dwelleth in a man," "sin existing within," thus distinguishing it from reigning sin; they assert that "the law of the mind" signifies "the law of the Spirit;" they explain in a corrupt manner the votive exclamation; and, lastly, they attribute a two-fold servitude to a regenerate man. In addition to these mistakes, they fall into others which are peculiar to their interpretation, but which are agreeable neither to the meaning of the apostle in this chapter, nor to the rest of the Scriptures, for, (1.) They are compelled to interpret that which, according to the meaning of the apostle, belongs to the continuous state of this man, as if it happened to him only occasionally, in contradiction to the express phraseology of the apostle, who says, "The good that I would, I do not; but the evil which I would not, that I do." This phraseology is by no means in accordance with the signification by which any one is said occasionally to perpetrate evil and to do good, as we have already rendered very manifest. (2.) They are under the necessity of interpreting the phrase, "The good that I would, I do not" by "I do not good in the perfection in which I ought," or, "I do not so much good as it is my will to do;" yet neither of these explanations is agreeable to the meaning of the apostle, as we have previously seen. (3.) They broadly assert, that while the regenerate are actually committing sin, they are unwilling to commit sin in the very act of sinning, in opposition to the whole of the Scriptures and to the nature of actual sin itself, which, if it be not voluntary, ceases to be sin. (4.) They are compelled to say contradictory things about this man. For they take away from sin, which exists within him, the dominion over him; and yet they attribute to it a habitation or indwelling, and they ascribe such force and efficacy to it, that it perpetrates evil itself in the man in opposition to his will, and brings him into captivity to the law of sin. These are most undoubted effects indeed of sin reigning and exercising dominion. (5.) Lastly, as there are many passages of Scripture, which attribute to the regenerate the willing of good, a delight in the law 0f God, and things of a similar kind, they are compelled to interpret those passages by this restrictive particle, "after the inward man," while, in the rest of the Scriptures, such attributes are simply ascribed to a regenerate man, because they have the predominance in him. But it is not necessary, at this time, to repeat all those things which we have before written and proved against that opinion. 3. But the opinion which I have undertaken to explain, is plain and perspicuous, under no necessity to affix any thing to the phraseology of the apostle, or to impinge against any other portions of holy writ. This may be perceived at one glance, by him who will cast his eyes upon these two things, that the man who is the subject of the present investigation, is said to be placed under the dominion of sin and under the law, that is, he is one in whom the law has discharged its entire office. (1.) For, as he is placed under the dominion of sin, the following affirmations are correctly and without any contortion made concerning him: "he is sold under sin; he does that which he wills not, and omits that which he wills; sin dwells in him, and in his flesh dwelleth no good thing; he cannot attain to the performance of that which is good; he does not perform that which is good, but he perpetrates evil; evil is present with him; the law of his members wages war with the law of his mind and overcomes it, and renders the man a captive under the law of sin which he has in his members; and, being thus entangled and bound down, he is detained by the body of this death, (that is, by the body of sin,) and required with his flesh to serve the law of sin." (2.) But, as he is said to be placed under the law, the following affirmations belong to him correctly and without any contortion: "He allows not (he approves not) that which he does; he wills that which he does not, and he wills not that which he does; he consents to the law of God that it is good; it is no longer he who commits evil; he has good dwelling in his mind; the good that he wills he does not, but the evil which he wills not, that he does; he delights in the law of God after the inward man; with the law of his mind he wages war against the law of his members; he is exceedingly desirous of deliverance; and with his mind he serves the law of God." Nay, these two united classes of attributes, joined as they intimately are, in the text of the apostle, cannot belong to any other man than to this as he is placed under the law, and at the same time under the dominion of sin. So far from these two relations not being capable of belonging at once to the same man, that he who is under the law necessarily endures the dominion of sin, that is, the law is too weak to be able to release and liberate the sinner from the tyranny of sin. This is the subject upon which the apostle treats through the whole of this chapter, and points it out in the person of that man who is placed under the law in a mode the most excellent of all, that is, one in whom the law has fulfilled not only some part of its office, (for that did not serve the purpose which he had in view,) but in whom the law had discharged all its offices and acts; for this was required by the necessity of the cause about which the apostle was treating; because "the weakness of the law" could not be taught by the example of him who had not within himself all those things which are usually effected by the law. For the Jews might have always objected that some other persons had made still further progress through the power and efficacy of the law. If this observation, as well as many others, be diligently considered, it will be of great potency in effecting a persuasion that the present chapter must be understood as relating to a man who is under the law. And I feel fully persuaded within myself, that if views similar to these had entered into the minds of our expositors, when they explained this portion of Scripture, they would undoubtedly have interpreted it in this manner; for such were their piety and their learning, that I cannot bring myself to feel any other persuasion than this concerning them. But it frequently happens, that the fear of falling into error or heresy, if any passage be explained in a manner different from that generally received, hinders those who are under the influence of such a fear from venturing the more diligently to inspect such passage, and to consider whether it may not be explained appropriately and agreeably to the analogy of faith, even by that mode which is said to be favourable to heresy. I likewise believe, that this interpretation of mine is rejected by many persons who have never once thought on the mode in which the Scriptures define that man whom I assert to be described in this chapter. If they had earnestly endeavoured to ascertain this point, they would assuredly have discovered that all these things may be most commodiously explained concerning a man who is under the law. I will add, as the result of my own experience, that I have found multitudes who have not only not considered with sufficient diligence, but who also have not exhibited any desire to consider, what these names and epithets properly signify, and how they must be accurately distinguished from each other--the natural man, the carnal man, the outward man, the old man, the sensual man, the earthly man, the worldly man--also, the spiritual man, the heavenly man, the inward man, the new man, the illuminated man, the regenerate man, &c. The same persons also have not manifested any inclination to distinguish in an accurate and suitable manner between the acts and operations of the Spirit--when making use of the law, and when employing the gospel--when preparing a home or abode for himself, and when actually the inhabitant of his own temple--of his enlightening, regenerating and sealing--of his bringing men to Christ, uniting them to Christ--and communicating to them the benefits of Christ--of his operating, co-operating, exciting, aiding, assisting, and confirming or strengthening--and of his infusing habits, and producing good actions. All these things seem to me to be of such a description that if any person were, without a consideration of these matters, to attempt a serious and solid explanation of those things of which the apostle is treating in this chapter, his conduct would appear to me like that of a man who should endeavour to construct a large and splendid edifice without stones and lime. 4. These remarks I offer, with a sincere and candid mind, to those pious and learned men, and those eminent servants of Christ, my beloved brethren in Christ and fellow-labourers in the work of the Lord, who ought ever to receive from me all due honour and deference, to be read, known, judged, and approved or disapproved; and I request and most earnestly beseech of them only one thing, in the name of our common saviour--that, if they shall discover me to have written anything, in the preceding treatise, which is either contrary to the analogy of faith or contrary to the sense and meaning of the apostle, they will admonish, teach and instruct me about it in a fraternal manner. If they find any such matter, I testify, before God, that I will not only lend an attentive and patient hearing to their admonitions, teaching and instruction, but will also yield them full compliance. I likewise protest, that if, in the present instance, any things of this description have escaped from me, (for we all know but in part,) I consider them as not written and as not spoken. But if they shall perceive that these very things are agreeable to the rest of the Scriptures and conformable to the mind of the apostle, then I may be permitted to request and intreat from them that they will grant a place to the truth, thus pointed out, in the church of Christ, which is the pillar and ground of the truth. I solemnly engage, that there is no cause for them to be afraid lest disturbances, quarrels, dissensions, or the occasions of such great evils, in the Christian church, should arise from such an examination and conference. They will have to discuss the subject with one--who knows in part how to distinguish between those doctrines which are simply necessary and fundamental, and those which have not in them an equal necessity, but are as the parts of a superstructure raised on a foundation--who, next to the necessity for truth, thinks all things should be yielded to the peace of the churches--who can, with Christian charity, bear with those that differ from him, provided they do not attempt "to have dominion over the faith of other persons"--who is not desirous with an officious hastiness to obtrude on the public either his own admissions, or those of other persons, which had been confided to each other for the sake of a mutual conference, but who knows how to retain them faithfully, and has skill enough to revolve them in his mind for nine long years, according to the ancient proverb, "One day is the disciple of another; our later meditations are wiser and more accurate than our early ones; we daily grow old and yet are learning many things" Lastly, they will have to discuss the subject with one who may be in error, but who cannot be a heretic, and whose will assuredly it is not to be one. Amicable, fraternal, and placid conferences of this description, instituted between professors of the same faith and of the same religion, are not only useful, but likewise necessary to the churches of Christ, for the further investigation of the truth, for retaining it firmly when discovered, and for boldly defending it against adversaries. From these friendly conferences, we may discover truth, since they are not undertaken through a desire for victory, or for the sake of defending some topic which had been formerly conceived and adopted. But from those others, which are not so much Christian conferences, as vehement, bitter and vexatious altercations, and which we perceive to be agitated by the followers and defenders of different religious professions, generally ensues the result that is comprised in the vulgar proverb, "Truth is lost in the midst of their wrangling." Such an issue is no ground of surprise when the very method and circumstances of the altercation very often declare that the whole affair was at its commencement undertaken, and afterwards prosecuted, without the spirit of truth, charity and peace; and that, as a necessary consequence, it has been conducted to a sad catastrophe, most lamentable to the churches of Christ. And let no man rashly persuade himself, that as long as the [visible] church shall be a sojourner in this world, and shall have, in the midst of her, unskillful, infirm and wicked persons, she will maintain the doctrine of Christ so correctly as not to require a still further investigation of the truth from the Scriptures, which are the inexhaustible fountain of divine wisdom, as to be able to dispense with the examination of those dogmas which are built up as a superstructure on the foundation of the Scriptures, and as not to be under the least necessity of confirming and defending Christian doctrine, by the force and weight of solid arguments, against ancient heresies which have been polished up after a new method, and against novel heresies which are daily springing up and becoming still more prevalent. It is not an act of arrogance to enter upon such an exercise and employment as this, but it is an act of true and solid piety towards God, which commands and prescribes that, as "a dispensation of the gospel has been committed to us," we ought to "stir up the gifts of God which are in us," to study and strive to augment the talents which have been divinely granted to us, and, with a pure conscience and in the fear of the Lord, to discharge the duties of this sacred ministry, to the sanctification of his name, the building up and edification of the church of Christ, and to the demolition and extirpation of the kingdom of Satan and of Antichrist--which may the God and Father of our Lord Jesus Christ vouchsafe to grant to us, through and for the sake of his only begotten Son, and in the power and efficacy of his Spirit. Amen. END OF DISSERTATION ON ROMANS.

A LETTER ADDRESSED TO HIPPOLYTUS A COLLIBUS

Ambassador from the most illustrious Prince, The elector Palatine, Frederick IV, To the Seven United Dutch Provinces: BY THE REV. JAMES ARMINIUS, D.D. OF OUDEWATER IN HOLLAND An Eminent Professor Of Sacred Theology, Likewise, CERTAIN ARTICLES To be subjected to a diligent examination, because some controversy has arisen about them among the Professors of the reformed Religion: In Which Arminius more fully declares his sentiments on the principal Articles of Christian Doctrine.

BENEVOLENT READER

IT cannot be a matter of secrecy to you, how various, uncertain and prodigious the rumors are which have been circulated through Holland, Germany, and Great Britain, concerning James Arminius, Professor of Divinity; and in what manner (I do not stop to discuss with how much zeal) some persons accuse this man of schism and others of heresy, some charge him with the crime of Pelagianism and others brand him with the black mark of Socinianism, while all of them execrate him as the pest of the reformed churches. On this account, those persons who feel a regard for the memory of this learned man, and who, not without good reason, are desirous of maintaining his reputation and character, and of defending him from those atrocious imputations and virulent calumnies, have lately published some of his erudite lucubrations, which are polished with the greatest care. They have thus placed them within the reach of the public, that the reader, who is eager in the pursuit after truth, may more easily and happily form his judgment about the station which Arminius is entitled to hold among posterity, not from fallacious rumors and the criminations of the malevolent, but from authentic documents, as if from the ingenuous confession itself of the accused speaking openly in his own cause, and mildly replying to the crimes with which he has been charged. With this object in view, the friends of Arminius have published, as separate treatises, his "Modest Examination of a Pamphlet, written some years ago by that very learned Divine, William Perkins, on Predestination: To which is added, an Analysis of the Ninth Chapter of the Epistle to the Romans," and his "Dissertation on the true and genuine Meaning of the Seventh Chapter of the Epistle to the Romans." But these two works are neither sufficient nor satisfactory to many dispositions that are prying or that indulge in surmises, and to other eminent men who abound with an acrimonious shrewdness of judgment; because they embrace neither the whole nor the chief of the perplexing difficulties of James Arminius. Some of those who attended his Academical Lectures, affirm that he frequently uttered novel and astounding paradoxes about other points of the orthodox doctrine [than are contained in the two works just mentioned]. Other persons relate, as a great secret, that Arminius addressed "A Letter" to Hippolytus a Collibus, in which he more fully discloses his own pestiferous sentiments; and that "CERTAIN ARTICLES" are circulated in a private manner, in which, while treating upon several of the chief heads of orthodox theology, he introduces his own poisonous dogmas. In this state of affairs, we may be permitted to give some assistance to an absent person, nay, to one who is dead, and to offer a reply to the accusations and criminations which we have now specified, by the evidence of witnesses who are worthy of credit, and by the publication of the very documents which we are thus challenged to produce. Perhaps, by this means, we shall be able to remove those sinister insinuations and suspicions. We shall, at least, meet the wishes of a number of persons, and shall terminate the anxieties of several minds that have till now been in a state of suspense. Accept, therefore, candid reader, of that "Letter" about which so many reports have been circulated, and which was addressed to Hippolytus a Collibus, Ambassador from Prince Frederick 4, the Electar Palatine. Accept, likewise, of those "ARTICLES" which are to be diligently examined and pondered, and which give us the sentiments of Arminius on the One and the Triune God, The Attributes of God, the Deity of the Son, Predestination and Divine Providence, Original Sin, Free Will, the Grace of God, Christ and his Satisfaction, Justification, Faith and Repentance, Regeneration, the Baptism of Infants, the Lords Supper, and On Magistracy. Accurately consider and candidly judge whatever he thought necessary to be amended or to be rendered more complete in the doctrine of the reformed churches. The writing of this man require no commendations from me, or from any other person: There is no need of ivy in this instance, for these productions will insure approbation.

A LETTER, BY THE REV. JAMES ARMINIUS, D.D. &c. &c. TO HIS EXCELLENCY, THE NOBLE LORD, HIPPOLYTUS A COLLIBUS, AMBASSADOR, FROM THE MOST ILLUSTRIOUS PRINCE, THE ELECTOR PALATINE, TO THE SEVEN UNITED DUTCH PROVINCES, JAMES ARMINIUS WISHETH HEALTH AND SUCCESS MOST NONOURABLE SIR

When I was lately admitted to a conversation with you, you had the kindness to intimate to me the reports which you understood had been circulated at Heidelberg about my heterodoxy in certain articles of our faith; and you gave me this information, not only that you might yourself hear from me personally the whole truth about the matter, but, much more, that, by the intervention of your good offices, the suspicions concerning me, which have been so unhandsomely conceived and propagated, might be removed from the minds of other persons, since this is a course which truth requires. I endeavoured at that interview, with diligence and seriousness to comply with your obliging request, and by returning a frank and open reply to each of those questions which your excellency proposed, I instantly disclosed my sentiments about those several Articles. For, in addition to my being bound to do this, by my duty as a Christian man, and especially as a divine, such a course of conduct was demanded from me by the great candour, condescension and benevolence which you exhibited towards me. But my explanation was so agreeable to your excellency, (which I ascribe to an act of the divine Benignity towards me,) as to induce you, on that occasion, to think it requisite that those propositions of mine should be committed to writing and transmitted to you, not only for the purpose of being thus enabled the more certainly and firmly to form your own judgment about the matter when you had maturely reflected upon it, but also with the design of communicating my written answers to others, that they might confute the calumny and vindicate my innocence. Having followed the counsel of your prudence, and firmly relying on the same hope, I now accede to your further wishes, in this letter; and I intreat your excellency to have the goodness to peruse its contents with the same candour and equanimity as were displayed when you listened to their delivery. Unless my mind greatly deceives me, your excellency will find in this letter that which will not only be able to obliterate, but also completely to eradicate, every unjust suspicion concerning me, from the minds of those good men who know that every one is the best interpreter of his own sentiments, and that the utmost credit is to be given to him who sacredly, and in the presence of God, bears testimony to his own meaning. The articles of doctrine about which your excellency made inquiries, were, as far as my memory serves me, the following: the Divinity of the Son of God, Providence, Divine Predestination, Grace and Free Will, and Justification. Beside these, you inquired about the things which concerned our opinions, in answer to the interrogatories of the States of Holland, concerning the mode of holding the proposed synod. But as the latter relate to that most eminent man, the Revelation John Uytenbogard, minister of the church at the Hague, as much as to me, I leave them to be explained by him, whose residence is much nearer to that of your excellency. With regard to all these doctrinal Articles, I confidently declare that I have never taught anything, either in the church or in the university, which contravenes the sacred writings, that ought to be with us the sole rule of thinking and of speaking, or which is opposed to the Dutch Confession of Faith, or to the Heidelberg Catechism, that are our stricter formularies of consent. In proof of this assertion I might produce, as most clear and unquestionable testimonies, the theses which I have composed on these several Articles, and which have been discussed as Public Disputations in the university; but as those theses are not entirely in readiness for every one, and can be with difficulty transmitted, I will now treat upon each of them specially, as far as I shall conceive it necessary.

THE DIVINITY OF THE SON OF GOD

Concerning the divinity of the Son of God, I have taught, and still teach, that the Father has never been without his Word and his Spirit, but that the Word and the Spirit are not to be considered in the Father under the notion of properties, as wisdom, goodness, justice, or power, but under that of really existing persons, to whom it belongs to be, to live, to understand, to will, to be capable, and to do or act, all of which, when united, are indications and proofs of a person, but that they are so in the Father as to be also from the Father, in a certain order of origin, not through collaterality, to be referred to the Father, and that they are from the Father neither by creation nor by decision but by a most wonderful and inexplicable internal emanation, which, with respect to the Son, the ancient church called generation, but with respect to the Holy Spirit, was denominated spiration or breathing, a term required by the very [etymon of the] word spirit. But about this breathing, I do not interpose my judgment --

whether it is from the Father and the Son, as the Latin fathers express themselves, or from the Father through the Son, as the Greek fathers prefer to define it, because this matter, I confess, far surpasses my capacity. If, on any subject, we ought to think and speak with sobriety, in my opinion, it must be on this. Since these are my sentiments on the divinity of the Son of God, no reason could exist why, on this point, I should endure the shafts of calumny. Yet this slander was first fabricated and spread through the whole of Germany by one in whom such conduct was exceedingly indecorous; because he was my pupil, and ought to have refrained from that course, having been taught by his own painful experience that he either possessed an unhappy memory, or was of doubtful credit; for he had previously been convicted of a similar calumny, and had openly confessed his fault before me, and requested my forgiveness. But, as I learned from a certain manuscript which was transmitted to Leyden out of Germany, and which the same youth had delivered to the Heidelberg divines, he took the groundwork of his calumny from those things which I had publicly taught concerning the economy of our salvation, as administered by the Father through the Son and the Holy Spirit. In the explanation of this economy, I had said "that we must have a diligent regard to this order, which the Scriptures in every part most religiously observe; and that we must distinctly consider what things are attributed as peculiar to the Father in this matter, what to the Son, and what to the Holy Spirit." After this, some other persons seized upon a different occasion for the same calumny, from my having said that the Son of God was not correctly called Autoqeon "very God," in the same sense in which that word signifies "God from himself." This audacious inclination for calumniating was promoted by the circumstance of my having explained in a different manner, certain passages of the Old and New Testament, which have been usually adduced to establish the Consubstantiality or the coessentiality of the trinity. But I can with ease in a moment shew, from the books of the Old and New Testament themselves, from the whole of antiquity, and from the sentiments of the ancient church, both Greek and Latin, as well as from the testimony of our own divines, that nothing can be deduced from those alleged misinterpreted passages, which is with the least semblance of probability, adverse to the sound and orthodox faith. In his able defense of Calvin, against the treatise of Hunnius, entitled "Calvin Judaizing," the learned Paraeus has taught that this last occasion was seized upon in vain; and he has liberated me from the necessity of this service. To spend any time in confuting the first slander, which was circulated by the young student, would not repay my trouble. Those who know that the Father in the Son hath reconciled the world unto himself, and administers the word of reconciliation through the Spirit, know, likewise, that, in the dispensation of salvation, an order must be considered among the persons of the Trinity, and their attributes must not be confounded, unless they be desirous of falling into the heresy of the Patripassionists. Respecting the second occasion, which concerns the word Autoqeon "very God," an answer somewhat more laboured must be undertaken, because there are not a few persons who are of a contrary opinion, and yet our church does not consider such persons as holding wrong sentiments concerning the trinity. This is the manner in which they propound their doctrine. "Because the essence of the Father and of the Son is one, and because it has its origin from no one, therefore, in this respect, the Son is correctly denominated Autoqeon that is, God from himself." But I reply, "The essence of the Son is from no one, or is from himself," is not the same as "the Son is from himself, or from no one." For, to speak in a proper and formal manner, the Son is not an essence, but having his essence by a certain mode Uparxewv of being or existence. They rejoin -- "The Son may be considered in two respects, "as he is the Son, and as he is God. As he is the Son, he is from the Father, and has his essence from the Father. But as he is God, he has his essence from himself or from no one." But the latter of these expressions is the most correct; for to have his essence from himself implies a contradiction. I reply, I admit this distinction; but it is extended much further than is allowable. For as he is God, he has the divine essence. As he is the Son, he has it from the Father. That is, by the word "God," is signified, generally, that which has the divine essence without any certain mode of subsistence. But, by the word "the Son," is signified a certain mode of having the divine essence, which is through communication from the Father, that is, through generation. Let these double ternaries be taken into consideration, which are opposed to each other, in one series, To have Deity -- To BE God To have Deity from the Father -- To BE the Son To have Deity from no one -- To BE the Father And it will be evident, that among themselves they mutually correspond with each other, thus: "to have Deity," and "to be God" -- "to have Deity from the Father," and "to be the Son" -- "to have Deity from no one," and "to be the Father" -- are consentaneous, though under the word "Father," as an affirmative, that is not signified which has its essence from no one; for this is signified by the word "ingenitus, inwardly born, which is attributed to the Father, though not with strictness, but only to signify that the Father has not his essence by the mode of generation. But the word "FATHER" by its own force and meaning is conclusive on this point: For where order is established, it is necessary that a beginning be made from some first person or thing, otherwise there will be confusion proceeding onwards ad infinitum. But, with respect to origin, he who is the first in this order has his origin from no one; he who is the second, has his origin from the first; he who is the third has his origin from the first and the second, or from the first through the second. Were not this the real state of the matter; there would be a Collaterality, which would make as many Gods as there were collateral persons laid down; since the Unity of the Deity in the trinity is defended against the Anti-trinitarians solely by the relation of origin and of order according to origin. But that it may evidently appear what were the sentiments of antiquity about this matter, I will here adduce from the ancient fathers, both of the Greek and Latin church, some passages which are applicable to this subject. BASIL THE GREAT According to the habit of causes to those things which are from them, we say that the Father has precedence before the Son. (Ever. lib. 1.) - because the Son has his source from the Father. According to this, the Father is the greater, as the cause and the source. Wherefore our Lord also has said, "My Father is greater than I," that is, because He is the Father. But what other signification can the word "FATHER" have, than the cause and the beginning of Him who is begotten from Him? (Ibid.) The Father is the root and the fountain of the Son and of the Holy Spirit. (Discourse against the Sabellians and Arius.) When I have said "one essence," I do not understand two [persons] distinguished from one, but the Son subsisting from the source of the Father, not the Father and Son from one superior essence. For we do not call them "brothers," but we confess them to be "the FATHER and the SON." But essence is identity, because the Son is from the Father, not made by command, but begotten from nature; not divided from the Father, but while he remains perfect, reflecting perfectly back again the light. But that you may not be able to charge these our assertions against us as a crime, and lest you should say, "He preaches two gods; he announces a multitude of deities;" there are not two gods, neither are there two fathers. He who produces two original sources, preaches two gods. (Ibid.) The way of the knowledge of God is, by one Spirit, through one Son, to one Father. And, on the contrary, natural goodness, natural sanctification, and royal dignity are transmitted from the Father, through the only begotten Son, to the Spirit. Thus we confess the persons [in the Godhead] and at the same time the pious doctrine of the unity is not undermined. (On the Holy Spirit, cap. 18.) GREGORY NAZIANZEN THE essence is common and equal to the Son with the Father, though the Son has it from the Father. (Fourth Discourse on Theology.) How is it possible for the same thing to be greater than itself and yet equal to itself? Is it not, therefore, plain, that the word "greater," which is attributed to the Father in reference to the Son, must be referred to CAUSE; but the word "equal," which is attributed to the Son, as to his equality with the Father, must be referred to Nature? (Ibid.) It may indeed be truly said, but not therefore so honourably, that, "with regard to the humanity, the Father is greater than the Son:" For what is there wonderful in God being greater than man? (Ibid.) AMBROSE Though Christ has redeemed us, yet "all things are of God," because from him is all the paternity. It is, therefore, of necessity that the person of the Father have the precedence. (On 2 Corinthians v. 18.) Consult also his remarks On 1 Corinthians 15. AUGUSTINE IF that which begets is the original source of that which is begotten, the Father is the source of the Son, because he begets him. (On the Trinity, lib. 5, cap. 14.) He did not say "whom the Father will send from me," as He said, "whom I will send from the Father," that is, plainly shewing the Father to be the source of the entire Deity. (Ibid. Lib. 4, Cap. 10.) - Therefore this was said concerning the Father: "He doeth the works;" because from Him also is the origin of the works, from whom the cooperating persons [in the Deity] have their existence: For both the Son is born of Him, and the Holy Spirit principally proceeds from Him, from whom the Son is born, and with whom the same Spirit is common with the Son. (Idem, tom. 10, fol. 11, col. 1.) Indeed God the Father is not God from another God; but God the Son is God from God the Father. But the Son is as much from the Father, as the Father is from no one. (Against Maximus, Lib. 3, cap. 23, col. 2.) HILARY There is no God who is eternal and without beginning, and who is God to that God from whom are all things. But the Father is God to the Son; for from Him He was born God. (Lib. 4, fol. 60.) The confession of the true faith is, God is so born of God, as light is from light, which, without detriment to itself, offers its own nature from itself, that it may bestow that which it has, and that it may have what it bestows, &c. (Lib. 6, fol 87.) It is apparent from these passages, according to the sentiments of the ancient church, that the Son, even as he is God, is from the Father, because he has received his Deity, according to which he is called "God," by being born of the Father; though the name of God does not indicate this mode of being or existence. From these quotations, it is also evident that, because the Father is the source of the Son, and of the Holy Spirit, he is called the source of the whole Deity; not indeed because God has any beginning or source, but because the Deity is communicated by the Father to the Son and the Holy Spirit. So far, therefore, is this from being a correct expression: "The Son of God as he is God, is from no one; and, with respect to his essence, is from himself or from no one." For he who has received his essence by being born of the Father, is from the Father with respect to his essence. I consider, therefore, that those who desire to think and to speak with orthodox antiquity, ought to abstain from these methods of expression; because, by adopting them, they seem to become the patrons of the opposing heresies of the Tritheists, and the Sabellians. Peruse the preface to the Dialogues of St. Athanasius On the Trinity, by Theodoure Beza; who excuses Calvin by saying, that he did not so solicitously observe the difference between the two phrases - - "He is the Son per se, through himself," and "He is the Son a se, from himself." If any one be desirous of knowing from me anything further on this point, I will not refuse to hold a placid conference with him either in writing or by conversation. I now proceed to the other topics, in the discussion of which I will consult brevity.

THE PROVIDENCE OF GOD

My sentiments respecting the providence of God are these: It is present with, and presides over, all things; and all things, according to their essences, quantities, qualities, relations, actions, passions, places, times, stations and habits, are subject to its governance, conservation, and direction. I except neither particular, sublunary, vile, nor contingent things, not even the free wills of men or of angels, either good or evil: And, what is still more, I do not take away from the government of the divine providence even sins themselves, whether we take into our consideration their commencement, their progress, or their termination. 1. With respect to the Beginning of Sin, I attribute the following acts to the providence of God: First. Permission, and that not idle, but which has united in it four positive acts: (1.) The preservation of the creature according to essence, life and capability. (2.) Care lest a greater or an equal power be placed in opposition. (3.) The offering of an object against which sin will be committed. (4.) The destined concession of its concurrence, which, on account of the dependence of a second on the first cause, is a necessary concurrence. Secondly. The administration of arguments and occasions, soliciting to the perpetration of sin. Thirdly. The determination of place, time, manner, and of similar circumstances. Fourthly. The immediate concurrence itself of God with the act of sin. 2. With respect to the Progress of sin, I attribute also the following four acts to the divine government: The First is the direction of sin that is already begun, to a certain object, at which the offending creature either has not aimed, or has not absolutely aimed. The Second act is the direction of sin to the end which God himself wills, whether the creature intend or do not intend that end, nay, though he intend another and quite opposite end. The Third act is the prescribing and determination of the time during which he wills or permits sin to endure. The Fourth act is the defining of its magnitude, by which limits are placed on sin, that it may not increase and assume greater strength. The whole of these acts, both concerning the commencement and the progress of sin, I consider distinctly in reference to the act itself, and to the anomy or transgression of the law, a course which, according to my judgment, is necessary and useful. 3. Lastly, with respect to the END and COMPLETION of sin, I attribute to divine providence either punishment through severity, or remission through grace; which are occupied about sin, in reference to its being sin and to its being a transgression, of the law. But I most solicitously avoid two causes of offense -- that God be not proposed as the author of sin, and that its liberty be not taken away from the human will. These are two points which, if any one knows how to avoid, he will think upon no act which I will not in that case most gladly allow to be ascribed to the providence of God, provided a just regard be had to the divine pre-eminence. But I have given a most ample explanation of these my sentiments, in the theses which were twice publicly disputed on the same subject in the university. On this account, therefore, I declare that I am much surprised, and not without good reason, at my being aspersed with this calumny - - that I hold corrupt opinions respecting the providence of God. If it be allowable to indulge in conjecture, I think this slander had its origin in the fact of my denying that, with respect to the decree of God, Adam necessarily sinned -- an assertion which I yet constantly deny, and think it one that ought not to be tolerated, unless the word "necessarily" be received in the acceptation of "infallibly," as it is by some persons; though this change does not agree with the etymology of the two words; for, necessity is an affection of being, but infallibility is an affection of the mind. Yet I easily endure the use of the first of these words, provided those two inconveniences to which I have recently alluded be faithfully avoided.

DIVINE PREDESTINATION

With respect to the article of predestination, my sentiments upon it are the following: It is an eternal and gracious decree of God in Christ, by which he determines to justify and adopt believers, and to endow them with life eternal, but to condemn unbelievers, and impenitent persons; as I have explained in the theses on the same subject, which were publicly disputed, and in which, no one found any thing to be reprehended as false or unsound. Only it was the opinion of some persons that those theses did not contain all the things which belong to this decree; nay, that the predestination about which there is the greatest controversy at this time, is not the subject of investigation in those theses. This indeed I confess; for I considered it the best course to discuss that decree of predestination which is the foundation of Christianity, of our salvation, and of the assurance of salvation, and upon which the apostle treats in the eighth and ninth chapters of the epistle to the Romans, and in the first chapter of that to the Ephesians- But such a decree as I have there described is not that by which God resolves to save some particular persons, and, that he may do this, resolves to endow them with faith, but to condemn others and not to endow them with faith. Yet many people declare, that this is the kind of predestination on which the apostle treats in the passages just cited. But I deny what they assert. I grant that there is a certain eternal decree of God, according to which he administers the means necessary to faith and salvation, and this he does in such a manner as he knows to be suited to righteousness, that is, to his mercy and his severity. But about this decree, I think nothing more is necessary to be known, than that faith is the mere gift of the gracious mercy of God; and that unbelief is partly to be attributed to the fault and wickedness of men, and partly to the just vengeance of God, which deserts, blinds and hardens sinners. But concerning that predestination by which God has decreed to save and to endow with faith some particular persons, but to damn others and not endow them with faith, so various are the sentiment, entertained even by the divines of our profession, that this very diversity of opinion easily declares the difficulty with which it is possible to determine any thing respecting it. For while some of them propose, as the object of predestination generally considered, that is, of election and reprobation, man as a sinner and fallen in Adam, others lay it down, man considered as created and placed "in puris naturalibus." Some of them consider this object to be, man to be created, or, as some of them express it, man as salvable and damnable, as capable of being created and of falling. Others of them lay down the object of election and reprobation, which they denominate Nonelection and Preterition, man considered in common and absolutely; but they lay down the object of reprobation, on which they bestow the appellation of Predamnation and Affirmative Reprobation, man a sinner and guilty in Adam. Lastly, some of them suppose that the object must be considered entirely in common, man as yet to be created, as created, and as fallen. I am aware that when this diversity of opinion is offered as an objection, it is usual to reply that, in the substance of the matter there is complete agreement, although some difference exists in the circumstances. But it would be in my power to prove, that the preceding opinions differ greatly in many of the things which conduce to the very matter and substance of this kind of predestination; but that of consent or agreement there is nothing except in the minds of those who hold such sentiments, and who are prepared to bear with those who dissent from them as far as these points extend. Such a mode of consent as this, [of which they are themselves the patrons,] is of the highest necessity in the Christian church -- as, without it, peace can by no means be preserved. I wish that I also was able to experience from them any such benevolent feelings towards me and my sentiments. In that species of predestination upon which I have treated, I define nothing that is not equally approved by all. On this point, alone, I differ -- I dare not with a safe conscience maintain in the affirmative any of the preceding opinions. I am also prepared to give a reason for this conscientious scruple when it shall be demanded by necessity, and can be done in a suitable manner.

GRACE AND FREE WILL

Concerning grace and free will, this is what I teach according to the Scriptures and orthodox consent: Free will is unable to begin or to perfect any true and spiritual good, without grace. That I may not be said, like Pelagius, to practice delusion with regard to the word "grace," I mean by it that which is the grace of Christ and which belongs to regeneration. I affirm, therefore, that this grace is simply and absolutely necessary for the illumination of the mind, the due ordering of the affections, and the inclination of the will to that which is good. It is this grace which operates on the mind, the affections, and the will; which infuses good thoughts into the mind, inspires good desires into the actions, and bends the will to carry into execution good thoughts and good desires. This grace goes before, accompanies, and follows; it excites, assists, operates that we will, and co-operates lest we will in vain. It averts temptations, assists and grants succour in the midst of temptations, sustains man against the flesh, the world and Satan, and in this great contest grants to man the enjoyment of the victory. It raises up again those who are conquered and have fallen, establishes and supplies them with new strength, and renders them more cautious. This grace commences salvation, promotes it, and perfects and consummates it. I confess that the mind of a natural and carnal man is obscure and dark, that his affections are corrupt and inordinate, that his will is stubborn and disobedient, and that the man himself is dead in sins. And I add to this -- that teacher obtains my highest approbation who ascribes as much as possible to divine grace, provided he so pleads the cause of grace, as not to inflict an injury on the justice of God, and not to take away the free will to that which is evil. I do not perceive what can be further required from me. Let it only be pointed out, and I will consent to give it, or I will shew that I ought not to give such an assent. Therefore, neither do I perceive with what justice I can be calumniated on this point, since I have explained these my sentiments, with sufficient plainness, in the theses on free will which were publicly disputed in the university.

JUSTIFICATION

The last article is on justification, about which these are my sentiments: Faith, and faith only, (though there is no faith alone without works,) is imputed for righteousness. By this alone are we justified before God, absolved from our sins, and are accounted, pronounced and declared righteous by God, who delivers his judgment from the throne of grace. I do not enter into the question be the active and the passive righteousness of Christ, or that of his death and of his life. On this subject, I walk at liberty: I say "Christ has been made of God to me righteousness" -- "he has been made sin for me, that through faith, I may be the righteousness of God in him." Nor yet do I refuse to confer with my brethren on this question, provided such conference be conducted without bitterness, and without an opinion of necessity, [that the partial view of any one should be generally received,] from which scarcely any other result can ensue than the existence of distraction, and of increased effervescence in the minds of men, especially if this discussion should occur between those who are hot controversialists, and too vehement in their zeal. But some persons charge me with this as a crime -- that I say the act itself of faith, that is, believing itself, is imputed for righteousness, and that in a proper sense, and not by a metonymy. I acknowledge this charge, as I have the apostle St. Paul, in Romans 4, and in other passages, as my precursor in the use of this phrase. But the conclusion which they draw from this affirmation, namely, "that Christ and his righteousness are excluded from our justification, and that our justification is thus attributed to the worthiness of our faith," I by no means concede it to be possible for them to deduce from my sentiments. For the word "to impute ," signifies that faith is not righteousness itself, but is graciously accounted for righteousness; by which circumstance all worthiness is taken away from faith, except that which is through the gracious condescending estimation of God. But this gracious condescension and estimation is not without Christ, but in reference to Christ, in Christ, and on account of Christ, whom God hath appointed as the propitiation through faith in his blood. I affirm, therefore, that faith is imputed to us for righteousness, on account of Christ and his righteousness. In this enunciation, faith is the object of imputation; but Christ and his obedience are the impetratory [procuring] or meritorious cause of justification. Christ and his obedience are the object of our faith, but not the object of justification or divine imputation, as if God imputes Christ and his righteousness to us for righteousness. This cannot possibly be, since the obedience of Christ is righteousness itself, taken according to the most severe rigor of the law. But I do not deny that the obedience of Christ is imputed to us; that is, that it is accounted or reckoned for us and for our benefit, because this very thing -- that God reckons the righteousness of Christ to have been performed for us and for our benefit -- is the cause why God imputes to us for righteousness our faith, which has Christ and his righteousness for its object and foundation, and why he justifies us by faith, from faith, or through faith. If any one will point out an error in this my opinion, I will gladly own it, because it is possible for me to err, but I am not willing to be a heretic. The preceding, then, as far as I remember, are the Articles which your excellency mentioned to me, with my explanations of them produced from sincerity of mind; and as thus sincere, I wish them to be accounted by all who see them. This one favour I wish I could obtain from my brethren, who are associated with me in the Lord by the profession of the same religion, that they would at least believe me to have some feeling of conscience towards God. And this favour ought to be easily granted by them, through the charity of Christ, if they be desirous to study his disposition and nature. Of what service to me can a dissension be which is undertaken merely through a reckless humour of mind, or a schism created in the church of Christ, of which, by the grace of God and Christ, I profess myself to be a member? If my brethren suppose that I am incited to such an enterprise through ambition or avarice, I sincerely declare in the Lord, that they know me not. But I can confess that I am so free from the latter of these vices, as never to have been tickled, on any occasion, with even the most enticing of its snares -- though it might be in my power to excuse or palliate it under some pretext or other. With regard to ambition, I possess it not, except to that honourable kind which impels me to this service -- to inquire with all earnestness in the Holy Scriptures for divine truth, and mildly and without contradiction to declare it when found, without prescribing it to any one, or labouring to extort consent, much less through a desire to "have dominion over the faith of others," but rather for the purpose of my winning some souls for Christ, that I may be a sweet savour to him, and may obtain an approved reputation in the church of the saints. This good name I hope I shall obtain by the grace of Christ, after a long period of patient endurance; though I be now a reproach to my brethren, and "made as the filth of the world and the offscouring of all things" to those who with me worship and invoke one God the Father, and one Lord Jesus Christ, in one spirit and with the same faith, and who have the same hope with me of obtaining the heavenly inheritance through the grace of our Lord Jesus Christ. I hope the Lord will grant unto me, that they and I may meekly meet together in his great name, and institute a Christian conference about those things which appertain to religion. O may the light of that sacred and happy day speedily shine upon me. In that assembly, I engage, through the grace of God, to manifest such moderation of mind, and such love for truth and peace, as ought deservedly to be required and expected from a servant of Christ Jesus. In the mean time [till this assembly can be convened], let my brethren themselves remain quiescent and suffer me to be quiet, that I may be at peace, and neither annoy them, nor create any uneasiness. If they entertain other thoughts concerning me, let them institute an [ecclesiastical] action against me; I will not shun or evade the authority of a competent judge, neither will I forfeit my recognizances by failing to appear. If it be supposed that the minds of those who hear me are preoccupied in my favour, at a distance, by some politic subtlety which I display, and that the matter is so managed through cunning, as makes my brethren neither to consider it advisable to arraign me before the judges, nor to account it sufficiently safe to commit to my care the youthful students; and therefore, that the black stain which I have deserved ought to be affixed to my reputation, that my pupils and hearers may be frightened away; therefore, lest the result of this should be that the deferring of such a conference be productive of certain danger, behold I now offer myself, that I may, in company with them, address, solicit, and intreat those high personages who are invested with the power of issuing a summons for a convention of this kind, or of granting it, not to suffer us any longer to continue in this anguish and disquietude of mind, but either themselves to apply a speedy remedy, or allow it to be applied by others, but still by their order and under their direction. I will not refuse to place myself before any assembly whatsoever, whether it be composed of all the ministers in our United Netherlands, or of some to be convoked from each of the seven provinces, or even of all the ministers of Holland and West Friesland, to which province our university at Leyden belongs, or of some ministers to be selected out of these, provided the whole affair be transacted under the cognizance of our lawful magistrates. Nor do I avoid or dread the presence of learned men, who may be invited from other countries, provided they be present at the conference on equitable conditions, and subject to the same laws as those under which I must be placed. To express the whole matter at once -- let a convention be summoned, consisting of many members or of few, provided some bright hope of success be afforded [to them], a hope, I repeat it, which I shall be able, by sound arguments, to prove destitute of good foundation. Behold me, this day, nay, this very hour, prepared and ready to enter into it. For I am weary of being daily aspersed with the filthy scum of fresh calumnies, and grieved at being burdened with the necessity of clearing myself from them. In this part of my conduct, I am assuredly dissimilar from heretics, who have either avoided ecclesiastical assemblies, or have managed matters so as to be able to confide in the number of their retainers, and to expect a certain victory. But I have finished. For I have occupied your attention, most honourable sir, a sufficient length of time; and I have made a serious encroachment on those valuable moments which you would have devoted to matters of greater importance. Your excellency will have the condescension to forgive the liberty which I have taken to address this letter to you, as it has been extorted from me by a degree of necessity -- and not to disdain to afford me your patronage and protection, just so far as divine truth and the peace and concord of the Christian church will allow you to vouchsafe. I pray and beseech Almighty God long to preserve your excellency in safety, to endue you yet more with the spirit of wisdom and prudence, by which you may be enabled to discharge the duties of the embassy which has been imposed upon you, and thus meet the wishes of the most illustrious prince, the Elector Palatine. And, after you have happily discharged those duties, may he benignantly and graciously grant to you a prosperous return to your own country and kindred. Thus prays Your excellency's most devoted servant,

JAMES ARMINIUS, Professor of Theology in the University of Leyden. LEYDEN, April 5, 1608
END OF THE LETTER TO HIPPOLYTUS A COLLIBUS

CERTAIN ARTICLES TO BE DILIGENTLY EXAMINED AND WEIGHED

BECAUSE SOME CONTROVERSY HAS ARISEN CONCERNING THEM AMONG EVEN THOSE WHO PROFESS THE REFORMED RELIGION

These articles are partly either denied or affirmed in a decisive manner, and partly either denied or affirmed in a doubting manner, each of which methods signified by certain indicative signs which are added to the different articles. I. ON THE

SCRIPTURE AND HUMAN TRADITIONS

The rule of theological verity is not two-fold, one primary and the other secondary; but it is one and simple, the Sacred Scriptures. 2. The Scriptures are the rule of all divine verity, from themselves, in themselves, and through themselves; and it is a rash assertion, "that they are indeed the rule, but only when understood according to the meaning of the confession of the Dutch churches, or when explained by the interpretation of the Heidelberg Catechism." 3. No writing composed by men -- by one man, by few men, or by many -- (with the exception of the Holy Scriptures,) is either axiopison "creditable of itself," or autopison "of itself deserving of implicit credence," and, therefore, is not exempted from an examination to be instituted by means of the Scriptures. 4. It is a thoughtless assertion, "that the Confession and Catechism are called in question, when they are subjected to examination;" for they have never been placed beyond the hazard of being called in doubt, nor can they be so placed. 5. It is tyrannical and popish to bind the consciences of men by human writings, and to hinder them from being submitted to a legitimate examination, under what pretext soever such tyrannical conduct is adopted.

II. ON GOD CONSIDERED ACCORDING TO HIS NATURE

GOD is good by a natural and internal necessity, not freely; which last word is stupidly explained by the terms "unconstrainedly" and "not slavishly." 2. God foreknows future things through the infinity of his essence, and through the pre-eminent perfection of his understanding and prescience, not as he willed or decreed that they should necessarily be done, though he would not foreknow them except as they were future, and they would not be future unless God had decreed either to perform or to permit them. 3. God loves righteousness and his creatures, yet he loves righteousness still more than the creatures, from which, two consequences follow: 4. The First, that God does not hate his creature, except on account of sin. 5. The Second, that God absolutely loves no creature to life eternal, except when considered as righteous, either by legal or evangelical righteousness. 6. The will of God is both correctly and usefully distinguished into that which is antecedent, and that which is consequent. 7. The distinction of the will of God into that which is secret or of his good pleasure, and that which is revealed or signified, cannot bear a rigid examination. 8. Punitive justice and mercy neither are, nor can they be "the only moving" or final causes of the first decree, or of its first operation. 9. God is blessed in himself and in the knowledge of his own perfection. He is, therefore, in want of nothing, neither does he require the demonstration of any of his properties by external operations: Yet if he do this, it is evident that he does it of His pure and free will; although, in this declaration [of any of His properties] a certain order must be observed according to the various egresses or "goings forth" of his goodness, and according to the prescript of his wisdom and justice.

III. ON GOD, CONSIDERED ACCORDING TO THE RELATION BETWEEN THE PERSONS IN THE TRINITY

The Son of God is not called by the ancient fathers "God from himself," and this is a dangerous expression. For, Autoqeov [as thus interpreted, God from himself,] properly signifies that the Son has not the divine essence from another -- But it is by a catachresis, or improperly, that the essence which the Son has is not from another; because the relation of the subject is thus changed: for "the Son," and "the divine essence," differ in relation. 2. The divine essence is communicated to the Son by the Father, and this properly and truly. Wherefore it is unskillfully asserted "that the divine essence is indeed properly said to be common to the Son and to the Father, but is improperly said to be communicated:" For it is not common to both except in reference to its being communicated. 3. The Son of God is correctly called Autoqeov "very God," as this word is received for that which is God himself, truly God. But he is erroneously designated by that epithet, so far as it signifies that he has an essence not communicated by the Father, yet has one in common with the Father. 4. "The Son of God, in regard to his essence, is from himself," is an ambiguous expression, and, on that account, dangerous. Neither is the ambiguity removed by saying "The Son, with respect to his absolute essence, or to his essence absolutely considered, is from himself." Besides, these modes of speaking are not only novel, but are also mere prattle. 5. The divine persons are not trowoi uparxewv or modes of being or of existing, or modes of the divine essence; For they are things with the mode of being or existing. 6. The divine persons are distinguished by a real distinction, not by the degree and mode of the thing. 7. A. person is an individual subsistence itself, not a characteristic property, nor is it an individual principle; though it be not an individual, nor a person, without a characteristic property or without an individual principle. 8. QUERIES. -- Is it not useful that the Trinity be considered, both as it exists in nature itself, according to the co-essential relation of the divine persons, and as it has been manifested in the economy of salvation, to be accomplished by God the Father, in Christ, through the Holy Spirit? And does not the former of these considerations appertain to religion universally, and to that which was prescribed to Adam, according to the law? But the latter consideration properly belongs to the gospel of Jesus Christ, yet not excluding that which I have mentioned as belonging to all religion universally, and therefore to that which is Christian.

IV. ON THE DECREE OF GOD

The decrees of God are the extrinsic acts of God, though they are internal, and, therefore, made by the free will of God, without any absolute necessity. Yet one decree seems to require the supposition of another, on account of a certain fitness of equity; as the decree concerning the creation of a rational creature, and the decree concerning the salvation or damnation [of that creature] on the condition of obedience or disobedience. The act of the creature also, when considered by God from eternity, may sometimes be the occasion, and sometimes the outwardly moving cause of making some decree; and this may be so fare that without such act [of the creature] the decree neither would nor could be made. 2. QUERY. -- Can the act of the creature impose a necessity on God of making some decree, and indeed a decree of a particular kind and no other -- and this not only according to some act to be performed respecting the creature and his act, but also according to a certain mode by which that act must be accomplished? 3. One and the same in number is the volition by which God decrees something and determines to do or to permit it, and by which he does or permits the very thing which he decreed. 4. About an object which is one and the same, and uniformly considered, there cannot be two decrees of God, or two volitions, either in reality, or according to any semblance of a contrary volition -- as to will to save man under conditions, and yet to will precisely and absolutely to condemn him. 5. A decree of itself imposes no necessity on any thing or event. But if any necessity exists through the decree of God, it exists through the intervention of the divine power, and indeed when he judges it proper to employ his irresistible power to effect what he has decreed. 6. Therefore, it is not correctly said, The will of God is the necessity of things." 7. Nor is this a just expression: "All things happen necessarily with respect to the divine decree." 8. As many distinct decrees are conceived by us, and must necessarily be conceived; as there are objects about which God is occupied in decreeing, or as there are axioms by which those decrees are enunciated. 9. Though all the decrees of God have been made from eternity, yet a certain order of priority and posteriority must be laid down, according to their nature, and the mutual relation between them.

ON PREDESTINATION TO SALVATION, AND ON DAMNATION CONSIDERED IN THE HIGHEST DEGREE

The first in order of the divine decrees is not that of predestination, by which God foreordained to supernatural ends, and by which he resolved to save and to condemn, to declare his mercy and his punitive justice, and to illustrate the glory of his saving grace, and of his wisdom and power which correspond with that most free grace. 2. The object of predestination to supernatural ends, to salvation and death, to the demonstration of the mercy and punitive justice, or of the saving grace, the wisdom, and the most free power of God, is not rational creatures indefinitely foreknown, and capable of salvation, of damnation, of creation, of falling, and of reparation or of being recovered. 3. Nor is the subject some particular creatures from among those who are considered in this manner. 4. The difference between the vessels to honour and those to dishonour, that is, of mercy and wrath, does not appertain to the adorning or perfection of the universe or of the house of God. 5. The entrance of sin into the world does not appertain to the beauty of the universe. 6. Creation in the upright state of original righteousness is not a means for executing the decree of predestination, or of election, or of reprobation. 7. It is horrid to affirm, that "the way of reprobation is creation in the upright state of original righteousness;" (Gomarus, in his Theses on Predestination;) and in this very assertion are propounded two contrary volitions of God concerning one and the same thing. 8. It is a horrible affirmation, that "God has predestinated whatsoever men he pleased not only to damnation, but likewise to the causes of damnation." (Beza, vol. I, fol. 417.) 9. It is a horrible affirmation, that "men are predestinated to eternal death by the naked will or choice of God, without any demerit on their part." (Calvin, Inst. l. I, c. 2, 3.) 10. This, also, is a horrible affirmation: "Some among men have been created unto life eternal, and others unto death eternal." 11. It is not a felicitous expression, that "preparation unto destruction is not to be referred to any other thing, than to the secret counsel of God." 12. Permission for the fall [of Adam] into sin, is not the means of executing the decree of predestination, or of election, or of reprobation. 13. It is an absurd assertion, that "the demerits of the reprobate are the subordinate means of bringing them onward to destined destruction." 14. It is a false assertion, that "the efficient and sufficient cause and matter of predestination are thus found in those who are reprobated." 15. The elect are not called "vessels of mercy" in the relation of means to the end, but because mercy is the only moving cause, by which is made the decree itself of predestination to salvation. 16. No small injury is inflicted on Christ as mediator, when he is called "the subordinate cause of destined salvation." 17. The predestination of angels and of men differ so much from each other, that no property of God can be prefixed to both of them unless it be received in an ambiguous acceptation.

ON THE CREATION, AND CHIEFLY THAT OF MAN

The creation of things out of nothing is the very first of all the external acts of God; nor is it possible for any act to be prior to this, or conceived to be prior to it; and the decree concerning creation is the first of all the decrees of God; because the properties according to which he performs and operates all things, are, in the first impulse of his nature, and in his first egress, occupied about nihility or nothing, when those properties are borne, ad extra, "outwards." 2. God has formed two creatures rational and capable of things divine; ONE of them is purely spiritual and invisible, and [that is the class of] angels; but the OTHER is partly corporeal and partly spiritual, visible and invisible, and [that is the class of] men; and the perfection of this universe seeing to have required the formation of these two [classes of] creatures. 3. QUERY. -- Did it not become the manifold wisdom of God, and was it not suitable to the difference by which these two rational creatures were distinguished at the very creation, that, in the mode and circumstances of imparting eternal life to angels and to men, he might act in a different manner with the former from that which he adopts towards the latter? It appears that he might do so. 4. But two general methods may be mentally conceived by us, ONE of which is through the strict observance of the law laid down, without hope of pardon if any transgression were committed; but the OTHER is through the remission of sins, though a law agreeable to their nature was likewise to be prescribed by a peremptory decree to men, with whom it was not the will of God to treat in a strict manner and according to the utmost rigor; and obedience was to be required from them without a promise or pardon. 5. The image and likeness of God, after which man was created, belongs partly to the very nature of man, so that, without it, man cannot be man; but it partly consists in those things which concern supernatural, heavenly and spiritual things. The former class comprises the understanding, the affections, and the will, which is free; but the latter, the knowledge of God and of things divine, righteousness, true holiness, &c. 6. With respect to essence and adequate objects, the faith by which Adam believed in God is not the same as that by which he believed in God after the promise made concerning the Blessed Seed, and not the same as that by which we believe the gospel of Christ. 7. Without doing any wrong to God, to Adam, and to the truth itself, it may be said, that in his primeval state Adam neither received or possessed a Proximate capability of understanding, believing, or performing any thing whatsoever which could be necessary to be understood, believed, or performed by him, in any state whatsoever at which it was possible for him to arrive, either by his own endeavours or by the gift of God, though he must have had a remote capability, otherwise something essential would still have been to be created within man himself. 8. The liberty of the will consists in this -- when all the requisites for willing or not willing are laid down, man is still indifferent to will or not to will, to will this rather than that. This indifference is removed by the previous determination, by which the will is circumscribed and absolutely determined to the one part or to the other of the contradiction or contrariety; and this predetermination, therefore, does not consist with the liberty of the will, which requires not only free capability, but also tree use in the very exercise of it. 9. Internal necessity is as repugnant to liberty as external necessity is; nay, external necessity does not necessitate to act except by the intervention of that which is internal. 10. Adam either possessed, or had ready and prepared for him, sufficient grace, whether it were habitual or assisting, to obey the command imposed on him, both that command which was symbolical and ceremonial, and that which was moral.

ON THE DOMINION OF GOD OVER THE CREATURES, AND CHIEFLY OVER MAN

The dominion of God over the creatures rests on the communication of the good which he has bestowed on them: And since this good is not infinite, neither is the dominion itself infinite. But that dominion is infinite according to which it may be lawful and proper for God to issue his commands to the creature, to impose on him all his works, to use him in all those things which his omnipotence might be able to command and to impose upon him, and to engage his services or attention. 2. Therefore the dominion of God does not extend itself so far as to be able to inflict eternal death on a rational creature, or to destine him to death eternal, without the demerits of the creature himself. 3. It is, therefore, falsely asserted, that "though God destined and created for destruction any creatures (indefinitely considered) without any consideration of sin as the meritorious cause, yet he cannot be accused of injustice, because he possesses an absolute right of dominion over them." (Gomar's Theses on Predestination.) 4. Another false assertion is this: "By the light of GLORY we shall understand by what right God can condemn an innocent person, or one who has not merited damnation, as by the light of GRACE we now understand by what right God saves unworthy and sinful men; yet this right we do not comprehend by the light of nature." (Luther On the Servitude of the Will.) 5. But still more false is the following assertion: "Man is bound to acquiesce in this will of God, nay, to give thanks to God, that he has made him an instrument of the divine glory, to be displayed through wrath and power in his eternal destruction." 6. God can make of his own whatsoever he wills. But he does not will, neither can he will, to make of that which is his own whatever it is possible for him to make according to his infinite and absolute power.

ON THE PROVIDENCE OF GOD 1

. The providence of God is subordinate to creation; and it is, therefore, necessary that it should not impinge against creation, which it would do, were it to inhibit or hinder the use of free will in man, or should deny to man its necessary concurrence, or should direct man to another end, or to destruction, than to that which is agreeable to the condition and state in which he was created; that is, if the providence of God should so rule and govern man that he should necessarily become corrupt, in order that God might manifest his own glory, both of justice and mercy, through the sin of man, according to his eternal counsel. 2. It appertains to the providence of God to act and permit; which two things are confounded when permission is changed into action under this pretext -- that it cannot be idle or unemployed. 3. Divine providence does not determine a free will to one part of a contradiction or contrariety, that is, by a determination preceding the actual volition itself; under other circumstances the concurrence of the very volition with the will is the concomitant cause, and thus determines the will with the volition itself, by an act which is not previous but simultaneous, as the schoolmen express themselves. 4. The permission of God by which he permits any one to fall into sin is not correctly defined as "the subtraction or withdrawing of divine grace, by which, while God executes the decrees of his will through his rational creatures, he either does not unfold to the creature his own will by which he wills that wicked work to be done, or he does not bend the will of the man to obey the divine will in that action." (Ursinus On Providence, tom. I, fol. 178.)

ON PREDESTINATION, CONSIDERED IN THE PRIMEVAL STATE OF MAN

It is not a true assertion, that "out of men considered in puris naturalibus, (either without supernatural things or with them,) God has determined, by the decree of election, to elevate to supernatural felicity some particular men, but to leave others in nature." 2. And it is rashly asserted that "it belongs to the relation or analogy of the universe, that some men be placed on the right and others on the left, even as the method of the master Builder requires, that some stones be placed on the left side, and others on the right, of a house which is to be built." 3. The permission by which God permits that some men wander from and miss the supernatural end, is unwisely made subordinate to this predestination; for it appertains to providence to lead and conduct a rational creature to supernatural felicity in a manner which is agreeable to the nature of that creature. 4. The permission, also, by which God permitted our first parents to fall into sin, is rashly said to be subordinate to this predestination.

ON THE CAUSE OF SIN UNIVERSALLY

Though sin can be committed by none except by a rational creature, and, therefore, ceases to be sin by this very circumstance if the cause of it be ascribed to God; yet it seems possible, by four arguments, to fasten this charge on our divines. "It follows from their doctrine that God is the author of sin." 2. First reason. -- Because they teach that, "without foresight of sin, God absolutely determined to declare his own glory through punitive justice and mercy, in the salvation of some men and in the damnation of others." Or, as others of them assert, "God resolved to illustrate his own glory by the demonstration of saving grace, wisdom, wrath, ability, and most free power, in the salvation of some particular men, and in the eternal damnation of others; which neither can be done, nor has been done, without the entrance of sin into the world." 3. Second reason. -- Because they teach "that, in order to attain to that chief and supreme end, God ordained that man should sin and become corrupt, by which thing God might open a way to himself for the execution of this decree." 4. Third reason. -- Because they teach "that God has either denied to man, or has withdrawn from man, before he sinned, grace necessary and sufficient to avoid sin;" which is equivalent to this -- as if God had imposed a law on man which was simply impossible to be performed or observed by his very nature. 5. Fourth reason. -- Because they attribute to God some acts, partly external, partly mediate, and partly immediate, which, being once laid down, man was not able to do otherwise than commit sin by necessity of a consequent and antecedent to the thing itself, which entirely takes away all liberty; yet without this liberty a man cannot be considered, or reckoned, as being guilty of the commission of sin. 6. A Fifth reason. -- Testimonies of the same description may be added in which our divines assert, in express words, that "the reprobate cannot escape the necessity of sinning, especially since this kind of necessity is injected through the appointment of God." (Calvin's Institutes, Lib. 2, 23.)

OF THE FALL OF ADAM

Adam was able to continue in goodness and to refrain from sinning, and this in reality and in reference to the issue, and not only by capability not to be brought into action on account of some preceding decree of God, or rather not possible to lead to an act by that preceding decree. 2. Adam sinned freely and voluntarily, without any necessity, either internal or external. 3. Adam did not fall through the decree of God, neither through being ordained to fall nor through desertion, but through the mere permission of God, which is placed in subordination to no predestination either to salvation or to death, but which belongs to providence so far as it is distinguished in opposition to predestination. 4. Adam did not fall necessarily, either with respect to a decree, appointment, desertion, or permission, from which it is evident what kind of judgment ought to be formed concerning expressions of the following description: 5. "I confess, indeed, that by the will of God all the sons of Adam have fallen into this miserable condition in which they are bound and fastened." (Calvin's Institute, lib. 3, cap. 23.) 6. "They deny, in express words, the existence of this fact - - that it was decreed by God that Adam should perish by his own defection." 7. "God foreknew what result man would have, became he thus ordained it by his decree." 8. "God not only foresaw the fall of the first man, but by his own will he ordained it."

ON ORIGINAL SIN

Original sin is not that actual sin by which Adam transgressed the law concerning the tree of knowledge of good and evil, and on account of which we have all been constituted sinners, and rendered obnoxious or liable to death and condemnation. 2. QUERIES. -- Is original sin only the absence or want of original righteousness and of primeval holiness, with an inclination to commit sin, which likewise formerly existed in man, though it was not so vehement nor so inordinate as now it is, on account of the lost favour of God, his malediction, and the loss of that good by which that inclination was reduced to order? Or is it a certain infused habit (or acquired ingress) contrary to righteousness and holiness, after that sin had been committed, 3. Does original sin render men obnoxious to the wrath of God, when they have been previously constituted sinners on account of the actual sin of Adam, and rendered liable to damnation? 4. Adam, when considered in this state, after sin and prior to restoration, was not bound at once to punishment and obedience, but only to punishment.

ON THE PREDESTINATION OF MAN CONSIDERED PARTLY IN HIS PRIMEVAL STATE, AND PARTLY IN THE FALL

IT is rashly asserted that "the matter of predestination, as it is opposed to reprobation, is man in common or absolutely, if regard be had to the foreordaining of the end; but if regard be had to the means for the end, it is man about to perish by and in himself and guilty in Adam." (Trelcatii Institut., lib. 2. On Predestination.) 2. With equal infelicity is it asserted that "one reprobation is negative or passive, another affirmative or active -- that the former is before all things and causes in things foreknown and considered, or that will arise from things; and that this act is respective of sin, and is called predamnation." 3. It may become a subject of discussion in what manner the following things can be said agreeably to this doctrine: "The impulsive cause of this predestination is the benevolent inclination of the will of God in Christ; and predestination is an eternal act of God, by which he resolves to make in Christ some creatures partakers of his grace and glory." 4. This is a stupid assertion: "The just desertion of God, by which he does not confer grace on a reprobate man, and which appertains to predestination and to its execution, is that of exploration or trial." This also cannot be reconciled with the expressions in the preceding paragraph.

ON PREDESTINATION CONSIDERED AFTER THE FALL

QUERIES. -- Out of the fallen human race, or out of the mass of corruption and perdition, has God absolutely chosen some particular men to life, and absolutely reprobated others to death, without any consideration of the good of the one or of the evil of the other? And from a just decree, which is both gracious and severe, is there such a requisite condition as this in the object which God is about to elect and to save, or to reprobate and condemn? 2. Is any man damned with death eternal, solely on account of the sin of Adam? 3. Are those who are thus the elect necessarily saved on account of the efficacy of grace, which has been destined to them only that they may not be able to do otherwise than assent to it, as it is irresistible, 4. Are those who are thus the reprobate necessarily damned, because either no grace at all, or not sufficient, has been destined to them, that they may assent to it and believe, 5. Or rather, according to St. Augustine, Are those who are thus the elect assuredly saved, because God decreed to employ grace on them as he knew was suitable and congruous that they might be persuaded and saved; though if regard be had to the internal efficacy of grace, they may not be advanced or benefited by it, 6. Are those who have thus been reprobated certainly damned, because God does not apply to them grace as he knows to be suitable and congruous, though in the mean time they are supplied with sufficient grace, that they may be able to yield their assent and be saved,

ON THE DECREES OF GOD WHICH CONCERN THE SALVATION OF SINFUL MEN, ACCORDING TO HIS OWN SENSE

The first decree concerning the salvation of sinful men, as that by which God resolves to appoint his Son Jesus Christ as a saviour, mediator, redeemer, high priest, and one who may expiate sins, by the merit of his own obedience may recover lost salvation, and dispense it by his efficacy. 2. The SECOND DECREE is that by which God resolves to receive into favour those who repent and believe, and to save in Christ, on account of Christ, and through Christ, those who persevere, but to leave under sin and wrath those who are impenitent and unbelievers, and to condemn them as aliens from Christ. 3. The THIRD DECREE is that by which God resolves to administer such means for repentance and faith as are necessary, sufficient, and efficacious. And this administration is directed according to the wisdom of God, by which he knows what is suitable or becoming to mercy and severity; it is also according to his righteousness, by which he is prepared to follow and execute [the directions] of his wisdom. 4. From these follows a FOURTH DECREE, concerning the salvation of these particular persons, and the damnation of those. This rests or depends on the prescience and foresight of God, by which he foreknew from all eternity what men would, through such administration, believe by the aid of preventing or preceding grace, and would persevere by the aid of subsequent or following grace, and who would not believe and persevere. 5. Hence, God is said to "know those who are his;" and the number both of those who are to be saved, and of those who are to be damned, is certain and fixed, and the quod and the qui, [the substance and the parties of whom it is composed,] or, as the phrase of the schools is, both materially and formally. 6. The second decree [described in § 2] is predestination to salvation, which is the foundation of Christianity, salvation, and of the assurance of salvation; it is also the matter of the gospel, and the substance of the doctrine taught by the apostles. 7. But that predestination by which God is said to have decreed to save particular creatures and persons and to endue them with faith, is neither the foundation of Christianity, of salvation, nor of the assurance of salvation.

ON CHRIST

QUERIES. -- After the entrance of sin into the world, was there no other remedy for the expiation of sin, or of rendering satisfaction to God, than through the death of the Son of God, 2. Had the human nature in Christ any other thing, than substance alone, immediately from the LOGOS, that is, without the intervention of the Holy Spirit, 3. Have the holy conception of Christ through the Holy Ghost, and his birth from the Virgin Mary, this tendency -- to cover the corruption of our nature lest it should come into the sight of God, 4. Does the holy life of Christ, in which he fulfilled all righteousness according to the prescript of the moral law concerning the love of God and of our neighbour, conduce only to this purpose -- that Christ may be a pure and innocent High Priest and an uncontaminated victim, But was it not like-wise for this purpose -- that this righteousness [of the holy life of Christ] may be our righteousness before God, and by this means performed by him for us, that is, in our name and in our stead, 5. Do those things which Christ suffered prior to his being placed before the tribunal of Pilate, concur with those which he afterwards endured, for the purging away and expiation of sins, and the redemption and reconciliation of sinners with God? 6. Was the oblation by which Christ offered himself to the Father as a victim for sin, so made on the cross that he has not offered himself and his blood to his Father in Heaven, 7. Is not the oblation by which Christ presents himself to his Father in heaven sprinkled with his own blood, a perpetual and continuous act, on which intercession rests or depends? 8. Is not the redemption which has been obtained by the blood of Christ, common to every man in particular, according to the love and affection of God by which he gave his Son for the world, though, according to the peremptory decree concerning the salvation of believers alone, it belongs only to some men?

ON THE VOCATION OF SINNERS TO COMMUNION WITH CHRIST, AND TO A PARTICIPATION OF HIS BENEFITS

Sinful man, after the perpetration of sin, has such a knowledge of the law as is sufficient for accusing, convicting, and condemning him; and this knowledge itself is capable of being employed by God when calling him to Christ, that he may, through it, compel man to repent and to flee to Christ. 2. An unregenerate man is capable of omitting more evil external works than he omits, and can perform more outward works which have been commanded by God than he actually performs; that is, it is possible for him to rule his inducements for abstaining in another and a better manner than that in which he does rule them; although if he were to do so, he would merit nothing by that deed. 3. The distribution of vocation into internal and external, is not the distribution of a genus into its species, or of a whole into its parts. 4. Internal vocation is granted even to those who do not comply with the call. 5. All unregenerate persons have freedom of will, and a capability of resisting the Holy Spirit, of rejecting the proffered grace of God, of despising the counsel of God against themselves, of refusing to accept the gospel of grace, and of not opening to Him who knocks at the door of the heart; and these things they can actually do, without any difference of the elect and of the reprobate. 6. Whomsoever God calls, he calls them seriously, with a will desirous of their repentance and salvation. Neither is there any volition of God about or concerning those whom he calls as being uniformly considered, that is, either affirmatively or negatively contrary to this will. 7. God is not bound to employ all the modes which are possible to him for the salvation of all men. He has performed his part, when he has employed either one or more of these possible means for saving. 8. "That man should be rendered inexcusable," is neither the proximate end, nor that which was intended by God, to the divine vocation when it is first made and has not been repulsed. 9. The doctrine which is manifested only for the purpose of rendering those who hear it inexcusable, cannot render them inexcusable either by right or by efficacy. 10. The right of God -- by which he can require faith in Christ from those who do not possess the capability of believing in him, and on whom he refuses to bestow the grace which is necessary and sufficient for believing, without any demerit on account of grace repulsed -- does not rest or depend on the fact that God gave to Adam, in his primeval state, and in him to all men, the capability of believing in Christ. 11. The right of God -- by which he can condemn those who reject the gospel of grace, and by which he actually condemns the disobedient -- does not rest or depend on this fact, that all men have, by their own fault, lost the capability of believing which they received in Adam. 12. Sufficient grace must necessarily be laid down; yet this sufficient grace, through the fault of him to whom it is granted, does not [always] obtain its effect. Were the fact otherwise, the justice of God could not be defended in his condemning those who do not believe. 13. The efficacy of saving grace is not consistent with that omnipotent act of God, by which he so inwardly acts in the heart and mind of man, that he on whom that act is impressed cannot do otherwise than consent to God who calls him; or, which is the same thing, grace is not an irresistible force. 14. QUERY. -- Are efficacious and sufficient grace correctly distinguished according to a congruous or suitable vocation and one that is incongruous, so that it may be called efficacious grace, which God employs according to his purpose of absolutely saving some particular man, as he knows it to be congruous or suitable that this man should be moved and persuaded to obedience; and so that it may be called sufficient grace which he employs, not for such a purpose, though, from his general love towards all mankind, some are affected or moved by it, on whom, by a peremptory decree, he had resolved not to have mercy? 15. The efficacy which is distinguished from efficiency itself, seems not to differ at all from sufficiency. 16. Those who are obedient to the vocation or call of God, freely yield their assent to grace; yet they are previously excited, impelled, drawn and assisted by grace; and in the very moment in which they actually assent, they possess the capability of not assenting. 17. In the very commencement of his conversion, man conducts himself in a purely passive manner; that is, though, by a vital act, that is, by feeling, he has a perception of the grace which calls him, yet he can do no other than receive it and feel it. But, when he feels grace affecting or inclining his mind and heart, he freely assents to it, so that he is able at the same time to withhold his assent.

ON PENITENCE

The doctrine concerning repentance is not legal but evangelical; that is, it appertains to the gospel and not to the law, although the law solicits and impels to repentance. 2. The knowledge or confession of sins, sorrow on account of sin and a desire for deliverance, with a resolution to avoid sin, are pleasing to God as the very beginnings of conversion. 3. In propriety of speech, these things are not the mortification itself of the flesh or of sin but necessarily precede it. 4. Repentance is prior to faith in Christ; but it is posterior to that faith by which we believe that God is willing to receive into his favour the penitent sinner. 5. QUERIES. -- Is the repentance of Judas properly called legal? 6. Was the penitence or repentance of the inhabitants of Tyre and Sidon, of which Christ speaks in Matt. xi. 21, dissembled and feigned, or true repentance?

ON FAITH

Justifying faith is not that by which any one believes that his sins are remitted to him for the sake of Christ; for the latter faith follows justification itself or remission of sins, which is the effect of justifying faith. 2. Justifying faith is not that by which any one believes himself to be elected. 3. All men are not bound to believe themselves to be elected. 4. The knowledge and faith by which any one knows and believes that he is in possession of faith, is prior by nature to that knowledge and faith by which any one knows and believes himself to be elected. 5. From these remarks, some judgment may be formed concerning that which is sometimes asserted, "A believing and elect person is bound to believe that he is elected." 6. Justifying faith is that by which men believe in Jesus Christ, as in the saviour of those universally who believe, and of each of them in particular, even the saviour of him who, through Christ, believes in God, who justifies the ungodly. 7. Evangelical and saving faith is of such vast excellency as to exceed the entire nature of man, and all his understanding, even that of Adam, when placed in a state of innocence. 8. God cannot of right require faith in Christ from that man whom, by an absolute will, he has reprobated, either without consideration of any sin, or as fallen in Adam; therefore, it was not his will that Christ should be of the least advantage to this man; or, rather, he willed that Christ should not profit him. 9. Faith is a gracious and gratuitous gift of God, bestowed according to the administration of the means necessary to conduce to the end, that is, according to such an administration as the justice of God requires, either towards the side of mercy or towards that of severity. It is a gift which is not bestowed according to an absolute will of saving some particular men; for it is a condition required in the object to be saved, and it is in fact a condition before it is the means for obtaining salvation. 10. Saving faith is that of the elect of God; it is not the faith of all men, of perverse and wicked men, not of those who repel the word of grace, and account themselves unworthy of life eternal, not of those who resist the Holy Spirit, not of those who reject the counsel of God against themselves, nor of those who have not been ordained to life eternal. No man believes in Christ except he has been previously disposed and prepared, by preventing or preceding grace, to receive life eternal on that condition on which God wills to bestow it, according to the following passage of Scripture: "If any man will do his will, he shall know of the doctrine, whether it be of God, or whether I speak of myself." (John vii. 17.)

ON REGENERATION AND THE REGENERATE

The proximate subject of regeneration, which is effected in the present life by the Spirit of Christ, is the mind and the affections of man, or the will considered according to the mode of nature, not the will considered according to the mode of liberty. It is not the body of man, though man, when renewed by regeneration through his mind and feelings, actually wills in a good manner, and performs well through the instruments of the body. 2. Though regeneration is not perfected in a moment, but by certain steps and intervals; yet, as soon as ever it is perfected according to its essence, that is, through the renovation of the mind and affections, it renders the man spiritual, and capable of resisting sin through the assisting grace of God. Hence, also, from the Spirit, which predominates in him, he is called spiritual and not carnal, though he still has within him the flesh lusting against the Spirit. For these two, a carnal man and a spiritual man, are so denominated in opposition, and according to [that which is in each of them] the more powerful, prevailing or predominant party. 3. The regenerate are able to perform more true good, and of such as is pleasing to God, than they actually perform, and to omit more evil than they omit; and, therefore, if they do not perform and omit what they ought to do, that must not be ascribed to any decree of God or inefficacy of divine grace, but it must be attributed to the negligence of the regenerate themselves. 4. He who asserts that "it is possible for the regenerate, through the grace of Christ, perfectly to fulfill the law in the present life," is neither a Pelagian, nor inflicts any injury on the grace of God, nor establishes justification through works. 5. The regenerate are capable of committing sin designedly and in opposition to their consciences, and of so laying waste their consciences, through sin, as to hear nothing from them except the sentence of condemnation. 6. The regenerate are capable of grieving the Holy Spirit by their sins, so that, for a season, until they suffer themselves to be brought back to repentance, he does not exert his power and efficacy in them. 7. Some of the regenerate actually thus sin, thus lay waste their conscience, and thus grieve the Holy Spirit. 8. If David had died in the very moment in which he had sinned against Uriah by adultery and murder, he would have been condemned to death eternal. 9. God truly hates the sins of the regenerate and of the elect of God, and indeed so much the more, as those who thus sin have received more benefits from God, and a greater power of resisting sin. 10. There are distinctions by which a man is said to sin with a full will, or with a will that is not full -- fully to destroy conscience, or not fully but only partly, and to sin according to his unregenerate part. When these distinctions are employed in the sense in which some persons use them, they are noxious to piety and injurious to good morals.

ON THE PERSEVERANCE OF SAINTS

QUERIES. -- Is it possible for true believers to fall away totally and finally: 2. Do some of them, in reality, totally and finally fall from the faith? 3. The opinion which denies "that true believers and regenerate persons are either capable of falling away or actually do fall away from the faith totally and finally," was never, from the very times of the apostles down to the present day, accounted by the church as a catholic doctrine. Neither has that which affirms the contrary ever been reckoned as a heretical opinion; nay, that which affirms it possible for believers to fall away from the faith, has always had more supporters in the church of Christ, than that which denies its possibility of its actually occurring.

ON THE ASSURANCE OF SALVATION

QUERIES. -- Is it possible for any believer, without a special revelation, to be certain or assured that he will not decline or fall away from the faith, 2. Are those who have faith, bound to believe that they will not decline from the faith? 3. The affirmative of either of these questions was never accounted in the church of Christ as a catholic doctrine; and the denial of either of them has never been adjudged by the church universal as a heresy. 4. The persuasion by which any believer assuredly persuades himself that it is impossible for him to decline from the faith, or that, at least, he will not decline from the faith, does not conduce so much to consolation against despair or against the doubting that is adverse to faith and hope, as it contributes to security, a thing directly opposed to that most salutary fear with which we are commanded to work out our salvation, and which is exceedingly necessary in this scene of temptations. 5. He who is of opinion that it is possible for him to decline from the faith, and who, therefore, is afraid lest he should decline, is neither destitute of necessary consolation, nor is he on this account, tormented with anxiety of mind. For it suffices to inspire consolation and to exclude anxiety, when he knows that he will decline from the faith through no force of Satan, of sin, or of the world, and through no inclination or weakness of his own flesh, unless he willingly and of his own accord, yield to temptation, and neglect to work out his salvation in a conscientious manner.

ON THE JUSTIFICATION OF MAN AS A SINNER, BUT YET A BELIEVER, BEFORE GOD

QUERIES. -- was it possible for the justice of God to be satisfied unless the law were likewise satisfied, 2. Is the satisfaction which has been rendered in Christ to the justice of God, the same as that rendered to the law through Christ? 3. Do legal righteousness and that of the gospel differ in essence? Or, Is the essence of both of them the same, that is, the matter -- the obedience performed to God, and the universal form -- the necessary conformity to the law? 4. Are there three parts of the righteousness of Christ by which believers are constituted righteous? Is the first of them the holiness of the nature of Christ, which is denominated habitual righteousness? Is the second those sufferings which, from infancy to the moment of his decease, he sustained on our account, and is this denominated his passive obedience, or that of his death? Is the third the most perfect, nay, the more than perfect fulfillment of the moral law, (add also that of the ceremonial law,) through the whole of his life to the period of his death; and is this denominated his active obedience, or that of his life? 5. Were not the acts of that obedience which Christ performed, and by which we are justified, imposed on him according to the peculiar command of the Father, and according to a peculiar compact or covenant entered into between him and the Father, in which he prescribed and stipulated those acts of obedience, with the addition of a promise that he should obtain eternal redemption for them, [the human race] and should see his seed, whom this obedience should justify through his knowledge, that is, through faith in him, 6. To which of the offices of Christ do those acts of obedience belong, 7. Is the righteousness of Christ the righteousness of a believer or of an elect person, before God imputes it to him? 8. Does God impute this righteousness to him before he justifies him through faith? 9. Or, which is the same thing, Is the object about which God is occupied in the act of justification, an elect person, unrighteous indeed in himself but righteous in Christ his head; so that he accounts him righteous because he is already righteous in Christ, that is, because the punishment due to him has been paid and endured by him in His Surety and Head, or because he has thus performed the obedience which was due from him? 10. Has an elect person really endured punishment in Christ and performed obedience, or only in the divine estimation or reckoning! And is this divine estimation, by which the elect person is reckoned to have endured punishment and performed obedience, an act preceding justification? 11. Does not the act of acceptation, by which God accepted the obedience of his Son, precede the oblation by which, through the gospel, he offers his Son for righteousness, 12. Is the accepted imputation of the righteousness of Christ justification itself, or a preliminary to justification? 13. Is not the act of apprehension, by which faith apprehends Christ and his righteousness, or Christ for righteousness, prior to justification itself? 14. If this act [of apprehension] be prior to justification, how is faith the instrumental cause of our justification; that is, at once the instrumental cause of the apprehending which precedes justification, and of justification itself which succeeds this apprehending, 15. Or, Does not faith apprehend Christ offered for righteousness, before faith is imputed for righteousness? 16. In this enunciation, "faith is imputed to the believer for righteousness," is the word "faith" to be properly received as the instrumental act by which Christ has been apprehended for righteousness? Or is it to be improperly received, that is, by a metonymy, for the very object which faith apprehends? 17. Is this phrase, "faith is received relatively and instrumentally," the same as "by the word Faith is signified, through a metonymy, the very object of faith"? 18. Or, Is it the same thing to say "we are justified by faith correlatively, and as it is an instrumental act, by which we apprehend Christ for righteousness" as we say "we are justified by obedience or righteousness"? 19. May the righteousness of Christ be correctly said to be graciously imputed for righteousness, or to be graciously accounted for righteousness? 20. When the apostle expresses himself in this manner, "Faith is imputed for righteousness," must not this be understood concerning the imputation which is made, not according to debt, but according to grace? 21. May that of which we are made partakers through faith, or by faith, be called the instrumental effect of faith? 22. When God has decreed to justify no one through grace and mercy, except him who believes in Christ, and, therefore, through the preaching of the gospel, requires faith in Christ from him who desires to be justified, can it not be said "when God is graciously judging according to the gospel, he is occupied about faith, as about a condition, which is required from, and performed by, him who appears before the throne of grace to be judged and justified"? 23. If this may be asserted, what crime is there in saying "through the gratuitous and gracious acceptance [of God] is faith accounted for righteousness on account of the obedience of Christ"? 24. Is "If the work of men who are born again were perfect, they might be justified by them, though they may have perpetrated many evil works when [or before] they obtain the remission of them" a correct assertion?

ON THE GOOD WORKS OF BELIEVERS

QUERIES. -- Is it truly said, concerning the good works of believers "they are unclean like a menstruous cloth", And does this confession, "We are all as an unclean thing, and all our righteousness are as filthy rags," &c., (Isa. lxiv. 6,) belong to those works? 2. In what sense is it correctly said "Believers sin mortally in every one of their good works"? 3. Do the good works of believers come into the judgment of God so far only as they are testimonies of faith; or like- wise so far as they have been prescribed by God, and sanctioned and honoured with the promise of a reward, although this reward be not bestowed on them except "of grace" united with mercy, and on account of Christ, whom God hath appointed and set forth as a propitiation through faith in his blood, and, therefore, with reference to faith in Christ?

ON PRAYER

QUERIES. -- Does prayer, or the invocation of God, hold relation only to the performance of worship to his honour? Or, does it likewise bear the relation of means necessary for obtaining that which is asked -- means, indeed, which God foresaw would be employed before he absolutely determined to bestow the blessing on the petitioner, 2. Is the faith with which we ought to pray, that faith by which he who prays believes assuredly that he will obtain what he asks? Or is it that faith by which he is assuredly persuaded, that he is asking according to the will of God, and will obtain what he asks, provided God knows that it will conduce to his glory and to the salvation of the petitioner?

ON THE INFANTS OF BELIEVERS WHEN THEY ARE OFFERED FOR BAPTISM

QUERY. -- When the children of believers are offered for baptism, are they considered as "the children of wrath," or as the children of God and of grace? And if they be considered in both ways, is this relation according to the same time, or according to different times?

ON THE SUPPER OF THE LORD

QUERY. -- Is not the proximate and most appropriate, and, therefore, the immediate end of the Lords Supper, both as it was at first instituted and as it is now used, the memory, or commemoration, or annunciation of the Lord's death, and this with thanksgiving for the gift of God, in delivering up his Son to death for us, and in having given his flesh to be eaten and his blood to be drank through faith in him?

ON MAGISTRACY

The chief magistrate is not correctly denominated political or secular, because those epithets are opposed to the ecclesiastical and spiritual power. 2. In the hands and at the disposal of the chief magistrate is placed, under God, the supreme and sovereign power of caring and providing for his subjects, and of governing them, with respect to animal and spiritual life. 3. The care of religion has been committed by God to the chief magistrate, more than to priests and to ecclesiastical persons. 4. It is in the power of the magistrate to enact laws concerning civil and ecclesiastical polity, yet not unless those persons have been asked and consulted who are the best versed in spiritual matters, and who are peculiarly designed for teaching the church. 5. It is the duty of the magistrate to preserve and defend the ecclesiastical ministry -- to appoint the ministers of God's word, after they have previously undergone a lawful examination before a presbytery -- to take care that they perform their duty -- to require an account of their ministry -- to admonish and incite those among them who are negligent -- to bestow rewards on those ministers who preside well over their flocks, and to remove such as are pertinaciously negligent, or who bring a scandal on the church. 6. Also to invoke councils, whether general, national or provincial; by his own authority to preside as moderator of the assembly, either in person or through deputies suitable for discharging such an office. 7. QUERY -- Is it useful to ecclesiastical conventions or assemblies, that those persons preside over them whose interest it is that matters of religion and church discipline should be transacted in this manner rather than in that? 8. For the discharge of these duties, the magistrate must understand those mysteries of religion which are absolutely necessary for the salvation of men; for in this part [of his high office] he cannot depend upon and confide in the conscience of another person. 9. The Christian magistrate both presides in those ecclesiastical assemblies in which he is present, and pronounces a decisive and definitive sentence, or has the right of delivering a decisive and definitive sentence.

ON THE CHURCH OF ROME

QUERIES. -- Must a difference be made between the court of Rome, (that is, the Roman pontiff, the cardinals, and the other sworn retainers and satelites of his kingdom,) and the Church which is denominated Romish? 2. Can those persons by no means be called "the church of Christ," who, having been deceived by the Roman pontiff consider him as the successor of St. Peter and the head of the church? 3. Has God sent a bill of divorcement to those persons, so that he does not at all acknowledge them as his, any more than he does Mahometans and Jews?

A LETTER ON THE SIN AGAINST THE HOLY GHOST TO JOHN UYTENBOGARD

HIS MOST DEAR AND PECULIARLY BELOVED BROTHER IN CHRIST, JAMES ARMINIUS WISHES HEALTH AND HIS WELFARE THROUGH CHRIST

Most Friendly Of Mankind: As You intend soon to preach before the members of your church on The Sin against the Holy Ghost, you request that I will disclose to you my meditations and musings on that subject, on which you had also previously asked my opinion; but at that time, it was not in my power to comply with your request; for I had formed no distinct conception in my mind respecting it, neither have my sentiments upon it yet attained to any certain and full persuasion. But my slight musings and meditations, I neither feel any desire of denying to you, nor would it be my duty to withhold them from one to whom I have long ago transferred the plenary fight of requiring and even commanding any thing from me. Nor will I suffer myself to be seduced from this desire of obeying you by any false and rustic shame, though I know that my contemplations on this question, are such as cannot satisfy you, since, in fact, they are not much approved by myself. For, of what kind soever they may be, I am aware that they deserve to obtain some excuse, as they are concerning that question, than which scarcely any one of greater difficulty can be found in the whole Scripture, as St. Augustine testifies when professedly treating upon this subject, (tom. 19, fol. 9,) in his explication of Matt. xii. 31,32. Besides, I hope and feel fully persuaded, that you will so polish these, my rough notes, that I may afterwards receive them from you not only with interest, but also others which will be able entirely to complete my wishes. But I will not at present examine what St. Augustine has produced on the same passage, when writing about this sin; nor what is found on this subject in the writings of other authors, whether among the ancients or in our own times, lest I should be unnecessarily prolix, especially as you are yourself extremely well furnished with their works, and are ready to make the necessary inquiry into their sentiments. I will transcribe for you my own meditations, not in that order which is suitable to the nature of the thing itself, (for how is it possible for me to do this, when it is not fully known by me?) but in the order which it is possible for me to observe in the confusion of various thoughts. It will not be useless, in the first place, to prefix to this investigation those passages of Scripture in which mention is made of this sin, or in which it seems at least to be made. "Wherefore I say unto you, All manner of sin and blasphemy shall be forgiven unto men; but the blasphemy against the Holy Ghost shall not be forgiven unto men. And whosoever speaketh against the Son of Man, it shall be forgiven him; but whosoever speaketh against the Holy Ghost, it shall not be forgiven him, neither in this world nor in the world to come. (Matt. xii. 31,32.) "Verily I say unto you All sins shall be forgiven unto the sons of men, and blasphemies wherewithsoever they shall blaspheme; but he that shall blaspheme against the Holy Ghost, hath never forgiveness, but is in danger of eternal damnation." (Mark iii. 28,29.) "and whosoever shall speak a word against the Son of man, it shall be forgiven him; but unto him that blasphemeth against the Holy Ghost, it shall not be forgiven." (Luke xii. 10.) There are, besides, two passages in the epistle to the Hebrews, the first of them in the sixth chapter, the other in the tenth, which it seems possible to refer to this subject without any great detriment. "For it is impossible for those who were once enlightened, and have tasted of the heavenly gift, and were made partakers of the Holy Ghost, and have tasted the good word of God, and the powers of the world to come, if they shall fall away, to renew them again to repentance; seeing they crucify to themselves the Son of God afresh, and put him to an open shame? (Heb. vi. 4-6.) "He that despised Moses' law, died without mercy under two or three witnesses; of how much sorer punishment, suppose ye, shall he be thought worthy, who hath trodden under foot the Son of God, and hath counted the blood of the covenant, wherewith he was sanctified, an unholy thing, and hath done despite unto the Spirit of grace?" (x, 28,29.) To these may be added a passage from St. John's first epistle: "If any man see his brother sin a sin which is not unto death, he shall ask, and he shall give him life for them that sin not unto death. There is a sin unto death: I do not say that he shall pray for it?" (1 John v. 16.) Let the following passage also, from the epistle to the Hebrews, be added, for the sake of explanation, not because it is on exactly the same subject: "For if the word spoken by angels was steadfast, and every transgression and disobedience received a just recompense of reward, how shall we escape if we neglect so great salvation, which at the first began to be spoken by the Lord, and was confirmed unto us by them that heard him, God also bearing them witness, both with signs and wonders, and with divers miracles, and gifts of the Holy Ghost, according to his own will?" (Heb. ii. 2-4.) To these, let another passage be subjoined from the Acts of the Apostles: "Ye stiff-necked and uncircumcised in heart and ears, ye do always resist the Holy Ghost. As did your fathers, so do ye." (Acts vii. 51.) But about the same persons, it was said, in a preceding chapter, "And they were not able to resist the wisdom and the Spirit by which Stephen spake." (vi, 10.) "And all that sat in the council looking steadfastly on him, saw his face as it had been the face of an angel." (vi, 15.) I unite these passages for no other reason than that I may be able to contemplate them all together at one glance, and may direct my thoughts according to them. And, first, we must see the appellations which the sin receives about which we are here treating. The Evangelists Matthew, Mark and Luke call it "the blasphemy of the Spirit," or "the blasphemy against the Holy Ghost." In the sixth chapter of the epistle to the Hebrews, it is called "a prolapsing" or "falling away," and in the tenth chapter of the same epistle, it is called "contumely poured on the Spirit of grace," or "a doing despite to the Spirit of grace." I might add, from the sixth chapter, "the crucifying afresh of the Son of God," and "the putting of him to an open shame;" and from the tenth, "the treading under foot of the Son of God," and "the profanation of the blood of the covenant," unless they were capable of being referred to some other thing, which we shall afterwards discuss. In 1 John v. 16, it is designated as "a sin unto death." The sin which is described in Hebrews ii. 2-4, is denominated "a neglecting of the salvation which was first announced by Christ and his apostles," and confirmed by God with infallible testimonies. In Acts vii. 51, it is called "a resisting of the Holy Ghost." We are permitted thus to employ these passages, because an inquiry is instituted into the genus of the sin. He, against whom the sin is committed, is styled by St. Matthew, Mark and Luke, "the Holy Spirit;" and, in Hebrews 10, he is called the "Spirit of grace;" by this addition of the epithet "of grace" to the Spirit, seems to be intimated that the person of the Holy Spirit himself is not so much the object of consideration in this passage, as some gracious act of his. The same Evangelists make a distinction between this sin and that against "the Son of Man," while in Hebrews 6 and 10, the same sin is said to redound to the ignominy of the Son of God and of his blood -- two declarations which must afterwards be reconciled, for each of them is true. But when the men who commit this sin are described, in Hebrews 6, as "those who were once enlightened, and have tasted of that heavenly gift, and were made partakers of the Holy Ghost, and have tasted the good word of God, and the powers of the world to come," in Hebrews 2, salvation is said to have been announced to them, and confirmed by indubitable testimonies. In Acts 6, it is attributed to them that "they were not able to resist the wisdom and Spirit by which Stephen spoke," and that they "saw his face as that of an angel." From these particulars, it seems proper to collect by what cause they were impelled who committed this sin. It is, moreover, attributed to this sin by Matthew, Mark and Luke, that it is irremissible, or not to be forgiven; by St. John that his unto death. The same thing is affirmed in Hebrews 6, but, as it appears to me, it is in the cause; for it is said to be impossible that he who has thus "fallen away should be renewed again unto repentance." In Hebrews 10, in the application of the comparison, this sin is said to deserve a more severe punishment than the despising of the law of Moses; and in the commencement of the same passage, the certainty of punishment is signified by these words: "He died without mercy," which seems also to be placed in the antapodosis, the repetition or summing up. In Hebrews 2, he who neglects this salvation is said "to receive a just recompense of reward." Besides, the cause why that sin is irremissible, unto death, and why the man who thus sins cannot be renewed unto repentance, seems to be rendered in Hebrews 6, in the following terms: "- seeing they crucify to themselves the Son of God afresh, and put him to an open shame." And in Hebrews 10, in the following words: "- who hath trodden under foot the Son of God, and hath counted the blood of the covenant, wherewith he was sanctified, an unholy thing." For it does not seem to me that these expressions can be placed collaterally with falling away and doing despite to the Spirit of grace; but I think they must be placed in subordination among themselves. Lastly, in Hebrews 2 a 10, is instituted a comparison between this sin and the violation and the despising of the law of Moses; for this likewise is worthy of consideration, that we may correctly determine concerning the kind of sin. From this comparison of it appears that the sin about which those passages treat, is not committed against the law of Moses. But from the contexture of those things which precede, and from a comparison of those which follow, is to be taken the occasion through which Christ, in the Evangelists, St. Paul in the epistle to the Hebrews, and St. John in his first epistle, have made mention of this sin. Let us now commence an inquiry into the matters which come under consideration in this sin, following, as far as possible, the guidance of those passages which we have premised and prefixed to this our disquisition. But to me it appears possible, most commodiously to circumscribe them within the following bounds: Let us, in the first place, (1.) enter into a discussion on the genus or kind of this sin; (2.) its object and mode; (3.) those who commit the sin; (4.) the impelling cause; (5.) the end of this sin; (6.) the degrees of this sin; (7.) the peculiar attribute of this sin -- its irremissibility or unpardonableness, and its cause. To these we shall subjoin the three other questions, which you mention in your letter. (1.) Can this sin be known by the human judgment, and what are the marks? (2.) Are those who are commonly considered to have perpetrated this sin, to be held as being guilty of it or not, (3.) Does not this distinction between the sin against the Son of Man, and that against the Holy Spirit, contribute to the confirmation of the truth of the personality of the Holy Ghost? 1. With respect to the genus or kind, it is a subject of much regret that a disquisition upon it is a matter of great difficulty. For it is produced from no other source than the too great fertility of sin, and its deduction and derivation into various species; yet it is not necessary to refer all the distributions and distinctions of sin to this point; we must descend commodiously by those degrees which may bring us down to this kind of sin. In order to do this, we must commence with that which is the highest. Sin, therefore, is the transgression of the divine law, of whatever description that law may be; for we are treating upon a sin of this kind. A transgression of the law is either special, against one or more of the precepts of the law; or it is universal, against the whole and entire law, which is called a rejection and abrogation of the law, and a defection from it, and which is as much against what is commanded or forbidden in the law, as against him who directly commanded it, through contempt for Him. This kind of sin, I suppose, is signified in the Old Testament by the phrase, to sin with a high or elevated hand; for the moral law consists of a preface which is contained in these words: "I am the Lord thy God, who brought thee out of the land of Egypt," &c., and of an enumeration of the precepts. Either the preface itself is rejected and God directly despised, or sin is committed against the precepts, none of which can in fact be violated without bringing ignominy on the divine Majesty and pouring contempt upon God. But every sin is not from a contempt for God. David committed adultery, which may be reductively or consequently referred to a contemning of God, and resolved into it; but he did not commit that sin through a contempt for God. The law of God is now two-fold -- the one of works, the other of faith; or, the precepts of the law are of two kinds: some, of the law properly so called, and others of the gospel. But this sin about which we are treating is not of the kind of those which are perpetrated against the law of God, whether it be a special or universal transgression and an apostasy from the law. This is evident from Hebrews x. 28,29; for this sin is there compared with the violation or abrogation of the law of Moses, as a greater sin with a smaller one. It is also evident from Hebrews ii. 2-4. This sin is also called "a doing despite unto the Spirit of grace," which is not that of the law, but the Spirit of Christ and of his gospel. It is easy to perceive the same thing in the Evangelists; for, in St. Matthew's gospel, Christ says, "but if I by the Spirit of God cast out devils, then the kingdom of God is come unto you." (xii, 28.) This sin, therefore, is committed against the Spirit who testifies that the kingdom of God has arrived; and, on this account, it is not committed against the law of God, but against the gospel of Jesus Christ. The same thing may be rendered evident from Hebrews 6, in which the apostle treats about a falling away from those gifts which are there enumerated, and which are the gifts of the gospel of Christ. Christ is also said "to be crucified afresh and put to an open shame "by this "falling away;" and, in Hebrews 10, he is said to be "trodden under foot," and "the blood of the covenant is said to be profaned." All these are sins committed, not against the law, but against the gospel of Christ. From these observations, it is evident, that those persons who assert that this sin is committed against the acknowledged truth concerning God, and concerning His will and works, have not taught concerning it with sufficient distinctness; they ought to have subjoined "against the truth of the gospel." But the commands of the gospel are two -- that of faith in Christ, and that of conversion to God. Concerning faith it is manifest. About conversion let us now inquire; for as aversion from God is produced by sin, the law accuses him who is thus averse or turned aside, and condemns him to cursing, without any hopes of pardon; but the gospel requires conversion and promises pardon. Therefore, conversion to God is an evangelical command, and not legal. But impenitence is opposed to conversion to God; and this, when final, condemns a man through the peremptory decree of God, that is, through that which is evangelical. This final impenitence, however, cannot be called "the sin against the Holy Ghost," which is the subject on which we are now treating. For (1.) final impenitence is common to all those who are to be condemned; while the sin against the Holy Ghost attaches to certain persons, or, rather, to very few. (2.) Final impenitence is not committed except at the closing period of life; but this sin is perpetrated while he is still running the space of life. This is apparent from 1 John v. 16: "There is a sin unto death; I do not say that he shall pray for it." (3.) Concerning him who commits the sin unto death it is said that "it is impossible for him to be renewed again to repentance;" but this would be a useless expression respecting one who was finally impenitent; for it is well known that all hopes of pardon are terminated by the short course of the present life. (4.) Respecting the sin against the Holy Ghost, it is affirmed that "it shall not be forgiven, neither in this world nor in that which is to come;" that is, it shall never be forgiven. But it is unnecessary to make such an affirmation concerning final impenitence. This sin, therefore, is a transgression of the precept which commands faith in Jesus Christ. But as the doctrine concerning faith in Jesus Christ is not only entire, but likewise consists of certain parts; from this may be assumed a difference in the transgression, that one is universal, the other special. The universal is that by which Christ is simply rejected and refused, and which may receive the general appellation of "infidelity" or "unbelief." The special is that by which Christ is not universally rejected, but is merely not accepted as he has been manifested in his word; and this is called "a heresy," that term being employed concerning those who, after having professed faith in Christ, do not preserve his doctrines entire and unsullied, but corrupt them. But the sin about which we are treating does not lie in this special transgression. It belongs, therefore, to the universal transgression of this precept concerning faith in Christ; and it is infidelity or unbelief. It is not all unbelief, of which there are various kinds. (1.) The infidelity of those who have heard nothing respecting Christ; but such persons do not commit the sin against the Holy Ghost. (2.) That of those persons who have indeed heard of Christ, but have not understood; (Matt. xiii. 19;) neither does the sin against the Holy Ghost attach to these men. (3.) The unbelief of those who have understood, but who have not been certainly persuaded and convinced in their consciences respecting the truth of the things understood; but these persons are not guilty of the sin against the Holy Ghost. (4.) That of those men who, being convinced in their consciences that Jesus is the Christ, by their infidelity still reject him; and, according to my judgment, to this class of persons belongs the sin against the Holy Ghost, about which we are now treating. Therefore, the genus or kind is a repulsion and rejection of Christ in opposition to conscience. It is not a mere abnegation or disowning; for that is the part of him who has previously made a profession. It is not an oppugnation or attack; for that belongs to further progress, [in the sin], as we shall, afterwards perceive. But it is worthy of observation, that in reality it is one and the same thing, whether it be called "a refusal of Christ," or "a rejection of the truth concerning Christ," provided a universal rejection be understood, and not a particular rejection in one doctrine or more. 2. Let us now come to the object. The object of this sin is said to be a person against whom the offense is committed, whether that person be God, or the offending mortal himself, or his neighbour. But we must take into our consideration not only the object, but also its mode, which the schoolmen denominate "the formal reason." This mode, when added to the object, causes the latter to be proper, adequate, and peculiar or suitable. A surface is an object of sight, but it is one which is coloured. An offense is committed against God by ingratitude, but it is against him as having merited better returns from us. We also sin against God by disobedience and contempt, as against him commanding, forbidding, promising, threatening, chastising, correcting, &c. Apostasy is committed against God, but it is against him when acknowledged as God, and to whose Deity and name he who falls away had devoted himself by oath. But, in this place, the object of the sin about which we are treating is Jesus Christ, and he immediately. This is the reason why I add the word "immediately," because he who rejects the Son, rejects also the Father. The mode of formal reason has been manifested and proved, [to the man who commits this sin,] nay, it has been known to be the Messiah and Redeemer of the world. This is evident from Hebrews vi. 6, in which those who thus "fall away" are said to "crucify to themselves the Son of God afresh and put him to an open shame." It is also evident from Hebrews x. 29, in which such persons are said to "tread under foot the Son of God, and to count the blood of the covenant an unholy thing." This is still more apparent from the words of the Pharisees, who said, "He casteth out devils by Beelzebub, the prince of devils," which are thus related by St. Mark: "For they said, he has an impure spirit," whether by these words they committed this sin, or not; for they contain the occasion on which Christ began to speak about the sin against the Holy Ghost. But because this mode agrees with the object through some gracious act, which proceeds principally and immediately from the Holy Spirit or the Spirit of grace; on this account this sin is called "the sin against the Holy Ghost" or against "the Spirit of grace;" because the offense is committed against that act of the Holy Spirit, either by despising the act, or by treating him also with ignominy. But that act of the Spirit is the act of testifying concerning Christ and the coming of his kingdom; an act not only sufficient to prove that Jesus is the Christ; but also efficacious, and assuredly convincing the mind and conscience of him to whom the testification is communicated concerning Christ; the operation and complete effect of which, in the mind of man, are an assured knowledge and persuasion of this truth, that "Jesus is the Christ, the Son of God." But of this sin the Holy Spirit is not the object; for it is not directed against his person. This is apparent from the end of the testifying and the object; for the end of this testification is Christ. But the object of this sin committed against the testification, and the object of the testification itself, are one and the same. And the end of the testifying is, not that the Holy Spirit, but that Jesus, be acknowledged and accepted for the Son of God and for the Anointed of the Lord. This is declared by Christ in the following words: "If I by the Spirit of God cast out devils, then is the kingdom of God come unto you." It also conduces to the same purpose that, not the Spirit out of Christ, but Christ himself in and through the Spirit, performed the miracles. From this, it appears, that the performing of miracles serves to prove the truth of the preaching of Christ concerning himself. From these remarks, I think, we may easily solve the difficulty which lies in the words of Christ, who distinguishes this "sin against the Holy Ghost" from "the sin against the Son of Man," and who declares that the former is irremissible or unpardonable, but that the latter is capable of forgiveness. For the sin against the Son of Man, without this testification of the Spirit, is remitted to many men; and it appears from the whole of this discussion, that regard is not had so much to the person against whom the sin is committed, as to the act of testification proceeding from the Holy Spirit, against whom the sin is perpetrated. With respect to the act, therefore, it is said to be perpetrated against the Holy Ghost, not against the Son of Man, but, with respect to the object, against the Son of Man, but who is known from the act of testifying. Since, then, regard is had rather to the act than to the object, in this respect this sin is called by Christ "the sin against the Holy Ghost," and is distinguished from the sin which is committed against Christ without any consideration of this mode and formal reason. I know there are among the fathers those who understand the appellation, "Son of Man," through a reduplication or reflection, to signify Jesus as he is the Son of Man, and the epithet, "Son of God," to signify Jesus as he is the Son of God. They also consider, that, when a sin committed against Jesus as he is the Son of Man, the offense is another and a less one than when he is sinned against as the Son of God. But such a consideration has no place here; for the testification of the Holy Spirit conduces to this end -- that the person who is sometimes denominated the Son of Man and sometimes the Son of God, be received as the true and only Messiah. Yet if any man be desirous of referring this consideration of some of the ancient fathers to the point under discussion, he will be able to say that a sin is committed against the Son of Man when Jesus is not recognized as the Son of God, but that a sin is committed against the Son of God, when it has been already proved, by undoubted testimonies, that he is the Son of God. The expressions in the Evangelist "Whosoever speaketh a word against the Son of Man, it shall be forgiven him," serve to favour this consideration, as do also those in the Epistle to the Hebrews, "crucifying to themselves the Son of God," and they who have "trodden under foot the Son of God," that is, Jesus, whom, through "the enlightening" of the Holy Spirit, they had previously accounted as "the Son of God." For it is manifest from the Scriptures that it was necessary to believe this attribute concerning Jesus of Nazareth, that he was the Christ, the Son of God, the saviour and Redeemer of the world, &c.; and as the object and the acts occupied about it have a mutual relation so that from an adequate object we can determine concerning the act, and from an act we can form a conclusion respecting the adequate object, it appears possible for us to conclude, from the acts which the apostle enumerates in Hebrews 6, and 10, that those persons who had thus sinned against Jesus, not only acknowledged him as the Son of God, but also sinned against him as against the Son of God whom they had so acknowledged. For, no one is said to "crucify the Son of God afresh," and to "tread him under foot," except that man who acknowledges him as the Son of God, and who sins against him under that consideration. For instance, the American Indians cannot be said to have "trodden under foot the gospel of Christ," when they trampled under their feet, and threw into the fire, the small volume of the four gospels, which was shewn to them by the Spaniards, who, in a boasting manner, represented it to them as the true gospel. 3. Let us now proceed to the description of the persons who commit this sin, that is, such as they are defined to us according to the Scriptures. But, generally, they are those who, through the testification of the Holy Spirit in their minds and consciences, are convinced of this truth -- that Jesus, the son of Mary, is Christ the Sod of God. Yet these persons may differ among themselves, and in reality do differ; for, after having been convinced of this truth, they either immediately reject Christ, never tendering him their names to be enrolled among his followers; or, having for a season embraced and professed Christ, they decline from him and fall away. Of the first of these two classes were the Pharisees, if, at the time when they said that" Christ cast out devils through Beelzebub," they were convinced in their consciences that such ejectment of the devils was truly the work of the Holy Spirit, as Christ had laid down his argument, "If I by the Spirit of God cast out devils, by whom do your sons cast them out?" Of the second class, are those of whom mention is made in Hebrews 6 and 10. For they who embrace Christ even with a temporary faith, do this through the illumination of the Holy Spirit; because "no man can say that Jesus is the Lord, except by the Holy Ghost." (1 Cor. xii. 3.) To these persons has been granted some "taste of the heavenly gift, of the good word of God, and of the powers of the world to come;" for the testification of the Holy Spirit concerning Jesus Christ the Son of God, when impressed with a full persuasion on the mind, can be followed by no other effect than the excitement of joy and gladness in the heart of him who professes Christ, as Christ himself declares, in Matthew xiii. 20, "But he that received the seed into stony places, the same is he that heareth the word, and anon with joy receiveth it," and as he also declares, in John v. 35, concerning those who "were willing for a season to rejoice in the light of John the Baptist." But on this subject consult Calvin's Institutes. (Lib. 3, cap. 2, sec. 11.) With regard to what is added in Heb. vi. 5, that the same persons "were made partakers of the Holy Ghost," this may be understood to relate to those extraordinary gifts of the Holy Spirit which at that period flourished in the church. This is likewise declared in Heb. ii. 4: "God likewise bare them witness, both with signs and wonders, and with divers miracles, and gifts of the Holy Ghost, according to his own will." In these persons, that abnegation or renouncing of Christ occurs which, in Hebrews 6, is denominated "a falling away," that is, from the truth which they have acknowledged, and from the confession of the name of Christ which they have made. About this renunciation of himself, Christ treats in a general manner in Luke xii. 9, subjoining to that passage a special mode in the particular deed which we are now discussing, and says, "Whosoever shall speak a word against the Son of Man, it shall be forgiven him; but unto him that blasphemeth against the Holy Ghost, it shall not be forgiven." To this genus of renunciation belongs the deed of Peter; but it is distinct, and differs greatly from this species, as will be very apparent in the next member that comes under our consideration. Therefore, the sin against the Holy Ghost is distinguished according to the mode of efficient causes, of which we have already adduced a distinction. 4. It follows that we now institute an inquiry into the cause of this sin.

The cause of all sin is commonly represented to be either ignorance, weakness, or malice. Ignorance, not negative, but privative of the knowledge which ought to be within, and, therefore, ignorance of the law. Weakness, too infirm to resist vehement passion and temptation, and the seductions which impel men to sin. Malice, by which any one knowingly and willingly, being enticed indeed by some temptation, but which can be easily resisted by the will, and which the will is able readily to overcome, is induced to sin. Though ignorance and infirmity are not directly and immediately the causes of sin, yet they are causes through the mode of prohibiting absence -- ignorance, through the mode of the absence of right knowledge and reason, which might be able to hinder from sin by instructing the will -- infirmity, through the mode of the absence of strength and capability, which might hinder from sin by confirming and invigourating the will. If, therefore, we be desirous accurately to examine this matter, the will is the proper, adequate and immediate cause of sin, and has two motives and incentives to commit sin, the one internal, the other external. The internal, which lies in man himself, is the love of himself and a concupiscence or lusting after temporal things, or of the blessings which are visible. The external motive is an object moving the appetite or desire; such objects are honours, riches, pleasures, life, health and soundness, friends, country, and similar things, the contraries to which the man hates and execrates, and is afraid of them, if he imagine them to be impending over him. But these motives do not move the will so efficaciously that the will is necessarily moved; for, in this case, the will would be excusable from sin; but they move the will through the mode of suasion and enticement. But now, when, through love of himself and the desire of some apparent good, (in which is included an avoiding or hatred of an apparent evil,) man is solicited or enticed to some act, which is indeed forbidden, but which he does not know to be sinful, then the will, following the appetite and erroneous reason, is said to sin through ignorance. But when, through the same motives, he is tempted to an act which he knows to be sin, then the will, following the appetite, sins indeed knowingly; but whether such sin is committed through infirmity or through malice, ought to be decided chiefly from the necessity of that good which the man is pursuing, and from the deep heinousness of the evil which he avoids. On this point, a judgment must also be formed from the vehemence of the appetite or passion, as well as from the inclination towards the person who seems desirous to hinder the completion or fulfilling of the desire, (a circumstance which does not on every occasion occur, but which for a certain reason I thought must be added in this place,) where a discrimination of the mode by which he endeavours to hinder, comes under consideration, whether it be good, lawful, and commanded, or whether it be evil, unlawful and forbidden. Let us now apply these remarks to our purpose. Paul persecuted the church of Christ, but he did it ignorantly, being inflamed with too great a zeal and desire for the law, as many of the Jews also crucified Christ, being ignorant that he was the Lord of glory; otherwise they would have refrained from such a nefarious crime. By those men, therefore, the sin about which we are treating was not committed. Peter denied Christ his Lord, whom he knew to be the true Messiah and the Anointed of the Lord, and his knowledge of this was obtained through an immediate revelation from the Father; but his conduct proceeded from a desire of life and a fear of death -- feelings which may attack even the bravest of mankind. he did it, therefore, through infirmity. Through fear of banishment, prescription, condemnation to the mines or to perpetual imprisonment, some persons have shrunk back from a confession of the name of Christ; and they must be considered as having thus sinned through infirmity. In order to recover the dignity of the sword, the official girdle, &c., which the emperor had threatened to take away from them unless they abjured Christ, some of the early Christians retained all their honours at the expense of denying Christ; yet still even these must be said to have sinned through infirmity. Some individual, having been vehemently tormented, afflicted, injured and stripped of his goods by a Christian prince, or by Christian people, breaks forth into passionate expressions of blasphemy against God and Christ; yet he must be considered as having acted thus through anger and dreadful commotion of spirit. But if the persons in the preceding instances were to add, to this their sin, hatred against Christ Himself and his doctrine, according to my judgment they would not be far from committing the sin against the Holy Ghost. To express and conclude the whole in one word, I affirm that this sin against the Holy Ghost is properly committed through malice. I understand, here, malice of two kinds: The one, by which no resistance is offered to concupiscence or desire, when that can easily be done, without much inconvenience; the other, by which Christ himself is hated, either because he endeavours, by his precepts, to hinder the completion or fulfillment of the unlawful desire; or because the enjoyment of such illicit desire is not permitted, on account of his cause and name. Both kinds of this malice were in those Jews with whom Christ had the transaction which is mentioned in Matthew 12. But they do not seem then to have been fully convinced in their consciences, that Jesus was the Christ and the promised Messiah. Let us add, therefore, to the other parts of the definition of this sin, that it is committed through malice and hatred against Christ, or through hatred of Christ and of the truth concerning him. This hatred I think is included in the words employed by the apostle in Hebrews 6 & 10; for such persons are there said "to crucify to themselves the Son of God afresh and put him to an open shame, to tread under foot the Son of God, to count the blood of the covenant an unholy thing, and to do despite unto the Spirit of grace." I suppose, by these words, are signified, not the results which happen to those who, beyond expectation, fall away or decline from Christ through their sin; but the acts which, of themselves, and by their own nature are allied to their sin, and which have an affinity with, and are consequences from, the same sin, not without the fixed purpose of those by whom it is committed. 5. To this cause, we will commodiously subjoin an end; for they correspond, for the most part, between themselves, and in a certain respect agree with each other. The end, therefore, is twofold. The one is the obtaining and the enjoyment of an apparent good which has been desired; the other is the completion of hatred, and the rejection of Christ and of his acknowledged truth, which Calvin has enunciated in these words:" -- for this purpose, that they may resist." By this very circumstance, is signified the malice of the man who thus sins, which, not content with obtaining the apparent good through the act of sin, is delighted even with the very act of sin as with its end or intention. This is a certain sign, that the will of this man has not been impelled by inclination or passion to perpetrate this crime, but that it has freely followed the inclination, and has added of its own this other thing -- hatred against Christ, from which, this hatred may be said to be entirely voluntary, and, therefore, arising from malice. For as appetite or desire is attributed to the concupiscible faculty, infirmity to the irascible, and ignorance to the reason or mind, so is malice attributed to the will. But from these things, considered in this manner, it seems the sin against the Holy Ghost may be thus defined: "The sin against the Holy Ghost is the rejection and refusing of Jesus Christ through determined malice and hatred against Christ, who, through the testifying of the Holy Spirit, has been assuredly acknowledged for the Son of God, (or, which is the same thing, the rejection and refusing of the acknowledged universal truth of the gospel,) against conscience and committed for this purpose -- that the sinner may fulfill and gratify his desire of the apparent good which is by no means necessary, and may reject Christ." 6. Let us subjoin these observations concerning the devotees of this sin. The following degrees of this sin, it seems to me possible to lay down in a commodious manner: The First is the rejection and refusal of Christ acknowledged, or of the acknowledged truth of the gospel. This degree is universal and primary; and it holds good under every circumstance, whether he who rejects and refuses Christ have for a season professed himself to be a disciple of Christ, or not -- a point which we have already discussed under the third head. The second degree is blasphemy against Christ the Son of God, and against the acknowledged truth of the gospel. The third is the assaulting and persecution of Christ, either in his own person or in those of his members, or the extirpation of the truth acknowledged. A fourth degree may be added, from the difference between the object, and the act by which that object is demonstrated and manifested; and this is blasphemy against the Spirit himself, or against the act of the Holy Spirit. For. he who calls Christ "a wine bibber," "a friend of publicans and sinners," "a seducer and false prophet," while he owns him to be the Son of God, sins in a different manner From him who says, that those miraculous operations of the Holy Spirit were performed by Beelzebub and were diabolical. 7. We have now arrived at the seventh division, which relates to the adjunct or attribute peculiar to this sin, that is, its being irremissible or unpardonable, and the cause why it is thus incapable of being forgiven. This sin is called "the sin unto death," not in the sense in which all sins merit death eternal, and that are, notwithstanding, remitted to many persons, as they have believed in Christ and are converted to God, but because no one who has committed this sin against the Holy Ghost, or who shall hereafter commit it, has at any time had the felicity, nor will he have it, of escaping death eternal. It is called "irremissible," not in the same manner as that in which unbelief and final impenitence are unpardonable, through this decree of God: "He that believeth not on the Son of God, is condemned," and "Unless ye repent and be converted, ye shall all likewise perish," &c. For these are conditions, without which sin is forgiven to no man. But it is called "unpardonable" in this sense, that, when it has once been perpetrated, the sinner never obtains remission from God, and never can obtain it, through the definitive and peremptory statute and decree of God, even though the offender should live many ages afterwards. But the proximate and immediate cause why this sin is unpardonable, seems to me to be comprehended in these words of the apostle in the epistle to the Hebrews: "It is impossible for those who shall thus fall away, to be renewed again unto repentance." The efficacy of this cause proceeds from the perpetual and immutable decree of God concerning the nonforgiveness of sins without repentance. But the mind cannot rest here; for it is further asked, "Why is it impossible for those who thus sin to be renewed again unto repentance?" The solution of this question, as it seems to me, must be taken partly from the causes of this "renewing again unto repentance," and partly from the heinousness of this sin, as described by the apostle in Hebrews 6 and 10. From a collation of these passages, it will be manifest why those who thus sin "cannot be renewed again to repentance." (1.) Let us treat on the causes of this renewing again. Renewing again to repentance seems to proceed from the mercy or grace of God in Christ, on account of the intercession of Christ, through the operation of the Holy Spirit, or the Spirit of grace. But this mercy of God, intercession of Christ, and operation of the Holy Spirit, are not infinite, that is, they do not operate according to the infinite omnipotence of God and Christ, and of his Spirit; but they are circumscribed by a certain mode of the equity and will of God, of Christ, and of the Spirit of God. This is apparent from particular passages of Scripture. Concerning the mercy of God, "God has mercy on whom he will have mercy; and whom he will, he hardeneth." Concerning the intercession of Christ, "I pray not for the world." Concerning the operation of the Holy Spirit, "whom the world cannot receive." (2.) Let us now consider the heinousness of this sin from the description of this apostle, who says, Those who thus sin, "crucify to themselves the Son of God afresh, and put him to an open shame; they tread under foot the Son of God, count the blood of the covenant an unholy thing, and do despite unto the Spirit of grace." But I account these acts to be so black and diabolical, that we must affirm, the mercy of God in Christ is circumscribed by no bounds whatsoever, the intercession of Christ is concluded within no space, and the Spirit of grace can be hindered by no malice, if God does not deny his mercy to such persons, if Christ intercedes for them, and if the Spirit of Grace is not deterred from them so as not to exert upon them his gracious efficacy. Take into consideration the difference of the sin which is committed against the law of God, and that against the gospel and the grace of God in Christ; and reflect how much more heinous it is to reject the remedy of the disease than to fall into the disease itself! To remove from his hearers their despair of pardon, St. Peter says to them, after having been convicted of the sin which they had committed against Christ, "Now, brethren, I wot that through ignorance ye did it." (Acts iii. 17.) St. Paul says to the Corinthians, "For had they known it, they would not have crucified the Lord of glory." (1 Cor. ii. 8.) He also says, concerning himself, "but I obtained mercy, because I did it ignorantly in unbelief." (1 Tim. i. 13.) Christ, when hanging on the Cross, and as the Scriptures express it in Isaiah liii. 12, while making intercession for the transgressors, said, "Father, forgive them, for they know not what they do." (Luke xxiii. 34.) The Scriptures declare, respecting the Holy Spirit, that he is capable not only of being grieved, (Ephes. iv. 30,) but likewise of being vexed, (Isa. lxiii. 10,) and of being quenched. (1 Thess. v. 19.) Whosoever they be who answer this description, and crucify Christ long acknowledged by them as the Son of God, and who tread under foot his blood, that blood by which God hath redeemed the church unto himself, which is the price of redemption, than which nothing is more precious, and by which alone the gratuitous covenant between God and men is confirmed and established -- who, against their consciences, treat the Holy Spirit with the greatest contempt and disgrace, and who sin so grievously against him that no sin can equal this in heinousness; it follows that, to people of this class, is justly and equitably denied their being renewed again to repentance, unless we completely divest God of justice, and remove from his free will the administration of divine mercy. When we have done this, and have ascribed the dispensing of salvation to the infinity of the divine mercy or goodness only, the very foundations of religion are then overturned, and by this means, life eternal is assigned to all men universally, and even to the devils. If any one supposes that the affirmations which are made in Hebrews 6 and 10, belong only to those who, after their open profession of Christianity, shall relapse and fall away, let him know that contumely and reproach are poured on "the Spirit of grace," by those who have never made a profession of Christianity, and that these words -- "to renew them again unto repentance," and "the blood through which he was sanctified," seem properly to belong to those who have not made a profession, and that the remaining parts of the description belong to the entire order of those who sin against the Holy Ghost. Having considered the preceding matters in this hasty and slight manner, let us now proceed to investigate those three questions which you proposed. I. With regard to the first, I think it may be known when any one has committed this sin; because, if this had been impossible, John would not have forbidden us to pray for that man. For we ought to pray for all those to whom, with even the least semblance of probability, the mercy of God has been manifested, for whom the intercession of Christ has been prepared, and to whom the grace of the Holy Spirit has not been denied. The ancient church formed a similar judgment, when she not only accounted it improper to pray for Julian, the apostate, but also actually prayed against him. But, according to my judgment, an indication of the knowledge of this sin is afforded by acts on the part of those who commit it. The first act is that profession of the name of Christ which is neither forced nor affected, but voluntary; the second is the rejection of Christ and the abandonment of all profession. If to these two acts be added blasphemy, opposition, &c., the judgment concerning this sin is rendered still more evident. From these remarks, it is manifest that the judgment of man can be formed only concerning those persons who have, at some time or other, made an open profession of Christianity, and have afterwards relapsed and fallen away. For it is impossible for us to know, except through [an act of] divine revelation, what effects the testification of the Holy Spirit has produced in the minds of those who reject Christ before they make an open profession of him and his religion. This seems to be intimated by St. John, when he says," If any man shall see his brother," that is, one who has made an open profession of faith in Christ, "sin a sin which is not unto death, he shall ask, and he shall give him life;" and it appears to be immediately repeated on the general principle, "There is a sin unto death," which, if a brother commit, I do not say that he shall pray for it." Let the whole history concerning Julian, the apostate, be taken into consideration, and it will be rendered manifest that the judgment of the church in that age was founded on the two acts which we have enumerated -- the former being the public profession of Christianity, and the latter the act of desertion, blasphemy and persecution. II. The second question is -- "Have Cain, Saul, Judas, Julian, Francis Spira, &c., perpetrated this crime?" In regard to this, I say, without any prejudice to the judgment of those who hold other and perhaps more correct sentiments on the subject, it seems to me that Cain did not perpetrate this crime. For this, a probable reason may, I think, be rendered: For he did not sin against grace through hatred to it, but through a perverse jealousy for grace, and through envy against his brother, because Abel had obtained that grace which was denied to himself, he committed crime of fratricide. Concerning the despair which is attributed to him, we know that interpreters differ in their opinions; and though he may have despaired of the mercy of God, yet it cannot be concluded from this that he had committed the sin about which we are treating; for despair is also a consequence of other sins, and not always, I think, an attendant on this sin. The sin of Saul was against David as a type of Christ, whom he persecuted in opposition to his conscience; but he committed it with this intention -- that he might afterwards preserve the kingdom safe and unimpaired for himself and his posterity. But as it is another thing to sin against the type of Christ, than to sin against Christ himself, (for Saul was in all likelihood ignorant of David being such a type,) and as he did not entirely decline from the Jewish religion, it has to me the air of probability that Saul did not commit the sin against the Holy Ghost. My opinion is different respecting Judas Iscariot; for I think that he sinned against the Holy Ghost, and this by the two indications which we have previously laid down. For as he lived three whole years in familiar converse with Christ, heard his discourses, saw his miracles, was himself sent forth with his fellow-disciples to preach the gospel, and was so far enlightened by the Holy Spirit as to be capable of executing that office, and actually did perform its duties, and, having been made a partaker of the Holy Ghost, he himself performed miracles, cast out devils, healed the sick, and raised the dead in the name of Christ, it cannot remain a matter of uncertainty that he assuredly and undoubtedly acknowledged his teacher, Jesus Christ, as the true Messiah and the Son of God. However, he not only deserted him whom he had thus acknowledged, but also delivered him up to his enemies, that sought to put him to death; and he did this not through weakness or some excusable necessity, but merely out of malice and pure hatred of Christ. This is evident from the history of the Evangelists, who relate that, at the moment when the "very precious ointment" was poured on the head of Christ, Judas departed and went to the chief priests, and bargained with them concerning the reward of his treason, which conduct was undoubtedly adopted by him to revenge himself upon Christ for the loss of the three hundred pence, for which the ointment might have been sold, and which were taken away from him, by Christ's permission. To this must be added, that the Scriptures reckon him among those against whom David, the type of Christ, formerly uttered the same petitions as those which St. Peter enumerates in that passage, (Acts i. 2,) as having had their accomplishment in Judas. I entertain a similar opinion respecting Julian the apostate, whom I consider to have completed every branch of this sin through consummate malice and the most bitter enmity against Christ. For he abandoned Christianity, poured infinite contumelies on Christ, and persecuted Christian people and the Christian truth in various ways, nay, by every method which it was possible for him to devise. He also attributed the miracles of Christ more to the devil than to the Son of God, for which reason, the church, in those early days, prayed against him, and her prayers were heard by God, and answered. With respect to Francis Spira, it would be with great reluctance that I should venture to pronounce him guilty of the sin against the Holy Ghost. On the contrary, I incline to the opposite opinion respecting him, and in this I follow the judgment of some learned men of the present age, who not only acquit him from the guilt of being charged with this sin, but who likewise do not even exclude him from the pardon of his sins. For (1.)he did not deny Christ himself, but declined to make such a confession of Christ as the Papists disapproved. (2.) He did not avoid this Protestant confession through malice and hatred of the truth known by him, but through weakness and too intense a desire for a good which appeared to him in some degree necessary; for he feared the forcible seizure and loss of his goods, without which he supposed it to be utterly impossible for him to gain a livelihood for himself and family. (3.) In the very agonies of his despair, he made frequent and honourable mention not only of Christ, but likewise of his truth which he had professed. (4.) Being asked by those who stood around him if he wished God to grant him pardon for that offense and to impress the assurance of it upon his mind, he replied, that there was nothing of which he was more desirous, nay, that he wished it could be purchased even by the greatest torments. The purchase of it, however, he knew to be an impossibility -- that no one might suppose that, by this his desire, he inflicted an injury on the blood of Christ. (5.) He diligently and seriously admonished those who visited him to apply themselves to the mortification of the flesh, to renounce the good things of the present life, and also to despise life itself if the cause of Christ and of truth were to be forsaken, lest they, having followed his example, should rush into the same abyss of despair and damnation. All these particulars [in His case] served as inducements to many persons [in the Venitian states] to withdraw from the papal church, and to unite themselves with the evangelical or reformed church; and to some of those who had entered into this union, they served as reasons for persevering in their profession. III. With respect to the third question, I answer, that this sin is not directly committed against the Holy Ghost himself, but that it is primarily, properly and immediately perpetrated against his gracious act. Yet this so redounds to the disgrace and contumely of the Holy Spirit himself, that he is said to be blasphemed and to be treated with ignominy by this sin; and that not accidentally, but per se, of itself. But I think, from this, by good consequence, may be deduced that the Holy Spirit is not some property, virtue, or power in God, usually considered by us under the mode of quality, but that it is something living, intelligent, willing and acting, distinct from the Father and the Son; upon which men are accustomed to bestow the appellation of "a person." To me, this seems possible to be proved by many arguments. (1.) Because he is distinguished in opposition to the Son, which ought not to be done, if he were a virtue or power not subsisting, communicated to Christ by the Father, by which he might perform miracles, as through a principle from which he has the dominion and power of his own act, and not through a principle which itself possesses such a dominion and power. (2.) Because it is said that men sin against the Holy Ghost, and blasphemy is said to be uttered against the Spirit, and he is treated with scorn and contempt. These phrases do not seem to me to indicate the inbeing of the Holy Ghost within God and Christ, but the existence and subsistence of the Holy Spirit; especially as this sin is distinguished from the sin against the Son of Man, which ought not to be done if this sin had been perpetrated against an act of the power which exists within Christ and is employed by him, and not against the act of the powerful and operating Holy Spirit himself; for as there are acts that appertain to persons, (though they operate through some natural property of their own,) so are there also passions belonging to persons. If any man rejects the gracious invitation of God to repentance, that sin is said to be committed against an act of the mercy of God; and, in this manner, he who has so sinned is said to sin against the mercy of God, but so that, by this very act the sin is properly committed against God, who is, himself, the author of this gracious invitation according to his own gratuitous mercy. Neither could he who thus sins against the mercy of God be said not to sin against God, but against his mercy; as he who sins against the gracious act of the Holy Spirit, is said, in this passage, (Matt. xii. 31,32) to sin, not against the Son of Man, against the Holy Spirit. IV. To these three questions might be added a FOURTH: "Can the mere thinking upon the perpetration of this sin, and the serious deliberation about its commission, come under the denomination of the sin itself, and receive such an appellation, in the same way as he is called a murderer who is angry with his brother, and as that man is said to have committed adultery in his heart who has looked upon the wife of his neighbour to lust after her?" I reply, that this does not seem to me to be the sin itself; for, as long as this deliberation continues, so long flourishes in that man the efficacy of the Holy Spirit employed to hinder that sin, until he finally and absolutely concludes about the commission of this sin, having spurned and rejected the resistance offered by the Holy Spirit. Such a conclusion is followed by the sin in that very moment, with regard to the refusing and rejection of Christ, not with regard to the other devotees enumerated, which the man produces at his own opportunities, even if his malice and hatred of Christ did not cease to impel him to the completion of those degrees. Amsterdam March 3d, 1599.

www.ingramcontent.com/pod-product-compliance
Lightning Source LLC
Chambersburg PA
CBHW060340100426
42812CB00003B/1064